PHILOSOPHICAL TEXTS

Philosophy 1A03

McMaster University

Barry Allen

2012

ANAXIMANDER

Fragments

Translated by John Burnet

Anaximander of Miletos, son of Praxiades, a fellow-citizen and associate of Thales, said that the material cause and first element of things was the unbounded aperion, he being the first to introduce this name for the material cause. He says it is neither water nor any other of the so-called elements, but a substance different from them, which is unbounded, from which arise all the heavens and the worlds within them. And into that from which things take their rise they pass away once more, "as is ordained; for they make reparation and satisfaction to one another for their injustice according to the appointed time," as he says in these somewhat poetical terms.

He says that the earth is cylindrical in form, and that its depth is as a third part of its breadth. He says that something capable of begetting hot and cold was separated off from the eternal at the origin of this world. From this arose a sphere of flame which grew round the air encircling the earth, as the bark grows round a tree. When this was torn off and enclosed in certain rings, the sun, moon, and stars came into existence.

He says that this is eternal and ageless, and that it encompasses all the worlds.

And besides this, there was an eternal motion, in the course of which was brought about the origin of the worlds. The earth swings free, held in its place by nothing. It stays where it is because of its equal distance from everything. Its shape is convex and round, and like a stone pillar. We are on one of the surfaces, and the other is on the opposite side. The heavenly bodies are wheels of fire separated off from the fire which encircles the world, and enclosed in air. And they have breathing-holes, certain pipe-like passages at which the heavenly bodies are seen. For this reason, too, when the breathing-holes are stopped, eclipses occur. And the moon appears now to wax and now to wane because of the stopping and opening of the passages. The circle of the sun is twenty-seven times that of the earth, while that of the moon is eighteen times as large. The sun is highest of all, and lowest are the wheels of the fixed stars. Living creatures arose from the moist element as it was evaporated by the sun. Man was like another animal, namely, a fish, in the beginning.

Rain was produced by the moisture drawn up from the earth by the sun.

Further, there cannot be a single, simple body which is unbounded, either, as some hold, one distinct from the elements, which they then derive from it, nor without this qualification. For there are some who make this (i.e. a body distinct from the elements) the infinite, and not air or water, in order that the other things may not be destroyed by their boundlessness. They are in opposition one to another—air is cold, water moist, and fire hot—and therefore, if any one of them were unbounded, the rest would have ceased to be by this time. Accordingly they say that is unbounded is something other than the elements, and from it the element arise.

Anaximander said the stars were hoop-like compressions of air, full of fire, breathing out flames at a certain point from orifices. The sun was highest of all, after it came the moon, and below these the fixed stars and the planets.

Anaximander said the sun was a ring twenty-eight times the size of the earth, like a cart-wheel with the felloe hollow and full of fire, showing the fire at a certain point, as if through the nozzle of a pair of bellows.

Anaximander held that thunder and lightning were caused by the blast. When it is shut up in a thick cloud and bursts forth with violence, then the breakage of the cloud makes the noise, and the rift gives the appearance of a flash by contrast with the darkness of the cloud.

Anaximander held that wind was a current of air which arose when its finest and moistest particles were set in motion or dissolved by the sun.

The sea is what is left of the original moisture. The fire has dried up most of it and turned the rest salt by scorching it.

The first animals were produced in the moisture, each enclosed in a prickly bark. As they advanced in age, they came out upon the drier part When the bark broke off, they survived for a short time.

He declares that at first human beings arose in the inside of fishes, and after having been reared like sharks, and become capable of protecting themselves, they were finally cast ashore and took to land.

XENOPHANES

Fragments

Translated by John Burnet

1

Now is the floor clean, and the hands and cups of all; one sets twisted garlands on our heads, another hands us fragrant ointment on a salver. The mixing bowl stands ready, full of gladness, and there is more wine at hand that promises never to leave us in the lurch, soft and smelling of flowers in the jars. In the midst the frankincense sends up its holy scent, and there is cold water, sweet and clean. Brown loaves are set before us and a lordly table laden with cheese and rich honey. The altar in the midst is clustered round with flowers; song and revel fill the halls.

But first it is meet that men should hymn the god with joy, with holy tales and pure words; then after libation and prayer made that we may have strength to do right—for that is in truth the first thing to do—no sin is it to drink as much as a man can take and get home without an attendant, so he be not stricken in years. And of all men is he to be praised who after drinking gives goodly proof of himself in the trial of skill, as memory and strength will serve him. Let him not sing of Titans and Giants—those fictions of the men of old—nor of turbulent civil broils in which is no good thing at all; but to give heedful reverence to the gods is ever good.

2

What if a man win victory in swiftness of foot, or in the pentathlon, at Olympia, where is the precinct of Zeus by Pisa's springs, or in wrestling,—what if by cruel boxing or that fearful sport men call pankration he become more glorious in the citizens' eyes, and win a place of honour in the sight of all at the games, his food at the public cost from the State, and a gift to be an heirloom for him,—what if he conquer in the chariot-race,—he will not deserve all this for his portion so much as I do. Far better is our wisdom than the strength of men and of horses! These are but thoughtless judgements, nor is it fitting to set strength before wisdom. Even if there arise a mighty boxer among a people, or one great in the pentathlon or at wrestling, or one excelling in swiftness of foot—and that stands in honour before all tasks of men at the games—the city would be none the better governed for that. It is but little joy a city gets of it if a man conquer at the games by Pisa's banks; it is not this that makes fat the store-houses of a city. . . .

10

Since all at first have learnt according to Homer . . . .

11

Homer and Hesiod have ascribed to the gods all things that are a shame and a disgrace among mortals, stealings and adulteries and deceivings of one another.

12

Since they have uttered many lawless deeds of the gods, stealings and adulteries and deceivings of one another.

14

But mortals deem that the gods are begotten as they are, and have clothes like theirs, and voice and form.

15

Yes, and if oxen and horses or lions had hands, and could paint with their hands, and produce works of art as men do, horses would paint the forms of the gods like horses, and oxen like oxen, and make their bodies in the image of their several kinds.

16

The Ethiopians make their gods black and snub-nosed; the Thracians say theirs have blue eyes and red hair.

18

The gods have not revealed all things to men from the beginning, but by seeking people find in time what is better.

23

One god, the greatest among gods and men, neither in form like unto mortals nor in thought.

24

He sees all over, thinks all over, and hears all over.

25

But without toil he moves all things by the thought of his mind.

26

And he abides ever in the selfsame place, moving not at all; nor does it befit him to go about now hither now thither.

27

All things come from the earth, and in earth all things end.

29

All things are earth and water that come into being and grow.

32

She that they call Iris [a rainbow] is a cloud likewise, purple, scarlet and green to behold.

33

For we all are born of earth and water.

34

There never was nor will be a man who has certain knowledge about the gods and about all the things I speak of. Even if he should chance to say the complete truth, yet he himself knows not that it is so. But all may have their fancy.

HERACLITUS

Fragments

Translated by John Burnet

1

It is wise to hearken, not to me, but to the Logos, and to confess that all things are one.

2

Though this Logos is true evermore, yet men are as unable to understand it when they hear it for the first time as before they have heard it at all. For, though all things come to pass in accordance with this Logos, men seem as if they had no experience of them, when they make trial of words and deeds such as I set forth, dividing each thing according to its kind and showing how it truly is. But other men know not what they are doing when awake, even as they forget what they do in sleep.

3

Fools when they do hear are like the deaf: of them does the saying bear witness that they are absent when present.

4

Eyes and ears are bad witnesses to men if they have souls that understand not their language.

5

The many do not take heed of such things as those they meet with, nor do they mark them when they are taught, though they think they do.

6

Knowing not how to listen nor how to speak.

7

If you do not expect the unexpected, you will not find it; for it is hard to be sought out and difficult.

8

Those who seek for gold dig up much earth and find a little.

10

Nature loves to hide.

11

The lord whose is the oracle at Delphi neither utters nor hides his meaning, but shows it by a sign.

13

The things that can be seen, heard, and learned are what I prize the most.

15

The eyes are more exact witnesses than the ears.

16

The learning of many things teacheth not understanding, else would it have taught Hesiod and Pythagoras, and again Xenophanes and Hekataios.

17

Pythagoras, son of Mnesarchos, practised scientific inquiry beyond all other men, and making a selection of these writings, claimed for his own wisdom what was but a knowledge of many things and an imposture.

18

Of all whose discourses I have heard, there is not one who attains to understanding that wisdom is apart from all.

19

Wisdom is one thing. It is to know the thought by which all things are steered through all things.

20

This world, which is the same for all, no one of gods or men has made; but it was ever, is now, and ever shall be an ever-living Fire, with measures of it kindling, and measures going out.

21

The transformations of Fire are, first of all, sea; and half of the sea is earth, half whirlwind.

22

All things are an exchange for Fire, and Fire for all things, even as wares for gold and gold for wares.

23

It becomes liquid sea, and is measured by the same tale as before it became earth.

24

Fire is want and surfeit.

25

Fire lives the death of air, and air lives the death of fire; water lives the death of earth, earth that of water.

26

Fire in its advance will judge and convict all things.

27

How can one hide from that which never sets?

28

It is the thunderbolt that steers the course of all things.

35

Hesiod is most men's teacher. Men are sure he knew very many things, a man who did not know day or night! They are one.

41

You cannot step twice into the same rivers; for fresh waters are ever flowing in upon you.

43

Homer was wrong in saying: "Would that strife might perish from among gods and men!" He did not see that he was praying for the destruction of the universe; for, if his prayer were heard, all things would pass away.

44

War is the father of all and the king of all; and some he has made gods and some men, some bond and some free.

45

Men do not know how what is at variance agrees with itself. It is an attunement of opposite tensions, like that of the bow and the lyre.

49

Men who love wisdom must be acquainted with very many things indeed.

51

Asses would rather have straw than gold. Oxen are happy when they find bitter vetches to eat.

52

The sea is the purest and the impurest water. Fish can drink it, and it is good for them; to men it is undrinkable and destructive.

57

Good and ill are one.

59

Couples are things whole and things not whole, what is drawn together and what is drawn asunder, the harmonious and the discordant. The one is made up of all things, and all things issue from the one.

61

To God all things are fair and good and right, but men hold some things wrong and some right.

62

We must know that war is common to all and strife is justice, and that all things come into being and pass away through strife.

64

All the things we see when awake are death, even as all we see in slumber are sleep.

65

The wise is one only. It is unwilling and willing to be called by the name of Zeus.

67

Mortals are immortals and immortals are mortals, the one living the others' death and dying the others' life.

69

The way up and the way down is one and the same.

70

In the circumference of a circle the beginning and end are common.

71

You will not find the boundaries of soul by traveling in any direction, so deep is the measure of it.

78

And it is the same thing in us that is quick and dead, awake and asleep, young and old; the former are shifted and become the latter, and the latter in turn are shifted and become the former.

79

Time is a child playing draughts, the kingly power is a child's.

80

I have sought for myself.

91

Thought is common to all. Those who speak with understanding must hold fast to what is common to all as a city holds fast to its law, and even more strongly. For all human laws are fed by the one divine law. It prevails as much as it will, and suffices for all things with something to spare.

92

So we must follow the common, yet though the Logos is common, the many live as if they had a wisdom of their own.

93

They are estranged from that with which they have most constant intercourse.

94

It is not meet to act and speak like men asleep.

95

The waking have one common world, but the sleeping turn aside each into a world of his own.

96

The way of man has no wisdom, but that of God has.

97

Man is called a baby by God, even as a child by a man.

98

The wisest man is an ape compared to God, just as the most beautiful ape is ugly compared to man.

100

The people must fight for its law as for its walls.

103

Wantonness needs putting out, even more than a house on fire.

111

For what thought or wisdom have they? They follow the poets and take the crowd as their teacher, knowing not that there are many bad and few good. For even the best of them choose one thing above all others, immortal glory among mortals, while most of them are glutted like beasts.

113

One is ten thousand to me, if he be the best.

115

Dogs bark at every one they do not know.

118

The most esteemed of them knows but fancies, and holds fast to them, yet of a truth justice shall overtake the artificers of lies and the false witnesses.

119

Homer should be turned out of the lists and whipped, and Archilochos likewise.

120

One day is like any other.

121

Man's character is his fate.

122

There awaits men when they die such things as they look not for nor dream of.

PARMENIDES

Fragments

Translated by John Burnet

1

The steeds that bear me carried me as far as ever my heart Desired, since they brought me and set me on the renowned Way of the goddess, who with her own hands conducts the man who knows through all things. On what way was I borne along; for on it did the wise steeds carry me, drawing my car, and maidens showed the way. And the axle, glowing in the socket—for it was urged round by the whirling wheels at each end—gave forth a sound as of a pipe, when the daughters of the Sun, hasting to convey me into the light, threw back their veils from off their faces and left the abode of Night.

There are the gates of the ways of Night and Day, fitted above with a lintel and below with a threshold of stone. They themselves, high in the air, are closed by mighty doors, and Avenging Justice keeps the keys that open them. Her did the maidens entreat with gentle words and skillfully persuade to unfasten without demur the bolted bars from the gates. Then, when the doors were thrown back, they disclosed a wide opening, when their brazen hinges swung backwards in the sockets fastened with rivets and nails.

Straight through them, on the broad way, did the maidens guide the horses and the car, and the goddess greeted me kindly, and took my right hand in hers, and spake to me these words: Welcome, noble youth, that comest to my abode on the car that bears thee tended by immortal charioteers! It is no ill chance, but justice and right that has sent thee forth to travel on this way. Far, indeed, does it lie from the beaten track of men! Meet it is that thou shouldst learn all things, as well the unshaken heart of persuasive truth, as the opinions of mortals in which is no true belief at all. Yet none the less shalt thou learn of these things also, since thou must judge approvedly of the things that seem to men as thou goest through all things in thy journey.

2

Come now, I will tell thee—and do thou hearken to my saying and carry it away—the only two ways of search that can be thought of. The first, namely, that It is, and that it is impossible for anything not to be, is the way of conviction, for truth is its companion. The other, namely, that It is not, and that something must needs not be,—that, I tell thee, is a wholly untrustworthy path. For you cannot know what is not—that is impossible—nor utter it.

3

For it is the same thing that can be thought and that can be.

4

It needs must be that what can be thought and spoken of is; for it is possible for it to be, and it is not possible for, what is nothing to be. This is what I bid thee ponder. I hold thee back from this first way of inquiry, and from this other also, upon which mortals knowing naught wander in two minds; for hesitation guides the wandering thought in their breasts, so that they are borne along stupefied like men deaf and blind. Undiscerning crowds, in whose eyes the same thing and not the same is and is not, and all things travel in opposite directions!

7

For this shall never be proved, that the things that are not are; and do thou restrain thy thought from this way of inquiry. Nor let habit force thee to cast a wandering eye upon this devious track, or to turn thither thy resounding ear or thy tongue; but do thou judge the subtle refutation of their discourse uttered by me.

8

One path only is left for us to speak of, namely, that It is. In it are very many tokens that what is, is uncreated and indestructible, alone, complete, immovable and without end. Nor was it ever, nor will it be; for now it is, all at once, a continuous one. For what kind of origin for it. will you look for? In what way and from what source could it have drawn its increase? I shall not let thee say nor think that it came from what is not; for it can neither be thought nor uttered that what is not is. And, if it came from nothing, what need could have made it arise later rather than sooner? Therefore must it either be altogether or be not at all.

Nor will the force of truth suffer aught to arise besides itself from that which in any way is. Wherefore, Justice does not loose her fetters and let anything come into being or pass away, but holds it fast. "Is it or is it not?" Surely it is adjudged, as it needs must be, that we are to set aside the one way as unthinkable and nameless (for it is no true way), and that the other path is real and true.

How, then, can what is be going to be in the future? Or how could it come into being? If it came into being, it is not; nor is it if it is going to be in the future. Thus is becoming extinguished and passing away not to be heard of.

Nor is it divisible, since it is all alike, and there is no more of it in one place than in another, to hinder it from holding together, nor less of it, but everything is full of what is. Wherefore all holds together; for what is; is in contact with what is.

Moreover, it is immovable in the bonds of mighty chains, without beginning and without end; since coming into being and passing away have been driven afar, and true belief has cast them away. It is the same, and it rests in the self-same place, abiding in itself. And thus it remaineth constant in its place; for hard necessity keeps it in the bonds of the limit that holds it fast on every side. Wherefore it is not permitted to what is to be infinite; for it is in need of nothing; while, if it were infinite, it would stand in need of everything.

It is the same thing that can be thought and for the sake of which the thought exists; for you cannot find thought without something that is, to which it is betrothed. And there is not, and never shall be, any time other, than that which is present, since fate has chained it so as to be whole and immovable.

Wherefore all these things are but the names which mortals have given, believing them, to be true—coming into being and passing away, being and not being, change of place and alteration of bright colour.

Where, then, it has its farthest boundary, it is complete on every side, equally poised from the centre in every direction, like the mass of a rounded sphere; for it cannot be greater or smaller in one place than in another. For there is nothing which is not that could keep it from reaching out equally, nor is it possible that there should be more of what is in this place and less in that, since it is all inviolable. For, since it is equal in all directions, it is equally confined within limits.

Here shall I close my trustworthy speech and thought about the truth. Henceforward learn the opinions of mortals, giving ear to the deceptive ordering of my words. Mortals have settled in their minds to speak of two forms, one of which they should have left out, and that is where they go astray from the truth.

They have assigned an opposite substance to each, and marks distinct from one another. To the one they allot the fire of heaven, light, thin, in every direction the same as itself, but not the same as the other. The other is opposite to it, dark night, a compact and heavy body.

Of these I tell thee the whole arrangement as it seems to men, in order that no mortal may surpass thee in knowledge.

PLATO
Euthyphro

Translated by Benjamin Jowett

PERSONS OF THE DIALOGUE: Socrates, Euthyphro.
THE SETTING: The Porch of the King Archon.

EUTHYPHRO: Why have you left the Lyceum, Socrates? and what are you doing in the Porch of the King Archon? Surely you cannot be concerned in a suit before the King, like myself?

SOCRATES: Not in a suit, Euthyphro; impeachment is the word which the Athenians use.

EUTHYPHRO: What! I suppose that some one has been prosecuting you, for I cannot believe that you are the prosecutor of another.

SOCRATES: Certainly not.

EUTHYPHRO: Then some one else has been prosecuting you?

SOCRATES: Yes.

EUTHYPHRO: And who is he?

SOCRATES: A young man who is little known, Euthyphro; and I hardly know him: his name is Meletus, and he is of the deme of Pitthis. Perhaps you may remember his appearance; he has a beak, and long straight hair, and a beard which is ill grown.

EUTHYPHRO: No, I do not remember him, Socrates. But what is the charge which he brings against you?

SOCRATES: What is the charge? Well, a very serious charge, which shows a good deal of character in the young man, and for which he is certainly not to be despised. He says he knows how the youth are corrupted and who are their corruptors. I fancy that he must be a wise man, and seeing that I am the reverse of a wise man, he has found me out, and is going to accuse me of corrupting his young friends. And of this our mother the state is to be the judge. Of all our political men he is the only one who seems to me to begin in the right way, with the cultivation of virtue in youth; like a good husbandman, he makes the young shoots his first care, and clears away us who are the destroyers of them. This is only the first step; he will afterwards attend to the elder branches; and if he goes on as he has begun, he will be a very great public benefactor.

EUTHYPHRO: I hope that he may; but I rather fear, Socrates, that the opposite will turn out to be the truth. My opinion is that in attacking you he is simply aiming a blow at the foundation of the state. But in what way does he say that you corrupt the young?

SOCRATES: He brings a wonderful accusation against me, which at first hearing excites surprise: he says that I am a poet or maker of gods, and that I invent new gods and deny the existence of old ones; this is the ground of his indictment.

EUTHYPHRO: I understand, Socrates; he means to attack you about the familiar sign which occasionally, as you say, comes to you. He thinks that you are a neologian, and he is going to have you up before the court for this. He knows that such a charge is readily received by the world, as I myself know too well; for when I speak in the assembly about divine things, and foretell the future to them, they laugh at me and think me a madman. Yet every word that I say is true. But they are jealous of us all; and we must be brave and go at them.

SOCRATES: Their laughter, friend Euthyphro, is not a matter of much consequence. For a man may be thought wise; but the Athenians, I suspect, do not much trouble themselves about him until he begins to impart his wisdom to others, and then for some reason or other, perhaps, as you say, from jealousy, they are angry.

EUTHYPHRO: I am never likely to try their temper in this way.

SOCRATES: I dare say not, for you are reserved in your behaviour, and seldom impart your wisdom. But I have a benevolent habit of pouring out myself to everybody, and would even pay for a listener, and I am afraid that the Athenians may think me too talkative. Now if, as I was saying, they would only laugh at me, as you say that they laugh at you, the time might pass gaily enough in the court; but perhaps they may be in earnest, and then what the end will be you soothsayers only can predict.

EUTHYPHRO: I dare say that the affair will end in nothing, Socrates, and that you will win your cause; and I think that I shall win my own.

SOCRATES: And what is your suit, Euthyphro? are you the pursuer or the defendant?

EUTHYPHRO: I am the pursuer.

SOCRATES: Of whom?

EUTHYPHRO: You will think me mad when I tell you.

SOCRATES: Why, has the fugitive wings?

EUTHYPHRO: Nay, he is not very volatile at his time of life.

SOCRATES: Who is he?

EUTHYPHRO: My father.

SOCRATES: Your father! my good man?

EUTHYPHRO: Yes.

SOCRATES: And of what is he accused?

EUTHYPHRO: Of murder, Socrates.

SOCRATES: By the powers, Euthyphro! how little does the common herd know of the nature of right and truth. A man must be an extraordinary man, and have made great strides in wisdom, before he could have seen his way to bring such an action. *

EUTHYPHRO: Indeed, Socrates, he must.

SOCRATES: I suppose that the man whom your father murdered was one of your relatives—clearly he was; for if he had been a stranger you would never have thought of prosecuting him.

EUTHYPHRO: I am amused, Socrates, at your making a distinction between one who is a relation and one who is not a relation; for surely the pollution is the same in either case, if you knowingly associate with the murderer when you ought to clear yourself and him by proceeding against him. The real question is whether the murdered man has been justly slain. If justly, then your duty is to let the matter alone; but if unjustly, then even if the murderer lives under the same roof with you and eats at the same table, proceed against him. Now the man who is dead was a poor dependant of mine who worked for us as a field labourer on our farm in Naxos, and one day in a fit of drunken passion he got into a quarrel with one of our domestic servants and slew him. My father bound him hand and foot and threw him into a ditch, and then sent to Athens to ask of a diviner what he should do with him. Meanwhile he never attended to him and took no care about him, for he regarded him as a murderer; and thought that no great harm would be done even if he did die.

Now this was just what happened. For such was the effect of cold and hunger and chains upon him, that before the messenger returned from the diviner, he was dead. And my father and family are angry with me for taking the part of the murderer and prosecuting my father. They say that he did not kill him, and that if he did, the dead man was but a murderer, and I ought not to take any notice, for that a son is impious who prosecutes a father. Which shows, Socrates, how little they know what the gods think about piety and impiety.

SOCRATES: Good heavens, Euthyphro! and is your knowledge of religion and of things pious and impious so very exact, that, supposing the circumstances to be as you state them, you are not afraid lest you too may be doing an impious thing in bringing an action against your father?

EUTHYPHRO: The best of Euthyphro, and that which distinguishes him, Socrates, from other men, is his exact knowledge of all such matters. What should I be good for without it?

SOCRATES: Rare friend! I think that I cannot do better than be your disciple. Then before the trial with Meletus comes on I shall challenge him, and say that I have always had a great interest in religious questions, and now, as he charges me with rash imaginations and innovations in religion, I have become your disciple. You, Meletus, as I shall say to him, acknowledge Euthyphro to be a great theologian, and sound in his opinions; and if you approve of him you ought to approve of me, and not have me into court; but if you disapprove, you should begin by indicting him who is my teacher, and who will be the ruin, not of the young, but of the old; that is to say, of myself whom he instructs, and of his old father whom he admonishes and chastises. And if Meletus refuses to listen to me, but will go on, and will not shift the indictment from me to you, I cannot do better than repeat this challenge in the court.

EUTHYPHRO: Yes, indeed, Socrates; and if he attempts to indict me I am mistaken if I do not find a flaw in him; the court shall have a great deal more to say to him than to me.

SOCRATES: And I, my dear friend, knowing this, am desirous of becoming your disciple. For I observe that no one appears to notice you—not even this Meletus; but his sharp eyes have found me out at once, and he has indicted me for impiety. And therefore, I adjure you to tell me the nature of piety and impiety, which you said that you knew so well, and of murder, and of other offences against the gods. What are they? Is not piety in every action always the same? and impiety, again—is it not always the opposite of piety, and also the same with itself, having, as impiety, one notion which includes whatever is impious?

EUTHYPHRO: To be sure, Socrates.

SOCRATES: And what is piety, and what is impiety?

EUTHYPHRO: Piety is doing as I am doing; that is to say, prosecuting any one who is guilty of murder, sacrilege, or of any similar crime—whether he be your father or mother, or whoever he may be—that makes no difference; and not to prosecute them is impiety. And please to consider, Socrates, what a notable proof I will give you of the truth of my words, a proof which I have already given to others:—of the principle, I mean, that the impious, whoever he may be, ought not to go unpunished. For do not men regard Zeus as the best and most righteous of the gods?—and yet they admit that he bound his father (Cronos) because he wickedly devoured his sons, and that he too had punished his own father (Uranus) for a similar reason, in a nameless manner. And yet when I proceed against my father, they are angry with me. So inconsistent are they in their way of talking when the gods are concerned, and when I am concerned.

SOCRATES: May not this be the reason, Euthyphro, why I am charged with impiety—that I cannot away with these stories about the gods? and therefore I suppose that people think me wrong. But, as you who are well informed about them approve of them, I cannot do better than assent to your superior wisdom. What else can I say, confessing as I do, that I know nothing about them? Tell me, for the love of Zeus, whether you really believe that they are true.

EUTHYPHRO: Yes, and things more wonderful still, of which the world is in ignorance.

SOCRATES: And do you really believe that the gods fought with one another, and had dire quarrels, battles, and the like, as the poets say, and as you may see represented in the works of great artists? The temples are full of them; and notably the robe of Athene, which is carried up to the Acropolis at the great Panathenaea, is embroidered with them. Are all these tales of the gods true?

EUTHYPHRO: Yes, Socrates; and, as I was saying, I can tell you, if you would like to hear them, many other things about the gods which would quite amaze you.

SOCRATES: I dare say; and you shall tell me them at some other time when I have leisure. But just at present I would rather hear from you a more precise answer, which you have not as yet given, my friend, to the question, What is 'piety'? When asked, you only replied, Doing as you do, charging your father with murder.

EUTHYPHRO: And what I said was true, Socrates.

SOCRATES: No doubt, Euthyphro; but you would admit there are many other pious acts?

EUTHYPHRO: There are.

SOCRATES: Remember that I did not ask you to give me two or three examples of piety, but to explain the general idea which makes all pious things to be pious. Do you not recollect that there was one idea which made the impious impious, and the pious pious?

EUTHYPHRO: I remember.

SOCRATES: Tell me what is the nature of this idea, and then I shall have a standard to which I may look, and by which I may measure actions, whether yours or those of any one else, and then I shall be able to say that such and such an action is pious, such another impious.

EUTHYPHRO: I will tell you, if you like.

SOCRATES: I should very much like.

EUTHYPHRO: Piety, then, is that which is dear to the gods, and impiety is that which is not dear to them.

SOCRATES: Very good, Euthyphro; you have now given me the sort of answer which I wanted. But whether what you say is true or not I cannot as yet tell, although I make no doubt that you will prove the truth of your words.

EUTHYPHRO: Of course.

SOCRATES: Come, then, and let us examine what we are saying. That thing or person which is dear to the gods is pious, and that thing or person which is hateful to the gods is impious, these two being the extreme opposites of one another. Was not that said?

EUTHYPHRO: It was.

SOCRATES: And well said?

EUTHYPHRO: Yes, Socrates, I thought so; it was certainly said.

SOCRATES: And further, Euthyphro, the gods were admitted to have enmities and hatreds and differences?

EUTHYPHRO: Yes, that was also said.

SOCRATES: And what sort of difference creates enmity and anger? Suppose that you and I, my good friend, differ about a number; do differences of this sort make us enemies and set us at variance with one another? Do we not go at once to arithmetic, and put an end to them by a sum?

EUTHYPHRO: True.

SOCRATES: Or suppose that we differ about magnitudes, do we not quickly end the differences by measuring?

EUTHYPHRO: Very true.

SOCRATES: And we end a controversy about heavy and light by resorting to weighing?

EUTHYPHRO: To be sure.

SOCRATES: But what differences are there which cannot be thus decided, and which therefore make us angry and set us at enmity with one another? I dare say the answer does not occur to you at the moment, and therefore I will suggest that these enmities arise when the matters of difference are the just and unjust, good and evil, honourable and dishonourable. Are not these the points about which men differ, and about which when we are unable satisfactorily to decide our differences, you and I and all of us quarrel, when we do quarrel?

EUTHYPHRO: Yes, Socrates, the nature of the differences about which we quarrel is such as you describe.

SOCRATES: And the quarrels of the gods, Euthyphro, when they occur, are of a like nature?

EUTHYPHRO: Certainly they are.

SOCRATES: They have differences of opinion, as you say, about good and evil, just and unjust, honourable and dishonourable: there would have been no quarrels among them, if there had been no such differences—would there now?

EUTHYPHRO: You are quite right.

SOCRATES: Does not every man love that which he deems noble and just and good, and hate the opposite of them?

EUTHYPHRO: Very true.

SOCRATES: But, as you say, people regard the same things, some as just and others as unjust,—about these they dispute; and so there arise wars and fightings among them.

EUTHYPHRO: Very true.

SOCRATES: Then the same things are hated by the gods and loved by the gods, and are both hateful and dear to them?

EUTHYPHRO: True.

SOCRATES: And upon this view the same things, Euthyphro, will be pious and impious?

EUTHYPHRO: So I should suppose.

SOCRATES: Then, my friend, I remark with surprise that you have not answered the question which I asked. For I certainly did not ask you to tell me what action is both pious and impious: but now it would seem that what is loved by the gods is also hated by them. And therefore, Euthyphro, in thus chastising your father you may very likely be doing what is agreeable to Zeus but disagreeable to Cronos or Uranus, and what is acceptable to Hephaestus but unacceptable to Here, and there may be other gods who have similar differences of opinion.

EUTHYPHRO: But I believe, Socrates, that all the gods would be agreed as to the propriety of punishing a murderer: there would be no difference of opinion about that.

SOCRATES: Well, but speaking of men, Euthyphro, did you ever hear any one arguing that a murderer or any sort of evil-doer ought to be let off?

EUTHYPHRO: I should rather say that these are the questions which they are always arguing, especially in courts of law: they commit all sorts of crimes, and there is nothing which they will not do or say in their own defence.

SOCRATES: But do they admit their guilt, and yet say that they ought not to be punished?

EUTHYPHRO: No; they do not.

SOCRATES: Then there are some things which they do not venture to say and do: for they do not venture to argue that the guilty are to be unpunished, but they deny their guilt, do they not?

EUTHYPHRO: Yes.

SOCRATES: Then they do not argue that the evil-doer should not be punished, but they argue about the fact of who the evil-doer is, and what he did and when?

EUTHYPHRO: True.

SOCRATES: And the gods are in the same case, if as you assert they quarrel about just and unjust, and some of them say while others deny that injustice is done among them. For surely neither God nor man will ever venture to say that the doer of injustice is not to be punished?

EUTHYPHRO: That is true, Socrates, in the main.

SOCRATES: But they join issue about the particulars—gods and men alike; and, if they dispute at all, they dispute about some act which is called in question, and which by some is affirmed to be just, by others to be unjust. Is not that true?

EUTHYPHRO: Quite true.

SOCRATES: Well then, my dear friend Euthyphro, do tell me, for my better instruction and information, what proof have you that in the opinion of all the gods a servant who is guilty of murder, and is put in chains by the master of the dead man, and dies because he is put in chains before he who bound him can learn from the interpreters of the gods what he ought to do with him, dies unjustly; and that on behalf of such an one a son ought to proceed against his father and accuse him of murder. How would you show that all the gods absolutely agree in approving of his act? Prove to me that they do, and I will applaud your wisdom as long as I live.

EUTHYPHRO: It will be a difficult task; but I could make the matter very clear to you.

SOCRATES: I understand; you mean to say that I am not so quick of apprehension as the judges: for to them you will be sure to prove that the act is unjust, and hateful to the gods.

EUTHYPHRO: Yes indeed, Socrates; at least if they will listen to me.

SOCRATES: But they will be sure to listen if they find that you are a good speaker. There was a notion that came into my mind while you were speaking; I said to myself: 'Well, and what if Euthyphro does prove to me that all the gods regarded the death of the serf as unjust, how do I know anything more of the nature of piety and impiety? for granting that this action may be hateful to the gods, still piety and impiety are not adequately defined by these distinctions, for that which is hateful to the gods has been shown to be also pleasing and dear to them.'

And therefore, Euthyphro, I do not ask you to prove this; I will suppose, if you like, that all the gods condemn and abominate such an action. But I will amend the definition so far as to say that what all the gods hate is impious, and what they love pious or holy; and what some of them love and others hate is both or neither. Shall this be our definition of piety and impiety? *

EUTHYPHRO: Why not, Socrates?

SOCRATES: Why not! certainly, as far as I am concerned, Euthyphro, there is no reason why not. But whether this admission will greatly assist you in the task of instructing me as you promised, is a matter for you to consider.

EUTHYPHRO: Yes, I should say that what all the gods love is pious and holy, and the opposite which they all hate, impious.

SOCRATES: Ought we to enquire into the truth of this, Euthyphro, or simply to accept the mere statement on our own authority and that of others? What do you say?

EUTHYPHRO: We should enquire; and I believe the statement will stand the test.

SOCRATES: We shall know better, my good friend, in a little while. The point which I should first wish to understand is whether the pious or holy is beloved by the gods because it is holy, or holy because it is beloved of the gods.

EUTHYPHRO: I do not understand your meaning, Socrates.

SOCRATES: I will endeavour to explain: we, speak of carrying and we speak of being carried, of leading and being led, seeing and being seen. You know that in all such cases there is a difference, and you know also in what the difference lies?

EUTHYPHRO: I think that I understand.

SOCRATES: And is not that which is beloved distinct from that which loves?

EUTHYPHRO: Certainly.

SOCRATES: Well; and now tell me, is that which is carried in this state of carrying because it is carried, or for some other reason?

EUTHYPHRO: No; that is the reason.

SOCRATES: And the same is true of what is led and of what is seen?

EUTHYPHRO: True.

SOCRATES: And a thing is not seen because it is visible, but conversely, visible because it is seen; nor is a thing led because it is in the state of being led, or carried because it is in the state of being carried, but the converse of this. And now I think, Euthyphro, that my meaning will be intelligible; and my meaning is, that any state of action or passion implies previous action or passion. It does not become because it is becoming, but it is in a state of becoming because it becomes; neither does it suffer because it is in a state of suffering, but it is in a state of suffering because it suffers. Do you not agree?

EUTHYPHRO: Yes.

SOCRATES: Is not that which is loved in some state either of becoming or suffering?

EUTHYPHRO: Yes.

SOCRATES: And the same holds as in the previous instances; the state of being loved follows the act of being loved, and not the act the state.

EUTHYPHRO: Certainly.

SOCRATES: And what do you say of piety, Euthyphro: is not piety, according to your definition, loved by all the gods?

EUTHYPHRO: Yes.

SOCRATES: Because it is pious or holy, or for some other reason?

EUTHYPHRO: No, that is the reason.

SOCRATES: It is loved because it is holy, not holy because it is loved?

EUTHYPHRO: Yes.

SOCRATES: And that which is dear to the gods is loved by them, and is in a state to be loved of them because it is loved of them?

EUTHYPHRO: Certainly.

SOCRATES: Then that which is dear to the gods, Euthyphro, is not holy, nor is that which is holy loved of God, as you affirm; but they are two different things.

EUTHYPHRO: How do you mean, Socrates?

SOCRATES: I mean to say that the holy has been acknowledged by us to be loved of God because it is holy, not to be holy because it is loved.

EUTHYPHRO: Yes.

SOCRATES: But that which is dear to the gods is dear to them because it is loved by them, not loved by them because it is dear to them.

EUTHYPHRO: True.

SOCRATES: But, friend Euthyphro, if that which is holy is the same with that which is dear to God, and is loved because it is holy, then that which is dear to God would have been loved as being dear to God; but if that which is dear to God is dear to him because loved by him, then that which is holy would have been holy because loved by him. But now you see that the reverse is the case, and that they are quite different from one another. For one is of a kind to be loved cause it is loved, and the other is loved because it is of a kind to be loved.

Thus you appear to me, Euthyphro, when I ask you what is the essence of holiness, to offer an attribute only, and not the essence—the attribute of being loved by all the gods. But you still refuse to explain to me the nature of holiness. And therefore, if you please, I will ask you not to hide your treasure, but to tell me once more what holiness or piety really is, whether dear to the gods or not (for that is a matter about which we will not quarrel); and what is impiety?

EUTHYPHRO: I really do not know, Socrates, how to express what I mean. For somehow or other our arguments, on whatever ground we rest them, seem to turn round and walk away from us.

SOCRATES: Your words, Euthyphro, are like the handiwork of my ancestor Daedalus; and if I were the sayer or propounder of them, you might say that my arguments walk away and will not remain fixed where they are placed because I am a descendant of his. But now, since these notions are your own, you must find some other gibe, for they certainly, as you yourself allow, show an inclination to be on the move.

EUTHYPHRO: Nay, Socrates, I shall still say that you are the Daedalus who sets arguments in motion; not I, certainly, but you make them move or go round, for they would never have stirred, as far as I am concerned.

SOCRATES: Then I must be a greater than Daedalus: for whereas he only made his own inventions to move, I move those of other people as well. And the beauty of it is, that I would rather not. For I would give the wisdom of Daedalus, and the wealth of Tantalus, to be able to detain them and keep them fixed. But enough of this. As I perceive that you are lazy, I will myself endeavour to show you how you might instruct me in the nature of piety; and I hope that you will not grudge your labour. Tell me, then—Is not that which is pious necessarily just?

EUTHYPHRO: Yes.

SOCRATES: And is, then, all which is just pious? or, is that which is pious all just, but that which is just, only in part and not all, pious?

EUTHYPHRO: I do not understand you, Socrates.

SOCRATES: And yet I know that you are as much wiser than I am, as you are younger. But, as I was saying, revered friend, the abundance of your wisdom makes you lazy. Please to exert yourself, for there is no real difficulty in understanding me. What I mean I may explain by an illustration of what I do not mean. The poet sings— 'Of Zeus, the author and creator of all these things, You will not tell: for where there is fear there is also reverence.' Now I disagree with this poet. Shall I tell you in what respect?

EUTHYPHRO: By all means.

SOCRATES: I should not say that where there is fear there is also reverence; for I am sure that many persons fear poverty and disease, and the like evils, but I do not perceive that they reverence the objects of their fear.

EUTHYPHRO: Very true.

SOCRATES: But where reverence is, there is fear; for he who has a feeling of reverence and shame about the commission of any action, fears and is afraid of an ill reputation.

EUTHYPHRO: No doubt.

SOCRATES: Then we are wrong in saying that where there is fear there is also reverence; and we should say, where there is reverence there is also fear. But there is not always reverence where there is fear; for fear is a more extended notion, and reverence is a part of fear, just as the odd is a part of number, and number is a more extended notion than the odd. I suppose that you follow me now?

EUTHYPHRO: Quite well.

SOCRATES: That was the sort of question which I meant to raise when I asked whether the just is always the pious, or the pious always the just; and whether there may not be justice where there is not piety; for justice is the more extended notion of which piety is only a part. Do you dissent?

EUTHYPHRO: No, I think that you are quite right.

SOCRATES: Then, if piety is a part of justice, I suppose that we should enquire what part? If you had pursued the enquiry in the previous cases; for instance, if you had asked me what is an even number, and what part of number the even is, I should have had no difficulty in replying, a number which represents a figure having two equal sides. Do you not agree?

EUTHYPHRO: Yes, I quite agree.

SOCRATES: In like manner, I want you to tell me what part of justice is piety or holiness, that I may be able to tell Meletus not to do me injustice, or indict me for impiety, as I am now adequately instructed by you in the nature of piety or holiness, and their opposites.

EUTHYPHRO: Piety or holiness, Socrates, appears to me to be that part of justice which attends to the gods, as there is the other part of justice which attends to men.

SOCRATES: That is good, Euthyphro; yet still there is a little point about which I should like to have further information, What is the meaning of 'attention'? For attention can hardly be used in the same sense when applied to the gods as when applied to other things. For instance, horses are said to require attention, and not every person is able to attend to them, but only a person skilled in horsemanship. Is it not so?

EUTHYPHRO: Certainly.

SOCRATES: I suppose that the art of horsemanship is the art of attending to horses?

EUTHYPHRO: Yes.

SOCRATES: Nor is every one qualified to attend to dogs, but only the huntsman?

EUTHYPHRO: True.

SOCRATES: And I suppose that the art of the huntsman is the art of attending to dogs?

EUTHYPHRO: Yes.

SOCRATES: As the art of the oxherd is the art of attending to oxen?

EUTHYPHRO: Very true.

SOCRATES: In like manner holiness or piety is the art of attending to the gods?—that would be your meaning, Euthyphro?

EUTHYPHRO: Yes.

SOCRATES: And is not attention always designed for the good or benefit of that to which the attention is given? As in the case of horses, you may observe that when attended to by the horseman's art they are benefited and improved, are they not?

EUTHYPHRO: True.

SOCRATES: As the dogs are benefited by the huntsman's art, and the oxen by the art of the oxherd, and all other things are tended or attended for their good and not for their hurt?

EUTHYPHRO: Certainly, not for their hurt.

SOCRATES: But for their good?

EUTHYPHRO: Of course.

SOCRATES: And does piety or holiness, which has been defined to be the art of attending to the gods, benefit or improve them? Would you say that when you do a holy act you make any of the gods better?

EUTHYPHRO: No, no; that was certainly not what I meant.

SOCRATES: And I, Euthyphro, never supposed that you did. I asked you the question about the nature of the attention, because I thought that you did not.

EUTHYPHRO: You do me justice, Socrates; that is not the sort of attention which I mean.

SOCRATES: Good: but I must still ask what is this attention to the gods that is called piety?

EUTHYPHRO: It is such, Socrates, as servants show to their masters.

SOCRATES: I understand—a sort of ministration to the gods.

EUTHYPHRO: Exactly.

SOCRATES: Medicine is also a sort of ministration or service, having in view the attainment of some object—would you not say of health?

EUTHYPHRO: I should.

SOCRATES: Again, there is an art which ministers to the ship-builder with a view to the attainment of some result?

EUTHYPHRO: Yes, Socrates, with a view to the building of a ship.

SOCRATES: As there is an art which ministers to the house-builder with a view to the building of a house?

EUTHYPHRO: Yes.

SOCRATES: And now tell me, my good friend, about the art which ministers to the gods: what work does that help to accomplish? For you must surely know if, as you say, you are of all men living the one who is best instructed in religion.

EUTHYPHRO: And I speak the truth, Socrates.

SOCRATES: Tell me then, oh tell me—what is that fair work which the gods do by the help of our ministrations?

EUTHYPHRO: Many and fair, Socrates, are the works which they do.

SOCRATES: Why, my friend, and so are those of a general. But the chief of them is easily told. Would you not say that victory in war is the chief of them?

EUTHYPHRO: Certainly.

SOCRATES: Many and fair, too, are the works of the husbandman, if I am not mistaken; but his chief work is the production of food from the earth?

EUTHYPHRO: Exactly.

SOCRATES: Of the many fair things done by the gods which is the chief or principal one?

EUTHYPHRO: I have told you already, Socrates, that to learn all these things accurately will be very tiresome. Let me simply say that piety or holiness is learning how to please the gods in word and deed, by prayers and sacrifices. Such piety is the salvation of families and states, just as the impious, which is unpleasing to the gods, is their ruin and destruction.

SOCRATES: I think that you could have answered in much fewer words the chief question which I asked, Euthyphro, if you had chosen. But I see plainly that you are not disposed to instruct me—clearly not: else why, when we reached the point, did you turn aside? Had you only answered me I should have truly learned of you by this time the nature of piety. Now, as the asker of a question is necessarily dependent on the answerer, whither he leads I must follow; and can only ask again, what is the pious, and what is piety? Do you mean that they are a sort of science of praying and sacrificing?

EUTHYPHRO: Yes, I do.

SOCRATES: And sacrificing is giving to the gods, and prayer is asking of the gods?

EUTHYPHRO: Yes, Socrates.

SOCRATES: Upon this view, then, piety is a science of asking and giving?

EUTHYPHRO: You understand me capitally, Socrates.

SOCRATES: Yes, my friend; the reason is that I am a votary of your science, and give my mind to it, and therefore nothing which you say will be thrown away upon me. Please then to tell me, what is the nature of this service to the gods? Do you mean we prefer requests and give gifts to them?

EUTHYPHRO: Yes, I do.

SOCRATES: Is not the right way of asking to ask of them what we want?

EUTHYPHRO: Certainly.

SOCRATES: And the right way of giving is to give to them in return what they want of us. There would be no meaning in an art which gives to any one that which he does not want.

EUTHYPHRO: Very true, Socrates.

SOCRATES: Then piety, Euthyphro, is an art which gods and men have of doing business with one another?

EUTHYPHRO: That is an expression which you may use, if you like.

SOCRATES: But I have no particular liking for anything but the truth. I wish, however, that you would tell me what benefit accrues to the gods from our gifts. There is no doubt about what they give to us; for there is no good thing which they do not give; but how we can give any good thing to them in return is far from being equally clear. If they give everything and we give nothing, that must be an affair of business in which we have very greatly the advantage of them.

EUTHYPHRO: Do you imagine that any benefit accrues to the gods from our gifts?

SOCRATES: But if not, Euthyphro, what is the meaning of gifts which are conferred by us upon the gods?

EUTHYPHRO: What else, but tributes of honour; and, as I was just now saying, what pleases them?

SOCRATES: Piety, then, is pleasing to the gods, but not beneficial or dear to them?

EUTHYPHRO: I should say that nothing could be dearer.

SOCRATES: Then once more the assertion is repeated that piety is dear to the gods?

EUTHYPHRO: Certainly.

SOCRATES: And when you say this, can you wonder at your words not standing firm, but walking away? Will you accuse me of being the Daedalus who makes them walk away, not perceiving that there is another and far greater artist than Daedalus who makes them go round in a circle, and he is yourself; for the argument, as you will perceive, comes round to the same point. Were we not saying that the holy or pious was not the same with that which is loved of the gods? Have you forgotten?

EUTHYPHRO: I quite remember.

SOCRATES: And are you not saying that what is loved of the gods is holy; and is not this the same as what is dear to them—do you see?

EUTHYPHRO: True.

SOCRATES: Then either we were wrong in our former assertion; or, if we were right then, we are wrong now.

EUTHYPHRO: One of the two must be true.

SOCRATES: Then we must begin again and ask, What is piety? That is an enquiry which I shall never be weary of pursuing as far as in me lies; and I entreat you not to scorn me, but to apply your mind to the utmost, and tell me the truth. For, if any man knows, you are he; and therefore I must detain you, like Proteus, until you tell. If you had not certainly known the nature of piety and impiety, I am confident that you would never, on behalf of a serf, have charged your aged father with murder. You would not have run such a risk of doing wrong in the sight of the gods, and you would have had too much respect for the opinions of men. I am sure, therefore, that you know the nature of piety and impiety. Speak out then, my dear Euthyphro, and do not hide your knowledge.

EUTHYPHRO: Another time, Socrates; for I am in a hurry, and must go now.

SOCRATES: Alas! my companion, and will you leave me in despair? I was hoping that you would instruct me in the nature of piety and impiety; and then I might have cleared myself of Meletus and his indictment. I would have told him that I had been enlightened by Euthyphro, and had given up rash innovations and speculations, in which I indulged only through ignorance, and that now I am about to lead a better life.

PLATO

Apology

Translated by Benjamin Jowett

Socrates addresses the Court of Athens.

How you, O Athenians, have been affected by my accusers, I cannot tell; but I know that they almost made me forget who I was—so persuasively did they speak; and yet they have hardly uttered a word of truth. But of the many falsehoods told by them, there was one which quite amazed me;—I mean when they said that you should be upon your guard and not allow yourselves to be deceived by the force of my eloquence. To say this, when they were certain to be detected as soon as I opened my lips and proved myself to be anything but a great speaker, did indeed appear to me most shameless—unless by the force of eloquence they mean the force of truth; for is such is their meaning, I admit that I am eloquent. But in how different a way from theirs!

Well, as I was saying, they have scarcely spoken the truth at all; but from me you shall hear the whole truth: not, however, delivered after their manner in a set oration duly ornamented with words and phrases. No, by heaven! but I shall use the words and arguments which occur to me at the moment; for I am confident in the justice of my cause: at my time of life I ought not to be appearing before you, O men of Athens, in the character of a juvenile orator—let no one expect it of me. And I must beg of you to grant me a favour:—If I defend myself in my accustomed manner, and you hear me using the words which I have been in the habit of using in the agora, at the tables of the money-changers, or anywhere else, I would ask you not to be surprised, and not to interrupt me on this account. For I am more than seventy years of age, and appearing now for the first time in a court of law, I am quite a stranger to the language of the place; and therefore I would have you regard me as if I were really a stranger, whom you would excuse if he spoke in his native tongue, and after the fashion of his country.

Am I making an unfair request of you? Never mind the manner, which may or may not be good; but think only of the truth of my words, and give heed to that: let the speaker speak truly and the judge decide justly. And first, I have to reply to the older charges and to my first accusers, and then I will go on to the later ones. For of old I have had many accusers, who have accused me falsely to you during many years; and I am more afraid of them than of Anytus and his associates, who are dangerous, too, in their own way. But far more dangerous are the others, who began when you were children, and took possession of your minds with their falsehoods, telling of one Socrates, a wise man, who speculated about the heaven above, and searched into the earth beneath, and made the worse appear the better cause.

The disseminators of this tale are the accusers whom I dread; for their hearers are apt to fancy that such enquirers do not believe in the existence of the gods. And they are many, and their charges against me are of ancient date, and they were made by them in the days when you were more impressible than you are now—in childhood, or it may have been in youth—and the cause when heard went by default, for there was none to answer. And hardest of all, I do not know and cannot tell the names of my accusers; unless in the chance case of a Comic poet. All who from envy and malice have persuaded you—some of them having first convinced themselves—all this class of men are most difficult to deal with; for I cannot have them up here, and cross-examine them, and therefore I must simply fight with shadows in my own defence, and argue when there is no one who answers.

I will ask you then to assume with me, as I was saying, that my opponents are of two kinds; one recent, the other ancient: and I hope that you will see the propriety of my answering the latter first, for these accusations you heard long before the others, and much oftener.

Well, then, I must make my defence, and endeavour to clear away in a short time, a slander which has lasted a long time. May I succeed, if to succeed be for my good and yours, or likely to avail me in my cause! The task is not an easy one; I quite understand the nature of it. And so leaving the event with God, in obedience to the law I will now make my defence. I will begin at the beginning, and ask what is the accusation which has given rise to the slander of me, and in fact has encouraged Meletus to proof this charge against me. Well, what do the slanderers say? They shall be my prosecutors, and I will sum up their words in an affidavit: 'Socrates is an evil-doer, and a curious person, who searches into things under the earth and in heaven, and he makes the worse appear the better cause; and he teaches the aforesaid doctrines to others.'

Such is the nature of the accusation: it is just what you have yourselves seen in the comedy of Aristophanes, who has introduced a man whom he calls Socrates, going about and saying that he walks in air, and talking a deal of nonsense concerning matters of which I do not pretend to know either much or little—not that I mean to speak disparagingly of any one who is a student of natural philosophy. I should be very sorry if Meletus could bring so grave a charge against me. But the simple truth is, O Athenians, that I have nothing to do with physical speculations. Very many of those here present are witnesses to the truth of this, and to them I appeal. Speak then, you who have heard me, and tell your neighbours whether any of you have ever known me hold forth in few words or in many upon such matters.

You hear their answer. And from what they say of this part of the charge you will be able to judge of the truth of the rest. As little foundation is there for the report that I am a teacher, and take money; this accusation has no more truth in it than the other. Although, if a man were really able to instruct mankind, to receive money for giving instruction would, in my opinion, be an honour to him. There is Gorgias of Leontium, and Prodicus of Ceos, and Hippias of Elis, who go the round of the cities, and are able to persuade the young men to leave their own citizens by whom they might be taught for nothing, and come to them whom they not only pay, but are thankful if they may be allowed to pay them.

There is at this time a Parian philosopher residing in Athens, of whom I have heard; and I came to hear of him in this way:—I came across a man who has spent a world of money on the Sophists, Callias, the son of Hipponicus, and knowing that he had sons, I asked him: 'Callias,' I said, 'if your two sons were foals or calves, there would be no difficulty in finding some one to put over them; we should hire a trainer of horses, or a farmer probably, who would improve and perfect them in their own proper virtue and excellence; but as they are human beings, whom are you thinking of placing over them? Is there any one who understands human and political virtue? You must have thought about the matter, for you have sons; is there any one?' 'There is,' he said. 'Who is he?' said I; 'and of what country? and what does he charge?' 'Evenus the Parian,' he replied; 'he is the man, and his charge is five minae.'

Happy is Evenus, I said to myself, if he really has this wisdom, and teaches at such a moderate charge. Had I the same, I should have been very proud and conceited; but the truth is that I have no knowledge of the kind. I dare say, Athenians, that some one among you will reply, 'Yes, Socrates, but what is the origin of these accusations which are brought against you; there must have been something strange which you have been doing? All these rumours and this talk about you would never have arisen if you had been like other men: tell us, then, what is the cause of them, for we should be sorry to judge hastily of you.' Now I regard this as a fair challenge, and I will endeavour to explain to you the reason why I am called wise and have such an evil fame. Please to attend then. And although some of you may think that I am joking, I declare that I will tell you the entire truth.

Men of Athens, this reputation of mine has come of a certain sort of wisdom which I possess. If you ask me what kind of wisdom, I reply, wisdom such as may perhaps be attained by man, for to that extent I am inclined to believe that I am wise; whereas the persons of whom I was speaking have a superhuman wisdom which I may fail to describe, because I have it not myself; and he who says that I have, speaks falsely, and is taking away my character. And here, O men of Athens, I must beg you not to interrupt me, even if I seem to say something extravagant. For the word which I will speak is not mine. I will refer you to a witness who is worthy of credit; that witness shall be the God of Delphi—he will tell you about my wisdom, if I have any, and of what sort it is.

You must have known Chaerephon; he was early a friend of mine, and also a friend of yours, for he shared in the recent exile of the people, and returned with you. Well, Chaerephon, as you know, was very impetuous in all his doings, and he went to Delphi and boldly asked the oracle to tell him whether—as I was saying, I must beg you not to interrupt—he asked the oracle to tell him whether anyone was wiser than I was, and the Pythian prophetess answered, that there was no man wiser. Chaerephon is dead himself; but his brother, who is in court, will confirm the truth of what I am saying. Why do I mention this? Because I am going to explain to you why I have such an evil name. When I heard the answer, I said to myself, What can the god mean? and what is the interpretation of his riddle? for I know that I have no wisdom, small or great. What then can he mean when he says that I am the wisest of men? And yet he is a god, and cannot lie; that would be against his nature.

After long consideration, I thought of a method of trying the question. I reflected that if I could only find a man wiser than myself, then I might go to the god with a refutation in my hand. I should say to him, 'Here is a man who is wiser than I am; but you said that I was the wisest.' Accordingly I went to one who had the reputation of wisdom, and observed him—his name I need not mention; he was a politician whom I selected for examination—and the result was as follows: When I began to talk with him, I could not help thinking that he was not really wise, although he was thought wise by many, and still wiser by himself; and thereupon I tried to explain to him that he thought himself wise, but was not really wise; and the consequence was that he hated me, and his enmity was shared by several who were present and heard me. So I left him, saying to myself, as I went away: Well, although I do not suppose that either of us knows anything really beautiful and good, I am better off than he is,— for he knows nothing, and thinks that he knows; I neither know nor think that I know. In this latter particular, then, I seem to have slightly the advantage of him.

Then I went to another who had still higher pretensions to wisdom, and my conclusion was exactly the same. Whereupon I made another enemy of him, and of many others besides him. Then I went to one man after another, being not unconscious of the enmity which I provoked, and I lamented and feared this: but necessity was laid upon me,—the word of God, I thought, ought to be considered first. And I said to myself, Go I must to all who appear to know, and find out the meaning of the oracle. And I swear to you, Athenians, by the dog I swear!—for I must tell you the truth—the result of my mission was just this: I found that the men most in repute were all but the most foolish; and that others less esteemed were really wiser and better. I will tell you the tale of my wanderings and of the 'Herculean' labours, as I may call them, which I endured only to find at last the oracle irrefutable.

After the politicians, I went to the poets; tragic, dithyrambic, and all sorts. And there, I said to myself, you will be instantly detected; now you will find out that you are more ignorant than they are. Accordingly, I took them some of the most elaborate passages in their own writings, and asked what was the meaning of them—thinking that they would teach me something. Will you believe me? I am almost ashamed to confess the truth, but I must say that there is hardly a person present who would not have talked better about their poetry than they did themselves. Then I knew that not by wisdom do poets write poetry, but by a sort of genius and inspiration; they are like diviners or soothsayers who also say many fine things, but do not understand the meaning of them. The poets appeared to me to be much in the same case; and I further observed that upon the strength of their poetry they believed themselves to be the wisest of men in other things in which they were not wise. So I departed, conceiving myself to be superior to them for the same reason that I was superior to the politicians.

At last I went to the artisans. I was conscious that I knew nothing at all, as I may say, and I was sure that they knew many fine things; and here I was not mistaken, for they did know many things of which I was ignorant, and in this they certainly were wiser than I was. But I observed that even the good artisans fell into the same error as the poets;—because they were good workmen they thought that they also knew all sorts of high matters, and this defect in them overshadowed their wisdom; and therefore I asked myself on behalf of the oracle, whether I would like to be as I was, neither having their knowledge nor their ignorance, or like them in both; and I made answer to myself and to the oracle that I was better off as I was.

This inquisition has led to my having many enemies of the worst and most dangerous kind, and has given occasion also to many calumnies. And I am called wise, for my hearers always imagine that I myself possess the wisdom which I find wanting in others: but the truth is, O men of Athens, that God only is wise; and by his answer he intends to show that the wisdom of men is worth little or nothing; he is not speaking of Socrates, he is only using my name by way of illustration, as if he said, He, O men, is the wisest, who, like Socrates, knows that his wisdom is in truth worth nothing.

And so I go about the world, obedient to the god, and search and make enquiry into the wisdom of any one, whether citizen or stranger, who appears to be wise; and if he is not wise, then in vindication of the oracle I show him that he is not wise; and my occupation quite absorbs me, and I have no time to give either to any public matter of interest or to any concern of my own, but I am in utter poverty by reason of my devotion to the god.

There is another thing:—young men of the richer classes, who have not much to do, come about me of their own accord; they like to hear the pretenders examined, and they often imitate me, and proceed to examine others; there are plenty of persons, as they quickly discover, who think that they know something, but really know little or nothing; and then those who are examined by them instead of being angry with themselves are angry with me: This confounded Socrates, they say; this villainous misleader of youth!—and then if somebody asks them, Why, what evil does he practise or teach? they do not know, and cannot tell; but in order that they may not appear to be at a loss, they repeat the ready-made charges which are used against all philosophers about teaching things up in the clouds and under the earth, and having no gods, and making the worse appear the better cause; for they do not like to confess that their pretence of knowledge has been detected—which is the truth; and as they are numerous and ambitious and energetic, and are drawn up in battle array and have persuasive tongues, they have filled your ears with their loud and inveterate calumnies.

And this is the reason why my three accusers, Meletus and Anytus and Lycon, have set upon me; Meletus, who has a quarrel with me on behalf of the poets; Anytus, on behalf of the craftsmen and politicians; Lycon, on behalf of the rhetoricians: and as I said at the beginning, I cannot expect to get rid of such a mass of calumny all in a moment. And this, O men of Athens, is the truth and the whole truth; I have concealed nothing, I have dissembled nothing. And yet, I know that my plainness of speech makes them hate me, and what is their hatred but a proof that I am speaking the truth?—Hence has arisen the prejudice against me; and this is the reason of it, as you will find out either in this or in any future enquiry.

I have said enough in my defence against the first class of my accusers; I turn to the second class. They are headed by Meletus, that good man and true lover of his country, as he calls himself. Against these, too, I must try to make a defence:—Let their affidavit be read: it contains something of this kind: It says that Socrates is a doer of evil, who corrupts the youth; and who does not believe in the gods of the state, but has other new divinities of his own. Such is the charge; and now let us examine the particular counts. He says that I am a doer of evil, and corrupt the youth; but I say, O men of Athens, that Meletus is a doer of evil, in that he pretends to be in earnest when he is only in jest, and is so eager to bring men to trial from a pretended zeal and interest about matters in which he really never had the smallest interest. And the truth of this I will endeavour to prove to you.

Come hither, Meletus, and let me ask a question of you. You think a great deal about the improvement of youth?

Yes, I do.

Tell the judges, then, who is their improver; for you must know, as you have taken the pains to discover their corrupter, and are citing and accusing me before them. Speak, then, and tell the judges who their improver is.—Observe, Meletus, that you are silent, and have nothing to say. But is not this rather disgraceful, and a very considerable proof of what I was saying, that you have no interest in the matter? Speak up, friend, and tell us who their improver is.

The laws.

But that, my good sir, is not my meaning. I want to know who the person is, who, in the first place, knows the laws.

The judges, Socrates, who are present in court.

What, do you mean to say, Meletus, that they are able to instruct and improve youth?

Certainly they are.

What, all of them, or some only and not others?

All of them.

By the goddess Here, that is good news! There are plenty of improvers, then. And what do you say of the audience,—do they improve them?

Yes, they do.

And the senators?

Yes, the senators improve them.

But perhaps the members of the assembly corrupt them?—or do they too improve them?

They improve them.

Then every Athenian improves and elevates them; all with the exception of myself; and I alone am their corrupter? Is that what you affirm?

That is what I stoutly affirm.

I am very unfortunate if you are right. But suppose I ask you a question: How about horses? Does one man do them harm and all the world good? Is not the exact opposite the truth? One man is able to do them good, or at least not many;—the trainer of horses, that is to say, does them good, and others who have to do with them rather injure them? Is not that true, Meletus, of horses, or of any other animals? Most assuredly it is; whether you and Anytus say yes or no. Happy indeed would be the condition of youth if they had one corrupter only, and all the rest of the world were their improvers. But you, Meletus, have sufficiently shown that you never had a thought about the young: your carelessness is seen in your not caring about the very things which you bring against me.

And now, Meletus, I will ask you another question—by Zeus I will: Which is better, to live among bad citizens, or among good ones? Answer, friend, I say; the question is one which may be easily answered. Do not the good do their neighbours good, and the bad do them evil?

Certainly.

And is there anyone who would rather be injured than benefited by those who live with him? Answer, my good friend, the law requires you to answer—does any one like to be injured?

Certainly not.

And when you accuse me of corrupting and deteriorating the youth, do you allege that I corrupt them intentionally or unintentionally?

Intentionally, I say.

But you have just admitted that the good do their neighbours good, and the evil do them evil. Now, is that a truth which your superior wisdom has recognized thus early in life, and am I, at my age, in such darkness and ignorance as not to know that if a man with whom I have to live is corrupted by me, I am very likely to be harmed by him; and yet I corrupt him, and intentionally, too—so you say, although neither I nor any other human being is ever likely to be convinced by you.

But either I do not corrupt them, or I corrupt them unintentionally; and on either view of the case you lie. If my offence is unintentional, the law has no cognizance of unintentional offences: you ought to have taken me privately, and warned and admonished me; for if I had been better advised, I should have left off doing what I only did unintentionally—no doubt I should; but you would have nothing to say to me and refused to teach me. And now you bring me up in this court, which is a place not of instruction, but of punishment.

It will be very clear to you, Athenians, as I was saying, that Meletus has no care at all, great or small, about the matter. But still I should like to know, Meletus, in what I am affirmed to corrupt the young. I suppose you mean, as I infer from your indictment, that I teach them not to acknowledge the gods which the state acknowledges, but some other new divinities or spiritual agencies in their stead. These are the lessons by which I corrupt the youth, as you say.

Yes, that I say emphatically.

Then, by the gods, Meletus, of whom we are speaking, tell me and the court, in somewhat plainer terms, what you mean! for I do not as yet understand whether you affirm that I teach other men to acknowledge some gods, and therefore that I do believe in gods, and am not an entire atheist—this you do not lay to my charge,—but only you say that they are not the same gods which the city recognizes—the charge is that they are different gods. Or, do you mean that I an atheist simply, and a teacher of atheism?

I mean the latter—that you are a complete atheist.

What an extraordinary statement! Why do you think so, Meletus? Do you mean that I do not believe in the godhead of the sun or moon, like other men? I assure you, judges, that he does not: for he says that the sun is stone, and the moon earth. Friend Meletus, you think that you are accusing Anaxagoras: and you have but a bad opinion of the judges, if you fancy them illiterate to such a degree as not to know that these doctrines are found in the books of Anaxagoras the Clazomenian, which are full of them. And so, forsooth, the youth are said to be taught them by Socrates, when there are not unfrequently exhibitions of them at the theatre (price of admission one drachma at the most); and they might pay their money, and laugh at Socrates if he pretends to father these extraordinary views. And so, Meletus, you really think that I do not believe in any god?

I swear by Zeus that you believe absolutely in none at all.

Nobody will believe you, Meletus, and I am pretty sure that you do not believe yourself. I cannot help thinking, men of Athens, that Meletus is reckless and impudent, and that he has written this indictment in a spirit of mere wantonness and youthful bravado. Has he not compounded a riddle, thinking to try me? He said to himself:—I shall see whether the wise Socrates will discover my facetious contradiction, or whether I shall be able to deceive him and the rest of them. For he certainly does appear to me to contradict himself in the indictment as much as if he said that Socrates is guilty of not believing in the gods, and yet of believing in them—but this is not like a person who is in earnest.

I should like you, O men of Athens, to join me in examining what I conceive to be his inconsistency; and do you, Meletus, answer. And I must remind the audience of my request that they would not make a disturbance if I speak in my accustomed manner:

Did ever man, Meletus, believe in the existence of human things, and not of human beings? I wish, men of Athens, that he would answer, and not be always trying to get up an interruption. Did ever any man believe in horsemanship, and not in horses? or in flute-playing, and not in flute-players? No, my friend; I will answer to you and to the court, as you refuse to answer for yourself. There is no man who ever did. But now please to answer the next question: Can a man believe in spiritual and divine agencies, and not in spirits or demigods?

He cannot.

How lucky I am to have extracted that answer, by the assistance of the court! But then you swear in the indictment that I teach and believe in divine or spiritual agencies (new or old, no matter for that); at any rate, I believe in spiritual agencies,—so you say and swear in the affidavit; and yet if I believe in divine beings, how can I help believing in spirits or demigods;—must I not? To be sure I must; and therefore I may assume that your silence gives consent.

Now what are spirits or demigods? Are they not either gods or the sons of gods? Certainly they are. But this is what I call the facetious riddle invented by you: the demigods or spirits are gods, and you say first that I do not believe in gods, and then again that I do believe in gods; that is, if I believe in demigods. For if the demigods are the illegitimate sons of gods, whether by the nymphs or by any other mothers, of whom they are said to be the sons—what human being will ever believe that there are no gods if they are the sons of gods? You might as well affirm the existence of mules, and deny that of horses and asses.

Such nonsense, Meletus, could only have been intended by you to make trial of me. You have put this into the indictment because you had nothing real of which to accuse me. But no one who has a particle of understanding will ever be convinced by you that the same men can believe in divine and superhuman things, and yet not believe that there are gods and demigods and heroes.

I have said enough in answer to the charge of Meletus: any elaborate defence is unnecessary, but I know only too well how many are the enmities which I have incurred, and this is what will be my destruction if I am destroyed;—not Meletus, nor yet Anytus, but the envy and detraction of the world, which has been the death of many good men, and will probably be the death of many more; there is no danger of my being the last of them.

Some one will say: And are you not ashamed, Socrates, of a course of life which is likely to bring you to an untimely end? To him I may fairly answer: There you are mistaken: a man who is good for anything ought not to calculate the chance of living or dying; he ought only to consider whether in doing anything he is doing right or wrong—acting the part of a good man or of a bad. Whereas, upon your view, the heroes who fell at Troy were not good for much, and the son of Thetis above all, who altogether despised danger in comparison with disgrace; and when he was so eager to slay Hector, his goddess mother said to him, that if he avenged his companion Patroclus, and slew Hector, he would die himself—'Fate,' she said, in these or the like words, 'waits for you next after Hector;' he, receiving this warning, utterly despised danger and death, and instead of fearing them, feared rather to live in dishonour, and not to avenge his friend. 'Let me die forthwith,' he replies, 'and be avenged of my enemy, rather than abide here by the beaked ships, a laughing-stock and a burden of the earth.' Had Achilles any thought of death and danger? For wherever a man's place is, whether the place which he has chosen or that in which he has been placed by a commander, there he ought to remain in the hour of danger; he should not think of death or of anything but of disgrace. And this, O men of Athens, is a true saying.

Strange, indeed, would be my conduct, O men of Athens, if I who, when I was ordered by the generals whom you chose to command me at Potidaea and Amphipolis and Delium, remained where they placed me, like any other man, facing death—if now, when, as I conceive and imagine, God orders me to fulfil the philosopher's mission of searching into myself and other men, I were to desert my post through fear of death, or any other fear; that would indeed be strange, and I might justly be arraigned in court for denying the existence of the gods, if I disobeyed the oracle because I was afraid of death, fancying that I was wise when I was not wise. For the fear of death is indeed the pretence of wisdom, not real wisdom, being a pretence of knowing the unknown; and no one knows whether death, which men in their fear apprehend to be the greatest evil, may not be the greatest good. Is not this ignorance of a disgraceful sort, the ignorance which is the conceit that a man knows what he does not know?

And in this respect only I believe myself to differ from men in general, and may perhaps claim to be wiser than they are:—that whereas I know but little of the world below, I do not suppose that I know: but I do know that injustice and disobedience to a better, whether God or man, is evil and dishonourable, and I will never fear or avoid a possible good rather than a certain evil.

And therefore if you let me go now, and are not convinced by Anytus, who said that since I had been prosecuted I must be put to death; (or if not that I ought never to have been prosecuted at all); and that if I escape now, your sons will all be utterly ruined by listening to my words—if you say to me, Socrates, this time we will not mind Anytus, and you shall be let off, but upon one condition, that you are not to enquire and speculate in this way any more, and that if you are caught doing so again you shall die;—if this was the condition on which you let me go, I should reply: Men of Athens, I honour and love you; but I shall obey God rather than you, and while I have life and strength I shall never cease from the practice and teaching of philosophy, exhorting any one whom I meet and saying to him after my manner: You, my friend,—a citizen of the great and mighty and wise city of Athens,—are you not ashamed of heaping up the greatest amount of money and honour and reputation, and caring so little about wisdom and truth and the greatest improvement of the soul, which you never regard or heed at all?

And if the person with whom I am arguing, says: Yes, but I do care; then I do not leave him or let him go at once; but I proceed to interrogate and examine and cross-examine him, and if I think that he has no virtue in him, but only says that he has, I reproach him with undervaluing the greater, and overvaluing the less. And I shall repeat the same words to every one whom I meet, young and old, citizen and alien, but especially to the citizens, inasmuch as they are my brethren. For know that this is the command of God; and I believe that no greater good has ever happened in the state than my service to the God. For I do nothing but go about persuading you all, old and young alike, not to take thought for your persons or your properties, but first and chiefly to care about the greatest improvement of the soul. I tell you that virtue is not given by money, but that from virtue comes money and every other good of man, public as well as private. This is my teaching, and if this is the doctrine which corrupts the youth, I am a mischievous person. But if any one says that this is not my teaching, he is speaking an untruth.

Wherefore, O men of Athens, I say to you, do as Anytus bids or not as Anytus bids, and either acquit me or not; but whichever you do, understand that I shall never alter my ways, not even if I have to die many times. Men of Athens, do not interrupt, but hear me; there was an understanding between us that you should hear me to the end: I have something more to say, at which you may be inclined to cry out; but I believe that to hear me will be good for you, and therefore I beg that you will not cry out.

I would have you know, that if you kill such an one as I am, you will injure yourselves more than you will injure me. Nothing will injure me, not Meletus nor yet Anytus—they cannot, for a bad man is not permitted to injure a better than himself. I do not deny that Anytus may, perhaps, kill him, or drive him into exile, or deprive him of civil rights; and he may imagine, and others may imagine, that he is inflicting a great injury upon him: but there I do not agree. For the evil of doing as he is doing—the evil of unjustly taking away the life of another—is greater far.

And now, Athenians, I am not going to argue for my own sake, as you may think, but for yours, that you may not sin against the God by condemning me, who am his gift to you. For if you kill me you will not easily find a successor to me, who, if I may use such a ludicrous figure of speech, am a sort of gadfly, given to the state by God; and the state is a great and noble steed who is tardy in his motions owing to his very size, and requires to be stirred into life. I am that gadfly which God has attached to the state, and all day long and in all places am always fastening upon you, arousing and persuading and reproaching you. You will not easily find another like me, and therefore I would advise you to spare me. I dare say that you may feel out of temper (like a person who is suddenly awakened from sleep), and you think that you might easily strike me dead as Anytus advises, and then you would sleep on for the remainder of your lives, unless God in his care of you sent you another gadfly.

When I say that I am given to you by God, the proof of my mission is this:—if I had been like other men, I should not have neglected all my own concerns or patiently seen the neglect of them during all these years, and have been doing yours, coming to you individually like a father or elder brother, exhorting you to regard virtue; such conduct, I say, would be unlike human nature. If I had gained anything, or if my exhortations had been paid, there would have been some sense in my doing so; but now, as you will perceive, not even the impudence of my accusers dares to say that I have ever exacted or sought pay of any one; of that they have no witness. And I have a sufficient witness to the truth of what I say—my poverty.

Some one may wonder why I go about in private giving advice and busying myself with the concerns of others, but do not venture to come forward in public and advise the state. I will tell you why. You have heard me speak at sundry times and in divers places of an oracle or sign which comes to me, and is the divinity which Meletus ridicules in the indictment. This sign, which is a kind of voice, first began to come to me when I was a child; it always forbids but never commands me to do anything which I am going to do. This is what deters me from being a politician. And rightly, as I think. For I am certain, O men of Athens, that if I had engaged in politics, I should have perished long ago, and done no good either to you or to myself.

And do not be offended at my telling you the truth: for the truth is, that no man who goes to war with you or any other multitude, honestly striving against the many lawless and unrighteous deeds which are done in a state, will save his life; he who will fight for the right, if he would live even for a brief space, must have a private station and not a public one. I can give you convincing evidence of what I say, not words only, but what you value far more—actions.

Let me relate to you a passage of my own life which will prove to you that I should never have yielded to injustice from any fear of death, and that 'as I should have refused to yield' I must have died at once. I will tell you a tale of the courts, not very interesting perhaps, but nevertheless true. The only office of state which I ever held, O men of Athens, was that of senator: the tribe Antiochis, which is my tribe, had the presidency at the trial of the generals who had not taken up the bodies of the slain after the battle of Arginusae; and you proposed to try them in a body contrary to law as you all thought afterwards; but at the time I was the only one of the Prytanes who was opposed to the illegality, and I gave my vote against you; and when the orators threatened to impeach and arrest me, and you called and shouted, I made up my mind that I would run the risk, having law and justice with me, rather than take part in your injustice because I feared imprisonment and death.

This happened in the days of the democracy. But when the oligarchy of the Thirty was in power, they sent for me and four others into the rotunda, and bade us bring Leon the Salaminian from Salamis, as they wanted to put him to death. This was a specimen of the sort of commands which they were always giving with the view of implicating as many as possible in their crimes; and then I showed, not in word only but in deed, that, if I may be allowed to use such an expression, I cared not a straw for death, and that my great and only care was lest I should do an unrighteous or unholy thing. For the strong arm of that oppressive power did not frighten me into doing wrong; and when we came out of the rotunda the other four went to Salamis and fetched Leon, but I went quietly home. For which I might have lost my life, had not the power of the Thirty shortly afterwards come to an end. And many will witness to my words.

Now do you really imagine that I could have survived all these years, if I had led a public life, supposing that like a good man I had always maintained the right and had made justice, as I ought, the first thing? No indeed, men of Athens, neither I nor any other man. But I have been always the same in all my actions, public as well as private, and never have I yielded any base compliance to those who are slanderously termed my disciples, or to any other.

Not that I have any regular disciples. But if any one likes to come and hear me while I am pursuing my mission, whether he be young or old, he is not excluded. Nor do I converse only with those who pay; but any one, whether he be rich or poor, may ask and answer me and listen to my words; and whether he turns out to be a bad man or a good one, neither result can be justly imputed to me; for I never taught or professed to teach him anything. And if any one says that he has ever learned or heard anything from me in private which all the world has not heard, let me tell you he is lying.

But I shall be asked, Why do people delight in continually conversing with you? I have told you already, Athenians, the whole truth about this matter: they like to hear the cross-examination of the pretenders to wisdom; there is amusement in it. Now this duty of cross-examining other men has been imposed upon me by God; and has been signified to me by oracles, visions, and in every way in which the will of divine power was ever intimated to any one. This is true, O Athenians, or, if not true, would be soon refuted.

If I am or have been corrupting the youth, those of them who are now grown up and have become sensible that I gave them bad advice in the days of their youth should come forward as accusers, and take their revenge; or if they do not like to come themselves, some of their relatives, fathers, brothers, or other kinsmen, should say what evil their families have suffered at my hands. Now is their time.

Many of them I see in the court. There is Crito, who is of the same age and of the same deme with myself, and there is Critobulus his son, whom I also see. Then again there is Lysanias of Sphettus, who is the father of Aeschines—he is present; and also there is Antiphon of Cephisus, who is the father of Epigenes; and there are the brothers of several who have associated with me. There is Nicostratus the son of Theosdotides, and the brother of Theodotus (now Theodotus himself is dead, and therefore he, at any rate, will not seek to stop him); and there is Paralus the son of Demodocus, who had a brother Theages; and Adeimantus the son of Ariston, whose brother Plato is present; and Aeantodorus, who is the brother of Apollodorus, whom I also see. I might mention a great many others, some of whom Meletus should have produced as witnesses in the course of his speech; and let him still produce them, if he has forgotten—I will make way for him.

And let him say, if he has any testimony of the sort which he can produce. Nay, Athenians, the very opposite is the truth. For all these are ready to witness on behalf of the corrupter, of the injurer of their kindred, as Meletus and Anytus call me; not the corrupted youth only—there might have been a motive for that—but their uncorrupted elder relatives. Why should they too support me with their testimony? Why, indeed, except for the sake of truth and justice, and because they know that I am speaking the truth, and that Meletus is a liar.

Well, Athenians, this and the like of this is all the defence which I have to offer. Yet a word more. Perhaps there may be some one who is offended at me, when he calls to mind how he himself on a similar, or even a less serious occasion, prayed and entreated the judges with many tears, and how he produced his children in court, which was a moving spectacle, together with a host of relations and friends; whereas I, who am probably in danger of my life, will do none of these things. The contrast may occur to his mind, and he may be set against me, and vote in anger because he is displeased at me on this account. Now if there be such a person among you,—mind, I do not say that there is,—to him I may fairly reply: My friend, I am a man, and like other men, a creature of flesh and blood, and not 'of wood or stone,' as Homer says; and I have a family, yes, and sons, O Athenians, three in number, one almost a man, and two others who are still young; and yet I will not bring any of them hither in order to petition you for an acquittal. And why not? Not from any self-assertion or want of respect for you.

Whether I am or am not afraid of death is another question, of which I will not now speak. But, having regard to public opinion, I feel that such conduct would be discreditable to myself, and to you, and to the whole state. One who has reached my years, and who has a name for wisdom, ought not to demean himself. Whether this opinion of me be deserved or not, at any rate the world has decided that Socrates is in some way superior to other men. And if those among you who are said to be superior in wisdom and courage, and any other virtue, demean themselves in this way, how shameful is their conduct! I have seen men of reputation, when they have been condemned, behaving in the strangest manner: they seemed to fancy that they were going to suffer something dreadful if they died, and that they could be immortal if you only allowed them to live; and I think that such are a dishonour to the state, and that any stranger coming in would have said of them that the most eminent men of Athens, to whom the Athenians themselves give honour and command, are no better than women.

And I say that these things ought not to be done by those of us who have a reputation; and if they are done, you ought not to permit them; you ought rather to show that you are far more disposed to condemn the man who gets up a doleful scene and makes the city ridiculous, than him who holds his peace. But setting aside the question of public opinion, there seems to be something wrong in asking a favour of a judge, and thus procuring an acquittal, instead of informing and convincing him. For his duty is not to make a present of justice but to give judgment; and he has sworn that he will judge according to the laws and not according to his own pleasure; and we ought not to encourage you, nor should you allow yourselves to be encouraged, in this habit of perjury—there can be no piety in that.

Do not then require me to do what I consider dishonourable and impious and wrong, especially now, when I am being tried for impiety on the indictment of Meletus. For if, O men of Athens, by force of persuasion and entreaty I could overpower your oaths, then I should be teaching you to believe that there are no gods, and in defending should simply convict myself of the charge of not believing in them. But that is not so—far otherwise. For I do believe that there are gods, and in a sense higher than that in which any of my accusers believe in them. And to you and to God I commit my cause, to be determined by you as is best for you and me.

•

There are many reasons why I am not grieved, O men of Athens, at the vote of condemnation. I expected it, and am only surprised that the votes are so nearly equal; for I had thought that the majority against me would have been far larger; but now, had thirty votes gone over to the other side, I should have been acquitted. And I may say, I think, that I have escaped Meletus. I may say more; for without the assistance of Anytus and Lycon, any one may see that he would not have had a fifth part of the votes, as the law requires, in which case he would have incurred a fine of a thousand drachmae. And so he proposes death as the penalty. And what shall I propose on my part, O men of Athens?

Clearly that which is my due. And what is my due? What return shall be made to the man who has never had the wit to be idle during his whole life; but has been careless of what the many care for—wealth, and family interests, and military offices, and speaking in the assembly, and magistracies, and plots, and parties. Reflecting that I was really too honest a man to be a politician and live, I did not go where I could do no good to you or to myself; but where I could do the greatest good privately to every one of you, thither I went, and sought to persuade every man among you that he must look to himself, and seek virtue and wisdom before he looks to his private interests, and look to the state before he looks to the interests of the state; and that this should be the order which he observes in all his actions. What shall be done to such an one?

Doubtless some good thing, O men of Athens, if he has his reward; and the good should be of a kind suitable to him. What would be a reward suitable to a poor man who is your benefactor, and who desires leisure that he may instruct you? There can be no reward so fitting as maintenance in the Prytaneum, O men of Athens, a reward which he deserves far more than the citizen who has won the prize at Olympia in the horse or chariot race, whether the chariots were drawn by two horses or by many. For I am in want, and he has enough; and he only gives you the appearance of happiness, and I give you the reality. And if I am to estimate the penalty fairly, I should say that maintenance in the Prytaneum is the just return.

Perhaps you think that I am braving you in what I am saying now, as in what I said before about the tears and prayers. But this is not so. I speak rather because I am convinced that I never intentionally wronged any one, although I cannot convince you—the time has been too short; if there were a law at Athens, as there is in other cities, that a capital cause should not be decided in one day, then I believe that I should have convinced you. But I cannot in a moment refute great slanders; and, as I am convinced that I never wronged another, I will assuredly not wrong myself. I will not say of myself that I deserve any evil, or propose any penalty.

Why should I? because I am afraid of the penalty of death which Meletus proposes? When I do not know whether death is a good or an evil, why should I propose a penalty which would certainly be an evil? Shall I say imprisonment? And why should I live in prison, and be the slave of the magistrates of the year—of the Eleven? Or shall the penalty be a fine, and imprisonment until the fine is paid? There is the same objection. I should have to lie in prison, for money I have none, and cannot pay. And if I say exile (and this may possibly be the penalty which you will affix), I must indeed be blinded by the love of life, if I am so irrational as to expect that when you, who are my own citizens, cannot endure my discourses and words, and have found them so grievous and odious that you will have no more of them, others are likely to endure me.

No indeed, men of Athens, that is not very likely. And what a life should I lead, at my age, wandering from city to city, ever changing my place of exile, and always being driven out! For I am quite sure that wherever I go, there, as here, the young men will flock to me; and if I drive them away, their elders will drive me out at their request; and if I let them come, their fathers and friends will drive me out for their sakes.

Some one will say: Yes, Socrates, but cannot you hold your tongue, and then you may go into a foreign city, and no one will interfere with you? Now I have great difficulty in making you understand my answer to this. For if I tell you that to do as you say would be a disobedience to the God, and therefore that I cannot hold my tongue, you will not believe that I am serious; and if I say again that daily to discourse about virtue, and of those other things about which you hear me examining myself and others, is the greatest good of man, and that the unexamined life is not worth living, you are still less likely to believe me. Yet I say what is true, although a thing of which it is hard for me to persuade you. Also, I have never been accustomed to think that I deserve to suffer any harm.

Had I money I might have estimated the offence at what I was able to pay, and not have been much the worse. But I have none, and therefore I must ask you to proportion the fine to my means. Well, perhaps I could afford a mina, and therefore I propose that penalty: Plato, Crito, Critobulus, and Apollodorus, my friends here, bid me say thirty minae, and they will be the sureties. Let thirty minae be the penalty; for which sum they will be ample security to you.

•

Not much time will be gained, O Athenians, in return for the evil name which you will get from the detractors of the city, who will say that you killed Socrates, a wise man; for they will call me wise, even although I am not wise, when they want to reproach you. If you had waited a little while, your desire would have been fulfilled in the course of nature. For I am far advanced in years, as you may perceive, and not far from death. I am speaking now not to all of you, but only to those who have condemned me to death.

And I have another thing to say to them: you think that I was convicted because I had no words of the sort which would have procured my acquittal—I mean, if I had thought fit to leave nothing undone or unsaid. Not so; the deficiency which led to my conviction was not of words—certainly not. But I had not the boldness or impudence or inclination to address you as you would have liked me to do, weeping and wailing and lamenting, and saying and doing many things which you have been accustomed to hear from others, and which, as I maintain, are unworthy of me. I thought at the time that I ought not to do anything common or mean when in danger: nor do I now repent of the style of my defence; I would rather die having spoken after my manner, than speak in your manner and live.

For neither in war nor yet at law ought I or any man to use every way of escaping death. Often in battle there can be no doubt that if a man will throw away his arms, and fall on his knees before his pursuers, he may escape death; and in other dangers there are other ways of escaping death, if a man is willing to say and do anything. The difficulty, my friends, is not to avoid death, but to avoid unrighteousness; for that runs faster than death. I am old and move slowly, and the slower runner has overtaken me, and my accusers are keen and quick, and the faster runner, who is unrighteousness, has overtaken them. And now I depart hence condemned by you to suffer the penalty of death, —they too go their ways condemned by the truth to suffer the penalty of villainy and wrong; and I must abide by my award—let them abide by theirs.

I suppose that these things may be regarded as fated,—and I think that they are well. And now, O men who have condemned me, I would fain prophesy to you; for I am about to die, and in the hour of death men are gifted with prophetic power. And I prophesy to you who are my murderers, that immediately after my departure punishment far heavier than you have inflicted on me will surely await you. Me you have killed because you wanted to escape the accuser, and not to give an account of your lives. But that will not be as you suppose: far otherwise. For I say that there will be more accusers of you than there are now; accusers whom hitherto I have restrained: and as they are younger they will be more inconsiderate with you, and you will be more offended at them. If you think that by killing men you can prevent some one from censuring your evil lives, you are mistaken; that is not a way of escape which is either possible or honourable; the easiest and the noblest way is not to be disabling others, but to be improving yourselves.

This is the prophecy which I utter before my departure to the judges who have condemned me. Friends, who would have acquitted me, I would like also to talk with you about the thing which has come to pass, while the magistrates are busy, and before I go to the place at which I must die. Stay then a little, for we may as well talk with one another while there is time. You are my friends, and I should like to show you the meaning of this event which has happened to me.

O my judges—for you I may truly call judges—I should like to tell you of a wonderful circumstance. Hitherto the divine faculty of which the internal oracle is the source has constantly been in the habit of opposing me even about trifles, if I was going to make a slip or error in any matter; and now as you see there has come upon me that which may be thought, and is generally believed to be, the last and worst evil. But the oracle made no sign of opposition, either when I was leaving my house in the morning, or when I was on my way to the court, or while I was speaking, at anything which I was going to say; and yet I have often been stopped in the middle of a speech, but now in nothing I either said or did touching the matter in hand has the oracle opposed me. What do I take to be the explanation of this silence?

I will tell you. It is an intimation that what has happened to me is a good, and that those of us who think that death is an evil are in error. For the customary sign would surely have opposed me had I been going to evil and not to good. Let us reflect in another way, and we shall see that there is great reason to hope that death is a good; for one of two things—either death is a state of nothingness and utter unconsciousness, or, as men say, there is a change and migration of the soul from this world to another. Now if you suppose that there is no consciousness, but a sleep like the sleep of him who is undisturbed even by dreams, death will be an unspeakable gain. For if a person were to select the night in which his sleep was undisturbed even by dreams, and were to compare with this the other days and nights of his life, and then were to tell us how many days and nights he had passed in the course of his life better and more pleasantly than this one, I think that any man, I will not say a private man, but even the great king will not find many such days or nights, when compared with the others.

Now if death be of such a nature, I say that to die is gain; for eternity is then only a single night. But if death is the journey to another place, and there, as men say, all the dead abide, what good, O my friends and judges, can be greater than this? If indeed when the pilgrim arrives in the world below, he is delivered from the professors of justice in this world, and finds the true judges who are said to give judgment there, Minos and Rhadamanthus and Aeacus and Triptolemus, and other sons of God who were righteous in their own life, that pilgrimage will be worth making. What would not a man give if he might converse with Orpheus and Musaeus and Hesiod and Homer? Nay, if this be true, let me die again and again. I myself, too, shall have a wonderful interest in there meeting and conversing with Palamedes, and Ajax the son of Telamon, and any other ancient hero who has suffered death through an unjust judgment; and there will be no small pleasure, as I think, in comparing my own sufferings with theirs.

Above all, I shall then be able to continue my search into true and false knowledge; as in this world, so also in the next; and I shall find out who is wise, and who pretends to be wise, and is not. What would not a man give, O judges, to be able to examine the leader of the great Trojan expedition; or Odysseus or Sisyphus, or numberless others, men and women too! What infinite delight would there be in conversing with them and asking them questions! In another world they do not put a man to death for asking questions: assuredly not. For besides being happier than we are, they will be immortal, if what is said is true.

Wherefore, O judges, be of good cheer about death, and know of a certainty, that no evil can happen to a good man, either in life or after death. He and his are not neglected by the gods; nor has my own approaching end happened by mere chance. But I see clearly that the time had arrived when it was better for me to die and be released from trouble; wherefore the oracle gave no sign. For which reason, also, I am not angry with my condemners, or with my accusers; they have done me no harm, although they did not mean to do me any good; and for this I may gently blame them.

Still I have a favour to ask of them. When my sons are grown up, I would ask you, O my friends, to punish them; and I would have you trouble them, as I have troubled you, if they seem to care about riches, or anything, more than about virtue; or if they pretend to be something when they are really nothing,—then reprove them, as I have reproved you, for not caring about that for which they ought to care, and thinking that they are something when they are really nothing. And if you do this, both I and my sons will have received justice at your hands.

The hour of departure has arrived, and we go our ways—I to die, and you to live. Which is better God only knows.

PLATO

Phaedo

Translated by Benjamin Jowett

PERSONS OF THE DIALOGUE: Phaedo, who is the narrator of the dialogue to Echecrates of Phlius. Socrates, Apollodorus, Simmias, Cebes, Crito, and an Attendant of the Prison.

THE SETTING: The Prison of Socrates.

ECHECRATES: Were you yourself, Phaedo, in the prison with Socrates on the day when he drank the poison?

PHAEDO: Yes, Echecrates, I was.

ECHECRATES: I should so like to hear about his death. What did he say in his last hours? We were informed that he died by taking poison, but no one knew anything more; for no Phliasian ever goes to Athens now, and it is a long time since any stranger from Athens has found his way hither; so that we had no clear account.

PHAEDO: Did you not hear of the proceedings at the trial?

ECHECRATES: Yes; some one told us about the trial, and we could not understand why, having been condemned, he should have been put to death, not at the time, but long afterwards. What was the reason of this?

PHAEDO: An accident, Echecrates: the stern of the ship which the Athenians send to Delos happened to have been crowned on the day before he was tried.

ECHECRATES: What is this ship?

PHAEDO: It is the ship in which, according to Athenian tradition, Theseus went to Crete when he took with him the fourteen youths, and was the saviour of them and of himself. And they were said to have vowed to Apollo at the time, that if they were saved they would send a yearly mission to Delos. Now this custom still continues, and the whole period of the voyage to and from Delos, beginning when the priest of Apollo crowns the stern of the ship, is a holy season, during which the city is not allowed to be polluted by public executions; and when the vessel is detained by contrary winds, the time spent in going and returning is very considerable. As I was saying, the ship was crowned on the day before the trial, and this was the reason why Socrates lay in prison and was not put to death until long after he was condemned.

ECHECRATES: What was the manner of his death, Phaedo? What was said or done? And which of his friends were with him? Or did the authorities forbid them to be present—so that he had no friends near him when he died?

PHAEDO: No; there were several of them with him.

ECHECRATES: If you have nothing to do, I wish that you would tell me what passed, as exactly as you can.

PHAEDO: I have nothing at all to do, and will try to gratify your wish. To be reminded of Socrates is always the greatest delight to me, whether I speak myself or hear another speak of him.

ECHECRATES: You will have listeners who are of the same mind with you, and I hope that you will be as exact as you can.

PHAEDO: I had a singular feeling at being in his company. For I could hardly believe that I was present at the death of a friend, and therefore I did not pity him, Echecrates; he died so fearlessly, and his words and bearing were so noble and gracious, that to me he appeared blessed. I thought that in going to the other world he could not be without a divine call, and that he would be happy, if any man ever was, when he arrived there, and therefore I did not pity him as might have seemed natural at such an hour. But I had not the pleasure which I usually feel in philosophical discourse (for philosophy was the theme of which we spoke). I was pleased, but in the pleasure there was also a strange admixture of pain; for I reflected that he was soon to die, and this double feeling was shared by us all; we were laughing and weeping by turns, especially the excitable Apollodorus—you know the sort of man?

ECHECRATES: Yes.

PHAEDO: He was quite beside himself; and I and all of us were greatly moved.

ECHECRATES: Who were present?

PHAEDO: Of native Athenians there were, besides Apollodorus, Critobulus and his father Crito, Hermogenes, Epigenes, Aeschines, Antisthenes; likewise Ctesippus of the deme of Paeania, Menexenus, and some others; Plato, if I am not mistaken, was ill.

ECHECRATES: Were there any strangers?

PHAEDO: Yes, there were; Simmias the Theban, and Cebes, and Phaedondes; Euclid and Terpison, who came from Megara.

ECHECRATES: And was Aristippus there, and Cleombrotus?

PHAEDO: No, they were said to be in Aegina.

ECHECRATES: Any one else?

PHAEDO: I think that these were nearly all.

ECHECRATES: Well, and what did you talk about?

PHAEDO: I will begin at the beginning, and endeavour to repeat the entire conversation.

On the previous days we had been in the habit of assembling early in the morning at the court in which the trial took place, and which is not far from the prison. There we used to wait talking with one another until the opening of the doors (for they were not opened very early); then we went in and generally passed the day with Socrates. On the last morning we assembled sooner than usual, having heard on the day before when we quitted the prison in the evening that the sacred ship had come from Delos, and so we arranged to meet very early at the accustomed place. On our arrival the jailer who answered the door, instead of admitting us, came out and told us to stay until he called us. 'For the Eleven,' he said, 'are now with Socrates; they are taking off his chains, and giving orders that he is to die to-day.' He soon returned and said that we might come in.

On entering we found Socrates just released from chains, and Xanthippe, whom you know, sitting by him, and holding his child in her arms. When she saw us she uttered a cry and said, as women will: 'O Socrates, this is the last time that either you will converse with your friends, or they with you.' Socrates turned to Crito and said: 'Crito, let some one take her home.' Some of Crito's people accordingly led her away, crying out and beating herself. And when she was gone, Socrates, sitting up on the couch, bent and rubbed his leg, saying, as he was rubbing:

"How singular is the thing called pleasure, and how curiously related to pain, which might be thought to be the opposite of it; for they are never present to a man at the same instant, and yet he who pursues either is generally compelled to take the other; their bodies are two, but they are joined by a single head. And I cannot help thinking that if Aesop had remembered them, he would have made a fable about God trying to reconcile their strife, and how, when he could not, he fastened their heads together; and this is the reason why when one comes the other follows, as I know by my own experience now, when after the pain in my leg which was caused by the chain pleasure appears to succeed."

Upon this Cebes said: I am glad, Socrates, that you have mentioned the name of Aesop. For it reminds me of a question which has been asked by many, and was asked of me only the day before yesterday by Evenus the poet —he will be sure to ask it again, and therefore if you would like me to have an answer ready for him, you may as well tell me what I should say to him:—he wanted to know why you, who never before wrote a line of poetry, now that you are in prison are turning Aesop's fables into verse, and also composing that hymn in honour of Apollo.

Tell him, Cebes, he replied, what is the truth—that I had no idea of rivalling him or his poems; to do so, as I knew, would be no easy task. But I wanted to see whether I could purge away a scruple which I felt about the meaning of certain dreams. In the course of my life I have often had intimations in dreams 'that I should compose music.' The same dream came to me sometimes in one form, and sometimes in another, but always saying the same or nearly the same words: 'Cultivate and make music,' said the dream. And hitherto I had imagined that this was only intended to exhort and encourage me in the study of philosophy, which has been the pursuit of my life, and is the noblest and best of music. The dream was bidding me do what I was already doing, in the same way that the competitor in a race is bidden by the spectators to run when he is already running.

But I was not certain of this, for the dream might have meant music in the popular sense of the word, and being under sentence of death, and the festival giving me a respite, I thought that it would be safer for me to satisfy the scruple, and, in obedience to the dream, to compose a few verses before I departed. And first I made a hymn in honour of the god of the festival, and then considering that a poet, if he is really to be a poet, should not only put together words, but should invent stories, and that I have no invention, I took some fables of Aesop, which I had ready at hand and which I knew—they were the first I came upon—and turned them into verse. Tell this to Evenus, Cebes, and bid him be of good cheer; say that I would have him come after me if he be a wise man, and not tarry; and that to-day I am likely to be going, for the Athenians say that I must.

Simmias said: What a message for such a man! having been a frequent companion of his I should say that, as far as I know him, he will never take your advice unless he is obliged.

Why, said Socrates,—is not Evenus a philosopher? I think that he is, said Simmias. Then he, or any man who has the spirit of philosophy, will be willing to die, but he will not take his own life, for that is held to be unlawful. Here he changed his position, and put his legs off the couch on to the ground, and during the rest of the conversation he remained sitting.

Why do you say, enquired Cebes, that a man ought not to take his own life, but that the philosopher will be ready to follow the dying?

Socrates replied: And have you, Cebes and Simmias, who are the disciples of Philolaus, never heard him speak of this?

Yes, but his language was obscure, Socrates.

My words, too, are only an echo; but there is no reason why I should not repeat what I have heard: and indeed, as I am going to another place, it is very meet for me to be thinking and talking of the nature of the pilgrimage which I am about to make. What can I do better in the interval between this and the setting of the sun?

Then tell me, Socrates, why is suicide held to be unlawful? as I have certainly heard Philolaus, about whom you were just now asking, affirm when he was staying with us at Thebes: and there are others who say the same, although I have never understood what was meant by any of them.

Do not lose heart, replied Socrates, and the day may come when you will understand. I suppose that you wonder why, when other things which are evil may be good at certain times and to certain persons, death is to be the only exception, and why, when a man is better dead, he is not permitted to be his own benefactor, but must wait for the hand of another.

Very true, said Cebes, laughing gently and speaking in his native Boeotian. I admit the appearance of inconsistency in what I am saying; but there may not be any real inconsistency after all. There is a doctrine whispered in secret that man is a prisoner who has no right to open the door and run away; this is a great mystery which I do not quite understand. Yet I too believe that the gods are our guardians, and that we are a possession of theirs. Do you not agree?

Yes, I quite agree, said Cebes. And if one of your own possessions, an ox or an ass, for example, took the liberty of putting himself out of the way when you had given no intimation of your wish that he should die, would you not be angry with him, and would you not punish him if you could?

Certainly, replied Cebes.

Then, if we look at the matter thus, there may be reason in saying that a man should wait, and not take his own life until God summons him, as he is now summoning me.

Yes, Socrates, said Cebes, there seems to be truth in what you say. And yet how can you reconcile this seemingly true belief that God is our guardian and we his possessions, with the willingness to die which we were just now attributing to the philosopher? That the wisest of men should be willing to leave a service in which they are ruled by the gods who are the best of rulers, is not reasonable; for surely no wise man thinks that when set at liberty he can take better care of himself than the gods take of him. A fool may perhaps think so—he may argue that he had better run away from his master, not considering that his duty is to remain to the end, and not to run away from the good, and that there would be no sense in his running away. The wise man will want to be ever with him who is better than himself. Now this, Socrates, is the reverse of what was just now said; for upon this view the wise man should sorrow and the fool rejoice at passing out of life.

The earnestness of Cebes seemed to please Socrates. Here, said he, turning to us, is a man who is always inquiring, and is not so easily convinced by the first thing which he hears. And certainly, added Simmias, the objection which he is now making does appear to me to have some force. For what can be the meaning of a truly wise man wanting to fly away and lightly leave a master who is better than himself? And I rather imagine that Cebes is referring to you; he thinks that you are too ready to leave us, and too ready to leave the gods whom you acknowledge to be our good masters.

Yes, replied Socrates; there is reason in what you say. And so you think that I ought to answer your indictment as if I were in a court?

We should like you to do so, said Simmias.

Then I must try to make a more successful defence before you than I did when before the judges. For I am quite ready to admit, Simmias and Cebes, that I ought to be grieved at death, if I were not persuaded in the first place that I am going to other gods who are wise and good (of which I am as certain as I can be of any such matters), and secondly (though I am not so sure of this last) to men departed, better than those whom I leave behind; and therefore I do not grieve as I might have done, for I have good hope that there is yet something remaining for the dead, and as has been said of old, some far better thing for the good than for the evil.

But do you mean to take away your thoughts with you, Socrates? said Simmias. Will you not impart them to us?—for they are a benefit in which we too are entitled to share. Moreover, if you succeed in convincing us, that will be an answer to the charge against yourself.

I will do my best, replied Socrates. But you must first let me hear what Crito wants; he has long been wishing to say something to me.

Only this, Socrates, replied Crito:—the attendant who is to give you the poison has been telling me, and he wants me to tell you, that you are not to talk much, talking, he says, increases heat, and this is apt to interfere with the action of the poison; persons who excite themselves are sometimes obliged to take a second or even a third dose.

Then, said Socrates, let him mind his business and be prepared to give the poison twice or even thrice if necessary; that is all.

I knew quite well what you would say, replied Crito; but I was obliged to satisfy him.

Never mind him, he said. And now, O my judges, I desire to prove to you that the real philosopher has reason to be of good cheer when he is about to die, and that after death he may hope to obtain the greatest good in the other world. And how this may be, Simmias and Cebes, I will endeavour to explain. For I deem that the true votary of philosophy is likely to be misunderstood by other men; they do not perceive that he is always pursuing death and dying; and if this be so, and he has had the desire of death all his life long, why when his time comes should he repine at that which he has been always pursuing and desiring?

Simmias said laughingly: Though not in a laughing humour, you have made me laugh, Socrates; for I cannot help thinking that the many when they hear your words will say how truly you have described philosophers, and our people at home will likewise say that the life which philosophers desire is in reality death, and that they have found them out to be deserving of the death which they desire.

And they are right, Simmias, in thinking so, with the exception of the words 'they have found them out'; for they have not found out either what is the nature of that death which the true philosopher deserves, or how he deserves or desires death. But enough of them:—let us discuss the matter among ourselves: Do we believe that there is such a thing as death?

To be sure, replied Simmias.

Is it not the separation of soul and body? And to be dead is the completion of this; when the soul exists in herself, and is released from the body and the body is released from the soul, what is this but death?

Just so, he replied.

There is another question, which will probably throw light on our present inquiry if you and I can agree about it:—Ought the philosopher to care about the pleasures—if they are to be called pleasures—of eating and drinking?

Certainly not, answered Simmias.

And what about the pleasures of love—should he care for them?

By no means.

And will he think much of the other ways of indulging the body, for example, the acquisition of costly raiment, or sandals, or other adornments of the body? Instead of caring about them, does he not rather despise anything more than nature needs? What do you say?

I should say that the true philosopher would despise them.

Would you not say that he is entirely concerned with the soul and not with the body? He would like, as far as he can, to get away from the body and to turn to the soul.

Quite true.

In matters of this sort philosophers, above all other men, may be observed in every sort of way to dissever the soul from the communion of the body.

Very true.

Whereas, Simmias, the rest of the world are of opinion that to him who has no sense of pleasure and no part in bodily pleasure, life is not worth having; and that he who is indifferent about them is as good as dead.

That is also true.

What again shall we say of the actual acquirement of knowledge?—is the body, if invited to share in the enquiry, a hinderer or a helper? I mean to say, have sight and hearing any truth in them? Are they not, as the poets tell us, inaccurate witnesses? and yet, if even they are inaccurate and indistinct, what is to be said of the other senses?—for you will allow that they are the best of them?

Certainly, he replied.

Then when does the soul attain truth?—for in attempting to consider anything in company with the body she is obviously deceived.

True.

Then must not true existence be revealed to her in thought, if at all?

Yes.

And thought is best when the mind is gathered into herself and none of these things trouble her—neither sounds nor sights nor pain nor any pleasure,—when she takes leave of the body, and has as little as possible to do with it, when she has no bodily sense or desire, but is aspiring after true being?

Certainly.

And in this the philosopher dishonours the body; his soul runs away from his body and desires to be alone and by herself?

That is true.

Well, but there is another thing, Simmias: Is there or is there not an absolute justice?

Assuredly there is.

And an absolute beauty and absolute good?

Of course.

But did you ever behold any of them with your eyes?

Certainly not.

Or did you ever reach them with any other bodily sense?—and I speak not of these alone, but of absolute greatness, and health, and strength, and of the essence or true nature of everything. Has the reality of them ever been perceived by you through the bodily organs? or rather, is not the nearest approach to the knowledge of their several natures made by him who so orders his intellectual vision as to have the most exact conception of the essence of each thing which he considers?

Certainly.

And he attains to the purest knowledge of them who goes to each with the mind alone, not introducing or intruding in the act of thought sight or any other sense together with reason, but with the very light of the mind in her own clearness searches into the very truth of each; he who has got rid, as far as he can, of eyes and ears and, so to speak, of the whole body, these being in his opinion distracting elements which when they infect the soul hinder her from acquiring truth and knowledge—who, if not he, is likely to attain the knowledge of true being?

What you say has a wonderful truth in it, Socrates, replied Simmias.

And when real philosophers consider all these things, will they not be led to make a reflection which they will express in words something like the following? 'Have we not found,' they will say, 'a path of thought which seems to bring us and our argument to the conclusion, that while we are in the body, and while the soul is infected with the evils of the body, our desire will not be satisfied? and our desire is of the truth. For the body is a source of endless trouble to us by reason of the mere requirement of food; and is liable also to diseases which overtake and impede us in the search after true being: it fills us full of loves, and lusts, and fears, and fancies of all kinds, and endless foolery, and in fact, as men say, takes away from us the power of thinking at all.

Whence come wars, and fightings, and factions? whence but from the body and the lusts of the body? wars are occasioned by the love of money, and money has to be acquired for the sake and in the service of the body; and by reason of all these impediments we have no time to give to philosophy; and, last and worst of all, even if we are at leisure and betake ourselves to some speculation, the body is always breaking in upon us, causing turmoil and confusion in our enquiries, and so amazing us that we are prevented from seeing the truth.

It has been proved to us by experience that if we would have pure knowledge of anything we must be quit of the body—the soul in herself must behold things in themselves: and then we shall attain the wisdom which we desire, and of which we say that we are lovers, not while we live, but after death; for if while in company with the body, the soul cannot have pure knowledge, one of two things follows—either knowledge is not to be attained at all, or, if at all, after death. For then, and not till then, the soul will be parted from the body and exist in herself alone. In this present life, I reckon that we make the nearest approach to knowledge when we have the least possible intercourse or communion with the body, and are not surfeited with the bodily nature, but keep ourselves pure until the hour when God himself is pleased to release us.

And thus having got rid of the foolishness of the body we shall be pure and hold converse with the pure, and know of ourselves the clear light everywhere, which is no other than the light of truth.' For the impure are not permitted to approach the pure. These are the sort of words, Simmias, which the true lovers of knowledge cannot help saying to one another, and thinking. You would agree; would you not?

Undoubtedly, Socrates.

But, O my friend, if this is true, there is great reason to hope that, going whither I go, when I have come to the end of my journey, I shall attain that which has been the pursuit of my life. And therefore I go on my way rejoicing, and not I only, but every other man who believes that his mind has been made ready and that he is in a manner purified.

Certainly, replied Simmias.

And what is purification but the separation of the soul from the body, as I was saying before; the habit of the soul gathering and collecting herself into herself from all sides out of the body; the dwelling in her own place alone, as in another life, so also in this, as far as she can;—the release of the soul from the chains of the body? Very true, he said. And this separation and release of the soul from the body is termed death?

To be sure, he said.

And the true philosophers, and they only, are ever seeking to release the soul. Is not the separation and release of the soul from the body their especial study?

That is true.

And, as I was saying at first, there would be a ridiculous contradiction in men studying to live as nearly as they can in a state of death, and yet repining when it comes upon them.

Clearly.

And the true philosophers, Simmias, are always occupied in the practice of dying, wherefore also to them least of all men is death terrible. Look at the matter thus:—if they have been in every way the enemies of the body, and are wanting to be alone with the soul, when this desire of theirs is granted, how inconsistent would they be if they trembled and repined, instead of rejoicing at their departure to that place where, when they arrive, they hope to gain that which in life they desired—and this was wisdom—and at the same time to be rid of the company of their enemy. Many a man has been willing to go to the world below animated by the hope of seeing there an earthly love, or wife, or son, and conversing with them. Will he who is a true lover of wisdom,and is strongly persuaded in like manner that only in the world below he can worthily enjoy her still repine at death? Will he not depart with joy?

Surely he will, O my friend, if he be a true philosopher. For he will have a firm conviction that there and there only, he can find wisdom in her purity. And if this be true, he would be very absurd, as I was saying, if he were afraid of death.

He would, indeed, replied Simmias.

And when you see a man who is repining at the approach of death, is not his reluctance a sufficient proof that he is not a lover of wisdom, but a lover of the body, and probably at the same time a lover of either money or power, or both?

Quite so, he replied.

And is not courage, Simmias, a quality which is specially characteristic of the philosopher?

Certainly.

There is temperance again, which even by the vulgar is supposed to consist in the control and regulation of the passions, and in the sense of superiority to them—is not temperance a virtue belonging to those only who despise the body, and who pass their lives in philosophy?

Most assuredly.

For the courage and temperance of other men, if you will consider them, are really a contradiction.

How so?

Well, he said, you are aware that death is regarded by men in general as a great evil.

Very true, he said.

And do not courageous men face death because they are afraid of yet greater evils?

That is quite true.

Then all but the philosophers are courageous only from fear, and because they are afraid; and yet that a man should be courageous from fear, and because he is a coward, is surely a strange thing.

Very true.

And are not the temperate exactly in the same case? They are temperate because they are intemperate—which might seem to be a contradiction, but is nevertheless the sort of thing which happens with this foolish temperance. For there are pleasures which they are afraid of losing; and in their desire to keep them, they abstain from some pleasures, because they are overcome by others; and although to be conquered by pleasure is called by men intemperance, to them the conquest of pleasure consists in being conquered by pleasure. And that is what I mean by saying that, in a sense, they are made temperate through intemperance. Such appears to be the case. Yet the exchange of one fear or pleasure or pain for another fear or pleasure or pain, and of the greater for the less, as if they were coins, is not the exchange of virtue.

O my blessed Simmias, is there not one true coin for which all things ought to be exchanged?—and that is wisdom; and only in exchange for this, and in company with this, is anything truly bought or sold, whether courage or temperance or justice. And is not all true virtue the companion of wisdom, no matter what fears or pleasures or other similar goods or evils may or may not attend her? But the virtue which is made up of these goods, when they are severed from wisdom and exchanged with one another, is a shadow of virtue only, nor is there any freedom or health or truth in her; but in the true exchange there is a purging away of all these things, and temperance, and justice, and courage, and wisdom herself are the purgation of them.

The founders of the mysteries would appear to have had a real meaning, and were not talking nonsense when they intimated in a figure long ago that he who passes unsanctified and uninitiated into the world below will lie in a slough, but that he who arrives there after initiation and purification will dwell with the gods. For 'many,' as they say in the mysteries, 'are the thyrsus- bearers, but few are the mystics,'—meaning, as I interpret the words, 'the true philosophers.' In the number of whom, during my whole life, I have been seeking, according to my ability, to find a place;—whether I have sought in a right way or not, and whether I have succeeded or not, I shall truly know in a little while, if God will, when I myself arrive in the other world—such is my belief.

And therefore I maintain that I am right, Simmias and Cebes, in not grieving or repining at parting from you and my masters in this world, for I believe that I shall equally find good masters and friends in another world. But most men do not believe this saying; if then I succeed in convincing you by my defence better than I did the Athenian judges, it will be well.

Cebes answered: I agree, Socrates, in the greater part of what you say. But in what concerns the soul, men are apt to be incredulous; they fear that when she has left the body her place may be nowhere, and that on the very day of death she may perish and come to an end—immediately on her release from the body, issuing forth dispersed like smoke or air and in her flight vanishing away into nothingness. If she could only be collected into herself after she has obtained release from the evils of which you are speaking, there would be good reason to hope, Socrates, that what you say is true. But surely it requires a great deal of argument and many proofs to show that when the man is dead his soul yet exists, and has any force or intelligence.

True, Cebes, said Socrates; and shall I suggest that we converse a little of the probabilities of these things?

I am sure, said Cebes, that I should greatly like to know your opinion about them.

I reckon, said Socrates, that no one who heard me now, not even if he were one of my old enemies, the Comic poets, could accuse me of idle talking about matters in which I have no concern:—If you please, then, we will proceed with the inquiry.

Suppose we consider the question whether the souls of men after death are or are not in the world below. There comes into my mind an ancient doctrine which affirms that they go from hence into the other world, and returning hither, are born again from the dead. Now if it be true that the living come from the dead, then our souls must exist in the other world, for if not, how could they have been born again? And this would be conclusive, if there were any real evidence that the living are only born from the dead; but if this is not so, then other arguments will have to be adduced.

Very true, replied Cebes.

Then let us consider the whole question, not in relation to man only, but in relation to animals generally, and to plants, and to everything of which there is generation, and the proof will be easier. Are not all things which have opposites generated out of their opposites? I mean such things as good and evil, just and unjust—and there are innumerable other opposites which are generated out of opposites. And I want to show that in all opposites there is of necessity a similar alternation; I mean to say, for example, that anything which becomes greater must become greater after being less.

True.

And that which becomes less must have been once greater and then have become less. Yes. And the weaker is generated from the stronger, and the swifter from the slower.

Very true.

And the worse is from the better, and the more just is from the more unjust.

Of course.

And is this true of all opposites? and are we convinced that all of them are generated out of opposites?

Yes.

And in this universal opposition of all things, are there not also two intermediate processes which are ever going on, from one to the other opposite, and back again; where there is a greater and a less there is also an intermediate process of increase and diminution, and that which grows is said to wax, and that which decays to wane?

Yes, he said.

And there are many other processes, such as division and composition, cooling and heating, which equally involve a passage into and out of one another. And this necessarily holds of all opposites, even though not always expressed in words—they are really generated out of one another, and there is a passing or process from one to the other of them?

Very true, he replied.

Well, and is there not an opposite of life, as sleep is the opposite of waking?

True, he said.

And what is it?

Death, he answered.

And these, if they are opposites, are generated the one from the other, and have there their two intermediate processes also?

Of course.

Now, said Socrates, I will analyze one of the two pairs of opposites which I have mentioned to you, and also its intermediate processes, and you shall analyze the other to me. One of them I term sleep, the other waking. The state of sleep is opposed to the state of waking, and out of sleeping waking is generated, and out of waking, sleeping; and the process of generation is in the one case falling asleep, and in the other waking up. Do you agree?

I entirely agree.

Then, suppose that you analyze life and death to me in the same manner. Is not death opposed to life?

Yes.

And they are generated one from the other?

Yes.

What is generated from the living?

The dead.

And what from the dead?

I can only say in answer—the living.

Then the living, whether things or persons, Cebes, are generated from the dead?

That is clear, he replied.

Then the inference is that our souls exist in the world below?

That is true.

And one of the two processes or generations is visible—for surely the act of dying is visible?

Surely, he said.

What then is the result? Shall we exclude the opposite process? Shall we suppose nature walks on one leg only? Must we not rather assign to death some corresponding process of generation?

Certainly, he replied.

And what is that process?

Return to life.

And return to life, if there be such a thing, is the birth of the dead into the world of the living?

Quite true.

Then here is a new way by which we arrive at the conclusion that the living come from the dead, just as the dead come from the living; and this, if true, affords a most certain proof that the souls of the dead exist in some place out of which they come again.

Yes, Socrates, he said; the conclusion seems to flow necessarily out of our previous admissions.

And that these admissions were not unfair, Cebes, he said, may be shown, I think, as follows: If generation were in a straight line only, and there were no compensation or circle in nature, no turn or return of elements into their opposites, then you know that all things would at last have the same form and pass into the same state, and there would be no more generation of them.

What do you mean? he said.

A simple thing enough, which I will illustrate by the case of sleep, he replied. You know that if there were no alternation of sleeping and waking, the tale of the sleeping Endymion would in the end have no meaning, because all other things would be asleep, too, and he would not be distinguishable from the rest. Or if there were composition only, and no division of substances, then the chaos of Anaxagoras would come again. And in like manner, my dear Cebes, if all things which partook of life were to die, and after they were dead remained in the form of death, and did not come to life again, all would at last die, and nothing would be alive—what other result could there be? For if the living spring from any other things, and they too die, must not all things at last be swallowed up in death?

There is no escape, Socrates, said Cebes; and to me your argument seems to be absolutely true.

Yes, he said, Cebes, it is and must be so, in my opinion; and we have not been deluded in making these admissions; but I am confident that there truly is such a thing as living again, and that the living spring from the dead, and that the souls of the dead are in existence, and that the good souls have a better portion than the evil.

Cebes added: Your favorite doctrine, Socrates, that knowledge is simply recollection, if true, also necessarily implies a previous time in which we have learned that which we now recollect. But this would be impossible unless our soul had been in some place before existing in the form of man; here then is another proof of the soul's immortality.

But tell me, Cebes, said Simmias, interposing, what arguments are urged in favour of this doctrine of recollection. I am not very sure at the moment that I remember them.

One excellent proof, said Cebes, is afforded by questions. If you put a question to a person in a right way, he will give a true answer of himself, but how could he do this unless there were knowledge and right reason already in him? And this is most clearly shown when he is taken to a diagram or to anything of that sort.

But if, said Socrates, you are still incredulous, Simmias, I would ask you whether you may not agree with me when you look at the matter in another way;—I mean, if you are still incredulous as to whether knowledge is recollection.

Incredulous, I am not, said Simmias; but I want to have this doctrine of recollection brought to my own recollection, and, from what Cebes has said, I am beginning to recollect and be convinced; but I should still like to hear what you were going to say.

This is what I would say, he replied. We should agree, if I am not mistaken, that what a man recollects he must have known at some previous time.

Very true.

And what is the nature of this knowledge or recollection? I mean to ask, Whether a person who, having seen or heard or in any way perceived anything, knows not only that, but has a conception of something else which is the subject, not of the same but of some other kind of knowledge, may not be fairly said to recollect that of which he has the conception?

What do you mean?

I mean what I may illustrate by the following instance:—The knowledge of a lyre is not the same as the knowledge of a man?

True.

And yet what is the feeling of lovers when they recognize a lyre, or a garment, or anything else which the beloved has been in the habit of using? Do not they, from knowing the lyre, form in the mind's eye an image of the youth to whom the lyre belongs? And this is recollection. In like manner any one who sees Simmias may remember Cebes; and there are endless examples of the same thing.

Endless, indeed, replied Simmias.

And recollection is most commonly a process of recovering that which has been already forgotten through time and inattention.

Very true, he said.

Well; and may you not also from seeing the picture of a horse or a lyre remember a man? and from the picture of Simmias, you may be led to remember Cebes?

True.

Or you may also be led to the recollection of Simmias himself?

Quite so.

And in all these cases, the recollection may be derived from things either like or unlike?

It may be.

And when the recollection is derived from like things, then another consideration is sure to arise, which is—whether the likeness in any degree falls short or not of that which is recollected?

Very true, he said.

And shall we proceed a step further, and affirm that there is such a thing as equality, not of one piece of wood or stone with another, but that, over and above this, there is absolute equality? Shall we say so?

Say so, yes, replied Simmias, and swear to it, with all the confidence in life.

And do we know the nature of this absolute essence?

To be sure, he said.

And whence did we obtain our knowledge? Did we not see equalities of material things, such as pieces of wood and stones, and gather from them the idea of an equality which is different from them? For you will acknowledge that there is a difference. Or look at the matter in another way:—Do not the same pieces of wood or stone appear at one time equal, and at another time unequal?

That is certain.

But are real equals ever unequal? or is the idea of equality the same as of inequality?

Impossible, Socrates.

Then these (so-called) equals are not the same with the idea of equality?

I should say, clearly not, Socrates.

And yet from these equals, although differing from the idea of equality, you conceived and attained that idea?

Very true, he said.

Which might be like, or might be unlike them?

Yes.

But that makes no difference; whenever from seeing one thing you conceived another, whether like or unlike, there must surely have been an act of recollection?

Very true.

But what would you say of equal portions of wood and stone, or other material equals? and what is the impression produced by them? Are they equals in the same sense in which absolute equality is equal? or do they fall short of this perfect equality in a measure?

Yes, he said, in a very great measure too.

And must we not allow, that when I or any one, looking at any object, observes that the thing which he sees aims at being some other thing, but falls short of, and cannot be, that other thing, but is inferior, he who makes this observation must have had a previous knowledge of that to which the other, although similar, was inferior?

Certainly.

And has not this been our own case in the matter of equals and of absolute equality?

Precisely.

Then we must have known equality previously to the time when we first saw the material equals, and reflected that all these apparent equals strive to attain absolute equality, but fall short of it?

Very true.

And this absolute equality has only been known and can only be known through the medium of sight or touch, or of some other of the senses, which are all alike in this respect?

Yes, Socrates, as far as the argument is concerned, one of them is the same as the other.

From the senses then is derived the knowledge that all sensible things aim at an absolute equality of which they fall short?

Yes.

Then before we began to see or hear or perceive in any way, we must have had a knowledge of absolute equality, or we could not have referred to that standard the equals which are derived from the senses?—for to that they all aspire, and of that they fall short. No other inference can be drawn from the previous statements. And did we not see and hear and have the use of our other senses as soon as we were born?

Certainly.

Then we must have acquired the knowledge of equality at some previous time?

Yes.

That is to say, before we were born, I suppose?

True.

And if we acquired this knowledge before we were born, and were born having the use of it, then we also knew before we were born and at the instant of birth not only the equal or the greater or the less, but all other ideas; for we are not speaking only of equality, but of beauty, goodness, justice, holiness, and of all which we stamp with the name of essence in the dialectical process, both when we ask and when we answer questions. Of all this we may certainly affirm that we acquired the knowledge before birth?

We may.

But if, after having acquired, we have not forgotten what in each case we acquired, then we must always have come into life having knowledge, and shall always continue to know as long as life lasts—for knowing is the acquiring and retaining knowledge and not forgetting. Is not forgetting, Simmias, just the losing of knowledge?

Quite true, Socrates.

But if the knowledge which we acquired before birth was lost by us at birth, and if afterwards by the use of the senses we recovered what we previously knew, will not the process we call learning be a recovering of the knowledge that is natural to us, and may not this be rightly termed recollection?

Very true.

So much is clear—that when we perceive something, either by the help of sight, or hearing, or some other sense, from that perception we are able to obtain a notion of some other thing like or unlike which is associated with it but has been forgotten. Whence, as I was saying, one of two alternatives follows:—either we had this knowledge at birth, and continued to know through life; or, after birth, those who are said to learn only remember, and learning is simply recollection.

Yes, that is quite true, Socrates.

And which alternative, Simmias, do you prefer? Had we the knowledge at our birth, or did we recollect the things which we knew previously to our birth?

I cannot decide at the moment.

At any rate you can decide whether he who has knowledge will or will not be able to render an account of his knowledge? What do you say?

Certainly, he will.

But do you think that every man is able to give an account of these very matters about which we are speaking?

Would that they could, Socrates, but I rather fear that to-morrow, at this time, there will no longer be any one alive who is able to give an account of them such as ought to be given.

Then you are not of opinion, Simmias, that all men know these things?

Certainly not.

They are in process of recollecting that which they learned before?

Certainly.

But when did our souls acquire this knowledge?—not since we were born as men?

Certainly not.

And therefore, previously?

Yes.

Then, Simmias, our souls must also have existed without bodies before they were in the form of man, and must have had intelligence.

Unless indeed you suppose, Socrates, that these notions are given us at the very moment of birth; for this is the only time which remains.

Yes, my friend, but if so, when do we lose them? for they are not in us when we are born—that is admitted. Do we lose them at the moment of receiving them, or if not at what other time?

No, Socrates, I perceive that I was unconsciously talking nonsense.

Then may we not say, Simmias, that if, as we are always repeating, there is an absolute beauty, and goodness, and an absolute essence of all things; and if to this, which is now discovered to have existed in our former state, we refer all our sensations, and with this compare them, finding these ideas to be pre-existent and our inborn possession—then our souls must have had a prior existence, but if not, there would be no force in the argument? There is the same proof that these ideas must have existed before we were born, as that our souls existed before we were born; and if not the ideas, then not the souls.

Yes, Socrates; I am convinced that there is precisely the same necessity for the one as for the other; and the argument retreats successfully to the position that the existence of the soul before birth cannot be separated from the existence of the essence of which you speak. For there is nothing which to my mind is so patent as that beauty, goodness, and the other notions of which you were just now speaking, have a most real and absolute existence; and I am satisfied with the proof.

Well, but is Cebes equally satisfied? for I must convince him too.

I think, said Simmias, that Cebes is satisfied: although he is the most incredulous of mortals, yet I believe that he is sufficiently convinced of the existence of the soul before birth. But that after death the soul will continue to exist is not yet proven even to my own satisfaction. I cannot get rid of the feeling of the many to which Cebes was referring—the feeling that when the man dies the soul will be dispersed, and that this may be the extinction of her. For admitting that she may have been born elsewhere, and framed out of other elements, and was in existence before entering the human body, why after having entered in and gone out again may she not herself be destroyed and come to an end?

Very true, Simmias, said Cebes; about half of what was required has been proven; to wit, that our souls existed before we were born:—that the soul will exist after death as well as before birth is the other half of which the proof is still wanting, and has to be supplied; when that is given the demonstration will be complete.

But that proof, Simmias and Cebes, has been already given, said Socrates, if you put the two arguments together—I mean this and the former one, in which we admitted that everything living is born of the dead. For if the soul exists before birth, and in coming to life and being born can be born only from death and dying, must she not after death continue to exist, since she has to be born again? Surely the proof which you desire has been already furnished. Still I suspect that you and Simmias would be glad to probe the argument further. Like children, you are haunted with a fear that when the soul leaves the body, the wind may really blow her away and scatter her; especially if a man should happen to die in a great storm and not when the sky is calm.

Cebes answered with a smile: Then, Socrates, you must argue us out of our fears—and yet, strictly speaking, they are not our fears, but there is a child within us to whom death is a sort of hobgoblin; him too we must persuade not to be afraid when he is alone in the dark.

Socrates said, Let the voice of the charmer be applied daily until you charm away the fear.

And where shall we find a good charmer of our fears, Socrates, when you are gone?

Hellas, he replied, is a large place, Cebes, and has many good men, and there are barbarous races not a few: seek for him among them all, far and wide, sparing neither pains nor money; for there is no better way of spending your money. And you must seek among yourselves too; for you will not find others better able to make the search.

The search, replied Cebes, shall certainly be made. And now, if you please, let us return to the point of the argument at which we digressed.

By all means, replied Socrates. Must we not, said Socrates, ask ourselves what that is which, as we imagine, is liable to be scattered, and about which we fear? and what again is that about which we have no fear? And then we may proceed further to enquire whether that which suffers dispersion is or is not of the nature of soul—our hopes and fears as to our own souls will turn upon the answers to these questions.

Very true, he said.

Now the compound or composite may be supposed to be naturally capable, as of being compounded, so also of being dissolved; but that which is uncompounded, and that only, must be, if anything is, indissoluble.

Yes; I should imagine so, said Cebes.

And the uncompounded may be assumed to be the same and unchanging, whereas the compound is always changing and never the same.

I agree, he said.

Then now let us return to the previous discussion. Is that idea or essence, which in the dialectical process we define as essence or true existence—whether essence of equality, beauty, or anything else—are these essences, I say, liable at times to some degree of change? or are they each of them always what they are, having the same simple self-existent and unchanging forms, not admitting of variation at all, or in any way, or at any time?

They must be always the same, Socrates, replied Cebes.

And what would you say of the many beautiful—whether men or horses or garments or any other things which are named by the same names and may be called equal or beautiful,—are they all unchanging and the same always, or quite the reverse? May they not rather be described as almost always changing and hardly ever the same, either with themselves or with one another?

The latter, replied Cebes; they are always in a state of change.

And these you can touch and see and perceive with the senses, but the unchanging things you can only perceive with the mind—they are invisible and are not seen?

That is very true, he said.

Well, then, added Socrates, let us suppose that there are two sorts of existences—one seen, the other unseen.

Let us suppose them.

The seen is the changing, and the unseen is the unchanging?

That may be also supposed.

And, further, is not one part of us body, another part soul?

To be sure.

And to which class is the body more alike and akin?

Clearly to the seen—no one can doubt that.

And is the soul seen or not seen?

Not by man, Socrates.

And what we mean by 'seen' and 'not seen' is that which is or is not visible to the eye of man?

Yes, to the eye of man.

And is the soul seen or not seen?

Not seen.

Unseen then?

Yes.

Then the soul is more like to the unseen, and the body to the seen?

That follows necessarily, Socrates.

And were we not saying long ago that the soul when using the body as an instrument of perception, that is to say, when using the sense of sight or hearing or some other sense (for the meaning of perceiving through the body is perceiving through the senses)—were we not saying that the soul too is then dragged by the body into the region of the changeable, and wanders and is confused; the world spins round her, and she is like a drunkard, when she touches change?

Very true.

But when returning into herself she reflects, then she passes into the other world, the region of purity, and eternity, and immortality, and unchangeableness, which are her kindred, and with them she ever lives, when she is by herself and is not let or hindered; then she ceases from her erring ways, and being in communion with the unchanging is unchanging. Is this state of the soul called wisdom?

That is well and truly said, Socrates, he replied.

And to which class is the soul more nearly alike and akin, as far as may be inferred from this argument, as well as from the preceding one?

I think, Socrates, that, in the opinion of every one who follows the argument, the soul will be infinitely more like the unchangeable—even the most stupid person will not deny that.

And the body is more like the changing?

Yes.

Yet once more consider the matter in another light: When the soul and the body are united, then nature orders the soul to rule and govern, and the body to obey and serve. Now which of these two functions is akin to the divine? and which to the mortal? Does not the divine appear to you to be that which naturally orders and rules, and the mortal to be that which is subject and servant?

True.

And which does the soul resemble?

The soul resembles the divine, and the body the mortal—there can be no doubt of that.

Then reflect, Cebes: of all which has been said is not this the conclusion?—that the soul is in the very likeness of the divine, and immortal, and intellectual, and uniform, and indissoluble, and unchangeable; and that the body is in the very likeness of the human, and mortal, and unintellectual, and multiform, and dissoluble, and changeable. Can this, my dear Cebes, be denied?

It cannot.

But if it be true, then is not the body liable to speedy dissolution? and is not the soul almost or altogether indissoluble?

Certainly.

And do you further observe, that after a man is dead, the body, or visible part of him, which is lying in the visible world, and is called a corpse, and would naturally be dissolved and decomposed and dissipated, is not dissolved or decomposed at once, but may remain for a for some time, nay even for a long time, if the constitution be sound at the time of death, and the season of the year favourable? For the body when shrunk and embalmed, as the manner is in Egypt, may remain almost entire through infinite ages; and even in decay, there are still some portions, such as the bones and ligaments, which are practically indestructible:—Do you agree?

Yes.

And is it likely that the soul, which is invisible, in passing to the place of the true Hades, which like her is invisible, and pure, and noble, and on her way to the good and wise God, whither, if God will, my soul is also soon to go,—that the soul, if this be her nature and origin, will be blown away and destroyed immediately on quitting the body, as the many say? That can never be, my dear Simmias and Cebes. The truth rather is, that the soul which is pure at departing and draws after her no bodily taint, having never voluntarily during life had connection with the body, which she is ever avoiding, herself gathered into herself;—and making such abstraction her perpetual study—which means she has been a true disciple of philosophy; and therefore has in fact been always engaged in the practice of dying? For is not philosophy the practice of death? Certainly, that soul, I say, herself invisible, departs to the invisible world—to the divine, immortal, and rational. Thither arriving, she is secure of bliss and is released from the error and folly of men, their fears and wild passions and all other human ills, and forever dwells in company with the gods. Is not this true, Cebes?

Yes, said Cebes, beyond a doubt.

But the soul which has been polluted, and is impure at the time of her departure, and is the companion and servant of the body always, and is in love with and fascinated by the body and by the desires and pleasures of the body, until she is led to believe that the truth only exists in a bodily form, which a man may touch and see and taste, and use for the purposes of his lusts,—the soul, I mean, accustomed to hate and fear and avoid the intellectual principle, which to the bodily eye is dark and invisible, and can be attained only by philosophy;—do you suppose that such a soul will depart pure and unalloyed? Impossible, he replied. She is held fast by the corporeal, which the continual association and constant care of the body have wrought into her nature.

Very true.

And this corporeal element, my friend, is heavy and weighty and earthy, and is that element of sight by which a soul is depressed and dragged down again into the visible world, because she is afraid of the invisible and of the world below—prowling about tombs and sepulchres, near which, as they tell us, are seen certain ghostly apparitions of souls which have not departed pure, but are cloyed with sight and therefore visible.

That is very likely, Socrates.

Yes, that is very likely, Cebes; and these must be the souls, not of the good, but of the evil, which are compelled to wander about such places in payment of the penalty of their former evil way of life; and they continue to wander until through the craving after the corporeal which never leaves them, they are imprisoned finally in another body. And they may be supposed to find their prisons in the same natures which they have had in their former lives.

What natures do you mean, Socrates?

What I mean is that men who have followed after gluttony, and wantonness, and drunkenness, and have had no thought of avoiding them, would pass into asses and animals of that sort. What do you think?

I think such an opinion to be exceedingly probable.

And those who have chosen the portion of injustice, and tyranny, and violence, will pass into wolves, or into hawks and kites;—whither else can we suppose them to go?

Yes, said Cebes; with such natures, beyond question.

And there is no difficulty, he said, in assigning to all of them places answering to their several natures and propensities?

There is not, he said.

Some are happier than others; and the happiest both in themselves and in the place to which they go are those who have practised the civil and social virtues which are called temperance and justice, and are acquired by habit and attention without philosophy and mind. Why are they the happiest? Because they may be expected to pass into some gentle and social kind which is like their own, such as bees or wasps or ants, or back again into the form of man, and just and moderate men may be supposed to spring from them.

Very likely.

No one who has not studied philosophy and who is not entirely pure at the time of his departure is allowed to enter the company of the Gods, but the lover of knowledge only. And this is the reason, Simmias and Cebes, why the true votaries of philosophy abstain from all fleshly lusts, and hold out against them and refuse to give themselves up to them,—not because they fear poverty or the ruin of their families, like the lovers of money, and the world in general; nor like the lovers of power and honour, because they dread the dishonour or disgrace of evil deeds.

No, Socrates, that would not become them, said Cebes.

No indeed, he replied; and therefore they who have any care of their own souls, and do not merely live moulding and fashioning the body, say farewell to all this; they will not walk in the ways of the blind: and when philosophy offers them purification and release from evil, they feel that they ought not to resist her influence, and whither she leads they turn and follow.

What do you mean, Socrates?

I will tell you, he said. The lovers of knowledge are conscious that the soul was simply fastened and glued to the body—until philosophy received her, she could only view real existence through the bars of a prison, not in and through herself; she was wallowing in the mire of every sort of ignorance; and by reason of lust had become the principal accomplice in her own captivity. This was her original state; and then, as I was saying, and as the lovers of knowledge are well aware, philosophy, seeing how terrible was her confinement, of which she was to herself the cause, received and gently comforted her and sought to release her, pointing out that the eye and the ear and the other senses are full of deception, and persuading her to retire from them, and abstain from all but the necessary use of them, and be gathered up and collected into herself, bidding her trust in herself and her own pure apprehension of pure existence, and to mistrust whatever comes to her through other channels and is subject to variation; for such things are visible and tangible, but what she sees in her own nature is intelligible and invisible. And the soul of the true philosopher thinks that she ought not to resist this deliverance, and therefore abstains from pleasures and desires and pains and fears, as far as she is able; reflecting that when a man has great joys or sorrows or fears or desires, he suffers from them, not merely the sort of evil which might be anticipated—as for example, the loss of his health or property which he has sacrificed to his lusts—but an evil greater far, which is the greatest and worst of all evils, and one of which he never thinks.

What is it, Socrates? said Cebes.

The evil is that when the feeling of pleasure or pain is most intense, every soul of man imagines the objects of this intense feeling to be then plainest and truest: but this is not so, they are really the things of sight.

Very true.

And is not this the state in which the soul is most enthralled by the body?

How so?

Why, because each pleasure and pain is a sort of nail which nails and rivets the soul to the body, until she becomes like the body, and believes that to be true which the body affirms to be true; and from agreeing with the body and having the same delights she is obliged to have the same habits and haunts, and is not likely ever to be pure at her departure to the world below, but is always infected by the body; and so she sinks into another body and there germinates and grows, and has therefore no part in the communion of the divine and pure and simple.

Most true, Socrates, answered Cebes.

And this, Cebes, is the reason why the true lovers of knowledge are temperate and brave; and not for the reason which the world gives. Certainly not. Certainly not! The soul of a philosopher will reason in quite another way; she will not ask philosophy to release her in order that when released she may deliver herself up again to the thraldom of pleasures and pains, doing a work only to be undone again, weaving instead of unweaving her Penelope's web. But she will calm passion, and follow reason, and dwell in the contemplation of her, beholding the true and divine (which is not matter of opinion), and thence deriving nourishment. Thus she seeks to live while she lives, and after death she hopes to go to her own kindred and to that which is like her, and to be freed from human ills. Never fear, Simmias and Cebes, that a soul which has been thus nurtured and has had these pursuits, will at her departure from the body be scattered and blown away by the winds and be nowhere and nothing.

When Socrates had done speaking, for a considerable time there was silence; he himself appeared to be meditating, as most of us were, on what had been said; only Cebes and Simmias spoke a few words to one another. And Socrates observing them asked what they thought of the argument, and whether there was anything wanting? For, said he, there are many points still open to suspicion and attack, if any one were disposed to sift the matter thoroughly. Should you be considering some other matter I say no more, but if you are still in doubt do not hesitate to say exactly what you think, and let us have anything better which you can suggest; and if you think that I can be of any use, allow me to help you.

Simmias said: I must confess, Socrates, that doubts did arise in our minds, and each of us was urging and inciting the other to put the question which we wanted to have answered and which neither of us liked to ask, fearing that our importunity might be troublesome under present at such a time.

Socrates replied with a smile: O Simmias, what are you saying? I am not very likely to persuade other men that I do not regard my present situation as a misfortune, if I cannot even persuade you that I am no worse off now than at any other time in my life. Will you not allow that I have as much of the spirit of prophecy in me as the swans? For they, when they perceive that they must die, having sung all their life long, do then sing more lustily than ever, rejoicing in the thought that they are about to go away to the god whose ministers they are.

But men, because they are themselves afraid of death, slanderously affirm of the swans that they sing a lament at the last, not considering that no bird sings when cold, or hungry, or in pain, not even the nightingale, nor the swallow, nor yet the hoopoe; which are said indeed to tune a lay of sorrow, although I do not believe this to be true of them any more than of the swans. But because they are sacred to Apollo, they have the gift of prophecy, and anticipate the good things of another world, wherefore they sing and rejoice in that day more than they ever did before. And I too, believing myself to be the consecrated servant of the same God, and the fellow-servant of the swans, and thinking that I have received from my master gifts of prophecy which are not inferior to theirs, would not go out of life less merrily than the swans. Never mind then, if this be your only objection, but speak and ask anything which you like, while the eleven magistrates of Athens allow.

Very good, Socrates, said Simmias; then I will tell you my difficulty, and Cebes will tell you his. I feel myself, (and I daresay that you have the same feeling), how hard or rather impossible is the attainment of any certainty about questions such as these in the present life. And yet I should deem him a coward who did not prove what is said about them to the uttermost, or whose heart failed him before he had examined them on every side. For he should persevere until he has achieved one of two things: either he should discover, or be taught the truth about them; or, if this be impossible, I would have him take the best and most irrefragable of human theories, and let this be the raft upon which he sails through life— not without risk, as I admit, if he cannot find some word of God which will more surely and safely carry him. And now, as you bid me, I will venture to question you, and then I shall not have to reproach myself hereafter with not having said at the time what I think. For when I consider the matter, either alone or with Cebes, the argument does certainly appear to me, Socrates, to be not sufficient.

Socrates answered: I dare say, my friend, that you may be right, but I should like to know in what respect the argument is insufficient.

In this respect, replied Simmias:—Suppose a person to use the same argument about harmony and the lyre—might he not say that harmony is a thing invisible, incorporeal, perfect, divine, existing in the lyre which is harmonized, but that the lyre and the strings are matter and material, composite, earthy, and akin to mortality? And when some one breaks the lyre, or cuts and rends the strings, then he who takes this view would argue as you do, and on the same analogy, that the harmony survives and has not perished—you cannot imagine, he would say, that the lyre without the strings, and the broken strings themselves which are mortal remain, and yet that the harmony, which is of heavenly and immortal nature and kindred, has perished—perished before the mortal. The harmony must still be somewhere, and the wood and strings will decay before anything can happen to that.

The thought, Socrates, must have occurred to your own mind that such is our conception of the soul; and that when the body is in a manner strung and held together by the elements of hot and cold, wet and dry, then the soul is the harmony or due proportionate admixture of them. But if so, whenever the strings of the body are unduly loosened or overstrained through disease or other injury, then the soul, though most divine, like other harmonies of music or of works of art, of course perishes at once, although the material remains of the body may last for a considerable time, until they are either decayed or burnt. And if any one maintains that the soul, being the harmony of the elements of the body, is first to perish in that which is called death, how shall we answer him?

Socrates looked fixedly at us as his manner was, and said with a smile: Simmias has reason on his side; and why does not some one of you who is better able than myself answer him? for there is force in his attack upon me. But perhaps, before we answer him, we had better also hear what Cebes has to say that we may gain time for reflection, and when they have both spoken, we may either assent to them, if there is truth in what they say, or if not, we will maintain our position. Please to tell me then, Cebes, he said, what was the difficulty which troubled you?

Cebes said: I will tell you. My feeling is that the argument is where it was, and open to the same objections which were urged before; for I am ready to admit that the existence of the soul before entering into the bodily form has been very ingeniously, and, if I may say so, quite sufficiently proven; but the existence of the soul after death is still, in my judgment, unproven. Now my objection is not the same as that of Simmias; for I am not disposed to deny that the soul is stronger and more lasting than the body, being of opinion that in all such respects the soul very far excels the body. Well, then, says the argument to me, why do you remain unconvinced?—When you see that the weaker continues in existence after the man is dead, will you not admit that the more lasting must also survive during the same period of time?

Now [Cebes continues] I will ask you to consider whether the objection, which, like Simmias, I will express in a figure, is of any weight. The analogy which I will adduce is that of an old weaver, who dies, and after his death somebody says:—He is not dead, he must be alive;—see, there is the coat which he himself wove and wore, and which remains whole and undecayed. And then he proceeds to ask of some one who is incredulous, whether a man lasts longer, or the coat which is in use and wear; and when he is answered that a man lasts far longer, thinks that he has thus certainly demonstrated the survival of the man, who is the more lasting, because the less lasting remains.

But that, Simmias, as I would beg you to remark, is a mistake; any one can see that he who talks thus is talking nonsense. For the truth is, that the weaver aforesaid, having woven and worn many such coats, outlived several of them, and was outlived by the last; but a man is not therefore proved to be slighter and weaker than a coat. Now the relation of the body to the soul may be expressed in a similar figure; and any one may very fairly say in like manner that the soul is lasting, and the body weak and shortlived in comparison. He may argue in like manner that every soul wears out many bodies, especially if a man live many years. While he is alive the body deliquesces and decays, and the soul always weaves another garment and repairs the waste. But of course, whenever the soul perishes, she must have on her last garment, and this will survive her; and then at length, when the soul is dead, the body will show its native weakness, and quickly decompose and pass away.

[Cebes continues:] I would therefore rather not rely on the argument from superior strength to prove the continued existence of the soul after death. For granting even more than you affirm to be possible, and acknowledging not only that the soul existed before birth, but also that the souls of some exist, and will continue to exist after death, and will be born and die again and again, and that there is a natural strength in the soul which will hold out and be born many times—nevertheless, we may be still inclined to think that she will weary in the labours of successive births, and may at last succumb in one of her deaths and utterly perish; and this death and dissolution of the body which brings destruction to the soul may be unknown to any of us, for no one of us can have had any experience of it: and if so, then I maintain that he who is confident about death has but a foolish confidence, unless he is able to prove that the soul is altogether immortal and imperishable. But if he cannot prove the soul's immortality, he who is about to die will always have reason to fear that when the body is disunited, the soul also may utterly perish.

All of us, as we afterwards remarked to one another, had an unpleasant feeling at hearing what they said. When we had been so firmly convinced before, now to have our faith shaken seemed to introduce a confusion and uncertainty, not only into the previous argument, but into any future one; either we were incapable of forming a judgment, or there were no grounds of belief.

ECHECRATES: There I feel with you—by heaven I do, Phaedo, and when you were speaking, I was beginning to ask myself the same question: What argument can I ever trust again? For what could be more convincing than the argument of Socrates, which has now fallen into discredit? That the soul is a harmony is a doctrine which has always had a wonderful attraction for me, and, when mentioned, came back to me at once, as my own original conviction. And now I must begin again and find another argument which will assure me that when the man is dead the soul survives. Tell me, I implore you, how did Socrates proceed? Did he appear to share the unpleasant feeling which you mention? or did he calmly meet the attack? And did he answer forcibly or feebly? Narrate what passed as exactly as you can.

PHAEDO: Often, Echecrates, I have wondered at Socrates, but never more than on that occasion. That he should be able to answer was nothing, but what astonished me was, first, the gentle and pleasant and approving manner in which he received the words of the young men, and then his quick sense of the wound which had been inflicted by the argument, and the readiness with which he healed it. He might be compared to a general rallying his defeated and broken army, urging them to accompany him and return to the field of argument.

ECHECRATES: What followed?

PHAEDO: You shall hear, for I was close to him on his right hand, seated on a sort of stool, and he on a couch which was a good deal higher. He stroked my head, and pressed the hair upon my neck—he had a way of playing with my hair; and then he said: To-morrow, Phaedo, I suppose that these fair locks of yours will be severed.

Yes, Socrates, I suppose that they will, I replied.

Not so, if you will take my advice.

What shall I do with them? I said.

To-day, he replied, and not to-morrow, if this argument dies and we cannot bring it to life again, you and I will both shave our locks; and if I were you, and the argument got away from me, and I could not hold my ground against Simmias and Cebes, I would myself take an oath, like the Argives, not to wear hair any more until I had renewed the conflict and defeated them.

Yes, I said, but Heracles himself is said not to be a match for two.

Summon me then, he said, and I will be your Iolaus until the sun goes down.

I summon you rather, I rejoined, not as Heracles summoning Iolaus, but as Iolaus might summon Heracles.

That will do as well, he said. But first let us take care that we avoid a danger.

Of what nature? I said.

Lest we become misologists, he replied, no worse thing can happen to a man than this. For as there are misanthropists or haters of men, there are also misologists or haters of ideas, and both spring from the same cause, which is ignorance of the world. Misanthropy arises out of the too great confidence of inexperience;—you trust a man and think him altogether true and sound and faithful, and then in a little while he turns out to be false and knavish; and then another and another, and when this has happened several times to a man, especially when it happens among those whom he deems to be his own most trusted and familiar friends, and he has often quarreled with them, he at last hates all men, and believes that no one has any good in him at all. You must have observed this trait of character?

I have.

And is not the feeling discreditable? Is it not obvious that such an one having to deal with other men, was clearly without any experience of human nature; for experience would have taught him the true state of the case, that few are the good and few the evil, and that the great majority are in the interval between them.

What do you mean? I said.

I mean, he replied, as you might say of the very large and very small, that nothing is more uncommon than a very large or very small man; and this applies generally to all extremes, whether of great and small, or swift and slow, or fair and foul, or black and white: and whether the instances you select be men or dogs or anything else, few are the extremes, but many are in the mean between them. Did you never observe this?

Yes, I said, I have.

And do you not imagine, he said, that if there were a competition in evil, the worst would be found to be very few?

Yes, that is very likely, I said.

Yes, that is likely, he replied; although in this respect arguments are unlike men—there I was led on by you to say more than I had intended; but the point of comparison was, that when a simple man who has no skill in dialectics believes an argument to be true which he afterwards imagines to be false, whether really false or not, and then another and another, he has no longer any faith left, and great disputers, as you know, come to think at last that they have grown to be the wisest of mankind; for they alone perceive the utter unsoundness and instability of all arguments, or indeed, of all things, which, like the currents in the Euripus, are going up and down in never-ceasing ebb and flow.

That is quite true, I said.

Yes, Phaedo, he replied, and how melancholy, if there be such a thing as truth or certainty or possibility of knowledge—that a man should have lighted upon some argument or other which at first seemed true and then turned out to be false, and instead of blaming himself and his own want of wit, because he is annoyed, should at last be too glad to transfer the blame from himself to arguments in general: and for ever afterwards should hate them, and lose truth and the knowledge of realities.

Yes, indeed, I said; that is very melancholy.

Let us then, in the first place, he said, be careful of allowing or of admitting into our souls the notion that there is no health or soundness in any arguments at all. Rather say that we have not yet attained to soundness in ourselves, and that we must struggle manfully and do our best to gain health of mind—you and all other men having regard to the whole of your future life, and I myself in the prospect of death. For at this moment I am sensible that I have not the temper of a philosopher; like the vulgar, I am only a partisan. Now the partisan, when he is engaged in a dispute, cares nothing about the rights of the question, but is anxious only to convince his hearers of his own assertions. And the difference between him and me at the present moment is merely this—that whereas he seeks to convince his hearers that what he says is true, I am rather seeking to convince myself; to convince my hearers is a secondary matter with me.

And do but see how much I gain by the argument. For if what I say is true, then I do well to be persuaded of the truth, but if there be nothing after death, still, during the short time that remains, I shall not distress my friends with lamentations, and my ignorance will not last, but will die with me, and therefore no harm will be done. This is the state of mind, Simmias and Cebes, in which I approach the argument. And I would ask you to be thinking of the truth and not of Socrates: agree with me, if I seem to you to be speaking the truth; or if not, withstand me might and main, that I may not deceive you as well as myself in my enthusiasm, and like the bee, leave my sting in you before I die.

And now let us proceed, he said. And first of all let me be sure that I have in my mind what you were saying. Simmias, if I remember rightly, has fears and misgivings whether the soul, although a fairer and diviner thing than the body, being as she is in the form of harmony, may not perish first. On the other hand, Cebes appeared to grant that the soul was more lasting than the body, but he said that no one could know whether the soul, after having worn out many bodies, might not perish herself and leave her last body behind her; and that this is death, which is the destruction not of the body but of the soul, for in the body the work of destruction is ever going on. Are not these, Simmias and Cebes, the points which we have to consider?

They both agreed to this statement of them. He proceeded:

And did you deny the force of the whole preceding argument, or of a part only?

Of a part only, they replied.

And what did you think, he said, of that part of the argument in which we said that knowledge was recollection, and hence inferred that the soul must have previously existed somewhere else before she was enclosed in the body?

Cebes said that he had been wonderfully impressed by that part of the argument, and that his conviction remained absolutely unshaken. Simmias agreed, and added that he himself could hardly imagine the possibility of his ever thinking differently.

But, rejoined Socrates, you will have to think differently, my Theban friend, if you still maintain that harmony is a compound, and that the soul is a harmony which is made out of strings set in the frame of the body; for you will surely never allow yourself to say that a harmony is prior to the elements which compose it.

Never, Socrates.

But do you not see that this is what you imply when you say that the soul existed before she took the form and body of man, and was made up of elements which as yet had no existence? For harmony is not like the soul, as you suppose; but first the lyre, and the strings, and the sounds exist in a state of discord, and then harmony is made last of all, and perishes first. And how can such a notion of the soul as this agree with the other?

Not at all, replied Simmias.

And yet, he said, there ought to be harmony in a discourse of which harmony is the theme.

There ought, replied Simmias.

But there is no harmony, he said, in the two propositions that knowledge is recollection, and that the soul is a harmony. Which of them will you retain?

I think, he replied, that I have a much stronger faith, Socrates, in the first of the two, which has been fully demonstrated to me, than in the latter, which has not been demonstrated at all, but rests only on probable and plausible grounds; and is therefore believed by the many. I know too well that these arguments from probabilities are impostors, and unless great caution is observed in the use of them, they are apt to be deceptive —in geometry, and in other things too. But the doctrine of knowledge and recollection has been proven to me on trustworthy grounds; and the proof was that the soul must have existed before she came into the body, because to her belongs the essence of which the very name implies existence. Having, as I am convinced, rightly accepted this conclusion, and on sufficient grounds, I must, as I suppose, cease to argue or allow others to argue that the soul is a harmony.

Let me put the matter, he said, in another point of view: Do you imagine that a harmony or any other composition can be in a state other than that of the elements, out of which it is compounded?

Certainly not.

Or do or suffer anything other than they do or suffer?

He agreed.

Then a harmony does not, properly speaking, lead the parts or elements which make up the harmony, but only follows them.

He assented.

For harmony cannot possibly have any motion, or sound, or other quality which is opposed to its parts.

That would be impossible, he replied.

And does not the nature of every harmony depend upon the manner in which the elements are harmonized?

I do not understand you, he said.

I mean to say that a harmony admits of degrees, and is more of a harmony, and more completely a harmony, when more truly and fully harmonized, to any extent which is possible; and less of a harmony, and less completely a harmony, when less truly and fully harmonized.

True.

But does the soul admit of degrees? or is one soul in the very least degree more or less, or more or less completely, a soul than another?

Not in the least.

Yet surely of two souls, one is said to have intelligence and virtue, and to be good, and the other to have folly and vice, and to be an evil soul: and this is said truly?

Yes, truly.

But what will those who maintain the soul to be a harmony say of this presence of virtue and vice in the soul?—will they say that here is another harmony, and another discord, and that the virtuous soul is harmonized, and herself being a harmony has another harmony within her, and that the vicious soul is inharmonical and has no harmony within her?

I cannot tell, replied Simmias; but I suppose that something of the sort would be asserted by those who say that the soul is a harmony.

And we have already admitted that no soul is more a soul than another; which is equivalent to admitting that harmony is not more or less harmony, or more or less completely a harmony?

Quite true.

And that which is not more or less a harmony is not more or less harmonized?

True.

And that which is not more or less harmonized cannot have more or less of harmony, but only an equal harmony?

Yes, an equal harmony.

Then one soul not being more or less a soul than another, is not more or less harmonized?

Exactly.

And therefore has neither more nor less of discord, nor yet of harmony?

She has not.

And having neither more nor less of harmony or of discord, one soul has no more vice or virtue than another, if vice be discord and virtue harmony?

Not at all more.

Or speaking more correctly, Simmias, the soul, if she is a harmony, will never have any vice; because a harmony, being absolutely a harmony, has no part in the inharmonical.

No.

And therefore a soul which is absolutely a soul has no vice?

How can she have, if the previous argument holds?

Then, if all souls are equally by their nature souls, all souls of all living creatures will be equally good?

I agree with you, Socrates, he said.

And can all this be true, think you? he said; for these are the consequences which seem to follow from the assumption that the soul is a harmony?

It cannot be true.

Once more, he said, what ruler is there of the elements of human nature other than the soul, and especially the wise soul? Do you know of any?

Indeed, I do not.

And is the soul in agreement with the affections of the body? or is she at variance with them? For example, when the body is hot and thirsty, does not the soul incline us against drinking? and when the body is hungry, against eating? And this is only one instance out of ten thousand of the opposition of the soul to the things of the body.

Very true.

But we have already acknowledged that the soul, being a harmony, can never utter a note at variance with the tensions and relaxations and vibrations and other affections of the strings out of which she is composed; she can only follow, she cannot lead them?

It must be so, he replied.

And yet do we not now discover the soul to be doing the exact opposite— leading the elements of which she is believed to be composed; almost always opposing and coercing them in all sorts of ways throughout life, sometimes more violently with the pains of medicine and gymnastic; then again more gently; now threatening, now admonishing the desires, passions, fears, as if talking to a thing which is not herself, as Homer in the Odyssee represents Odysseus doing in the words— 'He beat his breast, and thus reproached his heart: Endure, my heart; far worse hast thou endured!' Do you think that Homer wrote this under the idea that the soul is a harmony capable of being led by the affections of the body, and not rather of a nature which should lead and master them—herself a far diviner thing than any harmony?

Yes, Socrates, I quite think so.

Then, my friend, we can never be right in saying that the soul is a harmony, for we should contradict the divine Homer, and contradict ourselves.

True, he said.

Thus much, said Socrates, of Harmonia, your Theban goddess, who has graciously yielded to us; but what shall I say, Cebes, to her husband Cadmus, and how shall I make peace with him?

I think that you will discover a way of propitiating him, said Cebes; I am sure that you have put the argument with Harmonia in a manner that I could never have expected. For when Simmias was mentioning his difficulty, I quite imagined that no answer could be given to him, and therefore I was surprised at finding that his argument could not sustain the first onset of yours, and not impossibly the other, whom you call Cadmus, may share a similar fate.

Nay, my good friend, said Socrates, let us not boast, lest some evil eye should put to flight the word which I am about to speak. That, however, may be left in the hands of those above, while I draw near in Homeric fashion, and try the mettle of your words. Here lies the point:—You want to have it proven to you that the soul is imperishable and immortal, and the philosopher who is confident in death appears to you to have but a vain and foolish confidence, if he believes that he will fare better in the world below than one who has led another sort of life, unless he can prove this; and you say that the demonstration of the strength and divinity of the soul, and of her existence prior to our becoming men, does not necessarily imply her immortality.

Admitting the soul to be longlived, and to have known and done much in a former state, still she is not on that account immortal; and her entrance into the human form may be a sort of disease which is the beginning of dissolution, and may at last, after the toils of life are over, end in that which is called death. And whether the soul enters into the body once only or many times, does not, as you say, make any difference in the fears of individuals. For any man, who is not devoid of sense, must fear, if he has no knowledge and can give no account of the soul's immortality. This, or something like this, I suspect to be your notion, Cebes; and I designedly recur to it in order that nothing may escape us, and that you may, if you wish, add or subtract anything.

But, said Cebes, as far as I see at present, I have nothing to add or subtract: I mean what you say that I mean.

Socrates paused awhile, and seemed to be absorbed in reflection. At length he said: You are raising a tremendous question, Cebes, involving the whole nature of generation and corruption, about which, if you like, I will give you my own experience; and if anything which I say is likely to avail towards the solution of your difficulty you may make use of it.

I should very much like, said Cebes, to hear what you have to say.

Then I will tell you, said Socrates. When I was young, Cebes, I had a prodigious desire to know that department of philosophy which is called the investigation of nature; to know the causes of things, and why a thing is and is created or destroyed appeared to me to be a lofty profession; and I was always agitating myself with the consideration of questions such as these:—Is the growth of animals the result of some decay which the hot and cold principle contracts, as some have said? Is the blood the element with which we think, or the air, or the fire? or perhaps nothing of the kind—but the brain may be the originating power of the perceptions of hearing and sight and smell, and memory and opinion may come from them, and science may be based on memory and opinion when they have attained fixity. And then I went on to examine the corruption of them, and then to the things of heaven and earth, and at last I concluded myself to be utterly and absolutely incapable of these enquiries, as I will satisfactorily prove to you. For I was fascinated by them to such a degree that my eyes grew blind to things which I had seemed to myself, and also to others, to know quite well; I forgot what I had before thought self-evident truths; e.g. such a fact as that the growth of man is the result of eating and drinking; for when by the digestion of food flesh is added to flesh and bone to bone, and whenever there is an aggregation of congenial elements, the lesser bulk becomes larger and the small man great. Was not that a reasonable notion?

Yes, said Cebes, I think so.

Well; but let me tell you something more. There was a time when I thought that I understood the meaning of greater and less pretty well; and when I saw a great man standing by a little one, I fancied that one was taller than the other by a head; or one horse would appear to be greater than another horse: and still more clearly did I seem to perceive that ten is two more than eight, and that two cubits are more than one, because two is the double of one.

And what is now your notion of such matters? said Cebes.

I should be far enough from imagining, he replied, that I knew the cause of any of them, by heaven I should; for I cannot satisfy myself that, when one is added to one, the one to which the addition is made becomes two, or that the two units added together make two by reason of the addition. I cannot understand how, when separated from the other, each of them was one and not two, and now, when they are brought together, the mere juxtaposition or meeting of them should be the cause of their becoming two: neither can I understand how the division of one is the way to make two; for then a different cause would produce the same effect,—as in the former instance the addition and juxtaposition of one to one was the cause of two, in this the separation and subtraction of one from the other would be the cause. Nor am I any longer satisfied that I understand the reason why one or anything else is either generated or destroyed or is at all, but I have in my mind some confused notion of a new method, and can never admit the other.

Then I heard some one reading, as he said, from a book of Anaxagoras, that mind was the disposer and cause of all, and I was delighted at this notion, which appeared quite admirable, and I said to myself: If mind is the disposer, mind will dispose all for the best, and put each particular in the best place; and I argued that if any one desired to find out the cause of the generation or destruction or existence of anything, he must find out what state of being or doing or suffering was best for that thing, and therefore a man had only to consider the best for himself and others, and then he would also know the worse, since the same science comprehended both.

I rejoiced to think that I had found in Anaxagoras a teacher of the causes of existence such as I desired, and I imagined that he would tell me first whether the earth is flat or round; and whichever was true, he would proceed to explain the cause and the necessity of this being so, and then he would teach me the nature of the best and show that this was best; and if he said that the earth was in the centre, he would further explain that this position was the best, and I should be satisfied with the explanation given, and not want any other sort of cause. And I thought that I would then go on and ask him about the sun and moon and stars, and that he would explain to me their comparative swiftness, and their returnings and various states, active and passive, and how all of them were for the best. For I could not imagine that when he spoke of mind as the disposer of them, he would give any other account of their being as they are, except that this was best; and I thought that when he had explained to me in detail the cause of each and the cause of all, he would go on to explain to me what was best for each and what was good for all.

These hopes I would not have sold for a large sum of money, and I seized the books and read them as fast as I could in my eagerness to know the better and the worse. What expectations I had formed, and how grievously was I disappointed! As I proceeded, I found my philosopher altogether forsaking mind or any other principle of order, but having recourse to air, and ether, and water, and other eccentricities. I might compare him to a person who began by maintaining generally that mind is the cause of the actions of Socrates, but who, when he endeavoured to explain the causes of my several actions in detail, went on to show that I sit here because my body is made up of bones and muscles; and the bones, as he would say, are hard and have joints which divide them, and the muscles are elastic, and they cover the bones, which have also a covering or environment of flesh and skin which contains them; and as the bones are lifted at their joints by the contraction or relaxation of the muscles, I am able to bend my limbs, and this is why I am sitting here in a curved posture—that is what he would say, and he would have a similar explanation of my talking to you, which he would attribute to sound, and air, and hearing, and he would assign ten thousand other causes of the same sort, forgetting to mention the true cause, which is, that the Athenians have thought fit to condemn me, and accordingly I have thought it better and more right to remain here and undergo my sentence; for I am inclined to think that these muscles and bones of mine would have gone off long ago to Megara or Boeotia—by the dog they would, if they had been moved only by their own idea of what was best, and if I had not chosen the better and nobler part, instead of playing truant and running away, of enduring any punishment which the state inflicts.

There is surely a strange confusion of causes and conditions in all this. It may be said, indeed, that without bones and muscles and the other parts of the body I cannot execute my purposes. But to say that I do as I do because of them, and that this is the way in which mind acts, and not from the choice of the best, is a very careless and idle mode of speaking. I wonder that they cannot distinguish the cause from the condition, which the many, feeling about in the dark, are always mistaking and misnaming. And thus one man makes a vortex all round and steadies the earth by the heaven; another gives the air as a support to the earth, which is a sort of broad trough. Any power which in arranging them as they are arranges them for the best never enters into their minds; and instead of finding any superior strength in it, they rather expect to discover another Atlas of the world who is stronger and more everlasting and more containing than the good;—of the obligatory and containing power of the good they think nothing; and yet this is the principle which I would fain learn if any one would teach me. But as I have failed either to discover myself, or to learn of any one else, the nature of the best, I will exhibit to you, what I have found to be the second best mode of enquiring into the cause.

I should very much like to hear it, he replied.

Socrates proceeded:—I thought that as I had failed in the contemplation of true existence, I ought to be careful that I did not lose the eye of my soul; as people may injure their bodily eye by observing and gazing on the sun during an eclipse, unless they take the precaution of only looking at the image reflected in the water, or in some similar medium. So in my own case, I was afraid that my soul might be blinded altogether if I looked at things with my eyes or tried to apprehend them by the help of the senses.

I thought that I had better have recourse to the world of mind and seek there the truth of existence. I dare say that the simile is not perfect—for I am very far from admitting that he who contemplates existences through the medium of thought, sees them only 'through a glass darkly,' any more than he who considers them in action and operation. However, this was the method which I adopted: I first assumed some principle which I judged to be the strongest, and then I affirmed as true whatever seemed to agree with this, whether relating to the cause or to anything else; and that which disagreed I regarded as untrue. But I should like to explain my meaning more clearly, as I do not think that you as yet understand me.

No indeed, replied Cebes, not very well.

There is nothing new, he said, in what I am about to tell you; but only what I have been always and everywhere repeating in the previous discussion and on other occasions: I want to show you the nature of that cause which has occupied my thoughts. I shall have to go back to those familiar words which are in the mouth of every one, and first of all assume that there is an absolute beauty and goodness and greatness, and the like; grant me this, and I hope to be able to show you the nature of the cause, and to prove the immortality of the soul.

Cebes said: You may proceed at once with the proof, for I grant you this.

Well, he said, then I should like to know whether you agree with me in the next step; for I cannot help thinking, if there be anything beautiful other than absolute beauty should there be such, that it can be beautiful only in as far as it partakes of absolute beauty—and I should say the same of everything. Do you agree in this notion of the cause?

Yes, he said, I agree.

He proceeded: I know nothing and can understand nothing of any other of those wise causes which are alleged; and if a person says to me that the bloom of colour, or form, or any such thing is a source of beauty, I leave all that, which is only confusing to me, and simply and singly, and perhaps foolishly, hold and am assured in my own mind that nothing makes a thing beautiful but the presence and participation of beauty in whatever way or manner obtained; for as to the manner I am uncertain, but I stoutly contend that by beauty all beautiful things become beautiful. This appears to me to be the safest answer which I can give, either to myself or to another, and to this I cling, in the persuasion that this principle will never be overthrown, and that to myself or to any one who asks the question, I may safely reply, That by beauty beautiful things become beautiful. Do you not agree with me?

I do.

And that by greatness only great things become great and greater greater, and by smallness the less become less?

True.

Then if a person were to remark that A is taller by a head than B, and B less by a head than A, you would refuse to admit his statement, and would stoutly contend that what you mean is only that the greater is greater by, and by reason of, greatness, and the less is less only by, and by reason of, smallness; and thus you would avoid the danger of saying that the greater is greater and the less less by the measure of the head, which is the same in both, and would also avoid the monstrous absurdity of supposing that the greater man is greater by reason of the head, which is small. You would be afraid to draw such an inference, would you not?

Indeed, I should, said Cebes, laughing.

In like manner you would be afraid to say that ten exceeded eight by, and by reason of, two; but would say by, and by reason of, number; or you would say that two cubits exceed one cubit not by a half, but by magnitude?-for there is the same liability to error in all these cases.

Very true, he said.

Again, would you not be cautious of affirming that the addition of one to one, or the division of one, is the cause of two? And you would loudly asseverate that you know of no way in which anything comes into existence except by participation in its own proper essence, and consequently, as far as you know, the only cause of two is the participation in duality—this is the way to make two, and the participation in one is the way to make one. You would say: I will let alone puzzles of division and addition—wiser heads than mine may answer them; inexperienced as I am, and ready to start, as the proverb says, at my own shadow, I cannot afford to give up the sure ground of a principle. And if any one assails you there, you would not mind him, or answer him, until you had seen whether the consequences which follow agree with one another or not, and when you are further required to give an explanation of this principle, you would go on to assume a higher principle, and a higher, until you found a resting-place in the best of the higher; but you would not confuse the principle and the consequences in your reasoning, like the Eristics—at least if you wanted to discover real existence. Not that this confusion signifies to them, who never care or think about the matter at all, for they have the wit to be well pleased with themselves however great may be the turmoil of their ideas. But you, if you are a philosopher, will certainly do as I say.

What you say is most true, said Simmias and Cebes, both speaking at once.

ECHECRATES: Yes, Phaedo; and I do not wonder at their assenting. Any one who has the least sense will acknowledge the wonderful clearness of Socrates' reasoning.

PHAEDO: Certainly, Echecrates; and such was the feeling of the whole company at the time.

ECHECRATES: Yes, and equally of ourselves, who were not of the company, and are now listening to your recital. But what followed?

PHAEDO: After all this had been admitted, and they had that ideas exist, and that other things participate in them and derive their names from them, Socrates, if I remember rightly, said:

This is your way of speaking; and yet when you say that Simmias is greater than Socrates and less than Phaedo, do you not predicate of Simmias both greatness and smallness?

Yes, I do.

But still you allow that Simmias does not really exceed Socrates, as the words may seem to imply, because he is Simmias, but by reason of the size which he has; just as Simmias does not exceed Socrates because he is Simmias, any more than because Socrates is Socrates, but because he has smallness when compared with the greatness of Simmias?

True.

And if Phaedo exceeds him in size, this is not because Phaedo is Phaedo, but because Phaedo has greatness relatively to Simmias, who is comparatively smaller?

That is true.

And therefore Simmias is said to be great, and is also said to be small, because he is in a mean between them, exceeding the smallness of the one by his greatness, and allowing the greatness of the other to exceed his smallness. He added, laughing, I am speaking like a book, but I believe that what I am saying is true.

Simmias assented.

I speak as I do because I want you to agree with me in thinking, not only that absolute greatness will never be great and also small, but that greatness in us or in the concrete will never admit the small or admit of being exceeded: instead of this, one of two things will happen, either the greater will fly or retire before the opposite, which is the less, or at the approach of the less has already ceased to exist; but will not, if allowing or admitting of smallness, be changed by that; even as I, having received and admitted smallness when compared with Simmias, remain just as I was, and am the same small person. And as the idea of greatness cannot condescend ever to be or become small, in like manner the smallness in us cannot be or become great; nor can any other opposite which remains the same ever be or become its own opposite, but either passes away or perishes in the change.

That, replied Cebes, is quite my notion. Hereupon one of the company, though I do not exactly remember which of them, said: In heaven's name, is not this the direct contrary of what was admitted before—that out of the greater came the less and out of the less the greater, and that opposites were simply generated from opposites; but now this principle seems to be utterly denied.

Socrates inclined his head to the speaker and listened. I like your courage, he said, in reminding us of this. But you do not observe that there is a difference in the two cases. For then we were speaking of opposites in the concrete, and now of the essential opposite which, as is affirmed, neither in us nor in nature can ever be at variance with itself: then, my friend, we were speaking of things in which opposites are inherent and which are called after them, but now about the opposites which are inherent in them and which give their name to them; and these essential opposites will never, as we maintain, admit of generation into or out of one another. At the same time, turning to Cebes, he said: Are you at all disconcerted, Cebes, at our friend's objection?

No, I do not feel so, said Cebes; and yet I cannot deny that I am often disturbed by objections.

Then we are agreed after all, said Socrates, that the opposite will never in any case be opposed to itself?

To that we are quite agreed, he replied.

Yet once more let me ask you to consider the question from another point of view, and see whether you agree with me:—There is a thing which you term heat, and another thing which you term cold? Certainly. But are they the same as fire and snow?

Most assuredly not.

Heat is a thing different from fire, and cold is not the same with snow?

Yes.

And yet you will surely admit that when snow, as we said, is under the influence of heat, they will not remain snow and heat; but at the advance of the heat, the snow will either retire or perish?

Very true, he replied.

And the fire too at the advance of the cold will either retire or perish; and when the fire is under the influence of the cold, they will not remain as before, fire and cold.

That is true, he said.

And in some cases the name of the idea is not only attached to the idea in an eternal connection, but anything else which, not being the idea, exists only in the form of the idea, may also lay claim to it. I will try to make this clear by an example. An odd number is always called by the name of odd?

Very true.

But is this the only thing which is called odd? Are there not other things which have their own name, and yet are called odd, because, although not the same as oddness, they are never without oddness?—that is what I mean to ask—whether numbers such as the number three are not of the class of odd. And there are many other examples: would you not say, for example, that three may be called by its proper name, and also be called odd, which is not the same with three? and this may be said not only of three but also of five, and of every alternate number—each of them without being oddness is odd, and in the same way two and four, and the other series of alternate numbers, has every number even, without being evenness. Do you agree?

Of course.

Then now mark the point at which I am aiming:—not only do essential opposites exclude one another, but also concrete things, which, although not in themselves opposed, contain opposites; these, I say, likewise reject the idea which is opposed to that which is contained in them, and when it approaches them they either perish or withdraw. For example; Will not the number three endure annihilation or anything sooner than be converted into an even number, while remaining three?

Very true, said Cebes.

And yet, he said, the number two is certainly not opposed to the number three?

It is not.

Then not only do opposite ideas repel the advance of one another, but also there are other natures which repel the approach of opposites.

Very true, he said.

Suppose, he said, that we endeavour, if possible, to determine what these are.

By all means.

Are they not, Cebes, such as compel the things of which they have possession, not only to take their own form, but also the form of some opposite?

What do you mean?

I mean, as I was just now saying, and as I am sure that you know, that those things which are possessed by the number three must not only be three in number, but must also be odd.

Quite true.

And on this oddness of three the opposite idea will never intrude?

No.

And this impress was given by the odd principle?

Yes.

And to the odd is opposed the even?

True.

Then the idea of the even number will never arrive at three?

No.

Then three has no part in the even?

None.

Then the triad or number three is uneven?

Very true.

To return then to my distinction of natures which are not opposed, and yet do not admit opposites—as, in the instance given, three, although not opposed to the even, does not any the more admit of the even, but always brings the opposite into play on the other side; or as two does not receive the odd, or fire the cold—from these examples (and there are many more) you may be able to arrive at the general conclusion, that not only opposites will not receive opposites, but also that nothing which brings the opposite will admit the opposite of that which it brings, in that to which it is brought.

Here let me recapitulate—for there is no harm in repetition. The number five will not admit the nature of the even, any more than ten, which is the double of five, will admit the nature of the odd. The double has another opposite, and is not strictly opposed to the odd, but nevertheless rejects the odd altogether. Nor again will parts in the ratio 3:2, nor any fraction in which there is a half, nor again in which there is a third, admit the notion of the whole, although they are not opposed to the whole: You will agree?

Yes, he said, I entirely agree and go along with you in that.

And now, he said, let us begin again; and do not you answer my question in the words in which I ask it: let me have not the old safe answer of which I spoke at first, but another equally safe, of which the truth will be inferred by you from what has been just said. I mean that if any one asks you 'what that is, of which the inherence makes the body hot,' you will reply not heat (this is what I call the safe and stupid answer), but fire, a far superior answer, which we are now in a condition to give. Or if any one asks you 'why a body is diseased,' you will not say from disease, but from fever; and instead of saying that oddness is the cause of odd numbers, you will say that the monad is the cause of them: and so of things in general, as I dare say that you will understand sufficiently without my adducing any further examples.

Yes, he said, I quite understand you.

Tell me, then, what is that of which the inherence will render the body alive?

The soul, he replied.

And is this always the case?

Yes, he said, of course.

Then whatever the soul possesses, to that she comes bearing life?

Yes, certainly.

And is there any opposite to life?

There is, he said.

And what is that?

Death.

Then the soul, as has been acknowledged, will never receive the opposite of what she brings.

Impossible, replied Cebes.

And now, he said, what did we just now call that principle which repels the even?

The odd.

And that principle which repels the musical, or the just?

The unmusical, he said, and the unjust.

And what do we call the principle which does not admit of death?

The immortal, he said.

And does the soul admit of death?

No.

Then the soul is immortal?

Yes, he said.

And may we say that this has been proven?

Yes, abundantly proven, Socrates, he replied.

Supposing that the odd were imperishable, must not three be imperishable?

Of course.

And if that which is cold were imperishable, when the warm principle came attacking the snow, must not the snow have retired whole and unmelted—for it could never have perished, nor could it have remained and admitted the heat?

True, he said.

Again, if the uncooling or warm principle were imperishable, the fire when assailed by cold would not have perished or have been extinguished, but would have gone away unaffected?

Certainly, he said.

And the same may be said of the immortal: if the immortal is also imperishable, the soul when attacked by death cannot perish; for the preceding argument shows that the soul will not admit of death, or ever be dead, any more than three or the odd number will admit of the even, or fire or the heat in the fire, of the cold.

Yet a person may say: 'But although the odd will not become even at the approach of the even, why may not the odd perish and the even take the place of the odd?' Now to him who makes this objection, we cannot answer that the odd principle is imperishable; for this has not been acknowledged, but if this had been acknowledged, there would have been no difficulty in contending that at the approach of the even the odd principle and the number three took their departure; and the same argument would have held good of fire and heat and any other thing.

Very true.

And the same may be said of the immortal: if the immortal is also imperishable, then the soul will be imperishable as well as immortal; but if not, some other proof of her imperishableness will have to be given.

No other proof is needed, he said; for if the immortal, being eternal, is liable to perish, then nothing is imperishable.

Yes, replied Socrates, and yet all men will agree that God, and the essential form of life, and the immortal in general, will never perish. Yes, all men, he said—that is true; and what is more, gods, if I am not mistaken, as well as men. Seeing then that the immortal is indestructible, must not the soul, if she is immortal, be also imperishable? Most certainly. Then when death attacks a man, the mortal portion of him may be supposed to die, but the immortal retires at the approach of death and is preserved safe and sound?

True.

Then, Cebes, beyond question, the soul is immortal and imperishable, and our souls will truly exist in another world!

I am convinced, Socrates, said Cebes, and have nothing more to object; but if my friend Simmias, or any one else, has any further objection to make, he had better speak out, and not keep silence, since I do not know to what other season he can defer the discussion, if there is anything which he wants to say or to have said. But I have nothing more to say, replied Simmias; nor can I see any reason for doubt after what has been said. But I still feel and cannot help feeling uncertain in my own mind, when I think of the greatness of the subject and the feebleness of man.

Yes, Simmias, replied Socrates, that is well said: and I may add that first principles, even if they appear certain, should be carefully considered; and when they are satisfactorily ascertained, then, with a sort of hesitating confidence in human reason, you may, I think, follow the course of the argument; and if that be plain and clear, there will be no need for any further enquiry.

Very true.

But then, O my friends, he said, if the soul is really immortal, what care should be taken of her, not only in respect of the portion of time which is called life, but of eternity! And the danger of neglecting her from this point of view does indeed appear to be awful. If death had only been the end of all, the wicked would have had a good bargain in dying, for they would have been happily quit not only of their body, but of their own evil together with their souls.

But now, inasmuch as the soul is manifestly immortal, there is no release or salvation from evil except the attainment of the highest virtue and wisdom. For the soul when on her progress to the world below takes nothing with her but nurture and education; and these are said greatly to benefit or greatly to injure the departed, at the very beginning of his journey thither. For after death, as they say, the genius of each individual, to whom he belonged in life, leads him to a certain place in which the dead are gathered together, whence after judgment has been given they pass into the world below, following the guide, who is appointed to conduct them from this world to the other: and when they have there received their due and remained their time, another guide brings them back again after many revolutions of ages.

Now this way to the other world is not, as Aeschylus says in the Telephus, a single and straight path—if that were so no guide would be needed, for no one could miss it; but there are many partings of the road, and windings, as I infer from the rites and sacrifices which are offered to the gods below in places where three ways meet on earth. The wise and orderly soul follows in the straight path and is conscious of her surroundings; but the soul which desires the body, and which, as I was relating before, has long been fluttering about the lifeless frame and the world of sight, is after many struggles and many sufferings hardly and with violence carried away by her attendant genius,.

When she arrives at the place where the other souls are gathered, if she be impure and have done impure deeds, whether foul murders or other crimes which are the brothers of these, and the works of brothers in crime—from that soul every one flees and turns away; no one will be her companion, no one her guide, but alone she wanders in extremity of evil until certain times are fulfilled, and when they are fulfilled, she is borne irresistibly to her own fitting habitation; as every pure and just soul which has passed through life in the company and under the guidance of the gods has also her own proper home. Now the earth has divers wonderful regions, and is indeed in nature and extent very unlike the notions of geographers, as I believe on the authority of one who shall be nameless.

What do you mean, Socrates? said Simmias. I have myself heard many descriptions of the earth, but I do not know, and I should very much like to know, in which of these you put faith.

And I, Simmias, replied Socrates, if I had the art of Glaucus would tell you; although I know not that the art of Glaucus could prove the truth of my tale, which I myself should never be able to prove, and even if I could, I fear, Simmias, that my life would come to an end before the argument was completed. I may describe to you, however, the form and regions of the earth according to my conception of them.

That, said Simmias, will be enough.

Well, then, he said, my conviction is, that the earth is a round body in the centre of the heavens, and therefore has no need of air or any similar force to be a support, but is kept there and hindered from falling or inclining any way by the equability of the surrounding heaven and by her own equipoise. For that which, being in equipoise, is in the centre of that which is equably diffused, will not incline any way in any degree, but will always remain in the same state and not deviate. And this is my first notion.

Which is surely a correct one, said Simmias.

Also I believe that the earth is very vast, and that we who dwell in the region extending from the river Phasis to the Pillars of Heracles inhabit a small portion only about the sea, like ants or frogs about a marsh, and that there are other inhabitants of many other like places; for everywhere on the face of the earth there are hollows of various forms and sizes, into which the water and the mist and the lower air collect.

But the true earth is pure and situated in the pure heaven—there are the stars also; and it is the heaven which is commonly spoken of by us as the ether, and of which our own earth is the sediment gathering in the hollows beneath. But we who live in these hollows are deceived into the notion that we are dwelling above on the surface of the earth; which is just as if a creature who was at the bottom of the sea were to fancy that he was on the surface of the water, and that the sea was the heaven through which he saw the sun and the other stars, he having never come to the surface by reason of his feebleness and sluggishness, and having never lifted up his head and seen, nor ever heard from one who had seen, how much purer and fairer the world above is than his own.

Such is exactly our case: for we are dwelling in a hollow of the earth, and fancy that we are on the surface; and the air we call the heaven, in which we imagine that the stars move. But the fact is, that owing to our feebleness and sluggishness we are prevented from reaching the surface of the air: for if any man could arrive at the exterior limit, or take the wings of a bird and come to the top, then like a fish who puts his head out of the water and sees this world, he would see a world beyond; and, if the nature of man could sustain the sight, he would acknowledge that this other world was the place of the true heaven and the true light and the true earth.

For our earth, and the stones, and the entire region which surrounds us, are spoilt and corroded, as in the sea all things are corroded by the brine, neither is there any noble or perfect growth, but caverns only, and sand, and an endless slough of mud: and even the shore is not to be compared to the fairer sights of this world. And still less is this our world to be compared with the other. Of that upper earth which is under the heaven, I can tell you a charming tale, Simmias, which is well worth hearing.

And we, Socrates, replied Simmias, shall be charmed to listen to you.

The tale, my friend, he said, is as follows:—In the first place, the earth, when looked at from above, is in appearance streaked like one of those balls which have leather coverings in twelve pieces, and is decked with various colours, of which the colours used by painters on earth are in a manner samples. But there the whole earth is made up of them, and they are brighter far and clearer than ours; there is a purple of wonderful lustre, also the radiance of gold, and the white which is in the earth is whiter than any chalk or snow. Of these and other colours the earth is made up, and they are more in number and fairer than the eye of man has ever seen; the very hollows (of which I was speaking) filled with air and water have a colour of their own, and are seen like light gleaming amid the diversity of the other colours, so that the whole presents a single and continuous appearance of variety in unity.

And in this fair region everything that grows—trees, and flowers, and fruits—are in a like degree fairer than any here; and there are hills, having stones in them in a like degree smoother, and more transparent, and fairer in colour than our highly-valued emeralds and sardonyxes and jaspers, and other gems, which are but minute fragments of them: for there all the stones are like our precious stones, and fairer still. The reason is, that they are pure, and not, like our precious stones, infected or corroded by the corrupt briny elements which coagulate among us, and which breed foulness and disease both in earth and stones, as well as in animals and plants. They are the jewels of the upper earth, which also shines with gold and silver and the like, and they are set in the light of day and are large and abundant and in all places, making the earth a sight to gladden the beholder's eye.

And there are animals and men, some in a middle region, others dwelling about the air as we dwell about the sea; others in islands which the air flows round, near the continent: and in a word, the air is used by them as the water and the sea are by us, and the ether is to them what the air is to us. Moreover, the temperament of their seasons is such that they have no disease, and live much longer than we do, and have sight and hearing and smell, and all the other senses, in far greater perfection, in the same proportion that air is purer than water or the ether than air. Also they have temples and sacred places in which the gods really dwell, and they hear their voices and receive their answers, and are conscious of them and hold converse with them, and they see the sun, moon, and stars as they truly are, and their other blessedness is of a piece with this. Such is the nature of the whole earth, and of the things which are around the earth . . . .

When the dead arrive at the place to which the genius of each severally guides them, first of all, they have sentence passed upon them, as they have lived well and piously or not. And those who appear to have lived neither well nor ill, go to the river Acheron, and embarking in any vessels which they may find, are carried in them to the lake, and there they dwell and are purified of their evil deeds, and having suffered the penalty of the wrongs which they have done to others, they are absolved, and receive the rewards of their good deeds, each of them according to his deserts.

But those who appear to be incurable by reason of the greatness of their crimes—who have committed many and terrible deeds of sacrilege, murders foul and violent, or the like—such are hurled into Tartarus which is their suitable destiny, and they never come out. . . . Those too who have been pre-eminent for holiness of life are released from this earthly prison, and go to their pure home which is above, and dwell in the purer earth; and of these, such as have duly purified themselves with philosophy live henceforth altogether without the body, in mansions fairer still which may not be described, and of which the time would fail me to tell.

Wherefore, Simmias, seeing all these things, what ought not we to do that we may obtain virtue and wisdom in this life? Fair is the prize, and the hope great! A man of sense ought not to say, nor will I be very confident, that the description which I have given of the soul and her mansions is exactly true. But I do say that, inasmuch as the soul is shown to be immortal, he may venture to think, not improperly or unworthily, that something of the kind is true. The venture is a glorious one, and he ought to comfort himself with words like these, which is the reason why I lengthen out the tale.

Wherefore, I say, let a man be of good cheer about his soul, who having cast away the pleasures and ornaments of the body as alien to him and working harm rather than good, has sought after the pleasures of knowledge; and has arrayed the soul, not in some foreign attire, but in her own proper jewels, temperance, and justice, and courage, and nobility, and truth—in these adorned she is ready to go on her journey to the world below, when her hour comes. You, Simmias and Cebes, and all other men, will depart at some time or other. Me already, as the tragic poet would say, the voice of fate calls. Soon I must drink the poison; and I think that I had better repair to the bath first, in order that the women may not have the trouble of washing my body after I am dead.

When he had done speaking, Crito said: And have you any commands for us, Socrates—anything to say about your children, or any other matter in which we can serve you?

Nothing particular, Crito, he replied: only, as I have always told you, take care of yourselves; that is a service which you may be ever rendering to me and mine and to all of us, whether you promise to do so or not. But if you have no thought for yourselves, and care not to walk according to the rule which I have prescribed for you, not now for the first time, however much you may profess or promise at the moment, it will be of no avail.

We will do our best, said Crito: And in what way shall we bury you?

In any way that you like; but you must get hold of me, and take care that I do not run away from you. Then he turned to us, and added with a smile:—I cannot make Crito believe that I am the same Socrates who have been talking and conducting the argument; he fancies that I am the other Socrates whom he will soon see, a dead body—and he asks, How shall he bury me? And though I have spoken many words in the endeavour to show that when I have drunk the poison I shall leave you and go to the joys of the blessed,— these words of mine, with which I was comforting you and myself, have had, as I perceive, no effect upon Crito.

And therefore I want you to be surety for me to him now, as at the trial he was surety to the judges for me: but let the promise be of another sort; for he was surety for me to the judges that I would remain, and you must be my surety to him that I shall not remain, but go away and depart; and then he will suffer less at my death, and not be grieved when he sees my body being burned or buried. I would not have him sorrow at my hard lot, or say at the burial, Thus we lay out Socrates, or, Thus we follow him to the grave or bury him; for false words are not only evil in themselves, but they infect the soul with evil. Be of good cheer, then, my dear Crito, and say that you are burying my body only, and do with that whatever is usual, and what you think best.

When he had spoken these words, he arose and went into a chamber to bathe; Crito followed him and told us to wait. So we remained behind, talking and thinking of the subject of discourse, and also of the greatness of our sorrow; he was like a father of whom we were being bereaved, and we were about to pass the rest of our lives as orphans. When he had taken the bath his children were brought to him—(he had two young sons and an elder one); and the women of his family also came, and he talked to them and gave them a few directions in the presence of Crito; then he dismissed them and returned to us. The hour of sunset was near, for a good deal of time had passed while he was within.

When he came out, he sat down with us again after his bath, but not much was said. Soon the jailer, who was the servant of the Eleven, entered and stood by him, saying:—To you, Socrates, whom I know to be the noblest and gentlest and best of all who ever came to this place, I will not impute the angry feelings of other men, who rage and swear at me, when, in obedience to the authorities, I bid them drink the poison—indeed, I am sure that you will not be angry with me; for others, as you are aware, and not I, are to blame. And so fare you well, and try to bear lightly what must needs be—you know my errand. Then bursting into tears he turned away and went out.

Socrates looked at him and said: I return your good wishes, and will do as you bid. Then turning to us, he said, How charming the man is: since I have been in prison he has always been coming to see me, and at times he would talk to me, and was as good to me as could be, and now see how generously he sorrows on my account. We must do as he says, Crito; and therefore let the cup be brought, if the poison is prepared: if not, let the attendant prepare some.

Yet, said Crito, the sun is still upon the hill-tops, and I know that many a one has taken the draught late, and after the announcement has been made to him, he has eaten and drunk, and enjoyed the society of his beloved; do not hurry—there is time enough.

Socrates said: Yes, Crito, and they of whom you speak are right in so acting, for they think that they will be gainers by the delay; but I am right in not following their example, for I do not think that I should gain anything by drinking the poison a little later; I should only be ridiculous in my own eyes for sparing and saving a life which is already forfeit. Please do as I say, and do not refuse me.

Crito made a sign to the servant, who was standing by; and he went out, and having been absent for some time, returned with the jailer carrying the cup of poison.

Socrates said: You, my good friend, who are experienced in these matters, shall give me directions how I am to proceed.

The man answered: You have only to walk about until your legs are heavy, and then to lie down, and the poison will act. At the same time he handed the cup to Socrates, who in the easiest and gentlest manner, without the least fear or change of colour or feature, looking at the man with all his eyes, Echecrates, as his manner was, took the cup and said: What do you say about making a libation out of this cup to any god? May I, or not?

The man answered: We only prepare, Socrates, just so much as we deem enough.

I understand, he said: but I may and must ask the gods to prosper my journey from this to the other world—even so—and so be it according to my prayer. Then raising the cup to his lips, quite readily and cheerfully he drank off the poison. And hitherto most of us had been able to control our sorrow; but now when we saw him drinking, and saw too that he had finished the draught, we could no longer forbear, and in spite of myself my own tears were flowing fast; so that I covered my face and wept, not for him, but at the thought of my own calamity in having to part from such a friend. Nor was I the first; for Crito, when he found himself unable to restrain his tears, had got up, and I followed; and at that moment, Apollodorus, who had been weeping all the time, broke out in a loud and passionate cry which made cowards of us all. Socrates alone retained his calmness:

What is this strange outcry? he said. I sent away the women mainly in order that they might not misbehave in this way, for I have been told that a man should die in peace. Be quiet, then, and have patience. When we heard his words we were ashamed, and refrained our tears; and he walked about until, as he said, his legs began to fail, and then he lay on his back, according to the directions, and the man who gave him the poison now and then looked at his feet and legs; and after a while he pressed his foot hard, and asked him if he could feel; and he said, No; and then his leg, and so upwards and upwards, and showed us that he was cold and stiff. And he felt them himself, and said: When the poison reaches the heart, that will be the end. He was beginning to grow cold about the groin, when he uncovered his face, for he had covered himself up, and said—they were his last words—he said:

Crito, I owe a cock to Asclepius; will you remember to pay the debt?

The debt shall be paid, said Crito; is there anything else? There was no answer to this question; but in a minute or two a movement was heard, and the attendants uncovered him; his eyes were set, and Crito closed his eyes and mouth.

Such was the end, Echecrates, of our friend; concerning whom I may truly say, that of all the men of his time whom I have known, he was the wisest and justest and best.

PLATO

Symposium

Translated by Benjamin Jowett

PERSONS OF THE DIALOGUE: Apollodorus, who repeats to his companion the dialogue which he had heard from Aristodemus, and had already once narrated to Glaucon. Phaedrus, Pausanias, Eryximachus, Aristophanes, Agathon, Socrates, Alcibiades, A Troop of Revellers.

THE SETTING: The House of Agathon.

Concerning the things about which you ask to be informed I believe that I am not ill-prepared with an answer. For the day before yesterday I was coming from my own home at Phalerum to the city, and one of my acquaintance, who had caught a sight of me from behind, calling out playfully in the distance, said: Apollodorus, O thou Phalerian, halt! So I did as I was bid; and then he said, I was looking for you, Apollodorus, only just now, that I might ask you about the speeches in praise of love, which were delivered by Socrates, Alcibiades, and others, at Agathon's supper. Phoenix, the son of Philip, told another person who told me of them; his narrative was very indistinct, but he said that you knew, and I wish that you would give me an account of them. Who, if not you, should be the reporter of the words of your friend? And first tell me, he said, were you present at this meeting?

Your informant, Glaucon, I said, must have been very indistinct indeed, if you imagine that the occasion was recent; or that I could have been of the party.

Why, yes, he replied, I thought so.

Impossible: I said. Are you ignorant that for many years Agathon has not resided at Athens; and not three have elapsed since I became acquainted with Socrates, and have made it my daily business to know all that he says and does. There was a time when I was running about the world, fancying myself to be well employed, but I was really a most wretched being, no better than you are now. I thought that I ought to do anything rather than be a philosopher.

Well, he said, jesting apart, tell me when the meeting occurred.

In our boyhood, I replied, when Agathon won the prize with his first tragedy, on the day after that on which he and his chorus offered the sacrifice of victory.

Then it must have been a long while ago, he said; and who told you—did Socrates?

No indeed, I replied, but the same person who told Phoenix;—he was a little fellow, who never wore any shoes, Aristodemus, of the deme of Cydathenaeum. He had been at Agathon's feast; and I think that in those days there was no one who was a more devoted admirer of Socrates. Moreover, I have asked Socrates about the truth of some parts of his narrative, and he confirmed them.

Then, said Glaucon, let's have the tale again; isn't the road to Athens made for conversation?

And so we walked, and talked of the discourses on love; and therefore, as I said at first, I am not ill-prepared to comply with your request, and will have another rehearsal of them if you like. For to speak or to hear others speak of philosophy always gives me the greatest pleasure, to say nothing of the profit. But when I hear another strain, especially that of you rich men and traders, such conversation displeases me; and I pity you who are my companions, because you think that you are doing something when in reality you are doing nothing. And I dare say that you pity me in return, whom you regard as an unhappy creature, and very probably you are right. But I certainly know of you what you only think of me—there is the difference.

COMPANION: I see, Apollodorus, that you are just the same—always speaking evil of yourself, and of others; and I do believe that you pity all mankind, with the exception of Socrates, yourself first of all, true in this to your old name, which, however deserved, I know not how you acquired, of Apollodorus the madman; for you are always raging against yourself and everybody but Socrates.

APOLLODORUS: Yes, friend, and the reason why I am said to be mad, and out of my wits, is just because I have these notions of myself and you; no other evidence is required.

COMPANION: No more of that, Apollodorus; but let me renew my request that you would repeat the conversation.

APOLLODORUS: Well, the tale of love was on this wise:—But perhaps I had better begin at the beginning, and endeavour to give you the exact words of Aristodemus:

He said that he met Socrates fresh from the bath and sandalled; and as the sight of the sandals was unusual, he asked him whither he was going that he had been converted into such a beau. To a banquet at Agathon's, he replied, whose invitation to his sacrifice of victory I refused yesterday, fearing a crowd, but promising that I would come to-day instead; and so I have put on my finery, because he is such a fine man. What say you to going with me unasked?

I will do as you bid me, I replied.

Follow then, he said, and let us demolish the proverb:— 'To the feasts of inferior men the good unbidden go;' instead of which our proverb will run:— 'To the feasts of the good the good unbidden go;' and this alteration may be supported by the authority of Homer himself, who not only demolishes but literally outrages the proverb. For, after picturing Agamemnon as the most valiant of men, he makes Menelaus, who is but a fainthearted warrior, come unbidden to the banquet of Agamemnon, who is feasting and offering sacrifices, not the better to the worse, but the worse to the better.

I rather fear, Socrates, said Aristodemus, lest this may still be my case; and that, like Menelaus in Homer, I shall be the inferior person, who 'To the feasts of the wise unbidden goes.' But I shall say that I was bidden of you, and then you will have to make an excuse. 'Two going together,' he replied, in Homeric fashion, one or other of them may invent an excuse by the way.

This was the style of their conversation as they went along. Socrates dropped behind in a fit of abstraction, and desired Aristodemus, who was waiting, to go on before him. When he reached the house of Agathon he found the doors wide open, and a comical thing happened. A servant coming out met him, and led him at once into the banqueting-hall in which the guests were reclining, for the banquet was about to begin. Welcome, Aristodemus, said Agathon, as soon as he appeared—you are just in time to sup with us; if you come on any other matter put it off, and make one of us, as I was looking for you yesterday and meant to have asked you, if I could have found you. But what have you done with Socrates? I turned round, but Socrates was nowhere to be seen; and I had to explain that he had been with me a moment before, and that I came by his invitation to the supper.

You were quite right in coming, said Agathon; but where is he himself?

He was behind me just now, as I entered, he said, and I cannot think what has become of him.

Go and look for him, boy, said Agathon, and bring him in; and do you, Aristodemus, meanwhile take the place by Eryximachus. The servant then assisted him to wash, and he lay down, and presently another servant came in and reported that our friend Socrates had retired into the portico of the neighbouring house. 'There he is fixed,' said he, 'and when I call to him he will not stir.' How strange, said Agathon; then you must call him again, and keep calling him. Let him alone, said my informant; he has a way of stopping anywhere and losing himself without any reason. I believe that he will soon appear; do not therefore disturb him.

Well, if you think so, I will leave him, said Agathon. And then, turning to the servants, he added, 'Let us have supper without waiting for him. Serve up whatever you please, for there is no one to give you orders; hitherto I have never left you to yourselves. But on this occasion imagine that you are our hosts, and that I and the company are your guests; treat us well, and then we shall commend you.' After this, supper was served, but still no Socrates; and during the meal Agathon several times expressed a wish to send for him, but Aristodemus objected; and at last when the feast was about half over—for the fit, as usual, was not of long duration —Socrates entered.

Agathon, who was reclining alone at the end of the table, begged that he would take the place next to him; that 'I may touch you,' he said, 'and have the benefit of that wise thought which came into your mind in the portico, and is now in your possession; for I am certain that you would not have come away until you had found what you sought.'

How I wish, said Socrates, taking his place as he was desired, that wisdom could be infused by touch, out of the fuller into the emptier man, as water runs through wool out of a fuller cup into an emptier one; if that were so, how greatly should I value the privilege of reclining at your side! For you would have filled me full with a stream of wisdom plenteous and fair; whereas my own is of a very mean and questionable sort, no better than a dream. But yours is bright and full of promise, and was manifested forth in all the splendour of youth the day before yesterday, in the presence of more than thirty thousand Hellenes.

You are mocking, Socrates, said Agathon, and ere long you and I will have to determine who bears off the palm of wisdom—of this Dionysus shall be the judge; but at present you are better occupied with supper.

Socrates took his place on the couch, and supped with the rest; and then libations were offered, and after a hymn had been sung to the god, and there had been the usual ceremonies, they were about to commence drinking, when Pausanias said, And now, my friends, how can we drink with least injury to ourselves? I can assure you that I feel severely the effect of yesterday's potations, and must have time to recover; and I suspect that most of you are in the same predicament, for you were of the party yesterday. Consider then: How can the drinking be made easiest?

I entirely agree, said Aristophanes, that we should, by all means, avoid hard drinking, for I was myself one of those who were yesterday drowned in drink.

I think that you are right, said Eryximachus, the son of Acumenus; but I should still like to hear one other person speak: Is Agathon able to drink hard?

I am not equal to it, said Agathon.

Then, said Eryximachus, the weak heads like myself, Aristodemus, Phaedrus, and others who never can drink, are fortunate in finding that the stronger ones are not in a drinking mood. (I do not include Socrates, who is able either to drink or to abstain, and will not mind, whichever we do.) Well, as of none of the company seem disposed to drink much, I may be forgiven for saying, as a physician, that drinking deep is a bad practice, which I never follow, if I can help, and certainly do not recommend to another, least of all to any one who still feels the effects of yesterday's carouse.

I always do what you advise, and especially what you prescribe as a physician, rejoined Phaedrus the Myrrhinusian, and the rest of the company, if they are wise, will do the same.

It was agreed that drinking was not to be the order of the day, but that they were all to drink only so much as they pleased. Then, said Eryximachus, as you are all agreed that drinking is to be voluntary, and that there is to be no compulsion, I move, in the next place, that the flute-girl, who has just made her appearance, be told to go away and play to herself, or, if she likes, to the women who are within. To-day let us have conversation instead; and, if you will allow me, I will tell you what sort of conversation. This proposal having been accepted, Eryximachus proceeded as follows:—

I will begin, he said, after the manner of Melanippe in Euripides, 'Not mine the word' which I am about to speak, but that of Phaedrus. For often he says to me in an indignant tone:—'What a strange thing it is, Eryximachus, that, whereas other gods have poems and hymns made in their honour, the great and glorious god, Love, has no encomiast among all the poets who are so many. There are the worthy sophists too—the excellent Prodicus for example, who have descanted in prose on the virtues of Heracles and other heroes; and, what is still more extraordinary, I have met with a philosophical work in which the utility of salt has been made the theme of an eloquent discourse; and many other like things have had a like honour bestowed upon them. And only to think that there should have been an eager interest created about them, and yet that to this day no one has ever dared worthily to hymn Love's praises! So entirely has this great deity been neglected.'

Now in this Phaedrus seems to me to be quite right, and therefore I want to offer him a contribution; also I think that at the present moment we who are here assembled cannot do better than honour the god Love. If you agree with me, there will be no lack of conversation; for I mean to propose that each of us in turn, going from left to right, shall make a speech in honour of Love. Let him give us the best which he can; and Phaedrus, because he is sitting first on the left hand, and because he is the father of the thought, shall begin.

No one will vote against you, Eryximachus, said Socrates. How can I oppose your motion, who profess to understand nothing but matters of love; nor, I presume, will Agathon and Pausanias;

and there can be no doubt of Aristophanes, whose whole concern is with Dionysus and Aphrodite; nor will any one disagree of those whom I see around me. The proposal, as I am aware, may seem rather hard upon us whose place is last; but we shall be contented if we hear some good speeches first. Let Phaedrus begin the praise of Love, and good luck to him. All the company expressed their assent, and desired him to do as Socrates bade him.

Aristodemus did not recollect all that was said, nor do I recollect all that he related to me; but I will tell you what I thought most worthy of remembrance, and what the chief speakers said.

Phaedrus began by affirming that Love is a mighty god, and wonderful among gods and men, but especially wonderful in his birth. For he is the eldest of the gods, which is an honour to him; and a proof of his claim to this honour is, that of his parents there is no memorial; neither poet nor prose-writer has ever affirmed that he had any. As Hesiod says: 'First Chaos came, and then broad-bosomed Earth, The everlasting seat of all that is, And Love.' In other words, after Chaos, the Earth and Love, these two, came into being. Also Parmenides sings of Generation: 'First in the train of gods, he fashioned Love.' And Acusilaus agrees with Hesiod.

Thus numerous are the witnesses who acknowledge Love to be the eldest of the gods. And not only is he the eldest, he is also the source of the greatest benefits to us. For I know not any greater blessing to a young man who is beginning life than a virtuous lover, or to the lover than a beloved youth. For the principle which ought to be the guide of men who would nobly live—that principle, I say, neither kindred, nor honour, nor wealth, nor any other motive is able to implant so well as love.

Of what am I speaking? Of the sense of honour and dishonour, without which neither states nor individuals ever do any good or great work. And I say that a lover who is detected in doing any dishonourable act, or submitting through cowardice when any dishonour is done to him by another, will be more pained at being detected by his beloved than at being seen by his father, or by his companions, or by any one else. The beloved too, when he is found in any disgraceful situation, has the same feeling about his lover.

And if there were only some way of contriving that a state or an army should be made up of lovers and their loves, they would be the very best governors of their own city, abstaining from all dishonour, and emulating one another in honour; and when fighting at each other's side, although a mere handful, they would overcome the world. For what lover would not choose rather to be seen by all mankind than by his beloved, either when abandoning his post or throwing away his arms? He would be ready to die a thousand deaths rather than endure this. Or who would desert his beloved or fail him in the hour of danger? The veriest coward would become an inspired hero, equal to the bravest, at such a time; Love would inspire him. That courage which, as Homer says, the god breathes into the souls of some heroes, Love of his own nature infuses into the lover.

Love will make men dare to die for their beloved—love alone; and women as well as men. . . . These are my reasons for affirming that Love is the eldest and noblest and mightiest of the gods; and the chiefest author and giver of virtue in life, and of happiness after death.

This, or something like this, was the speech of Phaedrus; and some other speeches followed which Aristodemus did not remember; the next which he repeated was that of Pausanias.

Phaedrus, he said, the argument has not been set before us, I think, quite in the right form;—we should not be called upon to praise Love in such an indiscriminate manner. If there were only one Love, then what you said would be well enough; but since there are more Loves than one,—should have begun by determining which of them was to be the theme of our praises. I will amend this defect; and first of all I will tell you which Love is deserving of praise, and then try to hymn the praiseworthy one in a manner worthy of him. For we all know that Love is inseparable from Aphrodite, and if there were only one Aphrodite there would be only one Love; but as there are two goddesses there must be two Loves. And am I not right in asserting that there are two goddesses? The elder one, having no mother, who is called the heavenly Aphrodite—she is the daughter of Uranus; the younger, who is the daughter of Zeus and Dione —her we call common; and the Love who is her fellow-worker is rightly named common, as the other love is called heavenly.

All the gods ought to have praise given to them, but not without distinction of their natures; and therefore I must try to distinguish the characters of the two Loves. Now actions vary according to the manner of their performance. Take, for example, that which we are now doing, drinking, singing and talking—these actions are not in themselves either good or evil, but they turn out in this or that way according to the mode of performing them; and when well done they are good, and when wrongly done they are evil; and in like manner not every love, but only that which has a noble purpose, is noble and worthy of praise.

The Love who is the offspring of the common Aphrodite is essentially common, and has no discrimination, being such as the meaner sort of men feel, and is apt to be of women as well as of youths, and is of the body rather than of the soul—the most foolish beings are the objects of this love which desires only to gain an end, but never thinks of accomplishing the end nobly, and therefore does good and evil quite indiscriminately. The goddess who is his mother is far younger than the other, and she was born of the union of the male and female, and partakes of both. But the offspring of the heavenly Aphrodite is derived from a mother in whose birth the female has no part,—she is from the male only; this is that love which is of youths, and the goddess being older, there is nothing of wantonness in her.

Those who are inspired by this love turn to the male, and delight in him who is the more valiant and intelligent nature; any one may recognise the pure enthusiasts in the very character of their attachments. For they love not boys, but intelligent beings whose reason is beginning to be developed, much about the time at which their beards begin to grow. And in choosing young men to be their companions, they mean to be faithful to them, and pass their whole life in company with them, not to take them in their inexperience, and deceive them, and play the fool with them, or run away from one to another of them.

But the love of young boys should be forbidden by law, because their future is uncertain; they may turn out good or bad, either in body or soul, and much noble enthusiasm may be thrown away upon them; in this matter the good are a law to themselves, and the coarser sort of lovers ought to be restrained by force; as we restrain or attempt to restrain them from fixing their affections on women of free birth. These are the persons who bring a reproach on love; and some have been led to deny the lawfulness of such attachments because they see the impropriety and evil of them; for surely nothing that is decorously and lawfully done can justly be censured.

Now here and in Lacedaemon the rules about love are perplexing, but in most cities they are simple and easily intelligible; in Elis and Boeotia, and in countries having no gifts of eloquence, they are very straightforward; the law is simply in favour of these connexions, and no one, whether young or old, has anything to say to their discredit; the reason being, as I suppose, that they are men of few words in those parts, and therefore the lovers do not like the trouble of pleading their suit. In Ionia and other places, and generally in countries which are subject to the barbarians, the custom is held to be dishonourable; loves of youths share the evil repute in which philosophy and gymnastics are held, because they are inimical to tyranny; for the interests of rulers require that their subjects should be poor in spirit, and that there should be no strong bond of friendship or society among them, which love, above all other motives, is likely to inspire, as our Athenian tyrants learned by experience; for the love of Aristogeiton and the constancy of Harmodius had a strength which undid their power.

And, therefore, the ill-repute into which these attachments have fallen is to be ascribed to the evil condition of those who make them to be ill-reputed; that is to say, to the self- seeking of the governors and the cowardice of the governed; on the other hand, the indiscriminate honour which is given to them in some countries is attributable to the laziness of those who hold this opinion of them. In our own country a far better principle prevails, but, as I was saying, the explanation is rather perplexing.

For, observe that open loves are held to be more honourable than secret ones, and that the love of the noblest and highest, even if their persons are less beautiful than others, is especially honourable. Consider, too, how great is the encouragement which all the world gives to the lover; neither is he supposed to be doing anything dishonourable; but if he succeeds he is praised, and if he fail he is blamed. And in the pursuit of his love the custom of mankind allows him to do many strange things, which philosophy would bitterly censure if they were done from any motive of interest, or wish for office or power.

He may pray, and entreat, and supplicate, and swear, and lie on a mat at the door, and endure a slavery worse than that of any slave—in any other case friends and enemies would be equally ready to prevent him, but now there is no friend who will be ashamed of him and admonish him, and no enemy will charge him with meanness or flattery; the actions of a lover have a grace which ennobles them; and custom has decided that they are highly commendable and that there no loss of character in them; and, what is strangest of all, he only may swear and forswear himself (so men say), and the gods will forgive his transgression, for there is no such thing as a lover's oath.

Such is the entire liberty which gods and men have allowed the lover, according to the custom which prevails in our part of the world. From this point of view a man fairly argues that in Athens to love and to be loved is held to be a very honourable thing. But when parents forbid their sons to talk with their lovers, and place them under a tutor's care, who is appointed to see to these things, and their companions and equals cast in their teeth anything of the sort which they may observe, and their elders refuse to silence the reprovers and do not rebuke them—any one who reflects on all this will, on the contrary, think that we hold these practices to be most disgraceful.

But, as I was saying at first, the truth as I imagine is, that whether such practices are honourable or whether they are dishonourable is not a simple question; they are honourable to him who follows them honourably, dishonourable to him who follows them dishonourably. There is dishonour in yielding to the evil, or in an evil manner; but there is honour in yielding to the good, or in an honourable manner. Evil is the vulgar lover who loves the body rather than the soul, inasmuch as he is not even stable, because he loves a thing which is in itself unstable, and therefore when the bloom of youth which he was desiring is over, he takes wing and flies away, in spite of all his words and promises; whereas the love of the noble disposition is life-long, for it becomes one with the everlasting.

The custom of our country would have both of them proven well and truly, and would have us yield to the one sort of lover and avoid the other, and therefore encourages some to pursue, and others to fly; testing both the lover and beloved in contests and trials, until they show to which of the two classes they respectively belong. And this is the reason why, in the first place, a hasty attachment is held to be dishonourable, because time is the true test of this as of most other things; and secondly there is a dishonour in being overcome by the love of money, or of wealth, or of political power, whether a man is frightened into surrender by the loss of them, or, having experienced the benefits of money and political corruption, is unable to rise above the seductions of them. For none of these things are of a permanent or lasting nature; not to mention that no generous friendship ever sprang from them. There remains, then, only one way of honourable attachment which custom allows in the beloved, and this is the way of virtue; for as we admitted that any service which the lover does to him is not to be accounted flattery or a dishonour to himself, so the beloved has one way only of voluntary service which is not dishonourable, and this is virtuous service.

For we have a custom, and according to our custom any one who does service to another under the idea that he will be improved by him either in wisdom, or in some other particular of virtue —such a voluntary service, I say, is not to be regarded as a dishonour, and is not open to the charge of flattery. And these two customs, one the love of youth, and the other the practice of philosophy and virtue in general, ought to meet in one, and then the beloved may honourably indulge the lover. For when the lover and beloved come together, having each of them a law, and the lover thinks that he is right in doing any service which he can to his gracious loving one; and the other that he is right in showing any kindness which he can to him who is making him wise and good; the one capable of communicating wisdom and virtue, the other seeking to acquire them with a view to education and wisdom, when the two laws of love are fulfilled and meet in one—then, and then only, may the beloved yield with honour to the lover.

Nor when love is of this disinterested sort is there any disgrace in being deceived, but in every other case there is equal disgrace in being or not being deceived. For he who is gracious to his lover under the impression that he is rich, and is disappointed of his gains because he turns out to be poor, is disgraced all the same: for he has done his best to show that he would give himself up to any one's 'uses base' for the sake of money; but this is not honourable. And on the same principle he who gives himself to a lover because he is a good man, and in the hope that he will be improved by his company, shows himself to be virtuous, even though the object of his affection turn out to be a villain, and to have no virtue; and if he is deceived he has committed a noble error. For he has proved that for his part he will do anything for anybody with a view to virtue and improvement, than which there can be nothing nobler.

Thus noble in every case is the acceptance of another for the sake of virtue. This is that love which is the love of the heavenly godess, and is heavenly, and of great price to individuals and cities, making the lover and the beloved alike eager in the work of their own improvement. But all other loves are the offspring of the other, who is the common goddess. To you, Phaedrus, I offer this my contribution in praise of love, which is as good as I could make extempore.

Pausanias came to a pause—this is the balanced way in which I have been taught by the wise to speak; and Aristodemus said that the turn of Aristophanes was next, but either he had eaten too much, or from some other cause he had the hiccough, and was obliged to change turns with Eryximachus the physician, who was reclining on the couch below him.

Eryximachus, he said, you ought either to stop my hiccough, or to speak in my turn until I have left off.

I will do both, said Eryximachus: I will speak in your turn, and do you speak in mine; and while I am speaking let me recommend you to hold your breath, and if after you have done so for some time the hiccough is no better, then gargle with a little water; and if it still continues, tickle your nose with something and sneeze; and if you sneeze once or twice, even the most violent hiccough is sure to go. I will do as you prescribe, said Aristophanes, and now get on.

Eryximachus spoke as follows: Seeing that Pausanias made a fair beginning, and but a lame ending, I must endeavour to supply his deficiency. I think that he has rightly distinguished two kinds of love. But my art further informs me that the double love is not merely an affection of the soul of man towards the fair, or towards anything, but is to be found in the bodies of all animals and in productions of the earth, and I may say in all that is; such is the conclusion which I seem to have gathered from my own art of medicine, whence I learn how great and wonderful and universal is the deity of love, whose empire extends over all things, divine as well as human. And from medicine I will begin that I may do honour to my art.

There are in the human body these two kinds of love, which are confessedly different and unlike, and being unlike, they have loves and desires which are unlike; and the desire of the healthy is one, and the desire of the diseased is another; and as Pausanias said, that to indulge good men is honourable, and bad men dishonourable:—so too in the body the good and healthy elements are to be indulged, and the bad elements and the elements of disease are not to be indulged, but discouraged.

And this is what the physician has to do, and in this the art of medicine consists: for medicine may be regarded generally as the knowledge of the loves and desires of the body, and how to satisfy them or not; and the best physician is he who is able to separate fair love from foul, or to convert one into the other; and he who knows how to eradicate and how to implant love, whichever is required, and can reconcile the most hostile elements in the constitution and make them loving friends, is a skilful practitioner. Now the most hostile are the most opposite, such as hot and cold, bitter and sweet, moist and dry, and the like. And my ancestor, Asclepius, knowing how to implant friendship and accord in these elements, was the creator of our art, as our friends the poets here tell us, and I believe them; and not only medicine in every branch but the arts of gymnastic and husbandry are under his dominion.

Any one who pays the least attention to the subject will also perceive that in music there is the same reconciliation of opposites; and I suppose that this must have been the meaning of Heraclitus, although his words are not accurate; for he says that The One is united by disunion, like the harmony of the bow and the lyre. Now there is an absurdity saying that harmony is discord or is composed of elements which are still in a state of discord. But what he probably meant was, that harmony is composed of differing notes of higher or lower pitch which disagreed once, but are now reconciled by the art of music; for if the higher and lower notes still disagreed, there could be no harmony,—clearly not. For harmony is a symphony, and symphony is an agreement; but an agreement of disagreements while they disagree there cannot be; you cannot harmonize that which disagrees.

In like manner rhythm is compounded of elements short and long, once differing and now in accord; which accordance, as in the former instance, medicine, so in all these other cases, music implants, making love and unison to grow up among them; and thus music, too, is concerned with the principles of love in their application to harmony and rhythm. Again, in the essential nature of harmony and rhythm there is no difficulty in discerning love which has not yet become double. But when you want to use them in actual life, either in the composition of songs or in the correct performance of airs or metres composed already, which latter is called education, then the difficulty begins, and the good artist is needed. . . . Whence I infer that in music, in medicine, in all other things human as well as divine, both loves ought to be noted as far as may be, for they are both present.

The course of the seasons is also full of both these principles; and when, as I was saying, the elements of hot and cold, moist and dry, attain the harmonious love of one another and blend in temperance and harmony, they bring to men, animals, and plants health and plenty, and do them no harm; whereas the wanton love, getting the upper hand and affecting the seasons of the year, is very destructive and injurious, being the source of pestilence, and bringing many other kinds of diseases on animals and plants; for hoar-frost and hail and blight spring from the excesses and disorders of these elements of love, which to know in relation to the revolutions of the heavenly bodies and the seasons of the year is termed astronomy.

Furthermore all sacrifices and the whole province of divination, which is the art of communion between gods and men—these, I say, are concerned only with the preservation of the good and the cure of the evil love. For all manner of impiety is likely to ensue if, instead of accepting and honouring and reverencing the harmonious love in all his actions, a man honours the other love, whether in his feelings towards gods or parents, towards the living or the dead.

Wherefore the business of divination is to see to these loves and to heal them, and divination is the peacemaker of gods and men, working by a knowledge of the religious or irreligious tendencies which exist in human loves. Such is the great and mighty, or rather omnipotent force of love in general. And the love, more especially, which is concerned with the good, and which is perfected in company with temperance and justice, whether among gods or men, has the greatest power, and is the source of all our happiness and harmony, and makes us friends with the gods who are above us, and with one another.

I dare say that I too have omitted several things which might be said in praise of Love, but this was not intentional, and you, Aristophanes, may now supply the omission or take some other line of commendation; for I perceive that you are rid of the hiccough.

Yes, said Aristophanes, who followed, the hiccough is gone; not, however, until I applied the sneezing; and I wonder whether the harmony of the body has a love of such noises and ticklings, for I no sooner applied the sneezing than I was cured.

Eryximachus said: Beware, friend Aristophanes, although you are going to speak, you are making fun of me; and I shall have to watch and see whether I cannot have a laugh at your expense, when you might speak in peace.

You are right, said Aristophanes, laughing. I will unsay my words; but please do not watch me, as I fear that in the speech which I am about to make, instead of others laughing with me, which is to the manner born of our muse and would be all the better, I shall only be laughed at by them.

Do you expect to shoot your bolt and escape, Aristophanes? Well, perhaps if you are very careful and bear in mind that you will be called to account, I may be induced to let you off.

Aristophanes professed to open another vein of discourse; he had a mind to praise Love in another way, unlike that either of Pausanias or Eryximachus. Mankind, he said, judging by their neglect of him, have never, as I think, at all understood the power of Love. For if they had understood him they would surely have built noble temples and altars, and offered solemn sacrifices in his honour; but this is not done, and most certainly ought to be done: since of all the gods he is the best friend of men, the helper and the healer of the ills which are the great impediment to the happiness of the race. I will try to describe his power to you, and you shall teach the rest of the world what I am teaching you.

In the first place, let me treat of the nature of man and what has happened to it; for the original human nature was not like the present, but different. The sexes were not two as they are now, but originally three in number; there was man, woman, and the union of the two, having a name corresponding to this double nature, which had once a real existence, but is now lost, and the word 'Androgynous' is only preserved as a term of reproach.

In the second place, the primeval man was round, his back and sides forming a circle; and he had four hands and four feet, one head with two faces, looking opposite ways, set on a round neck and precisely alike; also four ears, two privy members, and the remainder to correspond. He could walk upright as men now do, backwards or forwards as he pleased, and he could also roll over and over at a great pace, turning on his four hands and four feet, eight in all, like tumblers going over and over with their legs in the air; this was when he wanted to run fast.

Now the sexes were three, and such as I have described them; because the sun, moon, and earth are three; and the man was originally the child of the sun, the woman of the earth, and the man-woman of the moon, which is made up of sun and earth, and they were all round and moved round and round like their parents. Terrible was their might and strength, and the thoughts of their hearts were great, and they made an attack upon the gods; of them is told the tale of Otys and Ephialtes who, as Homer says, dared to scale heaven, and would have laid hands upon the gods. Doubt reigned in the celestial councils. Should they kill them and annihilate the race with thunderbolts, as they had done the giants, then there would be an end of the sacrifices and worship which men offered to them; but, on the other hand, the gods could not suffer their insolence to be unrestrained.

At last, after a good deal of reflection, Zeus discovered a way. He said: 'Methinks I have a plan which will humble their pride and improve their manners; men shall continue to exist, but I will cut them in two and then they will be diminished in strength and increased in numbers; this will have the advantage of making them more profitable to us. They shall walk upright on two legs, and if they continue insolent and will not be quiet, I will split them again and they shall hop about on a single leg.'

He spoke and cut men in two, like a sorb-apple which is halved for pickling, or as you might divide an egg with a hair; and as he cut them one after another, he bade Apollo give the face and the half of the neck a turn in order that the man might contemplate the section of himself: he would thus learn a lesson of humility. Apollo was also bidden to heal their wounds and compose their forms. So he gave a turn to the face and pulled the skin from the sides all over that which in our language is called the belly, like the purses which draw in, and he made one mouth at the centre, which he fastened in a knot (the same which is called the navel); he also molded the breast and took out most of the wrinkles, much as a shoemaker might smooth leather upon a last; he left a few, however, in the region of the belly and navel, as a memorial of the primeval state.

After the division the two parts of man, each desiring his other half, came together, and throwing their arms about one another, entwined in mutual embraces, longing to grow into one, they were on the point of dying from hunger and self-neglect, because they did not like to do anything apart; and when one of the halves died and the other survived, the survivor sought another mate, man or woman as we call them,—being the sections of entire men or women,—and clung to that. They were being destroyed, when Zeus in pity of them invented a new plan: he turned the parts of generation round to the front, for this had not been always their position, and they sowed the seed no longer as hitherto like grasshoppers in the ground, but in one another; and after the transposition the male generated in the female in order that by the mutual embraces of man and woman they might breed, and the race might continue; or if man came to man they might be satisfied, and rest, and go their ways to the business of life: so ancient is the desire of one another which is implanted in us, reuniting our original nature, making one of two, and healing the state of man.

Each of us when separated, having one side only, like a flat fish, is but the indenture of a man, and he is always looking for his other half. Men who are a section of that double nature which was once called Androgynous are lovers of women; adulterers are generally of this breed, and also adulterous women who lust after men: the women who are a section of the woman do not care for men, but have female attachments; the female companions are of this sort. But they who are a section of the male follow the male, and while they are young, being slices of the original man, they hang about men and embrace them, and they are themselves the best of boys and youths, because they have the most manly nature.

Some indeed assert that they are shameless, but this is not true; for they do not act thus from any want of shame, but because they are valiant and manly, and have a manly countenance, and they embrace that which is like them. And these when they grow up become our statesmen, and these only, which is a great proof of the truth of what I am saying. When they reach manhood they are lovers of youth, and are not naturally inclined to marry or beget children,—if at all, they do so only in obedience to the law; but they are satisfied if they may be allowed to live with one another unwedded; and such a nature is prone to love and ready to return love, always embracing that which is akin to him.

And when one of them meets with his other half, the actual half of himself, whether he be a lover of youth or a lover of another sort, the pair are lost in an amazement of love and friendship and intimacy, and one will not be out of the other's sight, as I may say, even for a moment: these are the people who pass their whole lives together; yet they could not explain what they desire of one another. For the intense yearning which each of them has towards the other does not appear to be the desire of lover's intercourse, but of something else which the soul of either evidently desires and cannot tell, and of which she has only a dark and doubtful presentiment.

Suppose Hephaestus, with his instruments, to come to the pair who are lying side by side and to say to them, 'What do you people want of one another?' they would be unable to explain. And suppose further, that when he saw their perplexity he said: 'Do you desire to be wholly one; always day and night to be in one another's company? for if this is what you desire, I am ready to melt you into one and let you grow together, so that being two you shall become one, and while you live live a common life as if you were a single man, and after your death in the world below still be one departed soul instead of two—I ask whether this is what you lovingly desire, and whether you are satisfied to attain this?'—there is not a man of them who when he heard the proposal would deny or would not acknowledge that this meeting and melting into one another, this becoming one instead of two, was the very expression of his ancient need. And the reason is that human nature was originally one and we were a whole, and the desire and pursuit of the whole is called love.

There was a time, I say, when we were one, but now because of the wickedness of mankind God has dispersed us, as the Arcadians were dispersed into villages by the Lacedaemonians. And if we are not obedient to the gods, there is a danger that we shall be split up again and go about in basso-relievo, like the profile figures having only half a nose which are sculptured on monuments, and that we shall be like tallies. Wherefore let us exhort all men to piety, that we may avoid evil, and obtain the good, of which Love is to us the lord and minister; and let no one oppose him—he is the enemy of the gods who opposes him. For if we are friends of the God and at peace with him we shall find our own true loves, which rarely happens in this world at present.

I am serious, and therefore I must beg Eryximachus not to make fun or to find any allusion in what I am saying to Pausanias and Agathon, who, as I suspect, are both of the manly nature, and belong to the class which I have been describing. But my words have a wider application —they include men and women everywhere; and I believe that if our loves were perfectly accomplished, and each one returning to his primeval nature had his original true love, then our race would be happy. And if this would be best of all, the best in the next degree and under present circumstances must be the nearest approach to such an union; and that will be the attainment of a congenial love.

Wherefore, if we would praise him who has given to us the benefit, we must praise the god Love, who is our greatest benefactor, both leading us in this life back to our own nature, and giving us high hopes for the future, for he promises that if we are pious, he will restore us to our original state, and heal us and make us happy and blessed. This, Eryximachus, is my discourse of love, which, although different to yours, I must beg you to leave unassailed by the shafts of your ridicule, in order that each may have his turn; each, or rather either, for Agathon and Socrates are the only ones left.

Indeed, I am not going to attack you, said Eryximachus, for I thought your speech charming, and did I not know that Agathon and Socrates are masters in the art of love, I should be really afraid that they would have nothing to say, after the world of things which have been said already. But, for all that, I am not without hopes.

Socrates said: You played your part well, Eryximachus; but if you were as I am now, or rather as I shall be when Agathon has spoken, you would, indeed, be in a great strait. You want to cast a spell over me, Socrates, said Agathon, in the hope that I may be disconcerted at the expectation raised among the audience that I shall speak well.

I should be strangely forgetful, Agathon replied Socrates, of the courage and magnanimity which you showed when your own compositions were about to be exhibited, and you came upon the stage with the actors and faced the vast theatre altogether undismayed, if I thought that your nerves could be fluttered at a small party of friends.

Do you think, Socrates, said Agathon, that my head is so full of the theatre as not to know how much more formidable to a man of sense a few good judges are than many fools?

Nay, replied Socrates, I should be very wrong in attributing to you, Agathon, that or any other want of refinement. And I am quite aware that if you happened to meet with any whom you thought wise, you would care for their opinion much more than for that of the many. But then we, having been a part of the foolish many in the theatre, cannot be regarded as the select wise; though I know that if you chanced to be in the presence, not of one of ourselves, but of some really wise man, you would be ashamed of disgracing yourself before him—would you not?

Yes, said Agathon.

But before the many you would not be ashamed, if you thought that you were doing something disgraceful in their presence?

Here Phaedrus interrupted them, saying: not answer him, my dear Agathon; for if he can only get a partner with whom he can talk, especially a good- looking one, he will no longer care about the completion of our plan. Now I love to hear him talk; but just at present I must not forget the encomium on Love which I ought to receive from him and from every one. When you and he have paid your tribute to the god, then you may talk.

Very good, Phaedrus, said Agathon; I see no reason why I should not proceed with my speech, as I shall have many other opportunities of conversing with Socrates. Let me say first how I ought to speak, and then speak. The previous speakers, instead of praising the god Love, or unfolding his nature, appear to have congratulated mankind on the benefits he confers upon them. But I would rather praise the god first and then speak of his gifts; this is the right way of praising everything.

May I say without impiety or offence, that of all the blessed gods he is the most blessed because he is the fairest and best? And he is the fairest: for, in the first place, he is the youngest, and of his youth he is himself the witness, fleeing out of the way of age, who is swift enough, swifter truly than most of us like:—Love hates him and will not come near him; but youth and love live and move together—like to like, as the proverb says. Many things were said by Phaedrus about Love in which I agree with him; but I cannot agree that he is older than Iapetus and Kronos:—not so; I maintain him to be the youngest of the gods, and youthful ever.

The ancient doings among the gods of which Hesiod and Parmenides spoke, if the tradition of them be true, were done of Necessity and not of Love; had Love been in those days, there would have been no chaining or mutilation of the gods, or other violence, but peace and sweetness, as there is now in heaven, since the rule of Love began. Love is young and also tender; he ought to have a poet like Homer to describe his tenderness, as Homer says of Ate, that she is a goddess and tender:— 'Her feet are tender, for she sets her steps, Not on the ground but on the heads of men:' herein is an excellent proof of her tenderness,—that she walks not upon the hard but upon the soft. Let us adduce a similar proof of the tenderness of Love; for he walks not upon the earth, nor yet upon the skulls of men, which are not so very soft, but in the hearts and souls of both gods and men, which are of all things the softest: in them he walks and dwells and makes his home.

Not in every soul without exception, for where there is hardness he departs, where there is softness there he dwells; and nestling always with his feet and in all manner of ways in the softest of soft places, how can he be other than the softest of all things? Of a truth he is the tenderest as well as the youngest, and also he is of flexile form; for if he were hard and without flexure he could not enfold all things, or wind his way into and out of every soul of man undiscovered. And a proof of his flexibility and symmetry of form is his grace, which is universally admitted to be in an especial manner the attribute of Love; ungrace and love are always at war with one another. The fairness of his complexion is revealed by his habitation among the flowers; for he dwells not amid bloomless or fading beauties, whether of body or soul or aught else, but in the place of flowers and scents, there he sits and abides.

Concerning the beauty of the god I have said enough; and yet there remains much more which I might say. Of his virtue I have now to speak: his greatest glory is that he can neither do nor suffer wrong to or from any god or any man; for he suffers not by force if he suffers; force comes not near him, neither when he acts does he act by force. For all men in all things serve him of their own free will, and where there is voluntary agreement, there, as the laws which are the lords of the city say, is justice.

Not only is he just but exceedingly temperate, for Temperance is the acknowledged ruler of the pleasures and desires, and no pleasure ever masters Love; he is their master and they are his servants; and if he conquers them he must be temperate indeed. As to courage, even the God of War is no match for him; he is the captive and Love is the lord, for love, the love of Aphrodite, masters him, as the tale runs; and the master is stronger than the servant. And if he conquers the bravest of all others, he must be himself the bravest. Of his courage and justice and temperance I have spoken, but I have yet to speak of his wisdom; and according to the measure of my ability I must try to do my best.

In the first place he is a poet (and here, like Eryximachus, I magnify my art), and he is also the source of poesy in others, which he could not be if he were not himself a poet. And at the touch of him every one becomes a poet, even though he had no music in him before; this also is a proof that Love is a good poet and accomplished in all the fine arts; for no one can give to another that which he has not himself, or teach that of which he has no knowledge.

Who will deny that the creation of the animals is his doing? Are they not all the works of his wisdom, born and begotten of him? And as to the artists, do we not know that he only of them whom love inspires has the light of fame?—he whom Love touches not walks in darkness. The arts of medicine and archery and divination were discovered by Apollo, under the guidance of love and desire; so that he too is a disciple of Love. Also the melody of the Muses, the metallurgy of Hephaestus, the weaving of Athene, the empire of Zeus over gods and men, are all due to Love, who was the inventor of them. And so Love set in order the empire of the gods—the love of beauty, as is evident, for with deformity Love has no concern.

In the days of old, as I began by saying, dreadful deeds were done among the gods, for they were ruled by Necessity; but now since the birth of Love, and from the Love of the beautiful, has sprung every good in heaven and earth. Therefore, Phaedrus, I say of Love that he is the fairest and best in himself, and the cause of what is fairest and best in all other things. And there comes into my mind a line of poetry in which he is said to be the god who 'Gives peace on earth and calms the stormy deep, Who stills the winds and bids the sufferer sleep.'

This is he who empties men of disaffection and fills them with affection, who makes them to meet together at banquets such as these: in sacrifices, feasts, dances, he is our lord—who sends courtesy and sends away discourtesy, who gives kindness ever and never gives unkindness; the friend of the good, the wonder of the wise, the amazement of the gods; desired by those who have no part in him, and precious to those who have the better part in him; parent of delicacy, luxury, desire, fondness, softness, grace; regardful of the good, regardless of the evil: in every word, work, wish, fear—saviour, pilot, comrade, helper; glory of gods and men, leader best and brightest: in whose footsteps let every man follow, sweetly singing in his honour and joining in that sweet strain with which love charms the souls of gods and men. Such is the speech, Phaedrus, half-playful, yet having a certain measure of seriousness, which, according to my ability, I dedicate to the god.

When Agathon had done speaking, Aristodemus said that there was a general cheer; the young man was thought to have spoken in a manner worthy of himself, and of the god. And Socrates, looking at Eryximachus, said: Tell me, son of Acumenus, was there not reason in my fears? Was I not a prophet when I said that Agathon would make a wonderful oration, and that I should be in a strait?

The part of the prophecy which concerns Agathon, replied Eryximachus, appears to me to be true; but not the other part—that you will be in a strait.

Why, my dear friend, said Socrates, must not I or any one be in a strait who has to speak after he has heard such a rich and varied discourse? I am especially struck with the beauty of the concluding words—who could listen to them without amazement? When I reflected on the immeasurable inferiority of my own powers, I was ready to run away for shame, if there had been a possibility of escape. For I was reminded of Gorgias, and at the end of his speech I fancied that Agathon was shaking at me the Gorginian or Gorgonian head of the great master of rhetoric, which was simply to turn me and my speech into stone, as Homer says, and strike me dumb.

And then I perceived how foolish I had been in consenting to take my turn with you in praising love, and saying that I too was a master of the art, when I really had no conception how anything ought to be praised. For in my simplicity I imagined that the topics of praise should be true, and that this being presupposed, out of the true the speaker was to choose the best and set them forth in the best manner. I felt quite proud, thinking that I knew the nature of true praise, and should speak well. Whereas I now see that the intention was to attribute to Love every species of greatness and glory, whether really belonging to him or not, without regard to truth or falsehood—that was no matter; for the original proposal seems to have been not that each of you should really praise Love, but only that you should appear to praise him.

So you attribute to Love every imaginable form of praise which can be gathered anywhere; and you say that 'he is all this,' and 'the cause of all that,' making him appear the fairest and best of all to those who know him not, for you cannot impose upon those who know him. And a noble and solemn hymn of praise have you rehearsed. But as I misunderstood the nature of the praise when I said that I would take my turn, I must beg to be absolved from the promise which I made in ignorance, and which (as Euripides would say) was a promise of the lips and not of the mind. Farewell then to such a strain: for I do not praise in that way; no, indeed, I cannot.

But if you like to hear the truth about love, I am ready to speak in my own manner, though I will not make myself ridiculous by entering into any rivalry with you. Say then, Phaedrus, whether you would like to have the truth about love, spoken in any words and in any order which may happen to come into my mind at the time. Will that be agreeable to you? Aristodemus said that Phaedrus and the company bid him speak in any manner which he thought best. Then, he added, let me have your permission first to ask Agathon a few more questions, in order that I may take his admissions as the premisses of my discourse.

I grant the permission, said Phaedrus: put your questions.

Socrates then proceeded as follows:— In the magnificent oration which you have just uttered, I think that you were right, my dear Agathon, in proposing to speak of the nature of Love first and afterwards of his works—that is a way of beginning which I very much approve. And as you have spoken so eloquently of his nature, may I ask you further, Whether love is the love of something or of nothing? And here I must explain myself: I do not want you to say that love is the love of a father or the love of a mother—that would be ridiculous; but to answer as you would, if I asked is a father a father of something? to which you would find no difficulty in replying, of a son or daughter: and the answer would be right.

Very true, said Agathon.

And you would say the same of a mother?

He assented.

Yet let me ask you one more question in order to illustrate my meaning: Is not a brother to be regarded essentially as a brother of something?

Certainly, he replied.

That is, of a brother or sister?

Yes, he said.

And now, said Socrates, I will ask about Love:—Is Love of something or of nothing?

Of something, surely, he replied.

Keep in mind what this is, and tell me what I want to know—whether Love desires that of which love is.

Yes, surely.

And does he possess, or does he not possess, that which he loves and desires?

Probably not, I should say.

Nay, replied Socrates, I would have you consider whether 'necessarily' is not rather the word. The inference that he who desires something is in want of something, and that he who desires nothing is in want of nothing, is in my judgment, Agathon, absolutely and necessarily true. What do you think?

I agree with you, said Agathon.

Very good. Would he who is great desire to be great or he who is strong desire to be strong?

That would be inconsistent with our previous admissions.

True. For he who is anything cannot want to be that which he is?

Very true.

And yet, added Socrates, if a man being strong desired to be strong, or being swift desired to be swift, or being healthy desired to be healthy, in that case he might be thought to desire something which he already has or is. I give the example in order that we may avoid misconception. For the possessors of these qualities, Agathon, must be supposed to have their respective advantages at the time, whether they choose or not; and who can desire that which he has? Therefore, when a person says, I am well and wish to be well, or I am rich and wish to be rich, and I desire simply to have what I have —to him we shall reply: 'You, my friend, having wealth and health and strength, want to have the continuance of them; for at this moment, whether you choose or no, you have them. And when you say, I desire that which I have and nothing else, is not your meaning that you want to have what you now have in the future?' He must agree with us—must he not?

He must, replied Agathon.

Then, said Socrates, he desires that what he has at present may be preserved to him in the future, which is equivalent to saying that he desires something which is non-existent to him, and which as yet he has not got:

Very true, he said.

Then he and every one who desires, desires that which he has not already, and which is future and not present, and which he has not, and is not, and of which he is in want;—these are the sort of things which love and desire seek?

Very true, he said.

Then now, said Socrates, let us recapitulate the argument. First, is not love of something, and of something too which is wanting to a man?

Yes, he replied.

Remember further what you said in your speech, or if you do not remember I will remind you: you said that the love of the beautiful set in order the empire of the gods, for that of deformed things there is no love—did you not say something of that kind?

Yes, said Agathon.

Yes, my friend, and the remark was a just one. And if this is true, Love is the love of beauty and not of deformity?

He assented.

And Love is of something a man wants and has not?

True, he said.

Then Love wants and has not beauty?

Certainly, he replied.

And would you call that beautiful which wants and does not possess beauty?

Certainly not.

Then would you still say that love is beautiful?

Agathon replied: I fear that I did not understand what I was saying.

You made a very good speech, Agathon, replied Socrates; but there is yet one small question which I would fain ask:—Is not the good also the beautiful?

Yes.

Then in wanting the beautiful, love wants also the good?

I cannot refute you, Socrates, said Agathon:—Let us assume that what you say is true.

Say rather, beloved Agathon, that you cannot refute the truth; for Socrates is easily refuted.

And now, taking my leave of you, I would rehearse a tale of love which I heard from Diotima of Mantineia, a woman wise in this and in many other kinds of knowledge, who in the days of old, when the Athenians offered sacrifice before the coming of the plague, delayed the disease ten years. She was my instructress in the art of love, and I shall repeat to you what she said to me, beginning with the admissions made by Agathon, which are nearly if not quite the same which I made to the wise woman when she questioned me: I think that this will be the easiest way, and I shall take both parts myself as well as I can. As you, Agathon, suggested, I must speak first of the being and nature of Love, and then of his works.

First I said to her in nearly the same words which he used to me, that Love was a mighty god, and likewise fair; and she proved to me as I proved to him that, by my own showing, Love was neither fair nor good.

'What do you mean, Diotima,' I said, 'is love then evil and foul?'

'Hush,' she cried; 'must that be foul which is not fair?'

'Certainly,' I said. 'And is that which is not wise, ignorant? do you not see that there is a mean between wisdom and ignorance?'

'And what may that be?' I said. 'Right opinion,' she replied; 'which, as you know, being incapable of giving a reason, is not knowledge (for how can knowledge be devoid of reason? nor again, ignorance, for neither can ignorance attain the truth), but is clearly something which is a mean between ignorance and wisdom.'

'Quite true,' I replied.

'Do not then insist,' she said, 'that what is not fair is of necessity foul, or what is not good evil; or infer that because love is not fair and good he is therefore foul and evil; for he is in a mean between them.'

'Well,' I said, 'Love is surely admitted by all to be a great god.'

'By those who know or by those who do not know?'

'By all.'

'And how, Socrates,' she said with a smile, 'can Love be acknowledged to be a great god by those who say that he is not a god at all?'

'And who are they?' I said.

'You and I are two of them,' she replied.

'How can that be?' I said.

'It is quite intelligible,' she replied; 'for you yourself would acknowledge that the gods are happy and fair—of course you would—would you dare to say that any god was not?'

'Certainly not,' I replied.

'And you mean by the happy, those who are the possessors of things good or fair?'

'Yes.'

'And you admitted that Love, because he was in want, desires those good and fair things of which he is in want?'

'Yes, I did.'

'But how can he be a god who has no portion in what is either good or fair?'

'Impossible.'

'Then you see that you also deny the divinity of Love.'

'What then is Love?' I asked; 'Is he mortal?'

'No.'

'What then?'

'As in the former instance, he is neither mortal nor immortal, but in a mean between the two.'

'What is he, Diotima?'

'He is a great *daimon*, and like all spirits he is intermediate between divine and mortal.'

'And what,' I said, 'is his power?'

'He interprets,' she replied, 'between gods and men, conveying and taking across to the gods the prayers and sacrifices of men, and to men the commands and replies of the gods; he is the mediator who spans the chasm which divides them, and therefore in him all is bound together, and through him the arts of the prophet and the priest, their sacrifices and mysteries and charms, and all prophecy and incantation, find their way.

For God mingles not with man; but through Love all the intercourse and converse of God with man, whether awake or asleep, is carried on. The wisdom which understands this is spiritual; all other wisdom, such as that of arts and handicrafts, is mean and vulgar. Now these spirits or intermediate powers are many and diverse, and one of them is Love.'

'And who,' I said, 'was his father, and who his mother?'

'The tale,' she said, 'will take time; nevertheless I will tell you. On the birthday of Aphrodite there was a feast of the gods, at which the god Poros or Plenty, who is the son of Metis or Discretion, was one of the guests. When the feast was over, Penia or Poverty, as the manner is on such occasions, came about the doors to beg. Now Plenty who was the worse for nectar (there was no wine in those days), went into the garden of Zeus and fell into a heavy sleep, and Poverty considering her own straitened circumstances, plotted to have a child by him, and accordingly she lay down at his side and conceived Love, who partly because he is naturally a lover of the beautiful, and because Aphrodite is herself beautiful, and also because he was born on her birthday, is her follower and attendant.

And as his parentage is, so also are his fortunes. In the first place he is always poor, and anything but tender and fair, as the many imagine him; and he is rough and squalid, and has no shoes, nor a house to dwell in; on the bare earth exposed he lies under the open heaven, in the streets, or at the doors of houses, taking his rest; and like his mother he is always in distress. Like his father too, whom he also partly resembles, he is always plotting against the fair and good; he is bold, enterprising, strong, a mighty hunter, always weaving some intrigue or other, keen in the pursuit of wisdom, fertile in resources; a philosopher at all times, terrible as an enchanter, sorcerer, sophist.

He is by nature neither mortal nor immortal, but alive and flourishing at one moment when he is in plenty, and dead at another moment, and again alive by reason of his father's nature. But that which is always flowing in is always flowing out, and so he is never in want and never in wealth; and, further, he is in a mean between ignorance and knowledge.

The truth of the matter is this: No god is a philosopher or seeker after wisdom, for he is wise already; nor does any man who is wise seek after wisdom. Neither do the ignorant seek after wisdom. For herein is the evil of ignorance, that he who is neither good nor wise is nevertheless satisfied with himself: he has no desire for that of which he feels no want.'

'But who then,' I said, 'are the lovers of wisdom, if they are neither the wise nor the foolish?'

'A child may answer that question,' she replied; 'they are those who are in a mean between the two; Love is one of them. For wisdom is a most beautiful thing, and Love is of the beautiful; and therefore Love is also a philosopher or lover of wisdom, and being a lover of wisdom is in a mean between the wise and the ignorant. And of this too his birth is the cause; for his father is wealthy and wise, and his mother poor and foolish. Such, my dear Socrates, is the nature of the spirit Love.

The error in your conception of him was very natural, and as I imagine from what you say, has arisen out of a confusion of love and the beloved, which made you think that love was all beautiful. For the beloved is the truly beautiful, and delicate, and perfect, and blessed; but the principle of love is of another nature, and is such as I have described.'

I said, 'O thou stranger woman, thou sayest well; but, assuming Love to be such as you say, what is the use of him to men?'

'That, Socrates,' she replied, 'I will attempt to unfold: of his nature and birth I have already spoken; and you acknowledge that love is of the beautiful. But some one will say: Of the beautiful in what, Socrates and Diotima?—or rather let me put the question more clearly, and ask: When a man loves the beautiful, what does he desire?'

I answered her 'That the beautiful may be his.'

'The answer suggests a further question: What is given by the possession of beauty?'

'To what you have asked,' I replied, 'I have no answer ready.'

'Then,' she said, 'let me put the word "good" in the place of the beautiful, and repeat the question once more: If he who loves loves the good, what is it then that he loves?'

'The possession of the good,' I said.

'And what does he gain who possesses the good?'

'Happiness,' I replied; 'there is less difficulty in answering that question.'

'Yes,' she said, 'the happy are made happy by the acquisition of good things. Nor is there any need to ask why a man desires happiness; the answer is already final.'

'You are right.' I said.

'And is this wish and this desire common to all? and do all men always desire their own good, or only some men?—what say you?'

'All men,' I replied; 'the desire is common to all.'

'Why, then,' she rejoined, 'are not all men, Socrates, said to love, but only some of them? whereas you say that all men are always loving the same things.'

'I myself wonder,' I said, 'why this is.'

'There is nothing to wonder at,' she replied; 'the reason is that one part of love is separated off and receives the name of the whole, but the other parts have other names.'

'Give an illustration,' I said.

She answered me as follows: 'There is poetry, which, as you know, is complex and manifold. All creation or passage of non-being into being is poetry or making, and the processes of all art are creative; and the masters of arts are all poets or makers.'

'Very true.'

'Still,' she said, 'you know that they are not called poets, but have other names; only that portion of the art which is separated off from the rest, and is concerned with music and metre, is termed poetry, and they who possess poetry in this sense of the word are called poets.'

'Very true,' I said.

'And the same holds of love. For you may say generally that all desire of good and happiness is only the great and subtle power of love; but they who are drawn towards him by any other path, whether the path of money-making or gymnastics or philosophy, are not called lovers—the name of the whole is appropriated to those whose affection takes one form only—they alone are said to love, or to be lovers.'

'I dare say,' I replied, 'that you are right.'

'Yes,' she added, 'and you hear people say that lovers are seeking for their other half; but I say that they are seeking neither for the half of themselves, nor for the whole, unless the half or the whole be also a good. And they will cut off their own hands and feet and cast them away, if they are evil; for they love not what is their own, unless perchance there be some one who calls what belongs to him the good, and what belongs to another the evil. For there is nothing which men love but the good. Is there anything?'

'Certainly, I should say, that there is nothing.'

'Then,' she said, 'the simple truth is, that men love the good.'

'Yes,' I said.

'To which must be added that they love the possession of the good?'

'Yes, that must be added.'

'And not only the possession, but the everlasting possession of the good?'

'That must be added too.'

'Then love,' she said, 'may be described as the love of the everlasting possession of the good?'

'That is most true.'

'Then if this be the nature of love, can you tell me further,' she said, 'what is the manner of the pursuit? what are they doing who show all this eagerness and heat which is called love? and what is the object which they have in view? Answer me.'

'Nay, Diotima,' I replied, 'if I had known, I should not have wondered at your wisdom, neither should I have come to learn from you about this very matter.'

'Well,' she said, 'I will teach you:—The object which they have in view is birth in beauty, whether of body or soul.'

'I do not understand you,' I said; 'the oracle requires an explanation.'

'I will make my meaning clearer,' she replied. 'I mean to say, that all men are bringing to the birth in their bodies and in their souls. There is a certain age at which human nature is desirous of procreation—procreation which must be in beauty and not in deformity; and this procreation is the union of man and woman, and is a divine thing; for conception and generation are an immortal principle in the mortal creature, and in the inharmonious they can never be. But the deformed is always inharmonious with the divine, and the beautiful harmonious.

Beauty, then, is the destiny or goddess of parturition who presides at birth, and therefore, when approaching beauty, the conceiving power is propitious, and diffusive, and benign, and begets and bears fruit: at the sight of ugliness she frowns and contracts and has a sense of pain, and turns away, and shrivels up, and not without a pang refrains from conception. And this is the reason why, when the hour of conception arrives, and the teeming nature is full, there is such a flutter and ecstasy about beauty whose approach is the alleviation of the pain of travail. For love, Socrates, is not, as you imagine, the love of the beautiful only.'

'What then?'

'The love of generation and of birth in beauty.'

'Yes,' I said.

'Yes, indeed,' she replied.

'But why of generation?'

'Because to the mortal creature, generation is a sort of eternity and immortality,' she replied; 'and if, as has been already admitted, love is of the everlasting possession of the good, all men will necessarily desire immortality together with good: Wherefore love is of immortality.'

All this she taught me at various times when she spoke of love. And I remember her once saying to me, 'What is the cause, Socrates, of love, and the attendant desire? See you not how all animals, birds, as well as beasts, in their desire of procreation, are in agony when they take the infection of love, which begins with the desire of union; whereto is added the care of offspring, on whose behalf the weakest are ready to battle against the strongest even to the uttermost, and to die for them, and will let themselves be tormented with hunger or suffer anything in order to maintain their young. Man may be supposed to act thus from reason; but why should animals have these passionate feelings? Can you tell me why?'

Again I replied that I did not know. She said to me:

'And do you expect ever to become a master in the art of love, if you do not know this?' 'But I have told you already, Diotima, that my ignorance is the reason why I come to you; for I am conscious that I want a teacher; tell me then the cause of this and of the other mysteries of love.'

'Marvel not,' she said, 'if you believe that love is of the immortal, as we have several times acknowledged; for here again, and on the same principle too, the mortal nature is seeking as far as is possible to be everlasting and immortal: and this is only to be attained by generation, because generation always leaves behind a new existence in the place of the old. Nay even in the life of the same individual there is succession and not absolute unity: a man is called the same, and yet in the short interval which elapses between youth and age, and in which every animal is said to have life and identity, he is undergoing a perpetual process of loss and reparation—hair, flesh, bones, blood, and the whole body are always changing.

Which is true not only of the body, but also of the soul, whose habits, tempers, opinions, desires, pleasures, pains, fears, never remain the same in any one of us, but are always coming and going; and equally true of knowledge, and what is still more surprising to us mortals, not only do the sciences in general spring up and decay, so that in respect of them we are never the same; but each of them individually experiences a like change.

For what is implied in the word "recollection," but the departure of knowledge, which is ever being forgotten, and is renewed and preserved by recollection, and appears to be the same although in reality new, according to that law of succession by which all mortal things are preserved, not absolutely the same, but by substitution, the old worn-out mortality leaving another new and similar existence behind—unlike the divine, which is always the same and not another? And in this way, Socrates, the mortal body, or mortal anything, partakes of immortality; but the immortal in another way. Marvel not then at the love which all men have of their offspring; for that universal love and interest is for the sake of immortality.'

I was astonished at her words, and said: 'Is this really true, O thou wise Diotima?' And she answered with all the authority of an accomplished sophist:

'Of that, Socrates, you may be assured;—think only of the ambition of men, and you will wonder at the senselessness of their ways, unless you consider how they are stirred by the love of an immortality of fame. They are ready to run all risks greater far than they would have run for their children, and to spend money and undergo any sort of toil, and even to die, for the sake of leaving behind them a name which shall be eternal. Do you imagine that Alcestis would have died to save Admetus, or Achilles to avenge Patroclus, or your own Codrus in order to preserve the kingdom for his sons, if they had not imagined that the memory of their virtues, which still survives among us, would be immortal? Nay,' she said, 'I am persuaded that all men do all things, and the better they are the more they do them, in hope of the glorious fame of immortal virtue; for they desire the immortal.

'Those who are pregnant in the body only, betake themselves to women and beget children—this is the character of their love; their offspring, as they hope, will preserve their memory and giving them the blessedness and immortality which they desire in the future. But souls which are pregnant —for there certainly are men who are more creative in their souls than in their bodies—conceive that which is proper for the soul to conceive or contain. And what are these conceptions?—wisdom and virtue in general. And such creators are poets and all artists who are deserving of the name inventor.

But the greatest and fairest sort of wisdom by far is that which is concerned with the ordering of states and families, and which is called temperance and justice. And he who in youth has the seed of these implanted in him and is himself inspired, when he comes to maturity desires to beget and generate. He wanders about seeking beauty that he may beget offspring—for in deformity he will beget nothing—and naturally embraces the beautiful rather than the deformed body; above all when he finds a fair and noble and well-nurtured soul, he embraces the two in one person, and to such an one he is full of speech about virtue and the nature and pursuits of a good man; and he tries to educate him; and at the touch of the beautiful which is ever present to his memory, even when absent, he brings forth that which he had conceived long before, and in company with him tends that which he brings forth; and they are married by a far nearer tie and have a closer friendship than those who beget mortal children, for the children who are their common offspring are fairer and more immortal.

Who, when he thinks of Homer and Hesiod and other great poets, would not rather have their children than ordinary human ones? Who would not emulate them in the creation of children such as theirs, which have preserved their memory and given them everlasting glory? Or who would not have such children as Lycurgus left behind him to be the saviours, not only of Lacedaemon, but of Hellas, as one may say? There is Solon, too, who is the revered father of Athenian laws; and many others there are in many other places, both among Hellenes and barbarians, who have given to the world many noble works, and have been the parents of virtue of every kind; and many temples have been raised in their honour for the sake of children such as theirs; which were never raised in honour of any one, for the sake of his mortal children.

'These are the lesser mysteries of love, into which even you, Socrates, may enter; to the greater and more hidden ones which are the crown of these, and to which, if you pursue them in a right spirit, they will lead, I know not whether you will be able to attain. But I will do my utmost to inform you, and do you follow if you can. For he who would proceed aright in this matter should begin in youth to visit beautiful forms; and first, if he be guided by his instructor aright, to love one such form only—out of that he should create fair thoughts; and soon he will of himself perceive that the beauty of one form is akin to the beauty of another; and then if beauty of form in general is his pursuit, how foolish would he be not to recognize that the beauty in every form is and the same!

And when he perceives this he will abate his violent love of the one, which he will despise and deem a small thing, and will become a lover of all beautiful forms; in the next stage he will consider that the beauty of the mind is more honourable than the beauty of the outward form. So that if a virtuous soul have but a little comeliness, he will be content to love and tend him, and will search out and bring to the birth thoughts which may improve the young, until he is compelled to contemplate and see the beauty of institutions and laws, and to understand that the beauty of them all is of one family, and that personal beauty is a trifle; and after laws and institutions he will go on to the sciences, that he may see their beauty, being not like a servant in love with the beauty of one youth or man or institution, himself a slave mean and narrow-minded, but drawing towards and contemplating the vast sea of beauty, he will create many fair and noble thoughts and notions in boundless love of wisdom; until on that shore he grows and waxes strong, and at last the vision is revealed to him of a single science, which is the science of beauty everywhere.

To this I will proceed; please to give me your very best attention: 'He who has been instructed thus far in the things of love, and who has learned to see the beautiful in due order and succession, when he comes toward the end will suddenly perceive a nature of wondrous beauty (and this, Socrates, is the final cause of all our former toils)—a nature which in the first place is everlasting, not growing and decaying, or waxing and waning; secondly, not fair in one point of view and foul in another, or at one time or in one relation or at one place fair, at another time or in another relation or at another place foul, as if fair to some and foul to others, or in the likeness of a face or hands or any other part of the bodily frame, or in any form of speech or knowledge, or existing in any other being, as for example, in an animal, or in heaven, or in earth, or in any other place; but beauty absolute, separate, simple, and everlasting, which without diminution and without increase, or any change, is imparted to the ever-growing and perishing beauties of all other things.

He who from these ascending under the influence of true love, begins to perceive that beauty, is not far from the end. And the true order of going, or being led by another, to the things of love, is to begin from the beauties of earth and mount upwards for the sake of that other beauty, using these as steps only, and from one going on to two, and from two to all fair forms, and from fair forms to fair practices, and from fair practices to fair notions, until from fair notions he arrives at the notion of absolute beauty, and at last knows what the essence of beauty is.

This, my dear Socrates,' said the stranger of Mantineia, 'is that life above all others which man should live, in the contemplation of beauty absolute; a beauty which if you once beheld, you would see not to be after the measure of gold, and garments, and fair boys and youths, whose presence now entrances you; and you and many a one would be content to live seeing them only and conversing with them without meat or drink, if that were possible—you only want to look at them and to be with them. But what if man had eyes to see the true beauty—the divine beauty, I mean, pure and clear and unalloyed, not clogged with the pollutions of mortality and all the colours and vanities of human life—thither looking, and holding converse with the true beauty simple and divine?

Remember how in that communion only, beholding beauty with the eye of the mind, he will be enabled to bring forth, not images of beauty, but realities (for he has hold not of an image but of a reality), and bringing forth and nourishing true virtue to become the friend of God and be immortal, if mortal man may. Would that be an ignoble life?'

Such, Phaedrus—and I speak not only to you, but to all of you—were the words of Diotima; and I am persuaded of their truth. And being persuaded of them, I try to persuade others, that in the attainment of this end human nature will not easily find a helper better than love: And therefore, also, I say that every man ought to honour him as I myself honour him, and walk in his ways, and exhort others to do the same, and praise the power and spirit of love according to the measure of my ability now and ever. The words which I have spoken, you, Phaedrus, may call an encomium of love, or anything else which you please.

When Socrates had done speaking, the company applauded, and Aristophanes was beginning to say something in answer to the allusion which Socrates had made to his own speech, when suddenly there was a great knocking at the door of the house, as of revellers, and the sound of a flute-girl was heard. Agathon told the attendants to go and see who were the intruders. 'If they are friends of ours,' he said, 'invite them in, but if not, say that the drinking is over.'

A little while afterwards they heard the voice of Alcibiades resounding in the court; he was in a great state of intoxication, and kept roaring and shouting 'Where is Agathon? Lead me to Agathon,' and at length, supported by the flute-girl and some of his attendants, he found his way to them.

'Hail, friends,' he said, appearing at the door crowned with a massive garland of ivy and violets, his head flowing with ribands. 'Will you have a very drunken man as a companion of your revels? Or shall I crown Agathon, which was my intention in coming, and go away? For I was unable to come yesterday, and therefore I am here to-day, carrying on my head these ribands, that taking them from my own head, I may crown the head of this fairest and wisest of men, as I may be allowed to call him. Will you laugh at me because I am drunk? Yet I know very well that I am speaking the truth, although you may laugh. But first tell me; if I come in shall we have the understanding of which I spoke (supra Will you have a very drunken man? etc.)? Will you drink with me or not?'

The company were vociferous in begging that he would take his place among them, and Agathon specially invited him. Thereupon he was led in by the people who were with him; and as he was being led, intending to crown Agathon, he took the ribands from his own head and held them in front of his eyes; he was thus prevented from seeing Socrates, who made way for him, and Alcibiades took the vacant place between Agathon and Socrates, and in taking the place he embraced Agathon and crowned him. Take off his sandals, said Agathon, and let him make a third on the same couch.

By all means; but who makes the third partner in our revels? said Alcibiades, turning round and starting up as he caught sight of Socrates. By Heracles, he said, what is this? here is Socrates always lying in wait for me, and always, as his way is, coming out at all sorts of unsuspected places: and now, what have you to say for yourself, and why are you lying here, where I perceive that you have contrived to find a place, not by a joker or lover of jokes, like Aristophanes, but by the fairest of the company?

Socrates turned to Agathon and said: I must ask you to protect me, Agathon; for the passion of this man has grown quite a serious matter to me. Since I became his admirer I have never been allowed to speak to any other fair one, or so much as to look at them. If I do, he goes wild with envy and jealousy, and not only abuses me but can hardly keep his hands off me, and at this moment he may do me some harm. Please to see to this, and either reconcile me to him, or, if he attempts violence, protect me, as I am in bodily fear of his mad and passionate attempts.

There can never be reconciliation between you and me, said Alcibiades; but for the present I will defer your chastisement. And I must beg you, Agathon, to give me back some of the ribands that I may crown the marvellous head of this universal despot—I would not have him complain of me for crowning you, and neglecting him, who in conversation is the conqueror of all mankind; and this not only once, as you were the day before yesterday, but always. Whereupon, taking some of the ribands, he crowned Socrates, and again reclined.

Then he said: You seem, my friends, to be sober, which is a thing not to be endured; you must drink—for that was the agreement under which I was admitted—and I elect myself master of the feast until you are well drunk. Let us have a large goblet, Agathon, or rather, he said, addressing the attendant, bring me that wine-cooler. The wine-cooler which had caught his eye was a vessel holding more than two quarts—this he filled and emptied, and bade the attendant fill it again for Socrates. Observe, my friends, said Alcibiades, that this ingenious trick of mine will have no effect on Socrates, for he can drink any quantity of wine and not be at all nearer being drunk. Socrates drank the cup which the attendant filled for him.

Eryximachus said: What is this, Alcibiades? Are we to have neither conversation nor singing over our cups; but simply to drink as if we were thirsty?

Alcibiades replied: Hail, worthy son of a most wise and worthy sire!

The same to you, said Eryximachus; but what shall we do?

That I leave to you, said Alcibiades.

'The wise physician skilled our wounds to heal shall prescribe and we will obey. What do you want?

Well, said Eryximachus, before you appeared we had passed a resolution that each one of us in turn should make a speech in praise of love, and as good a one as he could: the turn was passed round from left to right; and as all of us have spoken, and you have not spoken but have well drunken, you ought to speak, and then impose upon Socrates any task which you please, and he on his right hand neighbour, and so on.

That is good, Eryximachus, said Alcibiades; and yet the comparison of a drunken man's speech with those of sober men is hardly fair; and I should like to know, sweet friend, whether you really believe what Socrates was just now saying; for I can assure you that the very reverse is the fact, and that if I praise any one but himself in his presence, whether God or man, he will hardly keep his hands off me.

For shame, said Socrates.

Hold your tongue, said Alcibiades, for by Poseidon, there is no one else whom I will praise when you are of the company.

Well then, said Eryximachus, if you like praise Socrates.

What do you think, Eryximachus? said Alcibiades: shall I attack him and inflict the punishment before you all? What are you about? said Socrates; are you going to raise a laugh at my expense? Is that the meaning of your praise? I am going to speak the truth, if you will permit me.

I not only permit, but exhort you to speak the truth. Then I will begin at once, said Alcibiades, and if I say anything which is not true, you may interrupt me if you will, and say 'that is a lie,' though my intention is to speak the truth. But you must not wonder if I speak any how as things come into my mind; for the fluent and orderly enumeration of all your singularities is not a task which is easy to a man in my condition.

And now, my boys, I shall praise Socrates in a figure which will appear to him to be a caricature, and yet I speak, not to make fun of him, but only for the truth's sake. I say, that he is exactly like the busts of Silenus, which are set up in the statuaries' shops, holding pipes and flutes in their mouths; and they are made to open in the middle, and have images of gods inside them. I say also that he is like Marsyas the satyr.

You yourself will not deny, Socrates, that your face is like that of a satyr. Aye, and there is a resemblance in other points too. For example, you are a bully, as I can prove by witnesses, if you will not confess. And are you not a flute-player? That you are, and a performer far more wonderful than Marsyas. He indeed with instruments used to charm the souls of men by the power of his breath, and the players of his music do so still: for the melodies of Olympus are derived from Marsyas who taught them, and these, whether they are played by a great master or by a miserable flute-girl, have a power which no others have; they alone possess the soul and reveal the wants of those who have need of gods and mysteries, because they are divine.

But you produce the same effect with your words only, and do not require the flute: that is the difference between you and him. When we hear any other speaker, even a very good one, he produces absolutely no effect upon us, or not much, whereas the mere fragments of you and your words, even at second-hand, and however imperfectly repeated, amaze and possess the souls of every man, woman, and child who comes within hearing of them. And if I were not afraid that you would think me hopelessly drunk, I would have sworn as well as spoken to the influence which they have always had and still have over me. For my heart leaps within me more than that of any Corybantian reveller, and my eyes rain tears when I hear them. And I observe that many others are affected in the same manner.

I have heard Pericles and other great orators, and I thought that they spoke well, but I never had any similar feeling; my soul was not stirred by them, nor was I angry at the thought of my own slavish state. But this Marsyas has often brought me to such a pass, that I have felt as if I could hardly endure the life which I am leading (this, Socrates, you will admit); and I am conscious that if I did not shut my ears against him, and fly as from the voice of the siren, my fate would be like that of others,—he would transfix me, and I should grow old sitting at his feet. For he makes me confess that I ought not to live as I do, neglecting the wants of my own soul, and busying myself with the concerns of the Athenians; therefore I hold my ears and tear myself away from him.

He is the only person who ever made me ashamed, which you might think not to be in my nature, and there is no one else who does the same. For I know that I cannot answer him or say that I ought not to do as he bids, but when I leave his presence the love of popularity gets the better of me. And therefore I run away and fly from him, and when I see him I am ashamed of what I have confessed to him. Many a time have I wished that he were dead, and yet I know that I should be much more sorry than glad, if he were to die: so that I am at my wit's end.

And this is what I and many others have suffered from the flute-playing of this satyr. Yet hear me once more while I show you how exact the image is, and how marvellous his power. For let me tell you; none of you know him; but I will reveal him to you; having begun, I must go on. See you how fond he is of the fair? He is always with them and is always being smitten by them, and then again he knows nothing and is ignorant of all things—such is the appearance which he puts on. Is he not like a Silenus in this?

To be sure he is: his outer mask is the carved head of the Silenus; but, O my companions in drink, when he is opened, what temperance there is residing within! Know you that beauty and wealth and honour, at which the many wonder, are of no account with him, and are utterly despised by him: he regards not at all the persons who are gifted with them; mankind are nothing to him; all his life is spent in mocking and flouting at them. But when I opened him, and looked within at his serious purpose, I saw in him divine and golden images of such fascinating beauty that I was ready to do in a moment whatever Socrates commanded: they may have escaped the observation of others, but I saw them.

Now I fancied that he was seriously enamoured of my beauty, and I thought that I should therefore have a grand opportunity of hearing him tell what he knew, for I had a wonderful opinion of the attractions of my youth. In the prosecution of this design, when I next went to him, I sent away the attendant who usually accompanied me (I will confess the whole truth, and beg you to listen; and if I speak falsely, do you, Socrates, expose the falsehood). Well, he and I were alone together, and I thought that when there was nobody with us, I should hear him speak the language which lovers use to their loves when they are by themselves, and I was delighted. Nothing of the sort; he conversed as usual, and spent the day with me and then went away. Afterwards I challenged him in the gym; and he wrestled and closed with me several times when there was no one present; I fancied that I might succeed in this manner. Not a bit; I made no way with him.

Lastly, as I had failed hitherto, I thought that I must take stronger measures and attack him boldly, and, as I had begun, not give him up, but see how matters stood between him and me. So I invited him to sup with me, just as if he were a fair youth, and I a designing lover. He was not easily persuaded to come; he did, however, after a while accept the invitation, and when he came the first time, he wanted to go away at once as soon as supper was over, and I had not the face to detain him. The second time, still in pursuance of my design, after we had supped, I went on conversing far into the night, and when he wanted to go away, I pretended that the hour was late and that he had much better remain.

So he lay down on the couch next to me, the same on which he had supped, and there was no one but ourselves sleeping in the apartment. All this may be told without shame to any one. But what follows I could hardly tell you if I were sober. Yet as the proverb says, 'In vino veritas,' whether with boys, or without them ; and therefore I must speak. Nor, again, should I be justified in concealing the lofty actions of Socrates when I come to praise him. Moreover I have felt the serpent's sting; and he who has suffered, as they say, is willing to tell his fellow-sufferers only, as they alone will be likely to understand him, and will not be extreme in judging of the sayings or doings which have been wrung from his agony.

For I have been bitten by a more than viper's tooth; I have known in my soul, or in my heart, or in some other part, that worst of pangs, more violent in ingenuous youth than any serpent's tooth, the pang of philosophy, which will make a man say or do anything. And you whom I see around me, Phaedrus and Agathon and Eryximachus and Pausanias and Aristodemus and Aristophanes, all of you, and I need not say Socrates himself, have had experience of the same madness and passion in your longing after wisdom. Therefore listen and excuse my doings then and my sayings now. But let the attendants and other profane and unmannered persons close up the doors of their ears.

When the lamp was put out and the servants had gone away, I thought that I must be plain with him and have no more ambiguity. So I gave him a shake, and I said: 'Socrates, are you asleep?' 'No,' he said. 'Do you know what I am meditating? 'What are you meditating?' he said.

'I think,' I replied, 'that of all the lovers whom I have ever had you are the only one who is worthy of me, and you appear to be too modest to speak. Now I feel that I should be a fool to refuse you this or any other favour, and therefore I come to lay at your feet all that I have and all that my friends have, in the hope that you will assist me in the way of virtue, which I desire above all things, and in which I believe that you can help me better than any one else. And I should certainly have more reason to be ashamed of what wise men would say if I were to refuse a favour to such as you, than of what the world, who are mostly fools, would say of me if I granted it.'

To these words he replied in the ironical manner which is so characteristic of him:—'Alcibiades, my friend, you have indeed an elevated aim if what you say is true, and if there really is in me any power by which you may become better; truly you must see in me some rare beauty of a kind infinitely higher than any which I see in you. And therefore, if you mean to share with me and to exchange beauty for beauty, you will have greatly the advantage of me; you will gain true beauty in return for appearance—like Diomede, gold in exchange for brass. But look again, sweet friend, and see whether you are not deceived in me. The mind begins to grow critical when the bodily eye fails, and it will be a long time before you get old.'

Hearing this, I said: 'I have told you my purpose, which is quite serious, and do you consider what you think best for you and me.'

'That is good,' he said; 'at some other time then we will consider and act as seems best about this and about other matters.'

Whereupon, I fancied that he was smitten, and that the words which I had uttered like arrows had wounded him, and so without waiting to hear more I got up, and throwing my coat about him crept under his threadbare cloak, as the time of year was winter, and there I lay during the whole night having this wonderful monster in my arms. This again, Socrates, will not be denied by you.

And yet, notwithstanding all, he was so superior to my solicitations, so contemptuous and derisive and disdainful of my beauty—which really, as I fancied, had some attractions—hear, O judges; for judges you shall be of the haughty virtue of Socrates—nothing more happened, but in the morning when I awoke (let all the gods and goddesses be my witnesses) I arose as from the couch of a father or an elder brother.

What do you suppose must have been my feelings, after this rejection, at the thought of my own dishonour? And yet I could not help wondering at his natural temperance and self-restraint and manliness. I never imagined that I could have met with a man such as he is in wisdom and endurance. And therefore I could not be angry with him or renounce his company, any more than I could hope to win him. For I well knew that if Ajax could not be wounded by steel, much less he by money; and my only chance of captivating him by my personal attractions had failed. So I was at my wit's end; no one was ever more hopelessly enslaved by another.

All this happened before he and I went on the expedition to Potidaea; there we messed together, and I had the opportunity of observing his extraordinary power of sustaining fatigue. His endurance was simply marvellous when, being cut off from our supplies, we were compelled to go without food—on such occasions, which often happen in time of war, he was superior not only to me but to everybody; there was no one to be compared to him. Yet at a festival he was the only person who had any real powers of enjoyment; though not willing to drink, he could if compelled beat us all at that,—wonderful to relate! no human being had ever seen Socrates drunk; and his powers, if I am not mistaken, will be tested before long.

His fortitude in enduring cold was also surprising. There was a severe frost, for the winter in that region is really tremendous, and everybody else either remained indoors, or if they went out had on an amazing quantity of clothes, and were well shod, and had their feet swathed in felt and fleeces: in the midst of this, Socrates with his bare feet on the ice and in his ordinary dress marched better than the other soldiers who had shoes, and they looked daggers at him because he seemed to despise them.

I have told you one tale, and now I must tell you another, which is worth hearing, 'Of the doings and sufferings of the enduring man' while he was on the expedition. One morning he was thinking about something which he could not resolve; he would not give it up, but continued thinking from early dawn until noon—there he stood fixed in thought; and at noon attention was drawn to him, and the rumour ran through the wondering crowd that Socrates had been standing and thinking about something ever since the break of day. At last, in the evening after supper, some Ionians out of curiosity (I should explain that this was not in winter but in summer), brought out their mats and slept in the open air that they might watch him and see whether he would stand all night.

There he stood until the following morning; and with the return of light he offered up a prayer to the sun, and went his way (compare supra). I will also tell, if you please—and indeed I am bound to tell—of his courage in battle; for who but he saved my life? Now this was the engagement in which I received the prize of valour: for I was wounded and he would not leave me, but he rescued me and my arms; and he ought to have received the prize of valour which the generals wanted to confer on me partly on account of my rank, and I told them so, (this, again, Socrates will not impeach or deny), but he was more eager than the generals that I and not he should have the prize.

There was another occasion on which his behaviour was very remarkable—in the flight of the army after the battle of Delium, where he served among the heavy-armed,—I had a better opportunity of seeing him than at Potidaea, for I was myself on horseback, and therefore comparatively out of danger. He and Laches were retreating, for the troops were in flight, and I met them and told them not to be discouraged, and promised to remain with them; and there you might see him, Aristophanes, as you describe, just as he is in the streets of Athens, stalking like a pelican, and rolling his eyes, calmly contemplating enemies as well as friends, and making very intelligible to anybody, even from a distance, that whoever attacked him would be likely to meet with a stout resistance; and in this way he and his companion escaped—for this is the sort of man who is never touched in war; those only are pursued who are running away headlong. I particularly observed how superior he was to Laches in presence of mind.

Many are the marvels which I might narrate in praise of Socrates; most of his ways might perhaps be paralleled in another man, but his absolute unlikeness to any human being that is or ever has been is perfectly astonishing. You may imagine Brasidas and others to have been like Achilles; or you may imagine Nestor and Antenor to have been like Pericles; and the same may be said of other famous men, but of this strange being you will never be able to find any likeness, however remote, either among men who now are or who ever have been—other than that which I have already suggested of Silenus and the satyrs; and they represent in a figure not only himself, but his words.

For, although I forgot to mention this to you before, his words are like the images of Silenus which open; they are ridiculous when you first hear them; he clothes himself in language that is like the skin of the wanton satyr—for his talk is of pack-asses and smiths and cobblers and curriers, and he is always repeating the same things in the same words, so that any ignorant or inexperienced person might feel disposed to laugh at him; but he who opens the bust and sees what is within will find that they are the only words which have a meaning in them, and also the most divine, abounding in fair images of virtue, and of the widest comprehension, or rather extending to the whole duty of a good and honourable man.

This, friends, is my praise of Socrates. I have added my blame of him for his ill-treatment of me; and he has ill-treated not only me, but Charmides the son of Glaucon, and Euthydemus the son of Diocles, and many others in the same way—beginning as their lover he has ended by making them pay their addresses to him. Wherefore I say to you, Agathon, 'Be not deceived by him; learn from me and take warning, and do not be a fool and learn by experience, as the proverb says.'

When Alcibiades had finished, there was a laugh at his outspokenness; for he seemed to be still in love with Socrates. You are sober, Alcibiades, said Socrates, or you would never have gone so far about to hide the purpose of your satyr's praises, for all this long story is only an ingenious circumlocution, of which the point comes in by the way at the end; you want to get up a quarrel between me and Agathon, and your notion is that I ought to love you and nobody else, and that you and you only ought to love Agathon. But the plot of this Satyric or Silenic drama has been detected, and you must not allow him, Agathon, to set us at variance.

I believe you are right, said Agathon, and I am disposed to think that his intention in placing himself between you and me was only to divide us; but he shall gain nothing by that move; for I will go and lie on the couch next to you.

Yes, yes, replied Socrates, by all means come here and lie on the couch below me.

Alas, said Alcibiades, how I am fooled by this man; he is determined to get the better of me at every turn. I do beseech you, allow Agathon to lie between us.

Certainly not, said Socrates, as you praised me, and I in turn praise my neighbour on the right, he will be out of order in praising me again when he ought rather to be praised by me, and I must entreat you to consent to this and not be jealous, for I have a great desire to praise the youth.

Hurrah! cried Agathon, I will rise instantly, that I may be praised by Socrates.

The usual way, said Alcibiades; where Socrates is, no one else has any chance with the fair; and now how readily has he invented a specious reason for attracting Agathon to himself.

Agathon arose in order that he might take his place on the couch by Socrates, when suddenly a band of revellers entered, and spoiled the order of the banquet. Some one who was going out having left the door open, they had found their way in, and made themselves at home; great confusion ensued, and every one was compelled to drink large quantities of wine. Aristodemus said that Eryximachus, Phaedrus, and others went away—he himself fell asleep, and as the nights were long took a good rest: he was awakened towards daybreak by a crowing of cocks, and when he awoke, the others were either asleep, or had gone away; there remained only Socrates, Aristophanes, and Agathon, who were drinking out of a large goblet which they passed round, and Socrates was discoursing to them.

Aristodemus was only half awake, and he did not hear the beginning of the discourse; the chief thing which he remembered was Socrates compelling the other two to acknowledge that the genius of comedy was the same with that of tragedy, and that the true artist in tragedy was an artist in comedy also. To this they were constrained to assent, being drowsy, and not quite following the argument. And first of all Aristophanes dropped off, then, when the day was already dawning, Agathon.

Socrates, having laid them to sleep, rose to depart; Aristodemus, as his manner was, following him. At the Lyceum he took a bath, and passed the day as usual. In the evening he retired to rest at his own home.

PLATO

Republic

Translated by Benjamin Jowett

Excerpt from **Book 6**

SOCRATES: . . . we have reached the end of one subject, but more remains to be discussed; how and by what studies and pursuits will the saviours of the constitution be created, and at what ages are they to apply themselves to their several studies?

GLAUCON: Certainly.

I omitted the troublesome business of the possession of women, and the procreation of children, and the appointment of the rulers, because I knew that the perfect State would be eyed with jealousy and was difficult of attainment; but that piece of cleverness was not of much service to me, for I had to discuss them all the same. The women and children are now disposed of, but the other question of the rulers must be investigated from the very beginning. We were saying, as you will remember, that they were to be lovers of their country, tried by the test of pleasures and pains, and neither in hardships, nor in dangers, nor at any other critical moment were to lose their patriotism— he was to be rejected who failed, but he who always came forth pure, like gold tried in the refiner's fire, was to be made a ruler, and to receive honors and rewards in life and after death. This was the sort of thing which was being said, and then the argument turned aside and veiled her face; not liking to stir the question which has now arisen.

I perfectly remember.

Yes, my friend, and I then shrank from hazarding the bold word; but now let me dare to say—that the perfect guardian must be a philosopher.

Yes, let that be affirmed.

And do not suppose that there will be many of them; for the gifts which were deemed by us to be essential rarely grow together; they are mostly found in shreds and patches.

What do you mean, Socrates?

You are aware that quick intelligence, memory, sagacity, cleverness, and similar qualities, do not often grow together, and that persons who possess them and are at the same time high-spirited and magnanimous are not so constituted by nature as to live orderly and in a peaceful and settled manner; they are driven any way by their impulses, and all solid principle goes out of them.

Very true.

On the other hand, those steadfast natures which can better be depended upon, which in a battle are impregnable to fear and immovable, are equally immovable when there is anything to be learned; they are always in a torpid state, and are apt to yawn and go to sleep over any intellectual toil.

Quite true.

And yet we were saying that both qualities were necessary in those to whom the higher education is to be imparted, and who are to share in any office or command.

Certainly.

And will they be a class which is rarely found?

Yes, indeed.

Then the aspirant must not only be tested in those labors and dangers and pleasures which we mentioned before, but there is another kind of probation which we did not mention— he must be exercised also in many kinds of knowledge, to see whether the soul will be able to endure the highest of all, or will faint under them, as in any other studies and exercises.

You are quite right to test them. But what do you mean by the highest of all knowledge?

You may remember that we divided the soul into three parts; and distinguished the several natures of justice, temperance, courage, and wisdom?

Indeed, if I had forgotten, I should not deserve to hear more.

And do you remember the word of caution which preceded the discussion of them?

To what do you refer?

We were saying, if I am not mistaken, that he who wanted to see them in their perfect beauty must take a longer and more circuitous way, at the end of which they would appear; but that we could add on a popular exposition of them on a level with the discussion which had preceded. And you replied that such an exposition would be enough for you, and so the inquiry was continued in what to me seemed to be a very inaccurate manner; whether you were satisfied or not, it is for you to say.

Yes, I thought and the others thought that you gave us a fair measure of truth.

But, my friend, a measure of such things which in any degree falls short of the whole truth is not fair measure; for nothing imperfect is the measure of anything, although persons are too apt to be contented and think that they need search no further.

Not an uncommon case, Socrates, when people are indolent.

Yes, and there cannot be any worse fault in a guardian of the State and of the laws.

True.

The guardian then, must be required to take the longer circuit, and toil at learning as well as at gymnastics, or he will never reach the highest knowledge of all which, as we were just now saying, is his proper calling.

What is there a knowledge still higher than this— higher than justice and the other virtues?

Yes there is. And of the virtues too we must behold not the outline merely, as at present— nothing short of the most finished picture should satisfy us. When little things are elaborated with an infinity of pains, in order that they may appear in their full beauty and utmost clearness, how ridiculous that we should not think the highest truths worthy of attaining the highest accuracy!

A right noble thought; but do you suppose that we shall refrain from asking you what is this highest knowledge?

Nay, ask if you will; but I am certain that you have heard the answer many times, and now you either do not understand me or, as I rather think, you are disposed to be troublesome; for you have often been told that the idea of good is the highest knowledge, and that all other things become useful and advantageous only by their use of this. You can hardly be ignorant that of this I was about to speak, concerning which, as you have often heard me say, we know so little; and, without which, any other knowledge or possession of any kind will profit us nothing. Do you think that the possession of all other things is of any value if we do not possess the good? or the knowledge of all other things if we have no knowledge of beauty and goodness?

Assuredly not, Socrates.

You are further aware that most people affirm pleasure to be the good, but the finer sort of wits say it is knowledge?

Yes.

And you are aware too that the latter cannot explain what they mean by knowledge, but are obliged after all to say knowledge of the good?

How ridiculous!

Yes, that they should begin by reproaching us with our ignorance of the good, and then presume our knowledge of it—for the good they define to be knowledge of the good, just as if we understood them when they use the term "good" —this is of course ridiculous.

Most true.

And those who make pleasure their good are in equal perplexity; for they are compelled to admit that there are bad pleasures as well as good.

Certainly.

And therefore to acknowledge that bad and good are the same?

True.

There can be no doubt about the numerous difficulties in which this question is involved.

There can be none.

Further, do we not see that many are willing to do or to have or to seem to be what is just and honorable without the reality; but no one is satisfied with the appearance of good— the reality is what they seek; in the case of the good, appearance is despised by everyone.

Very true.

Of this then, which every soul of man pursues and makes the end of all his actions, having a presentiment that there is such an end, and yet hesitating because neither knowing the nature nor having the same assurance of this as of other things, and therefore losing whatever good there is in other things— of a principle such and so great as this ought the best men in our State, to whom everything is intrusted, to be in the darkness of ignorance?

Certainly not.

I am sure that he who does not know how the beautiful and the just are likewise good will be but a sorry guardian of them; and I suspect that no one who is ignorant of the good will have a true knowledge of them.

That is a shrewd suspicion of yours.

And if we only have a guardian who has this knowledge, our State will be perfectly ordered?

Of course; but I wish that you would tell me whether you conceive this supreme principle of the good to be knowledge or pleasure, or different from either?

Aye, I knew all along that a fastidious gentleman like you would not be contented with the thoughts of other people about these matters.

True, Socrates; but I must say that one who like you has passed a lifetime in the study of philosophy should not be always repeating the opinions of others, and never telling his own.

Well, but has anyone a right to say positively what he does not know?

Not with the assurance of positive certainty; he has no right to do that: but he may say what he thinks, as a matter of opinion.

And do you not know that all mere opinions are bad, and the best of them blind? You would not deny that those who have any true notion without intelligence are only like blind men who feel their way along the road?

Very true.

And do you wish to behold what is blind and crooked and base, when others will tell you of brightness and beauty?

Still, I must implore you, Socrates, not to turn away just as you are reaching the goal; if you will only give such an explanation of the good as you have already given of justice and temperance and the other virtues, we shall be satisfied.

Yes, my friend, and I shall be at least equally satisfied, but I cannot help fearing that I shall fail, and that my indiscreet zeal will bring ridicule upon me. No, sweet sirs, let us not at present ask what is the actual nature of the good, for to reach what is now in my thoughts would be an effort too great for me. But of the child of the good who is likest him, I would fain speak, if I could be sure that you wished to hear—otherwise, not.

By all means tell us of the child and you shall remain in our debt for an account of the parent.

I do indeed wish that I could pay, and you receive, the account of the parent, and not, as now, of the offspring only; take, however, this latter by way of interest, and at the same time have a care that I do not render a false account, although I have no intention of deceiving you.

Yes, we will take all the care that we can: proceed.

Yes, but I must first come to an understanding with you, and remind you of what I have mentioned in the course of this discussion, and at many other times.

What?

The old story, that there is many a beautiful and many a good, and so of other things which we describe and define; to all of them the term "many" is implied.

True.

And there is an absolute beauty and an absolute good, and of other things to which the term "many" is applied there is an absolute; for they may be brought under a single idea, which is called the essence of each.

Very true.

The many, as we say, are seen but not known, and the ideas are known but not seen.

Exactly.

And what is the organ with which we see the visible things?

The sight.

And with the hearing, we hear, and with the other senses perceive the other objects of sense?

True.

But have you remarked that sight is by far the most costly and complex piece of workmanship which the artificer of the senses ever contrived?

No, I never have.

Then reflect: has the ear or voice need of any third or additional nature in order that the one may be able to hear and the other to be heard?

Nothing of the sort.

No, indeed, and the same is true of most, if not all, the other senses—you would not say that any of them requires such an addition?

Certainly not.

But you see that without the addition of some other nature there is no seeing or being seen?

How do you mean?

Sight being, as I conceive, in the eyes, and he who has eyes wanting to see; color being also present in them, still unless there be a third nature specially adapted to the purpose, the owner of the eyes will see nothing and the colors will be invisible.

Of what nature are you speaking?

Of that which you term light.

True.

Noble, then, is the bond which links together sight and visibility, and great beyond other bonds by no small difference of nature; for light is their bond, and light is no ignoble thing?

Nay, the reverse of ignoble.

And which of the gods in heaven would you say was the lord of this element? Whose is that light which makes the eye to see perfectly and the visible to appear?

You mean the sun, as you and all mankind say.

May not the relation of sight to this deity be described as follows?

How?

Neither sight nor the eye in which sight resides is the sun?

No.

Yet of all the organs of sense the eye is the most like the sun?

By far the most like.

And the power which the eye possesses is a sort of effluence which is dispensed from the sun?

Exactly.

Then the sun is not sight, but the author of sight who is recognized by sight?

True.

And this is he whom I call the child of the good, whom the good begat in his own likeness, to be in the visible world, in relation to sight and the things of sight, what the good is in the intellectual world in relation to mind and the things of mind:

Will you be a little more explicit?

Why, you know, that the eyes, when a person directs them toward objects on which the light of day is no longer shining, but the moon and stars only, see dimly, and are nearly blind; they seem to have no clearness of vision in them?

Very true.

But when they are directed toward objects on which the sun shines, they see clearly and there is sight in them?

Certainly.

And the soul is like the eye: when resting upon that on which truth and being shine, the soul perceives and understands, and is radiant with intelligence; but when turned toward the twilight of becoming and perishing, then she has opinion only, and goes blinking about, and is first of one opinion and then of another, and seems to have no intelligence?

Just so.

Now, that which imparts truth to the known and the power of knowing to the knower is what I would have you term the idea of good, and this you will deem to be the cause of science, and of truth in so far as the latter becomes the subject of knowledge; beautiful too, as are both truth and knowledge, you will be right in esteeming this other nature as more beautiful than either; and, as in the previous instance, light and sight may be truly said to be like the sun, and yet not to be the sun, so in this other sphere, science and truth may be deemed to be like the good, but not the good; the good has a place of honor yet higher.

What a wonder of beauty that must be, which is the author of science and truth, and yet surpasses them in beauty; for you surely cannot mean to say that pleasure is the good?

God forbid, but may I ask you to consider the image in another point of view?

In what point of view?

You would say, would you not? that the sun is not only the author of visibility in all visible things, but of generation and nourishment and growth, though he himself is not generation?

Certainly.

In like manner the good may be said to be not only the author of knowledge to all things known, but of their being and essence, and yet the good is not essence, but far exceeds essence in dignity and power.

By the light of heaven, how amazing!

Yes, and the exaggeration may be set down to you; for you made me utter my fancies.

And pray continue to utter them; at any rate let us hear if there is anything more to be said about the similitude of the sun.

Yes, there is a great deal more.

Then omit nothing, however slight.

I will do my best, but I should think that a great deal will have to be omitted.

I hope not.

You have to imagine, then, that there are two ruling powers, and that one of them is set over the intellectual world, the other over the visible. . . . May I suppose that you have this distinction of the visible and intelligible fixed in your mind?

I have.

Now take a line which has been cut into two unequal parts, and divide each of them again in the same proportion, and suppose the two main divisions to answer, one to the visible and the other to the intelligible, and then compare the subdivisions in respect of their clearness and want of clearness, and you will find that the first section in the sphere of the visible consists of images. And by images I mean, in the first place, shadows, and in the second place, reflections in water and in solid, smooth and polished bodies and the like: Do you understand?

Yes, I understand.

Imagine, now, the other section, of which this is only the resemblance, to include the animals which we see, and everything that grows or is made.

Very good.

Would you not admit that both the sections of this division have different degrees of truth, and that the copy is to the original as the sphere of opinion is to the sphere of knowledge?

Most undoubtedly.

Next proceed to consider the manner in which the sphere of the intellectual is to be divided.

In what manner?

Thus: There are two subdivisions, in the lower of which the soul uses the figures given by the former division as images; the inquiry can only be hypothetical, and instead of going upward to a principle descends to the other end; in the higher of the two, the soul passes out of hypotheses, and goes up to a principle which is above hypotheses, making no use of images as in the former case, but proceeding only in and through the ideas themselves.

I do not quite understand your meaning.

Then I will try again; you will understand me better when I have made some preliminary remarks. You are aware that students of geometry, arithmetic, and the kindred sciences assume the odd, and the even, and the figures, and three kinds of angles, and the like, in their several branches of science; these are their hypotheses, which they and everybody are supposed to know, and therefore they do not deign to give any account of them either to themselves or others; but they begin with them, and go on until they arrive at last, and in a consistent manner, at their conclusion?

Yes, I know.

And do you not know also that although they make use of the visible forms and reason about them, they are thinking not of these, but of the ideals which they resemble; not of the figures which they draw, but of the absolute square and the absolute diameter, and so on—the forms which they draw or make, and which have shadows and reflections in water of their own, are converted by them into images, but they are really seeking to behold the things themselves, which can only be seen with the eye of the mind?

That is true.

And of this kind I spoke as the intelligible, although in the search after it the soul is compelled to use hypotheses; not ascending to a first principle, because she is unable to rise above the region of hypothesis, but employing the objects of which the shadows below are resemblances in their turn as images, they having in relation to the shadows and reflections of them a greater distinctness, and therefore a higher value.

I understand that you are speaking of the province of geometry and the sister arts.

And when I speak of the other division of the intelligible, you will understand me to speak of that other sort of knowledge which reason herself attains by the power of dialectic, using the hypotheses not as first principles, but only as hypotheses—that is to say, as steps and points of departure into a world which is above hypotheses, in order that she may soar beyond them to the first principle of the whole; and clinging to this and then to that which depends on this, by successive steps she descends again without the aid of any sensible object, from ideas, through ideas, and in ideas she ends.

I understand you; not perfectly, for you seem to me to be describing a task which is really tremendous; but, at any rate, I understand you to say that knowledge and being, which the science of dialectic contemplates, are clearer than the notions of the arts, as they are termed, which proceed from hypotheses only: these are also contemplated by the understanding, and not by the senses: yet, because they start from hypotheses and do not ascend to a principle, those who contemplate them appear to you not to exercise the higher reason upon them, although when a first principle is added to them they are cognizable by the higher reason. And the habit which is concerned with geometry and the cognate sciences I suppose that you would term understanding, and not reason, as being intermediate between opinion and reason.

You have quite conceived my meaning; and now, corresponding to these four divisions, let there be four faculties in the soul—reason answering to the highest, understanding to the second, belief to the third, and perception of shadows to the last—and let there be a scale of them, and let us suppose that the several faculties have clearness in the same degree that their objects have truth.

I understand, and give my assent, and accept your arrangement.

Excerpt from **Book 7**

SOCRATES: And now, let me show in a figure how far our nature is enlightened or unenlightened: Behold! human beings living in an underground den, which has a mouth open toward the light and reaching all along the den; here they have been from their childhood, and have their legs and necks chained so that they cannot move, and can only see before them, being prevented by the chains from turning round their heads. Above and behind them a fire is blazing at a distance, and between the fire and the prisoners there is a raised way; and you will see, if you look, a low wall built along the way, like the screen which marionette-players have in front of them, over which they show the puppets.

GLAUCON: I see.

And do you see, men passing along the wall carrying all sorts of vessels, and statues and figures of animals made of wood and stone and various materials, which appear over the wall? Some of them are talking, others silent.

You have shown me a strange image, and they are strange prisoners.

Like ourselves. They see only their own shadows, or the shadows of one another, which the fire throws on the opposite wall of the cave?

How could they see anything but shadows if they were not allowed to move their heads?

And of the objects which are being carried in like manner they would only see the shadows?

Yes.

And if they were able to converse with one another, would they not suppose that they were naming what was actually before them?

Very true.

And suppose further that the prison had an echo which came from the other side, would they not be sure to fancy when one of the passers-by spoke that the voice which they heard came from the passing shadow?

No question.

To them, the truth would be literally nothing but the shadows of the images.

That is certain.

And now look again, and see what will naturally follow if the prisoners are released and disabused of their error. At first, when any of them is liberated and compelled suddenly to stand up and turn his neck round and walk and look toward the light, he will suffer sharp pains; the glare will distress him, and he will be unable to see the realities of which in his former state he had seen the shadows; and then conceive someone saying to him, that what he saw before was an illusion, but that now, when he is approaching nearer to being and his eye is turned toward more real existence, he has a clearer vision—what will be his reply? And you may further imagine that his instructor is pointing to the objects as they pass and requiring him to name them—will he not be perplexed? Will he not fancy that the shadows which he formerly saw are truer than the objects which are now shown to him?

Far truer.

And if he is compelled to look straight at the light, will he not have a pain in his eyes which will make him turn away to take refuge in the objects of vision which he can see, and which he will conceive to be in reality clearer than the things which are now being shown to him?

True.

And suppose once more, that he is reluctantly dragged up a steep and rugged ascent, and held fast until he is forced into the presence of the sun himself, is he not likely to be pained and irritated? When he approaches the light his eyes will be dazzled, and he will not be able to see anything at all of what are now called realities.

Not all in a moment.

He will require to grow accustomed to the sight of the upper world. And first he will see the shadows best, next the reflections of men and other objects in the water, and then the objects themselves; then he will gaze upon the light of the moon and the stars and the spangled heaven; and he will see the sky and the stars by night better than the sun or the light of the sun by day?

Certainly.

Last of all he will be able to see the sun, and not mere reflections of him in the water, but he will see him in his own proper place, and not in another; and he will contemplate him as he is.

Certainly.

He will then proceed to argue that this is he who gives the season and the years, and is the guardian of all that is in the visible world, and in a certain way the cause of all things which he and his fellows have been accustomed to behold?

Clearly, he would first see the sun and then reason about him.

And when he remembered his old habitation, and the wisdom of the den and his fellow-prisoners, do you not suppose that he would felicitate himself on the change, and pity him?

Certainly, he would.

And if they were in the habit of conferring honors among themselves on those who were quickest to observe the passing shadows and to remark which of them went before, and which followed after, and which were together; and who were therefore best able to draw conclusions as to the future, do you think that he would care for such honors and glories, or envy the possessors of them? Would he not say with Homer, "Better to be the poor servant of a poor master," and to endure anything, rather than think as they do and live after their manner?

Yes, I think that he would rather suffer anything than entertain these false notions and live in this miserable manner.

Imagine once more, such a one coming suddenly out of the sun to be replaced in his old situation; would he not be certain to have his eyes full of darkness?

To be sure.

And if there were a contest, and he had to compete in measuring the shadows with the prisoners who had never moved out of the den, while his sight was still weak, and before his eyes had become steady (and the time which would be needed to acquire this new habit of sight might be very considerable), would he not be ridiculous? Men would say of him that up he went and down he came without his eyes; and that it was better not even to think of ascending; and if anyone tried to loose another and lead him up to the light, let them only catch the offender, and they would put him to death.

No question.

This entire allegory you may now append, dear Glaucon, to the previous argument; the prison-house is the world of sight, the light of the fire is the sun, and you will not misapprehend me if you interpret the journey upward to be the ascent of the soul into the intellectual world according to my poor belief, which, at your desire, I have expressed—whether rightly or wrongly, God knows. But, whether true or false, my opinion is that in the world of knowledge the idea of good appears last of all, and is seen only with an effort; and, when seen, is also inferred to be the universal author of all things beautiful and right, parent of light and of the lord of light in this visible world, and the immediate source of reason and truth in the intellectual; and that this is the power upon which he who would act rationally either in public or private life must have his eye fixed.

I agree, as far as I am able to understand you.

Moreover, you must not wonder that those who attain to this beatific vision are unwilling to descend to human affairs; for their souls are ever hastening into the upper world where they desire to dwell; which desire of theirs is very natural, if our allegory may be trusted.

Yes, very natural.

And is there anything surprising in one who passes from divine contemplations to the evil state of man, misbehaving himself in a ridiculous manner; if, while his eyes are blinking and before he has become accustomed to the surrounding darkness, he is compelled to fight in courts of law, or in other places, about the images or the shadows of images of justice, and is endeavoring to meet the conceptions of those who have never yet seen absolute justice?

Anything but surprising.

Anyone who has common-sense will remember that the bewilderments of the eyes are of two kinds, and arise from two causes, either from coming out of the light or from going into the light, which is true of the mind's eye, quite as much as of the bodily eye; and he who remembers this when he sees anyone whose vision is perplexed and weak, will not be too ready to laugh; he will first ask whether that soul of man has come out of the brighter life, and is unable to see because unaccustomed to the dark, or having turned from darkness to the day is dazzled by excess of light. And he will count the one happy in his condition and state of being, and he will pity the other; or, if he have a mind to laugh at the soul which comes from below into the light, there will be more reason in this than in the laugh which greets him who returns from above out of the light into the den.

That is a very just distinction.

But then, if I am right, certain professors of education must be wrong when they say that they can put a knowledge into the soul which was not there before, like sight into blind eyes.

They undoubtedly say this.

Whereas, our argument shows that the power and capacity of learning exists in the soul already; and that just as the eye was unable to turn from darkness to light without the whole body, so too the instrument of knowledge can only by the movement of the whole soul be turned from the world of becoming into that of being, and learn by degrees to endure the sight of being, and of the brightest and best of being, or, in other words, of the good.

Very true.

And must there not be some art which will effect conversion in the easiest and quickest manner; not implanting the faculty of sight, for that exists already, but has been turned in the wrong direction, and is looking away from the truth?

Yes, such an art may be presumed.

And whereas the other so-called virtues of the soul seem to be akin to bodily qualities, for even when they are not originally innate they can be implanted later by habit and exercise, the virtue of wisdom more than anything else contains a divine element which always remains, and by this conversion is rendered useful and profitable; or, on the other hand, hurtful and useless. Did you never observe the narrow intelligence flashing from the keen eye of a clever rogue—how eager he is, how clearly his paltry soul sees the way to his end; he is the reverse of blind, but his keen eyesight is forced into the service of evil, and he is mischievous in proportion to his cleverness?

Very true.

But what if there had been a circumcision of such natures in the days of their youth; and they had been severed from those sensual pleasures, such as eating and drinking, which, like leaden weights, were attached to them at their birth, and which drag them down and turn the vision of their souls upon the things that are below—if, I say, they had been released from these impediments and turned in the opposite direction, the very same faculty in them would have seen the truth as keenly as they see what their eyes are turned to now.

Very likely.

Yes, and there is another thing which is likely, or rather a necessary inference from what has preceded, that neither the uneducated and uninformed of the truth, nor yet those who never make an end of their education, will be able ministers of the State; not the former, because they have no single aim of duty which is the rule of all their actions, private as well as public; nor the latter, because they will not act at all except upon compulsion, fancying that they are already dwelling apart in the islands of the blessed.

Very true.

Then, the business of us who are the founders of the State will be to compel the best minds to attain that knowledge which we have already shown to be the greatest of all—they must continue to ascend until they arrive at the good; but when they have ascended and seen enough we must not allow them to do as they do now.

What do you mean?

I mean that they remain in the upper world: but this must not be allowed; they must be made to descend again among the prisoners in the den, and partake of their labors and honors, whether they are worth having or not.

But is not this unjust? Ought we to give them a worse life, when they might have a better?

You have again forgotten, my friend, the intention of the legislator, who did not aim at making any one class in the State happy above the rest; the happiness was to be in the whole State, and he held the citizens together by persuasion and necessity, making them benefactors of the State, and therefore benefactors of one another; to this end he created them, not to please themselves, but to be his instruments in binding up the State.

True, I had forgotten.

Observe, Glaucon, that there will be no injustice in compelling our philosophers to have a care and providence of others; we shall explain to them that in other States, men of their class are not obliged to share in the toils of politics: and this is reasonable, for they grow up at their own sweet will, and the government would rather not have them. Being self-taught, they cannot be expected to show any gratitude for a culture which they have never received. But we have brought you into the world to be rulers of the hive, kings of yourselves and of the other citizens, and have educated you far better and more perfectly than they have been educated, and you are better able to share in the double duty.

Wherefore each of you, when his turn comes, must go down to the general underground abode, and get the habit of seeing in the dark. When you have acquired the habit, you will see ten thousand times better than the inhabitants of the den, and you will know what the several images are, and what they represent, because you have seen the beautiful and just and good in their truth. And thus our State, which is also yours, will be a reality, and not a dream only, and will be administered in a spirit unlike that of other States, in which men fight with one another about shadows only and are distracted in the struggle for power, which in their eyes is a great good. Whereas the truth is that the State in which the rulers are most reluctant to govern is always the best and most quietly governed, and the State in which they are most eager, the worst.

Quite true.

And will our pupils, when they hear this, refuse to take their turn at the toils of State, when they are allowed to spend the greater part of their time with one another in the heavenly light?

Impossible, for they are just men, and the commands which we impose upon them are just; there can be no doubt that every one of them will take office as a stern necessity, and not after the fashion of our present rulers of State.

Yes, my friend, and there lies the point. You must contrive for your future rulers another and a better life than that of a ruler, and then you may have a well-ordered State; for only in the State which offers this, will they rule who are truly rich, not in silver and gold, but in virtue and wisdom, which are the true blessings of life. Whereas, if they go to the administration of public affairs, poor and hungering after their own private advantage, thinking that hence they are to snatch the chief good, order there can never be; for they will be fighting about office, and the civil and domestic broils which thus arise will be the ruin of the rulers themselves and of the whole State.

Most true.

And the only life which looks down upon the life of political ambition is that of true philosophy. Do you know of any other?

Indeed, I do not.

And those who govern ought not to be lovers of the task? For, if they are, there will be rival lovers, and they will fight.

No question.

Who, then, are those whom we shall compel to be guardians?

Surely they will be the men who are wisest about affairs of State, and by whom the State is best administered, and who at the same time have other honors and another and a better life than that of politics?

They are the men, and I will choose them

ARISTOTLE
Metaphysics

Translated by W. D. Ross

Book 1
Chapter 1

All men by nature desire to know. An indication of this is the delight we take in our senses; for even apart from their usefulness they are loved for themselves; and above all others the sense of sight. For not only with a view to action, but even when we are not going to do anything, we prefer seeing (one might say) to everything else. The reason is that this, most of all the senses, makes us know and brings to light many differences between things.

By nature animals are born with the faculty of sensation, and from sensation memory is produced in some of them, though not in others. And therefore the former are more intelligent and apt at learning than those which cannot remember; those which are incapable of hearing sounds are intelligent though they cannot be taught, e.g. the bee, and any other race of animals that may be like it; and those which besides memory have this sense of hearing can be taught.

The animals other than man live by appearances and memories, and have but little of connected experience; but the human race lives also by art and reasonings. Now from memory experience is produced in men; for the several memories of the same thing produce finally the capacity for a single experience. And experience seems pretty much like science and art, but really science and art come to men through experience; for 'experience made art', as Polus says, 'but inexperience luck.' Now art arises when from many notions gained by experience one universal judgement about a class of objects is produced. For to have a judgement that when Callias was ill of this disease this did him good, and similarly in the case of Socrates and in many individual cases, is a matter of experience; but to judge that it has done good to all persons of a certain constitution, marked off in one class, when they were ill of this disease, e.g. to phlegmatic or bilious people when burning with fevers-this is a matter of art.

With a view to action experience seems in no respect inferior to art, and men of experience succeed even better than those who have theory without experience. (The reason is that experience is knowledge of individuals, art of universals, and actions and productions are all concerned with the individual; for the physician does not cure man, except in an incidental way, but Callias or Socrates or some other called by some such individual name, who happens to be a man. If, then, a man has the theory without the experience, and recognizes the universal but does not know the individual included in this, he will often fail to cure; for it is the individual that is to be cured.)

But yet we think that knowledge and understanding belong to art rather than to experience, and we suppose artists to be wiser than men of experience (which implies that Wisdom depends in all cases rather on knowledge); and this because the former know the cause, but the latter do not. For men of experience know that the thing is so, but do not know why, while the others know the 'why' and the cause. Hence we think also that the masterworkers in each craft are more honourable and know in a truer sense and are wiser than the manual workers, because they know the causes of the things that are done (we think the manual workers are like certain lifeless things which act indeed, but act without knowing what they do, as fire burns,-but while the lifeless things perform each of their functions by a natural tendency, the labourers perform them through habit); thus we view them as being wiser not in virtue of being able to act, but of having the theory for themselves and knowing the causes. And in general it is a sign of the man who knows and of the man who does not know, that the former can teach, and therefore we think art more truly knowledge than experience is; for artists can teach, and men of mere experience cannot.

Again, we do not regard any of the senses as Wisdom; yet surely these give the most authoritative knowledge of particulars. But they do not tell us the 'why' of anything—e.g. why fire is hot; they only say that it is hot.

At first he who invented any art whatever that went beyond the common perceptions of man was naturally admired by men, not only because there was something useful in the inventions, but because he was thought wise and superior to the rest. But as more arts were invented, and some were directed to the necessities of life, others to recreation, the inventors of the latter were naturally always regarded as wiser than the inventors of the former, because their branches of knowledge did not aim at utility. Hence when all such inventions were already established, the sciences which do not aim at giving pleasure or at the necessities of life were discovered, and first in the places where men first began to have leisure. This is why the mathematical arts were founded in Egypt; for there the priestly caste was allowed to be at leisure.

We have said in the *Ethics* what the difference is between art and science and the other kindred faculties; but the point of our present discussion is this, that all men suppose what is called Wisdom to deal with the first causes and the principles of things; so that, as has been said before, the man of experience is thought to be wiser than the possessors of any sense-perception whatever, the artist wiser than the men of experience, the masterworker than the mechanic, and the theoretical kinds of knowledge to be more of the nature of Wisdom than the productive. Clearly then Wisdom is knowledge about certain principles and causes.

Chapter 2

Since we are seeking this knowledge, we must inquire of what kind are the causes and the principles, the knowledge of which is Wisdom. If one were to take the notions we have about the wise man, this might perhaps make the answer more evident. We suppose first, then, that the wise man knows all things, as far as possible, although he has not knowledge of each of them in detail; secondly, that he who can learn things that are difficult, and not easy for man to know, is wise (sense-perception is common to all, and therefore easy and no mark of Wisdom); again, that he who is more exact and more capable of teaching the causes is wiser, in every branch of knowledge; and that of the sciences, also, that which is desirable on its own account and for the sake of knowing it is more of the nature of Wisdom than that which is desirable on account of its results, and the superior science is more of the nature of Wisdom than the ancillary; for the wise man must not be ordered but must order, and he must not obey another, but the less wise must obey him.

Such and so many are the notions, then, which we have about Wisdom and the wise. Now of these characteristics that of knowing all things must belong to him who has in the highest degree universal knowledge; for he knows in a sense all the instances that fall under the universal. And these things, the most universal, are on the whole the hardest for men to know; for they are farthest from the senses. And the most exact of the sciences are those which deal most with first principles; for those which involve fewer principles are more exact than those which involve additional principles, e.g. arithmetic than geometry. But the science which investigates causes is also instructive, in a higher degree, for the people who instruct us are those who tell the causes of each thing. And understanding and knowledge pursued for their own sake are found most in the knowledge of that which is most knowable (for he who chooses to know for the sake of knowing will choose most readily that which is most truly knowledge, and such is the knowledge of that which is most knowable); and the first principles and the causes are most knowable; for by reason of these, and from these, all other things come to be known, and not these by means of the things subordinate to them. And the science which knows to what end each thing must be done is the most authoritative of the sciences, and more authoritative than any ancillary science; and this end is the good of that thing, and in general the supreme good in the whole of nature. Judged by all the tests we have mentioned, then, the name in question falls to the same science; this must be a science that investigates the first principles and causes; for the good, i.e. the end, is one of the causes.

That it is not a science of production is clear even from the history of the earliest philosophers. For it is owing to their wonder that men both now begin and at first began to philosophize; they wondered originally at the obvious difficulties, then advanced little by little and stated difficulties about the greater matters, e.g. about the phenomena of the moon and those of the sun and of the stars, and about the genesis of the universe. And a man who is puzzled and wonders thinks himself ignorant (whence even the lover of myth is in a sense a lover of Wisdom, for the myth is composed of wonders); therefore since they philosophized order to escape from ignorance, evidently they were pursuing science in order to know, and not for any utilitarian end. And this is confirmed by the facts; for it was when almost all the necessities of life and the things that make for comfort and recreation had been secured, that such knowledge began to be sought. Evidently then we do not seek it for the sake of any other advantage; but as the man is free, we say, who exists for his own sake and not for another's, so we pursue this as the only free science, for it alone exists for its own sake.

Hence also the possession of it might be justly regarded as beyond human power; for in many ways human nature is in bondage, so that according to Simonides 'God alone can have this privilege', and it is unfitting that man should not be content to seek the knowledge that is suited to him. If, then, there is something in what the poets say, and jealousy is natural to the divine power, it would probably occur in this case above all, and all who excelled in this knowledge would be unfortunate. But the divine power cannot be jealous (nay, according to the proverb, 'bards tell a lie'), nor should any other science be thought more honourable than one of this sort. For the most divine science is also most honourable; and this science alone must be, in two ways, most divine. For the science which it would be most meet for God to have is a divine science, and so is any science that deals with divine objects; and this science alone has both these qualities; for (1) God is thought to be among the causes of all things and to be a first principle, and (2) such a science either God alone can have, or God above all others. All the sciences, indeed, are more necessary than this, but none is better.

Yet the acquisition of it must in a sense end in something which is the opposite of our original inquiries. For all men begin, as we said, by wondering that things are as they are, as they do about self-moving marionettes, or about the solstices or the incommensurability of the diagonal of a square with the side; for it seems wonderful to all who have not yet seen the reason, that there is a thing which cannot be measured even by the smallest unit. But we must end in the contrary and, according to the proverb, the better state, as is the case in these instances too when men learn the cause; for there is nothing which would surprise a geometer so much as if the diagonal turned out to be commensurable.

We have stated, then, what is the nature of the science we are searching for, and what is the mark which our search and our whole investigation must reach. . . .

Book 4

Chapter 1

There is a science which investigates being as being and the attributes which belong to this in virtue of its own nature. Now this is not the same as any of the so-called special sciences; for none of these others treats universally of being as being. They cut off a part of being and investigate the attribute of this part; this is what the mathematical sciences for instance do. Now since we are seeking the first principles and the highest causes, clearly there must be some thing to which these belong in virtue of its own nature. If then those who sought the elements of existing things were seeking these same principles, it is necessary that the elements must be elements of being not by accident but just because it is being. Therefore it is of being as being that we also must grasp the first causes.

Chapter 2

There are many senses in which a thing may be said to 'be', but all that 'is' is related to one central point, one definite kind of thing, and is not said to 'be' by a mere ambiguity. Everything which is healthy is related to health, one thing in the sense that it preserves health, another in the sense that it produces it, another in the sense that it is a symptom of health, another because it is capable of it. And that which is medical is relative to the medical art, one thing being called medical because it possesses it, another because it is naturally adapted to it, another because it is a function of the medical art. And we shall find other words used similarly to these.

So, too, there are many senses in which a thing is said to be, but all refer to one starting-point; some things are said to be because they are substances, others because they are affections of substance, others because they are a process towards substance, or destructions or privations or qualities of substance, or productive or generative of substance, or of things which are relative to substance, or negations of one of these thing of substance itself. It is for this reason that we say even of non-being that it is nonbeing.

As, then, there is one science which deals with all healthy things, the same applies in the other cases also. For not only in the case of things which have one common notion does the investigation belong to one science, but also in the case of things which are related to one common nature; for even these in a sense have one common notion. It is clear then that it is the work of one science also to study the things that are, qua being. But everywhere science deals chiefly with that which is primary, and on which the other things depend, and in virtue of which they get their names. If, then, this is substance, it will be of substances that the philosopher must grasp the principles and the causes.

Now for each one class of things, as there is one perception, so there is one science, as for instance grammar, being one science, investigates all articulate sounds. Hence to investigate all the species of being qua being is the work of a science which is generically one, and to investigate the several species is the work of the specific parts of the science.

If, now, being and unity are the same and are one thing in the sense that they are implied in one another as principle and cause are, not in the sense that they are explained by the same definition (though it makes no difference even if we suppose them to be like that—in fact this would even strengthen our case); for 'one man' and 'man' are the same thing, and so are 'existent man' and 'man', and the doubling of the words in 'one man and one existent man' does not express anything different (it is clear that the two things are not separated either in coming to be or in ceasing to be); and similarly 'one existent man' adds nothing to 'existent man', and that it is obvious that the addition in these cases means the same thing, and unity is nothing apart from being; and if, further, the substance of each thing is one in no merely accidental way, and similarly is from its very nature something that is.

All this being so, there must be exactly as many species of being as of unity. And to investigate the essence of these is the work of a science which is generically one—I mean, for instance, the discussion of the same and the similar and the other concepts of this sort; and nearly all contraries may be referred to this origin; let us take them as having been investigated in the 'Selection of Contraries'.

And there are as many parts of philosophy as there are kinds of substance, so that there must necessarily be among them a first philosophy and one which follows this. For being falls immediately into genera; for which reason the sciences too will correspond to these genera. For the philosopher is like the mathematician, as that word is used; for mathematics also has parts, and there is a first and a second science and other successive ones within the sphere of mathematics.

Now since it is the work of one science to investigate opposites, and plurality is opposed to unity—and it belongs to one science to investigate the negation and the privation because in both cases we are really investigating the one thing of which the negation or the privation is a negation or privation (for we either say simply that that thing is not present, or that it is not present in some particular class; in the latter case difference is present over and above what is implied in negation; for negation means just the absence of the thing in question, while in privation there is also employed an underlying nature of which the privation is asserted).

In view of all these facts, the contraries of the concepts we named above, the other and the dissimilar and the unequal, and everything else which is derived either from these or from plurality and unity, must fall within the province of the science above named. And contrariety is one of these concepts; for contrariety is a kind of difference, and difference is a kind of otherness. Therefore, since there are many senses in which a thing is said to be one, these terms also will have many senses, but yet it belongs to one science to know them all; for a term belongs to different sciences not if it has different senses, but if it has not one meaning and its definitions cannot be referred to one central meaning. And since all things are referred to that which is primary, as for instance all things which are called one are referred to the primary one, we must say that this holds good also of the same and the other and of contraries in general; so that after distinguishing the various senses of each, we must then explain by reference to what is primary in the case of each of the predicates in question, saying how they are related to it; for some will be called what they are called because they possess it, others because they produce it, and others in other such ways.

It is evident, then, that it belongs to one science to be able to give an account of these concepts as well as of substance (this was one of the questions in our book of problems), and that it is the function of the philosopher to be able to investigate all things. For if it is not the function of the philosopher, who is it who will inquire whether Socrates and Socrates seated are the same thing, or whether one thing has one contrary, or what contrariety is, or how many meanings it has? And similarly with all other such questions. Since, then, these are essential modifications of unity qua unity and of being qua being, not qua numbers or lines or fire, it is clear that it belongs to this science to investigate both the essence of these concepts and their properties.

Those who study these properties err not by leaving the sphere of philosophy, but by forgetting that substance, of which they have no correct idea, is prior to these other things. For number qua number has peculiar attributes, such as oddness and evenness, commensurability and equality, excess and defect, and these belong to numbers either in themselves or in relation to one another. And similarly the solid and the motionless and that which is in motion and the weightless and that which has weight have other peculiar properties. So too there are certain properties peculiar to being as such, and it is about these that the philosopher has to investigate the truth.

An indication of this may be mentioned: dialecticians and sophists assume the same guise as the philosopher, for sophistic is Wisdom which exists only in semblance, and dialecticians embrace all things in their dialectic, and being is common to all things; but evidently their dialectic embraces these subjects because these are proper to philosophy.-For sophistic and dialectic turn on the same class of things as philosophy, but this differs from dialectic in the nature of the faculty required and from sophistic in respect of the purpose of the philosophic life. Dialectic is merely critical where philosophy claims to know, and sophistic is what appears to be philosophy but is not.

Again, in the list of contraries one of the two columns is privative, and all contraries are reducible to being and non-being, and to unity and plurality, as for instance rest belongs to unity and movement to plurality. And nearly all thinkers agree that being and substance are composed of contraries; at least all name contraries as their first principles-some name odd and even, some hot and cold, some limit and the unlimited, some love and strife. And all the others as well are evidently reducible to unity and plurality (this reduction we must take for granted), and the principles stated by other thinkers fall entirely under these as their genera.

It is obvious then from these considerations too that it belongs to one science to examine being qua being. For all things are either contraries or composed of contraries, and unity and plurality are the starting-points of all contraries. And these belong to one science, whether they have or have not one single meaning. Probably the truth is that they have not; yet even if 'one' has several meanings, the other meanings will be related to the primary meaning (and similarly in the case of the contraries), even if being or unity is not a universal and the same in every instance or is not separable from the particular instances (as in fact it probably is not; the unity is in some cases that of common reference, in some cases that of serial succession). And for this reason it does not belong to the geometer to inquire what is contrariety or completeness or unity or being or the same or the other, but only to presuppose these concepts and reason from this starting-point.

Obviously then it is the work of one science to examine being qua being, and the attributes which belong to it qua being, and the same science will examine not only substances but also their attributes, both those above named and the concepts 'prior' and 'posterior', 'genus' and 'species', 'whole' and 'part', and the others of this sort.

Chapter 3

We must state whether it belongs to one or to different sciences to inquire into the truths which are in mathematics called axioms, and into substance. Evidently, the inquiry into these also belongs to one science, and that the science of the philosopher; for these truths hold good for everything that is, and not for some special genus apart from others. And all men use them, because they are true of being qua being and each genus has being. But men use them just so far as to satisfy their purposes; that is, as far as the genus to which their demonstrations refer extends.

Therefore since these truths clearly hold good for all things qua being (for this is what is common to them), to him who studies being qua being belongs the inquiry into these as well. And for this reason no one who is conducting a special inquiry tries to say anything about their truth or falsity, neither the geometer nor the arithmetician. Some natural philosophers indeed have done so, and their procedure was intelligible enough; for they thought that they alone were inquiring about the whole of nature and about being. But since there is one kind of thinker who is above even the natural philosopher (for nature is only one particular genus of being), the discussion of these truths also will belong to him whose inquiry is universal and deals with primary substance.

Physics also is a kind of Wisdom, but it is not the first kind.-And the attempts of some of those who discuss the terms on which truth should be accepted, are due to a want of training in logic; for they should know these things already when they come to a special study, and not be inquiring into them while they are listening to lectures on it. Evidently then it belongs to the philosopher, i.e. to him who is studying the nature of all substance, to inquire also into the principles of syllogism. But he who knows best about each genus must be able to state the most certain principles of his subject, so that he whose subject is existing things qua existing must be able to state the most certain principles of all things.

This is the philosopher, and the most certain principle of all is that regarding which it is impossible to be mistaken; for such a principle must be both the best known (for all men may be mistaken about things which they do not know), and non-hypothetical. For a principle which every one must have who understands anything that is, is not a hypothesis; and that which every one must know who knows anything, he must already have when he comes to a special study.

Evidently then such a principle is the most certain of all; which principle this is, let us proceed to say. It is, that the same attribute cannot at the same time belong and not belong to the same subject and in the same respect; we must presuppose, to guard against dialectical objections, any further qualifications which might be added. This, then, is the most certain of all principles, since it answers to the definition given above. For it is impossible for any one to believe the same thing to be and not to be, as some think Heraclitus says.

For what a man says, he does not necessarily believe; and if it is impossible that contrary attributes should belong at the same time to the same subject (the usual qualifications must be presupposed in this premiss too), and if an opinion which contradicts another is contrary to it, obviously it is impossible for the same man at the same time to believe the same thing to be and not to be; for if a man were mistaken on this point he would have contrary opinions at the same time. It is for this reason that all who are carrying out a demonstration reduce it to this as an ultimate belief; for this is naturally the starting-point even for all the other axioms. . . .

Book 12
Chapter 6

Since there were three kinds of substance, two of them physical and one unmovable, regarding the latter we must assert that it is necessary that there should be an eternal unmovable substance. For substances are the first of existing things, and if they are all destructible, all things are destructible. But it is impossible that movement should either have come into being or cease to be (for it must always have existed), or that time should. For there could not be a before and an after if time did not exist. Movement also is continuous, then, in the sense in which time is; for time is either the same thing as movement or an attribute of movement. And there is no continuous movement except movement in place, and of this only that which is circular is continuous.

But if there is something which is capable of moving things or acting on them, but is not actually doing so, there will not necessarily be movement; for that which has a potency need not exercise it. Nothing, then, is gained even if we suppose eternal substances, as the believers in the Forms do, unless there is to be in them some principle which can cause change; nay, even this is not enough, nor is another substance besides the Forms enough; for if it is not to act, there will be no movement. Further even if it acts, this will not be enough, if its essence is potency; for there will not be eternal movement, since that which is potentially may possibly not be. There must, then, be such a principle, whose very essence is actuality. Further, then, these substances must be without matter; for they must be eternal, if anything is eternal. Therefore they must be actuality.

Yet there is a difficulty; for it is thought that everything that acts is able to act, but that not everything that is able to act acts, so that the potency is prior. But if this is so, nothing that is need be; for it is possible for all things to be capable of existing but not yet to exist.

Yet if we follow the theologians who generate the world from night, or the natural philosophers who say that 'all things were together', the same impossible result ensues. For how will there be movement, if there is no actually existing cause? Wood will surely not move itself—the carpenter's art must act on it; nor will the menstrual blood nor the earth set themselves in motion, but the seeds must act on the earth and the semen on the menstrual blood.

This is why some suppose eternal actuality; e.g. Leucippus and Plato. They say there is always movement, but why and what this movement is they do say, nor, if the world moves in this way or that, do they tell us the cause of its doing so. Now nothing is moved at random, but there must always be something present to move it; e.g. as a matter of fact a thing moves in one way by nature, and in another by force or through the influence of reason or something else. (Further, what sort of movement is primary? This makes a vast difference.)

But again for Plato, at least, it is not permissible to name here that which he sometimes supposes to be the source of movement-that which moves itself; for the soul is later, and coeval with the heavens, according to his account. To suppose potency prior to actuality, then, is in a sense right, and in a sense not; and we have specified these senses. That actuality is prior is testified by Anaxagoras (for his 'reason' is actuality) and by Empedocles in his doctrine of love and strife, and by those who say that there is always movement, e.g. Leucippus. Therefore chaos or night did not exist for an infinite time, but the same things have always existed (either passing through a cycle of changes or obeying some other law), since actuality is prior to potency.

If, then, there is a constant cycle, something must always remain, acting in the same way. And if there is to be generation and destruction, there must be something else which is always acting in different ways. This must, then, act in one way in virtue of itself, and in another in virtue of something else—either of a third agent, therefore, or of the first. Now it must be in virtue of the first. For otherwise this again causes the motion both of the second agent and of the third.

Therefore it is better to say 'the first'. For it was the cause of eternal uniformity; and something else is the cause of variety, and evidently both together are the cause of eternal variety. This, accordingly, is the character which the motions actually exhibit. What need then is there to seek for other principles?

Chapter 7

Since (1) this is a possible account of the matter, and (2) if it were not true, the world would have proceeded out of night and 'all things together' and out of non-being, these difficulties may be taken as solved. There is, then, something which is always moved with an unceasing motion, which is motion in a circle; and this is plain not in theory only but in fact.

Therefore the first heaven must be eternal. There is therefore also something which moves it. And since that which moves and is moved is intermediate, there is something which moves without being moved, being eternal, substance, and actuality. And the object of desire and the object of thought move in this way; they move without being moved.

The primary objects of desire and of thought are the same. For the apparent good is the object of appetite, and the real good is the primary object of rational wish. But desire is consequent on opinion rather than opinion on desire; for the thinking is the starting-point. And thought is moved by the object of thought, and one of the two columns of opposites is in itself the object of thought; and in this, substance is first, and in substance, that which is simple and exists actually. (The one and the simple are not the same; for 'one' means a measure, but 'simple' means that the thing itself has a certain nature.) But the beautiful, also, and that which is in itself desirable are in the same column; and the first in any class is always best, or analogous to the best.

That a final cause may exist among unchangeable entities is shown by the distinction of its meanings. For the final cause is (a) some being for whose good an action is done, and (b) something at which the action aims; and of these the latter exists among unchangeable entities though the former does not. The final cause, then, produces motion as being loved, but all other things move by being moved. Now if something is moved it is capable of being otherwise than as it is. Therefore if its actuality is the primary form of spatial motion, then in so far as it is subject to change, in this respect it is capable of being otherwise,-in place, even if not in substance. But since there is something which moves while itself unmoved, existing actually, this can in no way be otherwise than as it is. For motion in space is the first of the kinds of change, and motion in a circle the first kind of spatial motion; and this the first mover produces. The first mover, then, exists of necessity; and in so far as it exists by necessity, its mode of being is good, and it is in this sense a first principle. For the necessary has all these senses—that which is necessary perforce because it is contrary to the natural impulse, that without which the good is impossible, and that which cannot be otherwise but can exist only in a single way.

On such a principle, then, depend the heavens and the world of nature. And it is a life such as the best which we enjoy, and enjoy for but a short time (for it is ever in this state, which we cannot be), since its actuality is also pleasure. (And for this reason are waking, perception, and thinking most pleasant, and hopes and memories are so on account of these.) And thinking in itself deals with that which is best in itself, and that which is thinking in the fullest sense with that which is best in the fullest sense. And thought thinks on itself because it shares the nature of the object of thought; for it becomes an object of thought in coming into contact with and thinking its objects, so that thought and object of thought are the same. For that which is capable of receiving the object of thought, i.e. the essence, is thought. But it is active when it possesses this object.

Therefore the possession rather than the receptivity is the divine element which thought seems to contain, and the act of contemplation is what is most pleasant and best. If, then, God is always in that good state in which we sometimes are, this compels our wonder; and if in a better this compels it yet more. And God is in a better state. And life also belongs to God; for the actuality of thought is life, and God is that actuality; and God's self-dependent actuality is life most good and eternal. We say therefore that God is a living being, eternal, most good, so that life and duration continuous and eternal belong to God; for this is God.

Those who suppose, as the Pythagoreans and Speusippus do, that supreme beauty and goodness are not present in the beginning, because the beginnings both of plants and of animals are causes, but beauty and completeness are in the effects of these, are wrong in their opinion. For the seed comes from other individuals which are prior and complete, and the first thing is not seed but the complete being; e.g. we must say that before the seed there is a man,-not the man produced from the seed, but another from whom the seed comes.

It is clear then from what has been said that there is a substance which is eternal and unmovable and separate from sensible things. It has been shown also that this substance cannot have any magnitude, but is without parts and indivisible (for it produces movement through infinite time, but nothing finite has infinite power; and, while every magnitude is either infinite or finite, it cannot, for the above reason, have finite magnitude, and it cannot have infinite magnitude because there is no infinite magnitude at all). But it has also been shown that it is impassive and unalterable; for all the other changes are posterior to change of place.

EPICURUS

Letter to Menoeceus

Translated by Erik Anderson

Epicurus to Menoeceus, Greetings!

Let no one hesitate to study philosophy while young, and let no one tire of it when old, for it is never too soon nor too late to devote oneself to the well-being of the soul. Whoever says that the time for philosophy has not yet come or that it has already passed is saying that it is too soon or too late for happiness. Therefore both the young and the old should study philosophy so that, while old, one may still be young with all the joy he has gathered from the past; and while young, one may at the same time be old through fearlessness of the future.

We must practice what produces happiness because when we have it, we have everything, and if we lack it, we shall be doing everything necessary to regain it. So I encourage you, as always, to study and practice my teachings, for they are the basic ingredients of a happy life.

Don't Fear the Gods

A god is an immortal and happy being. This is well-known, but do not believe anything about divine nature other than what is congenial for an eternally happy existence. The gods do exist because we have preconceived notions of them, but they are not like how most people describe them. Most people embellish their notions of the gods with false beliefs. They credit the gods for delivering rewards and punishments because they commend those who share their own ways and condemn those who do not. Rejecting the popular myths does not make one impious; preaching them is what demonstrates impiety.

Don't Fear Death

Death is no concern to us. All things good and bad are experienced through sensation, but sensation ceases at death. So death is nothing to us, and to know this makes a mortal life happy. Life is not improved by adding infinite time; removing the desire for immortality is what's required. There is no reason why one who is convinced that there is nothing to fear at death should fear anything about it during life. And whoever says that he dreads death not because it's painful to experience, but only because it's painful to contemplate, is foolish. It is pointless to agonize over something that brings no trouble when it arrives. So death, the most dreaded of evils, is nothing to us, because when we exist, death is not present, and when death is present, we do not exist. It neither concerns the living nor the dead, since death does not exist for the living, and the dead no longer exist.

Most people, however, either dread death as the greatest of suffering or long for it as a relief from suffering. One who is wise neither renounces life nor fears not living. Life does not offend him, nor does he suppose that not living is any kind of suffering. For just as he would not choose the greatest amount of food over what is most delicious, so too he does not seek the longest possible life, but rather the happiest. And he who advises the young man to live well and the old man to die well is also foolish – not only because it's desirable to live, but because the art of living well and the art of dying well are the same. And he was still more wrong who said it would be better to have never been born, but that "Once born, be quick to pass through the gates of Hades!" (Theognis) If he was being serious, why wasn't he himself quick to end his life? Certainly the means were available if this was what he really wanted to do. But if he was not serious, then we have even less reason to believe him.

Future days are neither wholly ours, nor wholly not ours. We must neither depend on them as sure to come nor despair that we won't live to see them.

Master Your Desires

Among desires, some are natural and some are vain. Of those that are natural, some are necessary and some unnecessary. Of those that are necessary, some are necessary for happiness, some for health, and some for life itself. A clear recognition of desires enables one to base every choice and avoidance upon whether it secures or upsets bodily comfort and peace of mind—the goal of a happy life.

Everything we do is for the sake of freedom from pain and anxiety. Once this is achieved, the storms in the soul are stilled. Nothing else and nothing more are needed to perfect the well-being of the body and soul. It is when we feel pain that we must seek relief, which is pleasure. And when we no longer feel pain, we have all the pleasure we need.

Pleasure, we declare, is the beginning and end of the happy life. We are endowed by nature to recognize pleasure as the greatest good. Every choice and avoidance we make is guided by pleasure as our standard for judging the goodness of everything.

Although pleasure is the greatest good, not every pleasure is worth choosing. We may instead avoid certain pleasures when, by doing so, we avoid greater pains. We may also choose to accept pain if, by doing so, it results in greater pleasure. So while every pleasure is naturally good, not every pleasure should be chosen. Likewise, every pain is naturally evil, but not every pain is to be avoided. Only upon considering all consequences should we decide. Thus, sometimes we might regard the good as evil, and conversely: the evil as good.

We regard self-sufficiency as a great virtue—not so that we may only enjoy a few things, but so that we may be satisfied with a few things if those are all we have. We are firmly convinced that those who least yearn for luxury enjoy it most, and that while natural desires are easily fulfilled, vain desires are insatiable. Plain meals offer the same pleasure as luxurious fare, so long as the pain of hunger is removed. Bread and water offer the greatest pleasure for those in need of them. Accustoming oneself to a simple lifestyle is healthy and it doesn't sap our motivation to perform the necessary tasks of life. Doing without luxuries for long intervals allows us to better appreciate them and keeps us fearless against changes of fortune.

When we say that pleasure is the goal, we do not mean the pleasure of debauchery or sensuality. Despite whatever may be said by those who misunderstand, disagree with, or deliberately slander our teachings, the goal we do seek is this: freedom from pain in the body and freedom from turmoil in the soul. For it is not continuous drinking and revelry, the sexual enjoyment of women and boys, or feasting upon fish and fancy cuisine which result in a happy life. Sober reasoning is what is needed, which decides every choice and avoidance and liberates us from the false beliefs which are the greatest source of anxiety.

Live Wisely

The greatest virtue and the basis for all virtues is prudence. Prudence, the art of practical wisdom, is something even more valuable than philosophy, because all other virtues spring from it. It teaches us that it is not possible to live pleasurably unless one also lives prudently, honorably, and justly; nor is it possible to live prudently, honestly, and justly without living pleasurably. For the virtues are inseparable from a happy life, and living happily is inseparable from the virtues.

Who could conceivably be better off than one who is wise? No one could be more content than one who simply reveres the gods, who is utterly unafraid of death, and who has discovered the natural goal of life. He understands that pleasure, the greatest good, is easily supplied to absolute fullness, while pain, the greatest evil, lasts only a moment when intense and is easily tolerated when prolonged.

Some believe that everything is ruled by fate, but we should dismiss this. One who is wise knows that the greater power of decision lies within oneself. He understands that while some things are indeed caused by fate, other things happen by chance or by choice. He sees that fate is irreproachable and chance unreliable, but choices deserve either praise or blame because what is decided by choice is not subject to any external power. One would be better off believing in the myths about the gods than to be enslaved by the determinism proclaimed by certain physicists. At least the myths offer hope of winning divine favors through prayer, but fate can never be appealed.

Some believe that chance is a god, but we should dismiss this also. One who is wise knows the gods do not act randomly. He does not believe that everything is randomly caused. Nor does he believe, in cases when they are, that chance is doling out good and evil with the intent of making human lives happy or unhappy. He would actually prefer to suffer setbacks while acting wisely than to have miraculous luck while acting foolishly; for it would be better that well-planned actions should perchance fail than ill-planned actions should perchance succeed.

Conclusion

Practice these teachings daily and nightly. Study them on your own or in the company of a like-minded friend, and you shall not be disturbed while awake or asleep. You shall live like a god among men, because one whose life is fortified by immortal blessings in no way resembles a mortal being.

EPICURUS

Principal Doctrines

Translated by Erik Anderson

The four-fold cure for anxiety: Don't fear the gods; Nor death; Goods are easy to obtain; Evils are easy to endure.

1. A blessed and imperishable being neither has trouble itself nor does it cause trouble for anyone else; therefore, it does not experience feelings of anger or indebtedness, for such feelings signify weakness.

2. Death is nothing to us, because a body that has been dispersed into elements experiences no sensations, and the absence of sensation is nothing to us. death

3. Pleasure reaches its maximum limit at the removal of all sources of pain. When such pleasure is present, for as long as it lasts, there is no cause of physical nor mental pain present – nor of both together.

4. Continuous physical pain does not last long. Instead, extreme pain lasts only a very short time, and even less-extreme pain does not last for many days at once. Even protracted diseases allow periods of physical comfort that exceed feelings of pain.

Pleasure and virtue are interdependent

5. It is impossible to live pleasantly without living wisely and honorably and justly, and it is impossible to live wisely and honorably and justly without living pleasantly. Whenever any one of these is lacking (when, for instance, one is not able to live wisely, though he lives honorably and justly) it is impossible for him to live a pleasant life.

Social and financial status have recognizable costs and benefits

6. That natural benefit of kingship and high office is (and only is) the degree to which they provide security from other men.

7. Some seek fame and status, thinking that they could thereby protect themselves against other men. If their lives really are secure, then they have attained a natural good; if, however, they're insecure, they still lack what they originally sought by natural instinct.

8. No pleasure is a bad thing in itself, but some pleasures are only obtainable at the cost of excessive troubles.

Through the study of Nature, we discern the limits of things

9. If every pleasure could be prolonged to endure in both body or mind, pleasures would never differ from one another.

10. If the things which debauched men find pleasurable put an end to all fears (such as concerns about the heavenly bodies, death, and pain) and if they revealed how we ought to limit our desires, we would have no reason to reproach them, for they would be fulfilled with pleasures from every source while experiencing no pain, neither in mind nor body, which is the chief evil of life.

11. If we were never troubled by how phenomena in the sky or death might concern us, or by our failures to grasp the limits of pains and desires, we would have no need to study nature.

12. One cannot rid himself of his primal fears if he does not understand the nature of the universe but instead suspects the truth of some mythical story. So without the study of nature, there can be no enjoyment of pure pleasure.

13. One gains nothing by securing protection from other men if he still has apprehensions about things above and beneath the earth and throughout the infinite universe.

Unlike social and financial status, which are unlimited,
peace of mind can be wholly secured

14. Supreme power and great wealth may, to some degree, protect us from other men; but security in general depends upon peace of mind and social detachment.

15. Natural wealth is both limited and easily obtained, but vanity is insatiable.

16. Chance has little effect upon the wise man, for his greatest and highest interests are directed by reason throughout the course of life.

17. The just man is the freest of anyone from anxiety; but the unjust man is perpetually haunted by it.

18. When pain arising from need has been removed, bodily pleasure cannot increase—it merely varies. But the limit of mental pleasure is reached after we reflect upon these bodily pleasures and the related mental distress prior to fulfillment.

19. Infinite and finite time afford equal pleasure, if one measures its limits by reason.

20. Bodily pleasure seems unlimited, and to provide it would require unlimited time. But the mind, recognizing the limits of the body, and dismissing apprehensions about eternity, furnishes a complete and optimal life, so we no longer have any need of unlimited time. Nevertheless, the mind does not shun pleasure; moreover, when the end of life approaches, it does not feel remorse, as if it fell short in any way from living the best life possible.

21. He who understands the limits of life knows that things which remove pain arising from need are easy to obtain, and furnish a complete and optimal life. Thus he no longer needs things that are troublesome to attain.

Happiness depends on foresight and friendship

22. We must consider the ultimate goal to be real, and reconcile our opinions with sensory experience; otherwise, life will be full of confusion and disturbance.

23. If you argue against all your sensations, you will then have no criterion to declare any of them false.

24. If you arbitrarily reject any one sensory experience and fail to differentiate between an opinion awaiting confirmation and what is already perceived by the senses, feelings, and every intuitive faculty of mind, you will impute trouble to all other sensory experiences, thereby rejecting every criterion. And if you concurrently affirm what awaits confirmation as well as actual sensory experience, you will still blunder, because you will foster equal reasons to doubt the truth and falsehood of everything.

25. If you do not reconcile your behavior with the goal of nature, but instead use some other criterion in matters of choice and avoidance, then there will be a conflict between theory and practice.

26. All desires which create no pain when unfulfilled are not necessary; such desires may easily be dispelled when they are seen as difficult to fulfill or likely to produce harm.

27. Of all things that wisdom provides for living one's entire life in happiness, the greatest by far is the possession of friendship.

28. The same conviction which inspires confidence that nothing terrible lasts forever, or even for long, also enables us to see that in the midst of life's limited evils, nothing enhances our security so much as friendship.

29. Among desires some are natural and necessary, some natural but not necessary, and others neither natural nor necessary, but due to baseless opinion.

30. Those natural desires which create no pain when unfulfilled, though pursued with an intense effort, are also due to baseless opinion; and if they are not dispelled, it is not because of their own nature, but because of human vanity.

The benefits of natural justice are far-reaching

31. Natural justice is the advantage conferred by mutual agreements not to inflict nor allow harm.

32. For all living creatures incapable of making agreements not to harm one another, nothing is ever just or unjust; and so it is likewise for all tribes of men which have been unable or unwilling to make such agreements.

33. Absolute justice does not exist. There are only mutual agreements among men, made at various times and places, not to inflict nor allow harm.

34. Injustice is not an evil in itself, but only in consequence of the accompanying fear of being unable to escape those assigned to punish unjust acts.

35. It is not possible for one who secretly violates the provisos of the agreement not to inflict nor allow harm to be confident that he won't get caught, even if he has gotten away with it a thousand times before. For up until the time of death, there is no certainty that he will indeed escape detection.

36. Justice is essentially the same for all peoples insofar as it benefits human interaction. But the details of how justice is applied in particular countries or circumstances may vary.

37. Among actions legally recognized as just, that which is confirmed by experience as mutually beneficial has the virtue of justice, whether it is the same for all peoples or not. But if a law is made which results in no such advantage, then it no longer carries the hallmark of justice. And if something that used to be mutually beneficial changes, though for some time it conformed to our concept of justice, it is still true that it really was just during that time—at least for those who do not fret about technicalities and instead prefer to examine and judge each case for themselves.

38. Where, without any change in circumstances, things held to be just by law are revealed to be in conflict with the essence of justice, such laws were never really just. But wherever or whenever laws have ceased to be advantageous because of a change in circumstances, in that case or time the

laws were just when they benefitted human interaction, and ceased to be just only when they were no longer beneficial.

Happiness can be secured in all circumstances

39. He who desires to live in tranquility with nothing to fear from other men ought to make friends. Those of whom he cannot make friends, he should at least avoid rendering enemies; and if that is not in his power, he should, as much as possible, avoid all dealings with them, and keep them aloof, insofar as it is in his interest to do so.

40. The happiest men are those who enjoy the condition of having nothing to fear from those who surround them. Such men live among one another most agreeably, having the firmest grounds for confidence in one another, enjoying the benefits of friendship in all their fullness, and they do not mourn a friend who dies before they do, as if there was a need for pity.

EPICTETUS
Enchiridion

Translated by Elizabeth Carter

Some things are in our control and others not. Things in our control are opinion, pursuit, desire, aversion, and, in a word, whatever are our own actions. Things not in our control are body, property, reputation, command, and, in one word, whatever are not our own actions.

1. The things in our control are by nature free, unrestrained, unhindered; but those not in our control are weak, slavish, restrained, belonging to others. Remember, then, that if you suppose that things which are slavish by nature are also free, and that what belongs to others is your own, then you will be hindered. You will lament, you will be disturbed, and you will find fault both with gods and men. But if you suppose that only to be your own which is your own, and what belongs to others such as it really is, then no one will ever compel you or restrain you. Further, you will find fault with no one or accuse no one. You will do nothing against your will. No one will hurt you, you will have no enemies, and you not be harmed.

Aiming therefore at such great things, remember that you must not allow yourself to be carried, even with a slight tendency, towards the attainment of lesser things. Instead, you must entirely quit some things and for the present postpone the rest. But if you would both have these great things, along with power and riches, then you will not gain even the latter, because you aim at the former too: but you will absolutely fail of the former, by which alone happiness and freedom are achieved.

Work, therefore to be able to say to every harsh appearance, "You are but an appearance, and not absolutely the thing you appear to be." And then examine it by those rules which you have, and first, and chiefly, by this: whether it concerns the things which are in our own control, or those which are not; and, if it concerns anything not in our control, be prepared to say that it is nothing to you.

2. Remember that following desire promises the attainment of that of which you are desirous; and aversion promises the avoiding that to which you are averse. However, he who fails to obtain the object of his desire is disappointed, and he who incurs the object of his aversion wretched. If, then, you confine your aversion to those objects only which are contrary to the natural use of your faculties, which you have in your own control, you will never incur anything to which you are averse. But if you are averse to sickness, or death, or poverty, you will be wretched. Remove aversion, then, from all things that are not in our control, and transfer it to things contrary to the nature of what is in our control. But, for the present, totally suppress desire: for, if you desire any of the things which are not in your own control, you must necessarily be disappointed; and of those which are, and which it would be laudable to desire, nothing is yet in your possession. Use only the appropriate actions of pursuit and avoidance; and even these lightly, and with gentleness and reservation.

3. With regard to whatever objects give you delight, are useful, or are deeply loved, remember to tell yourself of what general nature they are, beginning from the most insignificant things. If, for example, you are fond of a specific ceramic cup, remind yourself that it is only ceramic cups in general of which you are fond. Then, if it breaks, you will not be disturbed. If you kiss your child, or your wife, say that you only kiss things which are human, and thus you will not be disturbed if either of them dies.

4. When you are going about any action, remind yourself what nature the action is. If you are going to bathe, picture to yourself the things which usually happen in the bath: some people splash the water, some push, some use abusive language, and others steal. Thus you will more safely go about this action if you say to yourself, "I will now go bathe, and keep my own mind in a state conformable to nature." And in the same manner with regard to every other action. For thus, if any hindrance arises in bathing, you will have it ready to say, "It was not only to bathe that I desired, but to keep my mind in a state conformable to nature; and I will not keep it if I am bothered at things that happen.

5. Men are disturbed, not by things, but by the principles and notions which they form concerning things. Death, for instance, is not terrible, else it would have appeared so to Socrates. But the

terror consists in our notion of death that it is terrible. When therefore we are hindered, or disturbed, or grieved, let us never attribute it to others, but to ourselves; that is, to our own principles. An uninstructed person will lay the fault of his own bad condition upon others. Someone just starting instruction will lay the fault on himself. Some who is perfectly instructed will place blame neither on others nor on himself.

6. Don't be prideful with any excellence that is not your own. If a horse should be prideful and say, " I am handsome," it would be supportable. But when you are prideful, and say, " I have a handsome horse," know that you are proud of what is, in fact, only the good of the horse. What, then, is your own? Only your reaction to the appearances of things. Thus, when you behave conformably to nature in reaction to how things appear, you will be proud with reason; for you will take pride in some good of your own.

7. Consider when, on a voyage, your ship is anchored; if you go on shore to get water you may along the way amuse yourself with picking up a shellfish, or an onion. However, your thoughts and continual attention ought to be bent towards the ship, waiting for the captain to call on board; you must then immediately leave all these things, otherwise you will be thrown into the ship, bound neck and feet like a sheep. So it is with life. If, instead of an onion or a shellfish, you are given a wife or child, that is fine. But if the captain calls, you must run to the ship, leaving them, and regarding none of them. But if you are old, never go far from the ship: lest, when you are called, you should be unable to come in time.

8. Don't demand that things happen as you wish, but wish that they happen as they do happen, and you will go on well.

9. Sickness is a hindrance to the body, but not to your ability to choose, unless that is your choice. Lameness is a hindrance to the leg, but not to your ability to choose. Say this to yourself with regard to everything that happens, then you will see such obstacles as hindrances to something else, but not to yourself.

10. With every accident, ask yourself what abilities you have for making a proper use of it. If you see an attractive person, you will find that self-restraint is the ability you have against your desire. If you are in pain, you will find fortitude. If you hear unpleasant language, you will find patience. And thus habituated, the appearances of things will not hurry you away along with them.

11. Never say of anything, "I have lost it"; but, "I have returned it." Is your child dead? It is returned. Is your wife dead? She is returned. Is your estate taken away? Well, and is not that likewise returned? "But he who took it away is a bad man." What difference is it to you who the giver assigns to take it back? While he gives it to you to possess, take care of it; but don't view it as your own, just as travelers view a hotel.

12. If you want to improve, reject such reasonings as these: "If I neglect my affairs, I'll have no income; if I don't correct my servant, he will be bad." For it is better to die with hunger, exempt from grief and fear, than to live in affluence with perturbation; and it is better your servant should be bad, than you unhappy.

Begin therefore from little things. Is a little oil spilt? A little wine stolen? Say to yourself, "This is the price paid for apathy, for tranquillity, and nothing is to be had for nothing." When you call your servant, it is possible that he may not come; or, if he does, he may not do what you want. But he is by no means of such importance that it should be in his power to give you any disturbance.

13. If you want to improve, be content to be thought foolish and stupid with regard to external things. Don't wish to be thought to know anything; and even if you appear to be somebody important to others, distrust yourself. For, it is difficult to both keep your faculty of choice in a state con-

formable to nature, and at the same time acquire external things. But while you are careful about the one, you must of necessity neglect the other.

14. If you wish your children, and your wife, and your friends to live for ever, you are stupid; for you wish to be in control of things which you cannot, you wish for things that belong to others to be your own. So likewise, if you wish your servant to be without fault, you are a fool; for you wish vice not to be vice," but something else. But, if you wish to have your desires undisappointed, this is in your own control. Exercise, therefore, what is in your control. He is the master of every other person who is able to confer or remove whatever that person wishes either to have or to avoid. Whoever, then, would be free, let him wish nothing, let him decline nothing, which depends on others else he must necessarily be a slave.

15. Remember that you must behave in life as at a dinner party. Is anything brought around to you? Put out your hand and take your share with moderation. Does it pass by you? Don't stop it. Is it not yet come? Don't stretch your desire towards it, but wait till it reaches you. Do this with regard to children, to a wife, to public posts, to riches, and you will eventually be a worthy partner of the feasts of the gods. And if you don't even take the things which are set before you, but are able even to reject them, then you will not only be a partner at the feasts of the gods, but also of their empire. For, by doing this, Diogenes, Heraclitus and others like them, deservedly became, and were called, divine.

16. When you see anyone weeping in grief because his son has gone abroad, or is dead, or because he has suffered in his affairs, be careful that the appearance may not misdirect you. Instead, distinguish within your own mind, and be prepared to say, "It's not the accident that distresses this person., because it doesn't distress another person; it is the judgment which he makes about it." As far as words go, however, don't reduce yourself to his level, and certainly do not moan with him. Do not moan inwardly either.

17. Remember that you are an actor in a drama, of such a kind as the author pleases to make it. If short, of a short one; if long, of a long one. If it is his pleasure you should act a poor man, a cripple, a governor, or a private person, see that you act it naturally. For this is your business, to act well the character assigned you; to choose it is another's.

18. When a raven happens to croak unluckily, don't allow the appearance hurry you away with it, but immediately make the distinction to yourself, and say, "None of these things are foretold to me; but either to my paltry body, or property, or reputation, or children, or wife. But to me all omens are lucky, if I will. For whichever of these things happens, it is in my control to derive advantage from it."

19. You may be unconquerable, if you enter into no combat in which it is not in your own control to conquer. When, therefore, you see anyone eminent in honors, or power, or in high esteem on any other account, take heed not to be hurried away with the appearance, and to pronounce him happy; for, if the essence of good consists in things in our own control, there will be no room for envy or emulation. But, for your part, don't wish to be a general, or a senator, or a consul, but to be free; and the only way to this is a contempt of things not in our own control.

20. Remember, that not he who gives ill language or a blow insults, but the principle which represents these things as insulting. When, therefore, anyone provokes you, be assured that it is your own opinion which provokes you. Try, therefore, in the first place, not to be hurried away with the appearance. For if you once gain time and respite, you will more easily command yourself.

21. Let death and exile, and all other things which appear terrible be daily before your eyes, but chiefly death, and you win never entertain any abject thought, nor too eagerly covet anything.

22. If you have an earnest desire of attaining to philosophy, prepare yourself from the very first to be laughed at, to be sneered by the multitude, to hear them say,." He is returned to us a philosopher all at once," and " Whence this supercilious look?" Now, for your part, don't have a supercilious look indeed; but keep steadily to those things which appear best to you as one appointed by God to this station. For remember that, if you adhere to the same point, those very persons who at first ridiculed will afterwards admire you. But if you are conquered by them, you will incur a double ridicule.

23. If you ever happen to turn your attention to externals, so as to wish to please anyone, be assured that you have ruined your scheme of life. Be contented, then, in everything with being a philosopher; and, if you wish to be thought so likewise by anyone, appear so to yourself, and it will suffice you.

24. Don't allow such considerations as these distress you. "I will live in dishonor, and be nobody anywhere." For, if dishonor is an evil, you can no more be involved in any evil by the means of another, than be engaged in anything base. Is it any business of yours, then, to get power, or to be admitted to an entertainment? By no means. How, then, after all, is this a dishonor? And how is it true that you will be nobody anywhere, when you ought to be somebody in those things only which are in your own control, in which you may be of the greatest consequence? "But my friends will be unassisted." — What do you mean by unassisted? They will not have money from you, nor will you make them Roman citizens. Who told you, then, that these are among the things in our own control, and not the affair of others? And who can give to another the things which he has not himself? "Well, but get them, then, that we too may have a share."

If I can get them with the preservation of my own honor and fidelity and greatness of mind, show me the way and I will get them; but if you require me to lose my own proper good that you may gain what is not good, consider how inequitable and foolish you are. Besides, which would you rather have, a sum of money, or a friend of fidelity and honor? Rather assist me, then, to gain this character than require me to do those things by which I may lose it. Well, but my country, say you, as far as depends on me, will be unassisted. Here again, what assistance is this you mean? "It will not have porticoes nor baths of your providing." And what signifies that? Why, neither does a smith provide it with shoes, or a shoemaker with arms. It is enough if everyone fully performs his own proper business. And were you to supply it with another citizen of honor and fidelity, would not he be of use to it? Yes. Therefore neither are you yourself useless to it. "What place, then, say you, will I hold in the state?" Whatever you can hold with the preservation of your fidelity and honor. But if, by desiring to be useful to that, you lose these, of what use can you be to your country when you are become faithless and void of shame.

25. Is anyone preferred before you at an entertainment, or in a compliment, or in being admitted to a consultation? If these things are good, you ought to be glad that he has gotten them; and if they are evil, don't be grieved that you have not gotten them. And remember that you cannot, without using the same means [which others do] to acquire things not in our own control, expect to be thought worthy of an equal share of them. For how can he who does not frequent the door of any [great] man, does not attend him, does not praise him, have an equal share with him who does? You are unjust, then, and insatiable, if you are unwilling to pay the price for which these things are sold, and would have them for nothing.

For how much is lettuce sold? Fifty cents, for instance. If another, then, paying fifty cents, takes the lettuce, and you, not paying it, go without them, don't imagine that he has gained any advantage over you. For as he has the lettuce, so you have the fifty cents which you did not give. So, in the present case, you have not been invited to such a person's entertainment, because you have not paid him the price for which a supper is sold. It is sold for praise; it is sold for attendance. Give him then the value, if it is for your advantage. But if you would, at the same time, not pay the one and yet receive the other, you are insatiable, and a blockhead. Have you nothing, then, instead of the supper? Yes, indeed, you have: the not praising him, whom you don't like to praise; the not bearing with his behavior at coming in.

26. The will of nature may be learned from those things in which we don't distinguish from each other. For example, when our neighbor's boy breaks a cup, or the like, we are presently ready to say, "These things will happen." Be assured, then, that when your own cup likewise is broken, you ought to be affected just as when another's cup was broken. Apply this in like manner to greater things. Is the child or wife of another dead? There is no one who would not say, "This is a human accident." but if anyone's own child happens to die, it is presently, "Alas I how wretched am I!" But it should be remembered how we are affected in hearing the same thing concerning others.

27. As a mark is not set up for the sake of missing the aim, so neither does the nature of evil exist in the world.

28. If a person gave your body to any stranger he met on his way, you would certainly be angry. And do you feel no shame in handing over your own mind to be confused and mystified by anyone who happens to verbally attack you?

29. In every affair consider what precedes and follows, and then undertake it. Otherwise you will begin with spirit; but not having thought of the consequences, when some of them appear you will shamefully desist. "I would conquer at the Olympic games." But consider what precedes and follows, and then, if it is for your advantage, engage in the affair. You must conform to rules, submit to a diet, refrain from dainties; exercise your body, whether you choose it or not, at a stated hour, in heat and cold; you must drink no cold water, nor sometimes even wine. In a word, you must give yourself up to your master, as to a physician. Then, in the combat, you may be thrown into a ditch, dislocate your arm, turn your ankle, swallow dust, be whipped, and, after all, lose the victory. When you have evaluated all this, if your inclination still holds, then go to war. Otherwise, take notice, you will behave like children who sometimes play like wrestlers, sometimes gladiators, sometimes blow a trumpet, and sometimes act a tragedy when they have seen and admired these shows. Thus you too will be at one time a wrestler, at another a gladiator, now a philosopher, then an orator; but with your whole soul, nothing at all. Like an ape, you mimic all you see, and one thing after another is sure to please you, but is out of favor as soon as it becomes familiar. For you have never entered upon anything considerately, nor after having viewed the whole matter on all sides, or made any scrutiny into it, but rashly, and with a cold inclination.

Thus some, when they have seen a philosopher and heard a man speaking like Euphrates (though, indeed, who can speak like him?), have a mind to be philosophers too. Consider first, man, what the matter is, and what your own nature is able to bear. If you would be a wrestler, consider your shoulders, your back, your thighs; for different persons are made for different things. Do you think that you can act as you do, and be a philosopher? That you can eat and drink, and be angry and discontented as you are now? You must watch, you must labor, you must get the better of certain appetites, must quit your acquaintance, be despised by your servant, be laughed at by those you meet; come off worse than others in everything, in magistracies, in honors, in courts of judicature. When you have considered all these things round, approach, if you please; if, by parting with them, you have a mind to purchase apathy, freedom, and tranquillity. If not, don't come here; don't, like children, be one while a philosopher, then a publican, then an orator, and then one of Caesar's officers. These things are not consistent. You must be one man, either good or bad. You must cultivate either your own ruling faculty or externals, and apply yourself either to things within or without you; that is, be either a philosopher, or one of the vulgar.

30. Duties are universally measured by relations. Is anyone a father? If so, it is implied that the children should take care of him, submit to him in everything, patiently listen to his reproaches, his correction. But he is a bad father. Is you naturally entitled, then, to a good father? No, only to a father. Is a brother unjust? Well, keep your own situation towards him. Consider not what he does, but what you are to do to keep your own faculty of choice in a state conformable to nature. For another will not hurt you unless you please. You will then be hurt when you think you are hurt. In this manner, there-

fore, you will find, from the idea of a neighbor, a citizen, a general, the corresponding duties if you accustom yourself to contemplate the several relations.

31. Be assured that the essential property of piety towards the gods is to form right opinions concerning them, as existing "I and as governing the universe with goodness and justice. And fix yourself in this resolution, to obey them, and yield to them, and willingly follow them in all events, as produced by the most perfect understanding. For thus you will never find fault with the gods, nor accuse them as neglecting you. And it is not possible for this to be effected any other way than by withdrawing yourself from things not in our own control, and placing good or evil in those only which are. For if you suppose any of the things not in our own control to be either good or evil, when you are disappointed of what you wish, or incur what you would avoid, you must necessarily find fault with and blame the authors. For every animal is naturally formed to fly and abhor things that appear hurtful, and the causes of them; and to pursue and admire those which appear beneficial, and the causes of them.

It is impractical, then, that one who supposes himself to be hurt should be happy about the person who, he thinks, hurts him, just as it is impossible to be happy about the hurt itself. Hence, also, a father is reviled by a son, when he does not impart to him the things which he takes to be good; and the supposing empire to be a good made Polynices and Eteocles mutually enemies. On this account the husbandman, the sailor, the merchant, on this account those who lose wives and children, revile the gods. For where interest is, there too is piety placed. So that, whoever is careful to regulate his desires and aversions as he ought, is, by the very same means, careful of piety likewise. But it is also incumbent on everyone to offer libations and sacrifices and first fruits, conformably to the customs of his country, with purity, and not in a slovenly manner, nor negligently, nor sparingly, nor beyond his ability.

32. When you have recourse to divination, remember that you know not what the event will be, and you come to learn it of the diviner; but of what nature it is you know before you come, at least if you are a philosopher. For if it is among the things not in our own control, it can by no means be either good or evil. Don't, therefore, bring either desire or aversion with you to the diviner (else you will approach him trembling), but first acquire a distinct knowledge that every event is indifferent and nothing to you., of whatever sort it may be, for it will be in your power to make a right use of it, and this no one can hinder; then come with confidence to the gods, as your counselors, and afterwards, when any counsel is given you, remember what counselors you have assumed, and whose advice you will neglect if you disobey.

Come to divination, as Socrates prescribed, in cases of which the whole consideration relates to the event, and in which no opportunities are afforded by reason, or any other art, to discover the thing proposed to be learned. When, therefore, it is our duty to share the danger of a friend or of our country, we ought not to consult the oracle whether we will share it with them or not. For, though the diviner should forewarn you that the victims are unfavorable, this means no more than that either death or mutilation or exile is portended. But we have reason within us, and it directs, even with these hazards, to the greater diviner, the Pythian god, who cast out of the temple the person who gave no assistance to his friend while another was murdering him.

33. Immediately prescribe some character and form of conduce to yourself, which you may keep both alone and in company.

Be for the most part silent, or speak merely what is necessary, and in few words. We may, however, enter, though sparingly, into discourse sometimes when occasion calls for it, but not on any of the common subjects, of gladiators, or horse races, or athletic champions, or feasts, the vulgar topics of conversation; but principally not of men, so as either to blame, or praise, or make comparisons. If you are able, then, by your own conversation bring over that of your company to proper subjects; but, if you happen to be taken among strangers, be silent. Don't allow your laughter be much, nor on many occasions, nor profuse. Avoid swearing, if possible, altogether; if not, as far as you are able. Avoid public and vulgar entertainments; but, if ever an occasion calls you to them, keep your attention upon the stretch, that you may not imperceptibly slide into vulgar manners. For be assured that if a person be ever so sound himself, yet, if his companion be infected, he who converses with him will be infected likewise.

Provide things relating to the body no further than mere use; as meat, drink, clothing, house, family. But strike off and reject everything relating to show and delicacy. As far as possible, before marriage, keep yourself pure from familiarities with women, and, if you indulge them, let it be lawfully. But don't therefore be troublesome and full of reproofs to those who use these liberties, nor frequently boast that you yourself don't. If anyone tells you that such a person speaks ill of you, don't make excuses about what is said of you, but answer: "He does not know my other faults, else he would not have mentioned only these."

It is not necessary for you to appear often at public spectacles; but if ever there is a proper occasion for you to be there, don't appear more solicitous for anyone than for yourself; that is, wish things to be only just as they are, and him only to conquer who is the conqueror, for thus you will meet with no hindrance. But abstain entirely from declamations and derision and violent emotions. And when you come away, don't discourse a great deal on what has passed, and what does not contribute to your own amendment. For it would appear by such discourse that you were immoderately struck with the show.

Go not of your own accord to the rehearsals of any [theatrical productions], nor appear at them readily. But, if you do appear, keep your gravity and sedateness, and at the same time avoid being morose.

When you are going to confer with anyone, and particularly of those in a superior station, represent to yourself how Socrates or Zeno would behave in such a case, and you will not be at a loss to make a proper use of whatever may occur.

When you are going to any of the people in power, represent to yourself that you will not find him at home; that you will not be admitted; that the doors will not be opened to you; that he will take no notice of you. If, with all this, it is your duty to go, bear what happens, and never say to yourself, "It was not worth so much." For this is vulgar, and like a man dazed by external things.

In parties of conversation, avoid a frequent and excessive mention of your own actions and dangers. For, however agreeable it may be to yourself to mention the risks you have run, it is not equally agreeable to others to hear your adventures. Avoid, likewise, an endeavor to excite laughter. For this is a slippery point, which may throw you into vulgar manners, and, besides, may be apt to lessen you in the esteem of your acquaintance. Approaches to indecent discourse are likewise dangerous. Whenever, therefore, anything of this sort happens, if there be a proper opportunity, rebuke him who makes advances that way; or, at least, by silence and blushing and a forbidding look, show yourself to be displeased by such talk.

34. If you are struck by the appearance of any promised pleasure, guard yourself against being hurried away by it; but let the affair wait your leisure, and procure yourself some delay. Then bring to your mind both points of time: that in which you will enjoy the pleasure, and that in which you will repent and reproach yourself after you have enjoyed it; and set before you, in opposition to these, how you will be glad and applaud yourself if you abstain. And even though it should appear to you a seasonable gratification, take heed that its enticing, and agreeable and attractive force may not subdue you; but set in opposition to this how much better it is to be conscious of having gained so great a victory.

35. When you do anything from a clear judgment that it ought to be done, never shun the being seen to do it, even though the world should make a wrong supposition about it; for, if you don't act right, shun the action itself; but, if you do, why are you afraid of those who censure you wrongly?

36. As the proposition, "Either it is day or it is night," is extremely proper for a disjunctive argument, but quite improper in a conjunctive one, so, at a feast, to choose the largest share is very suitable to the bodily appetite, but utterly inconsistent with the social spirit of an entertainment. When you eat with another, then, remember not only the value of those things which are set before you to

the body, but the value of that behavior which ought to be observed towards the person who gives the entertainment.

37. If you have assumed any character above your strength, you have both made an ill figure in that and quitted one which you might have supported.

38. When walking, you are careful not to step on a nail or turn your foot; so likewise be careful not to hurt the ruling faculty of your mind. And, if we were to guard against this in every action, we should undertake the action with the greater safety.

39. The body is to everyone the measure of the possessions proper for it, just as the foot is of the shoe. If, therefore, you stop at this, you will keep the measure; but if you move beyond it, you must necessarily be carried forward, as down a cliff; as in the case of a shoe, if you go beyond its fitness to the foot, it comes first to be gilded, then purple, and then studded with jewels. For to that which once exceeds a due measure, there is no bound.

40. Women from fourteen years old are flattered with the title of "mistresses" by the men. Therefore, perceiving that they are regarded only as qualified to give the men pleasure, they begin to adorn themselves, and in that to place ill their hopes. We should, therefore, fix our attention on making them sensible that they are valued for the appearance of decent, modest and discreet behavior.

41. It is a mark of want of genius to spend much time in things relating to the body, as to be long in our exercises, in eating and drinking, and in the discharge of other animal functions. These should be done incidentally and slightly, and our whole attention be engaged in the care of the understanding.

42. When any person harms you, or speaks badly of you, remember that he acts or speaks from a supposition of its being his duty. Now, it is not possible that he should follow what appears right to you, but what appears so to himself. Therefore, if he judges from a wrong appearance, he is the person hurt, since he too is the person deceived. For if anyone should suppose a true proposition to be false, the proposition is not hurt, but he who is deceived about it. Setting out, then, from these principles, you will meekly bear a person who reviles you, for you will say upon every occasion, "It seemed so to him."

43. Everything has two handles, the one by which it may be carried, the other by which it cannot. If your brother acts unjustly, don't lay hold on the action by the handle of his injustice, for by that it cannot be carried; but by the opposite, that he is your brother, that he was brought up with you; and thus you will lay hold on it, as it is to be carried.

44. These reasonings are unconnected: "I am richer than you, therefore I am better"; "I am more eloquent than you, therefore I am better." The connection is rather this: "I am richer than you, therefore my property is greater than yours;" "I am more eloquent than you, therefore my style is better than yours." But you, after all, are neither property nor style.

45. Does anyone bathe in a mighty little time? Don't say that he does it ill, but in a mighty little time. Does anyone drink a great quantity of wine? Don't say that he does ill, but that he drinks a great quantity. For, unless you perfectly understand the principle from which anyone acts, how should you know if he acts ill? Thus you will not run the hazard of assenting to any appearances but such as you fully comprehend.

46. Never call yourself a philosopher, nor talk a great deal among the unlearned about theorems, but act conformably to them. Thus, at an entertainment, don't talk how persons ought to eat, but eat as you ought. For remember that in this manner Socrates also universally avoided all ostentation.

And when persons came to him and desired to be recommended by him to philosophers, he took and recommended them, so well did he bear being overlooked.

So that if ever any talk should happen among the unlearned concerning philosophic theorems, be you, for the most part, silent. For there is great danger in immediately throwing out what you have not digested. And, if anyone tells you that you know nothing, and you are not nettled at it, then you may be sure that you have begun your business. For sheep don't throw up the grass to show the shepherds how much they have eaten; but, inwardly digesting their food, they outwardly produce wool and milk. Thus, therefore, do you likewise not show theorems to the unlearned, but the actions produced by them after they have been digested.

47. When you have brought yourself to supply the necessities of your body at a small price, don't pique yourself upon it; nor, if you drink water, be saying upon every occasion, "I drink water." But first consider how much more sparing and patient of hardship the poor are than we. But if at any time you would inure yourself by exercise to labor, and bearing hard trials, do it for your own sake, and not for the world; don't grasp statues, but, when you are violently thirsty, take a little cold water in your mouth, and spurt it out and tell nobody.

48. The condition and characteristic of a vulgar person, is, that he never expects either benefit or hurt from himself, but from externals. The condition and characteristic of a philosopher is, that he expects all hurt and benefit from himself. The marks of a proficient are, that he censures no one, praises no one, blames no one, accuses no one, says nothing concerning himself as being anybody, or knowing anything: when he is, in any instance, hindered or restrained, he accuses himself; and, if he is praised, he secretly laughs at the person who praises him; and, if he is censured, he makes no defense. But he goes about with the caution of sick or injured people, dreading to move anything that is set right, before it is perfectly fixed. He suppresses all desire in himself; he transfers his aversion to those things only which thwart the proper use of our own faculty of choice; the exertion of his active powers towards anything is very gentle; if he appears stupid or ignorant, he does not care, and, in a word, he watches himself as an enemy, and one in ambush.

49. When anyone shows himself overly confident in ability to understand and interpret the works of Chrysippus, say to yourself, "Unless Chrysippus had written obscurely, this person would have had no subject for his vanity. But what do I desire? To understand nature and follow her. I ask, then, who interprets her, and, finding Chrysippus does, I have recourse to him. I don't understand his writings. I seek, therefore, one to interpret them." So far there is nothing to value myself upon. And when I find an interpreter, what remains is to make use of his instructions. This alone is the valuable thing. But, if I admire nothing but merely the interpretation, what do I become more than a grammarian instead of a philosopher? Except, indeed, that instead of Homer I interpret Chrysippus. When anyone, therefore, desires me to read Chrysippus to him, I rather blush when I cannot show my actions agreeable and consonant to his discourse.

50. Whatever moral rules you have deliberately proposed to yourself. abide by them as they were laws, and as if you would be guilty of impiety by violating any of them. Don't regard what anyone says of you, for this, after all, is no concern of yours. How long, then, will you put off thinking yourself worthy of the highest improvements and follow the distinctions of reason? You have received the philosophical theorems, with which you ought to be familiar, and you have been familiar with them. What other master, then, do you wait for, to throw upon that the delay of reforming yourself? You are no longer a boy, but a grown man. If, therefore, you will be negligent and slothful, and always add procrastination to procrastination, purpose to purpose, and fix day after day in which you will attend to yourself, you will insensibly continue without proficiency, and, living and dying, persevere in being one of the vulgar.

This instant, then, think yourself worthy of living as a man grown up, and a proficient. Let whatever appears to be the best be to you an inviolable law. And if any instance of pain or pleasure, or glory or disgrace, is set before you, remember that now is the combat, now the Olympiad comes on, nor can it be put off. By once being defeated and giving way, proficiency is lost, or by the contrary preserved. Thus Socrates became perfect, improving himself by everything. attending to nothing but reason. And though you are not yet a Socrates, you ought, however, to live as one desirous of becoming a Socrates.

51. The first and most necessary topic in philosophy is that of the use of moral theorems, such as, "We ought not to lie;" the second is that of demonstrations, such as, "What is the origin of our obligation not to lie;" the third gives strength and articulation to the other two, such as, "What is the origin of this is a demonstration." For what is demonstration? What is consequence? What contradiction? What truth? What falsehood? The third topic, then, is necessary on the account of the second, and the second on the account of the first. But the most necessary, and that whereon we ought to rest, is the first. But we act just on the contrary. For we spend all our time on the third topic, and employ all our diligence about that, and entirely neglect the first. Therefore, at the same time that we lie, we are immediately prepared to show how it is demonstrated that lying is not right.

52. Upon all occasions we ought to have these maxims ready at hand:

> Conduct me, Jove, and you, O Destiny,
> Wherever your decrees have fixed my station. (Cleanthes)

> I follow cheerfully; and, did I not,
> Wicked and wretched, I must follow still
> Whoever yields properly to Fate, is deemed
> Wise among men, and knows the laws of heaven. (Euripides)

And this third:

> O Crito, if it thus pleases the gods, thus let it be. Anytus and Melitus may kill me indeed, but hurt me they cannot. (Plato)

RENÉ DESCARTES
Meditations on First Philosophy

Translated by Jonathan Bennett

First Meditation
On What Can Be Called into Doubt

Some years ago I was struck by how many false things I had believed, and by how doubtful was the structure of beliefs that I had based on them. I realized that if I wanted to establish anything in the sciences that was stable and likely to last, I needed—just once in my life—to demolish everything completely and start again from the foundations. It looked like an enormous task, and I decided to wait until I was old enough to be sure that there was nothing to be gained from putting it off any longer. I have now delayed it for so long that I have no excuse for going on planning to do it rather than getting to work. So today I have set all my worries aside and arranged for myself a clear stretch of free time. I am here quite alone, and at last I will devote myself, sincerely and without holding back, to demolishing my opinions.

I can do this without showing that all my beliefs are false, which is probably more than I could ever manage. My reason tells me that as well as withholding assent from propositions that are obviously false, I should also withhold it from ones that are not completely certain and indubitable. So all I need, for the purpose of rejecting all my opinions, is to find in each of them at least some reason for doubt. I can do this without going through them one by one, which would take forever: once the foundations of a building have been undermined, the rest collapses of its own accord; so I will go straight for the basic principles on which all my former beliefs rested.

Whatever I have accepted until now as most true has come to me through my senses. But occasionally I have found that they have deceived me, and it is unwise to trust completely those who have deceived us even once.

Hopeful: Yet although the senses sometimes deceive us about objects that are very small or distant, that doesn't apply to my belief that I am here, sitting by the fire, wearing a winter dressing-gown, holding this piece of paper in my hands, and so on. It seems to be quite impossible to doubt beliefs like these, which come from the senses. Another example: how can I doubt that these hands or this whole body are mine? To doubt such things I would have to liken myself to brain-damaged madmen who are convinced they are kings when really they are paupers, or say they are dressed in purple when they are naked, or that they are pumpkins, or made of glass. Such people are insane, and I would be thought equally mad if I modeled myself on them.

Doubtful (sarcastically): What a brilliant piece of reasoning! As if I were not a man who sleeps at night and often has all the same experiences while asleep as madmen do when awake—indeed sometimes even more improbable ones. Often in my dreams I am convinced of just such familiar events —that I am sitting by the fire in my dressing-gown—when in fact I am lying undressed in bed!

Hopeful: Yet right now my eyes are certainly wide open when I look at this piece of paper; I shake my head and it isn't asleep; when I rub one hand against the other, I do it deliberately and know what I am doing. This wouldn't all happen with such clarity to someone asleep.

Doubtful: Indeed! As if I didn't remember other occasions when I have been tricked by exactly similar thoughts while asleep! As I think about this more carefully, I realize that there is never any reliable way of distinguishing being awake from being asleep. This discovery makes me feel dizzy, which itself reinforces the notion that I may be asleep! Suppose then that I am dreaming—it isn't true that I, with my eyes open, am moving my head and stretching out my hands. Suppose, indeed that I don't even have hands or any body at all. Still, it has to be admitted that the visions that come in sleep are like paintings: they must have been made as copies of real things; so at least these general kinds of things—eyes, head, hands and the body as a whole—must be real and not imaginary.

For even when painters try to depict sirens and satyrs with the most extraordinary bodies, they simply jumble up the limbs of different kinds of real animals, rather than inventing natures that are entirely new. If they do succeed in thinking up something completely fictitious and unreal—not remotely like anything ever seen before—at least the colours used in the picture must be real. Similarly, although these general kinds of things— eyes, head, hands and so on—could be imaginary, there is no denying that certain even simpler and more universal kinds of things are real. These are the elements out of which we make all our mental images of things—the true and also the false ones.

These simpler and more universal kinds include body, and extension; the shape of extended things; their quantity, size and number; the places things can be in, the time through which they can last, and so on.

So it seems reasonable to conclude that physics, astronomy, medicine, and all other sciences dealing with things that have complex structures are doubtful; while arithmetic, geometry and other studies of the simplest and most general things—whether they really exist in nature or not—contain something certain and indubitable. For whether I am awake or asleep, two plus three makes five, and a square has only four sides. It seems impossible to suspect that such obvious truths might be false.

However, I have for many years been sure that there is an all-powerful God who made me to be the sort of creature that I am. How do I know that he hasn't brought it about that there is no earth, no sky, nothing that takes up space, no shape, no size, no place, while making sure that all these things appear to me to exist? Anyway, I sometimes think that others go wrong even when they think they have the most perfect knowledge; so how do I know that I myself don't go wrong every time I add two and three or count the sides of a square? Well, you might say, God would not let me be deceived like that, because he is said to be supremely good. But, I reply, if God's goodness would stop him from letting me be deceived all the time, you would expect it to stop him from allowing me to be deceived even occasionally; yet clearly I sometimes am deceived.

Some people would deny the existence of such a powerful God rather than believe that everything else is uncertain. Let us grant them—for purposes of argument—that there is no God, and theology is fiction. On their view, then, I am a product of fate or chance or a long chain of causes and effects. But the less powerful they make my original cause, the more likely it is that I am so imperfect as to be deceived all the time—because deception and error seem to be imperfections. Having no answer to these arguments, I am driven back to the position that doubts can properly be raised about any of my former beliefs. I don't reach this conclusion in a flippant or casual manner, but on the basis of powerful and well thought-out reasons. So in future, if I want to discover any certainty, I must withhold my assent from these former beliefs just as carefully as I withhold it from obvious falsehoods.

It isn't enough merely to have noticed this, though; I must make an effort to remember it. My old familiar opinions keep coming back, and against my will they capture my belief. It is as though they had a right to a place in my belief-system as a result of long occupation and the law of custom. These habitual opinions of mine are indeed highly probable; although they are in a sense doubtful, as I have shown, it is more reasonable to believe than to deny them.

But if I go on viewing them in that light I shall never get out of the habit of confidently assenting to them. To conquer that habit, therefore, I had better switch right around and pretend (for a while) that these former opinions of mine are utterly false and imaginary. I shall do this until I have something to counterbalance the weight of old opinion, and the distorting influence of habit no longer prevents me from judging correctly. However far I go in my distrustful attitude, no actual harm will come of it, because my project won't affect how I act, but only how I go about acquiring knowledge.

So I shall suppose that some malicious, powerful, cunning demon has done all he can to deceive me—rather than this being done by God, who is supremely good and the source of truth. I shall think that the sky, the air, the earth, colours, shapes, sounds and all external things are merely dreams that the demon has contrived as traps for my judgment. I shall consider myself as having no hands or eyes, or flesh, or blood or senses, but as having falsely believed that I had all these things. I shall stubbornly persist in this train of thought; and even if I can't learn any truth, I shall at least do what I can do, which is to be on my guard against accepting any falsehoods, so that the deceiver—however powerful and cunning he may be—will be unable to affect me in the slightest.

This will be hard work, though, and a kind of laziness pulls me back into my old ways. Like a prisoner who dreams that he is free, starts to suspect that it is merely a dream, and wants to go on dreaming rather than waking up, so I am content to slide back into my old opinions; I fear being shaken out of them because I am afraid that my peaceful sleep may be followed by hard labour when I wake, and that I shall have to struggle not in the light but in the imprisoning darkness of the problems I have raised.

Second Meditation
The Nature of the Human Mind, and How It is Better Known than the Body

Yesterday's meditation raised doubts—ones that are too serious to be ignored—which I can see no way of resolving. I feel like someone who is suddenly dropped into a deep whirlpool that tumbles him around so that he can neither stand on the bottom nor swim to the top. However, I shall force my way up, and try once more to carry out the project that I started on yesterday. I will set aside anything that admits of the slightest doubt, treating it as though I had found it to be outright false; and I will carry on like that until I find something certain, or—at worst—until I become certain that there is no certainty.

Archimedes said that if he had one firm and immovable point he could lift the world ·with a long enough lever·; so I too can hope for great things if I manage to find just one little thing that is solid and certain. I will suppose, then, that everything I see is fictitious. I will believe that my memory tells me nothing but lies. I have no senses. Body, shape, extension, movement and place are illusions. So what remains true? Perhaps just the one fact that nothing is certain!

Hopeful: Still, how do I know that there isn't something— not on that list—about which there is no room for even the slightest doubt? Isn't there a God (call him what you will) who gives me the thoughts I am now having?

Doubtful: But why do I think this, since I might myself be the author of these thoughts?

Hopeful: But then doesn't it follow that I am, at least, something?

Doubtful: This is very confusing, because I have just said that I have no senses and no body, and I am so bound up with a body and with senses that one would think that I can't exist without them. Now that I have convinced myself that there is nothing in the world—no sky, no earth, no minds, no bodies—does it follow that I don't exist either?

Hopeful: No it does not follow; for if I convinced myself of something then I certainly existed.

Doubtful: But there is a supremely powerful and cunning deceiver who deliberately deceives me all the time!

Hopeful: Even then, if he is deceiving me I undoubtedly exist: let him deceive me all he can, he will never bring it about that I am nothing while I think I am something. So after thoroughly thinking the matter through I conclude that this proposition, I am, I exist, must be true whenever I assert it or think it.

But this 'I' that must exist—I still don't properly understand what it is; so I am at risk of confusing it with something else, thereby falling into error in the very item of knowledge that I maintain is the most certain and obvious of all. To get straight about what this 'I' is, I shall go back and think some more about what I believed myself to be before I started this meditation. I will eliminate from those beliefs anything that could be even slightly called into question by the arguments I have been using, which will leave me with only beliefs about myself that are certain and unshakable.

Well, then, what did I think I was? A man. But what is a man? Shall I say 'a rational animal'? No; for then I should have to ask what an animal is, and what rationality is—each question would lead me on to other still harder ones, and this would take more time than I can spare. Let me focus instead on the beliefs that spontaneously and naturally came to me whenever I thought about what I was. The first such belief was that I had a face, hands, arms and the whole structure of bodily parts that corpses also have—I call it the body. The next belief was that I ate and drank, that I moved about, and that I engaged in sense-perception and thinking; these things, I thought, were done by the soul.

If I gave any thought to what this soul was like, I imagined it to be something thin and filmy — like a wind or fire or ether—permeating my more solid parts. I was more sure about the body, though, thinking that I knew exactly what sort of thing it was. If I had tried to put my conception of the body into words, I would have said this:

By a 'body' I understand whatever has a definite shape and position, and can occupy a region of space in such a way as to keep every other body out of it; it can be perceived by touch, sight, hearing, taste or smell, and can be moved in various ways.

I would have added that a body can't start up movements by itself, and can move only through being moved by other things that bump into it. It seemed to me quite out of character for a body to be able to initiate movements, or to able to sense and think, and I was amazed that certain bodies—namely, human ones—could do those things. But now that I am supposing there is a supremely powerful and malicious deceiver who has set out to trick me in every way he can—now what shall I say that I am? Can I now claim to have any of the features that I used to think belong to a body? When I think about them really carefully, I find that they are all open to doubt: I shan't waste time by showing this about each of them separately.

Now, what about the features that I attributed to the soul? Nutrition or movement? Since now I am pretending that I don't have a body, these are mere fictions. Sense-perception? One needs a body in order to perceive; and, besides, when dreaming I have seemed to perceive through the senses many things that I later realized I had not perceived in that way. Thinking? At last I have discovered it—thought! This is the one thing that can't be separated from me. I am, I exist—that is certain.

But for how long? For as long as I am thinking. But perhaps no longer than that; for it might be that if I stopped thinking I would stop existing; and I have to treat that possibility as though it were actual, because my present policy is to reject everything that isn't necessarily true. Strictly speaking, then, I am simply a thing that thinks—a mind, or soul, or intellect, or reason, these being words whose meaning I have only just come to know. Still, I am a real, existing thing. What kind of a thing? I have answered that: a thinking thing.

What else am I? I will use my imagination to see if I am anything more. I am not that structure of limbs and organs that is called a human body; nor am I a thin vapour that permeates the limbs—a wind, fire, air, breath, or whatever I imagine; for I have supposed all these things to be nothing because I have supposed all bodies to be nothing. Even if I go on supposing them to be nothing, I am still something. But these things that I suppose to be nothing because they are unknown to me—might they not in fact be identical with the I of which I am aware? I don't know; and just now I shan't discuss the matter, because I can form opinions only about things that I know. I know that I exist, and I am asking: what is this I that I know? My knowledge of it can't depend on things of whose existence I am still unaware; so it can't depend on anything that I invent in my imagination.

The word 'invent' points to what is wrong with relying on my imagination in this matter: if I used imagination to show that I was something or other, that would be mere invention, mere story-telling; for imagining is simply contemplating the shape or image of a bodily thing. That makes imagination suspect, for while I know for sure that I exist, I know that everything relating to the nature of body including imagination could be mere dreams; so it would be silly for me to say 'I will use my imagination to get a clearer understanding of what I am'—as silly, indeed, as to say 'I am now awake, and see some truth; but I shall deliberately fall asleep so as to see even more, and more truly, in my dreams'! If my mind is to get a clear understanding of its own nature, it had better not look to the imagination for it.

Well, then, what am I? A thing that thinks. What is that? A thing that doubts, understands, affirms, denies, wants, refuses, and also imagines and senses. That is a long list of attributes for me to have—and it really is I who have them all. Why should it not be? Isn't it one and the same 'I' who now doubts almost everything, understands some things, affirms this one thing—namely, that I exist and think, denies everything else, wants to know more, refuses to be deceived, imagines many things involuntarily, and is aware of others that seem to come from the senses?

Isn't all this just as true as the fact that I exist, even if I am in a perpetual dream, and even if my creator is doing his best to deceive me? Which of all these activities is distinct from my thinking? Which of them can be said to be separate from myself? The fact that it is I who doubt and understand and want is so obvious that I can't see how to make it any clearer. But the 'I' who imagines is also this same 'I'. For even if (as I am pretending) none of the things that I imagine really exist, I really do imagine them, and this is part of my thinking. Lastly, it is also this same 'I' who senses, or is aware of bodily things seemingly through the senses. Because I may be dreaming, I can't say for sure that I now see the flames, hear the wood crackling, and feel the heat of the fire; but I certainly seem to see, to hear, and to be warmed. This cannot be false; what is called 'sensing' is strictly just this seeming, and when 'sensing' is understood in this restricted sense of the word it too is simply thinking.

All this is starting to give me a better understanding of what I am. But I still can't help thinking that bodies—of which I form mental images and which the senses investigate—are much more clearly known to me than is this puzzling 'I' that can't be pictured in the imagination. It would be surprising if this were right, though; for it would be surprising if I had a clearer grasp of things that I realize are doubtful, unknown and foreign to me—namely, bodies—than I have of what is true and known—namely my own self. But I see what the trouble is: I keep drifting towards that error because my mind likes to wander freely, refusing to respect the boundaries that truth lays down. Very well, then; I shall let it run free for a while, so that when the time comes to rein it in it won't be so resistant to being pulled back.

Let us consider the things that people ordinarily think they understand best of all, namely the bodies that we touch and see. I don't mean bodies in general—for our general thoughts are apt to be confused—but one particular body: this piece of wax, for example. It has just been taken from the honeycomb; it still tastes of honey and has the scent of the flowers from which the honey was gathered; its colour, shape and size are plain to see; it is hard, cold and can be handled easily; if you rap it with your knuckle it makes a sound. In short, it has everything that seems to be needed for a body to be known perfectly clearly.

But as I speak these words I hold the wax near to the fire, and look! The taste and smell vanish, the colour changes, the shape is lost, the size increases; the wax becomes liquid and hot; you can hardly touch it, and it no longer makes a sound when you strike it. But is it still the same wax? Of course it is; no one denies this. So what was it about the wax that I understood so clearly? Evidently it was not any of the features that the senses told me of; for all of them— brought to me through taste, smell, sight, touch or hearing—have now altered, yet it is still the same wax.

Perhaps what I now think about the wax indicates what its nature was all along. If that is right, then the wax was not the sweetness of the honey, the scent of the flowers, the whiteness, the shape, or the sound, but was rather a body that recently presented itself to me in those ways but now appears differently. But what exactly is this thing that I am now imagining? Well, if we take away whatever doesn't belong to the wax (that is, everything that the wax could be without), what is left is merely something extended, flexible and changeable. What do 'flexible' and 'changeable' mean here? I can imaginatively picture this piece of wax changing from round to square, from square to triangular, and so on. But that isn't what changeability is. In knowing that the wax is changeable I understand that it can go through endlessly many changes of that kind, far more than I can depict in my imagination; so it isn't my imagination that gives me my grasp of the wax as flexible and changeable.

Also, what does 'extended' mean? Is the wax's extension also unknown? It increases if the wax melts, and increases again if it boils; the wax can be extended in many more ways (that is, with many more shapes) than I will ever bring before my imagination. I am forced to conclude that the nature of this piece of wax isn't revealed by my imagination, but is perceived by the mind alone. (I am speaking of this particular piece of wax; the point is even clearer with regard to wax in general.) This wax that is perceived by the mind alone is, of course, the same wax that I see, touch, and picture in my imagination—in short the same wax I thought it to be from the start. But although my perception of it seemed to be a case of vision and touch and imagination, it isn't so and it never was. Rather, it is purely a scrutiny by the mind alone—formerly an imperfect and confused one, but now vivid and clear because I am now concentrating carefully on what the wax consists in.

As I reach this conclusion I am amazed at how prone to error my mind is. For although I am thinking all this out within myself, silently, I do it with the help of words, and I am at risk of being led astray by them. When the wax is in front of us, we say that we see it, not that we judge it to be there from its colour or shape; and this might make me think that knowledge of the wax comes from what the eye sees rather than from the perception of the mind alone. But this is clearly wrong, as the following example shows. If I look out of the window and see men crossing the square, as I have just done, I say that I see the men themselves, just as I say that I see the wax; yet do I see any more than hats and coats that could conceal robots? I judge that they are men. Something that I thought I saw with my eyes, therefore, was really grasped solely by my mind's faculty of judgment.

However, someone who wants to know more than the common crowd should be ashamed to base his doubts on ordinary ways of talking. Let us push ahead, then, and ask: When was my perception of the wax's nature more perfect and clear? Was it when I first looked at the wax, and thought I knew it through my senses? Or is it now, after I have enquired more carefully into the wax's nature and into how it is known? It would be absurd to hesitate in answering the question; for what clarity and sharpness was there in my earlier perception of the wax? Was there anything in it that a lower animal couldn't have? But when I consider the wax apart from its outward forms—take its clothes off, so to speak, and consider it naked—then although my judgment may still contain errors, at least I am now having a perception of a sort that requires a human mind.

But what am I to say about this mind, or about myself? (So far, remember, I don't admit that there is anything to me except a mind.) What, I ask, is this 'I' that seems to perceive the wax so clearly? Surely, I am aware of my own self in a truer and more certain way than I am of the wax, and also in a much more distinct and evident way. What leads me to think that the wax exists—namely, that I see it— leads much more obviously to the conclusion that I exist. What I see might not really be the wax; perhaps I don't even have eyes with which to see anything. But when I see or think I see (I am not here distinguishing the two), it is simply not possible that I who am now thinking am not something. Similarly, that I exist follows from the other bases for judging that the wax exists—that I touch it, that I imagine it, or any other basis—and similarly for my bases for judging that anything else exists outside me.

As I came to perceive the wax more distinctly by applying not just sight and touch but other considerations, all this too contributed to my knowing myself even more distinctly, because whatever goes into my perception of the wax or of any other body must do even more to establish the nature of my own mind. What comes to my mind from bodies, therefore, helps me to know my mind distinctly; yet all of that pales into insignificance—it is hardly worth mentioning—when compared with what my mind contains within itself that enables me to know it distinctly.

See! With no effort I have reached the place where I wanted to be! I now know that even bodies are perceived not by the senses or by imagination but by the intellect alone, not through their being touched or seen but through their being understood; and this helps me to know plainly that I can perceive my own mind more easily and clearly than I can anything else. Since the grip of old opinions is hard to shake off, however, I want to pause and meditate for a while on this new knowledge of mine, fixing it more deeply in my memory.

THOMAS HOBBES
Leviathan

First Part
Of Man

Chapter 1
Of Sense

CONCERNING the thoughts of man, I will consider them first singly, and afterwards in train or dependence upon one another. Singly, they are every one a representation or appearance of some quality, or other accident of a body without us, which is commonly called an object. Which object worketh on the eyes, ears, and other parts of man's body, and by diversity of working produceth diversity of appearances.

The original of them all is that which we call sense, (for there is no conception in a man's mind which hath not at first, totally or by parts, been begotten upon the organs of sense). The rest are derived from that original.

To know the natural cause of sense is not very necessary to the business now in hand; and I have elsewhere written of the same at large. Nevertheless, to fill each part of my present method, I will briefly deliver the same in this place.

The cause of sense is the external body, or object, which presseth the organ proper to each sense, either immediately, as in the taste and touch; or mediately, as in seeing, hearing, and smelling: which pressure, by the mediation of nerves and other strings and membranes of the body, continued inwards to the brain and heart, causeth there a resistance, or counter-pressure, or endeavour of the heart to deliver itself: which endeavour, because outward, seemeth to be some matter without. And this seeming, or fancy, is that which men call sense; and consisteth, as to the eye, in a light, or colour figured; to the ear, in a sound; to the nostril, in an odour; to the tongue and palate, in a savour; and to the rest of the body, in heat, cold, hardness, softness, and such other qualities as we discern by feeling.

All which qualities called sensible are in the object that causeth them but so many several motions of the matter, by which it presseth our organs diversely. Neither in us that are pressed are they anything else but diverse motions (for motion produceth nothing but motion). But their appearance to us is fancy, the same waking that dreaming. And as pressing, rubbing, or striking the eye makes us fancy a light, and pressing the ear produceth a din; so do the bodies also we see, or hear, produce the same by their strong, though unobserved action. For if those colours and sounds were in the bodies or objects that cause them, they could not be severed from them, as by glasses and in echoes by reflection we see they are: where we know the thing we see is in one place; the appearance, in another. And though at some certain distance the real and very object seem invested with the fancy it begets in us; yet still the object is one thing, the image or fancy is another. So that sense in all cases is nothing else but original fancy caused (as I have said) by the pressure that is, by the motion of external things upon our eyes, ears, and other organs, thereunto ordained.

But the philosophy schools, through all the universities of Christendom, grounded upon certain texts of Aristotle, teach another doctrine; and say, for the cause of vision, that the thing seen sendeth forth on every side a visible species, (in English) a visible show, apparition, or aspect, or a being seen; the receiving whereof into the eye is seeing. And for the cause of hearing, that the thing heard sendeth forth an audible species, that is, an audible aspect, or audible being seen; which, entering at the ear, maketh hearing. Nay, for the cause of understanding also, they say the thing understood sendeth forth an intelligible species, that is, an intelligible being seen; which, coming into the understanding, makes us understand. I say not this, as disapproving the use of universities: but because I am to speak hereafter of their office in a Commonwealth, I must let you see on all occasions by the way what things would be amended in them; amongst which the frequency of insignificant speech is one.

Chapter 2
Of Imagination

THAT when a thing lies still, unless somewhat else stir it, it will lie still for ever, is a truth that no man doubts of. But that when a thing is in motion, it will eternally be in motion, unless somewhat else stay it, though the reason be the same (namely, that nothing can change itself), is not so easily assented to. For men measure, not only other men, but all other things, by themselves: and because they find themselves subject after motion to pain and lassitude, think everything else grows weary of motion, and seeks repose of its own accord; little considering whether it be not some other motion wherein that desire of rest they find in themselves consisteth. From hence it is that the schools say, heavy bodies fall downwards out of an appetite to rest, and to conserve their nature in that place which is most proper for them; ascribing appetite, and knowledge of what is good for their conservation (which is more than man has), to things inanimate, absurdly.

When a body is once in motion, it moveth (unless something else hinder it) eternally; and whatsoever hindreth it, cannot in an instant, but in time, and by degrees, quite extinguish it: and as we see in the water, though the wind cease, the waves give not over rolling for a long time after; so also it happeneth in that motion which is made in the internal parts of a man, then, when he sees, dreams, etc. For after the object is removed, or the eye shut, we still retain an image of the thing seen, though more obscure than when we see it. And this is it the Latins call imagination, from the image made in seeing, and apply the same, though improperly, to all the other senses. But the Greeks call it fancy, which signifies appearance, and is as proper to one sense as to another. Imagination, therefore, is nothing but decaying sense; and is found in men and many other living creatures, as well sleeping as waking.

The decay of sense in men waking is not the decay of the motion made in sense, but an obscuring of it, in such manner as the light of the sun obscureth the light of the stars; which stars do no less exercise their virtue by which they are visible in the day than in the night. But because amongst many strokes which our eyes, ears, and other organs receive from external bodies, the predominant only is sensible; therefore the light of the sun being predominant, we are not affected with the action of the stars. And any object being removed from our eyes, though the impression it made in us remain, yet other objects more present succeeding, and working on us, the imagination of the past is obscured and made weak, as the voice of a man is in the noise of the day.

From whence it followeth that the longer the time is, after the sight or sense of any object, the weaker is the imagination. For the continual change of man's body destroys in time the parts which in sense were moved: so that distance of time, and of place, hath one and the same effect in us. For as at a great distance of place that which we look at appears dim, and without distinction of the smaller parts, and as voices grow weak and inarticulate: so also after great distance of time our imagination of the past is weak; and we lose, for example, of cities we have seen, many particular streets; and of actions, many particular circumstances. This decaying sense, when we would express the thing itself (I mean fancy itself), we call imagination, as I said before. But when we would express the decay, and signify that the sense is fading, old, and past, it is called memory. So that imagination and memory are but one thing, which for diverse considerations hath diverse names.

Much memory, or memory of many things, is called experience. Again, imagination being only of those things which have been formerly perceived by sense, either all at once, or by parts at several times; the former (which is the imagining the whole object, as it was presented to the sense) is simple imagination, as when one imagineth a man, or horse, which he hath seen before. The other is compounded, when from the sight of a man at one time, and of a horse at another, we conceive in our mind a centaur. So when a man compoundeth the image of his own person with the image of the actions of another man, as when a man imagines himself a Hercules or an Alexander (which happeneth often to them that are much taken with reading of romances), it is a compound imagination, and properly but a fiction of the mind. There be also other imaginations that rise in men, though waking, from the great impression made in sense: as from gazing upon the sun, the impression leaves an image of the sun before our eyes a long time after; and from being long and vehemently attent upon geometrical figures, a man shall in the dark, though awake, have the images of lines and angles before his eyes; which kind of fancy hath no particular name, as being a thing that doth not commonly fall into men's discourse.

The imaginations of them that sleep are those we call dreams. And these also (as all other imaginations) have been before, either totally or by parcels, in the sense. And because in sense, the brain and nerves, which are the necessary organs of sense, are so benumbed in sleep as not easily to be moved by the action of external objects, there can happen in sleep no imagination, and therefore no dream, but what proceeds from the agitation of the inward parts of man's body; which inward parts, for the connexion they have with the brain and other organs, when they be distempered do keep the same in motion; whereby the imaginations there formerly made, appear as if a man were waking; saving that the organs of sense being now benumbed, so as there is no new object which can master and obscure them with a more vigorous impression, a dream must needs be more clear, in this silence of sense, than are our waking thoughts.

And hence it cometh to pass that it is a hard matter, and by many thought impossible, to distinguish exactly between sense and dreaming. For my part, when I consider that in dreams I do not often nor constantly think of the same persons, places, objects, and actions that I do waking, nor remember so long a train of coherent thoughts dreaming as at other times; and because waking I often observe the absurdity of dreams, but never dream of the absurdities of my waking thoughts, I am well satisfied that, being awake, I know I dream not; though when I dream, I think myself awake.

And seeing dreams are caused by the distemper of some of the inward parts of the body, diverse distempers must needs cause different dreams. And hence it is that lying cold breedeth dreams of fear, and raiseth the thought and image of some fearful object, the motion from the brain to the inner parts, and from the inner parts to the brain being reciprocal; and that as anger causeth heat in some parts of the body when we are awake, so when we sleep the overheating of the same parts causeth anger, and raiseth up in the brain the imagination of an enemy. In the same manner, as natural kindness when we are awake causeth desire, and desire makes heat in certain other parts of the body; so also too much heat in those parts, while we sleep, raiseth in the brain an imagination of some kindness shown. In sum, our dreams are the reverse of our waking imaginations; the motion when we are awake beginning at one end, and when we dream, at another. . . .

The imagination that is raised in man (or any other creature endued with the faculty of imagining) by words, or other voluntary signs, is that we generally call understanding, and is common to man and beast. For a dog by custom will understand the call or the rating of his master; and so will many other beasts. That understanding which is peculiar to man is the understanding not only his will, but his conceptions and thoughts, by the sequel and contexture of the names of things into affirmations, negations, and other forms of speech: and of this kind of understanding I shall speak hereafter.

Chapter 3
Of the Consequence or Train of Imaginations

BY CONSEQUENCE, or train of thoughts, I understand that succession of one thought to another which is called, to distinguish it from discourse in words, mental discourse.

When a man thinketh on anything whatsoever, his next thought after is not altogether so casual as it seems to be. Not every thought to every thought succeeds indifferently. But as we have no imagination, whereof we have not formerly had sense, in whole or in parts; so we have no transition from one imagination to another, whereof we never had the like before in our senses. The reason whereof is this. All fancies are motions within us, relics of those made in the sense; and those motions that immediately succeeded one another in the sense continue also together after sense: in so much as the former coming again to take place and be predominant, the latter followeth, by coherence of the matter moved, in such manner as water upon a plain table is drawn which way any one part of it is guided by the finger. But because in sense, to one and the same thing perceived, sometimes one thing, sometimes another, succeedeth, it comes to pass in time that in the imagining of anything, there is no certainty what we shall imagine next; only this is certain, it shall be something that succeeded the same before, at one time or another.

This train of thoughts, or mental discourse, is of two sorts. The first is unguided, without design, and inconstant; wherein there is no passionate thought to govern and direct those that follow to itself as the end and scope of some desire, or other passion; in which case the thoughts are said to wander, and seem impertinent one to another, as in a dream. Such are commonly the thoughts of men that are not only without company, but also without care of anything; though even then their thoughts are as busy as at other times, but without harmony; as the sound which a lute out of tune would yield to any man; or in tune, to one that could not play. And yet in this wild ranging of the mind, a man may oft-times perceive the way of it, and the dependence of one thought upon another. For in a discourse of our present civil war, what could seem more impertinent than to ask, as one did, what was the value of a Roman penny? Yet the coherence to me was manifest enough. For the thought of the war introduced the thought of the delivering up the King to his enemies; the thought of that brought in the thought of the delivering up of Christ; and that again the thought of the 30 pence, which was the price of that treason: and thence easily followed that malicious question; and all this in a moment of time, for thought is quick.

The second is more constant, as being regulated by some desire and design. For the impression made by such things as we desire, or fear, is strong and permanent, or (if it cease for a time) of quick return: so strong it is sometimes as to hinder and break our sleep. From desire ariseth the thought of some means we have seen produce the like of that which we aim at; and from the thought of that, the thought of means to that mean; and so continually, till we come to some beginning within our own power. And because the end, by the greatness of the impression, comes often to mind, in case our thoughts begin to wander they are quickly again reduced into the way: which, observed by one of the seven wise men, made him give men this precept, which is now worn out: respice finem; that is to say, in all your actions, look often upon what you would have, as the thing that directs all your thoughts in the way to attain it.

The train of regulated thoughts is of two kinds: one, when of an effect imagined we seek the causes or means that produce it; and this is common to man and beast. The other is, when imagining anything whatsoever, we seek all the possible effects that can by it be produced; that is to say, we imagine what we can do with it when we have it. Of which I have not at any time seen any sign, but in man only; for this is a curiosity hardly incident to the nature of any living creature that has no other passion but sensual, such as are hunger, thirst, lust, and anger. In sum, the discourse of the mind, when it is governed by design, is nothing but seeking, or the faculty of invention, which the Latins call *sagacitas*, and *solertia*; a hunting out of the causes of some effect, present or past; or of the effects of some present or past cause. Sometimes a man seeks what he hath lost; and from that place, and time, wherein he misses it, his mind runs back, from place to place, and time to time, to find where and when he had it; that is to say, to find some certain and limited time and place in which to begin a method of seeking. Again, from thence, his thoughts run over the same places and times to find what action or other occasion might make him lose it. This we call remembrance, or calling to mind: the Latins call it *reminiscentia*, as it were a re-conning of our former actions.

Chapter 4
Of Speech

. . . THE GENERAL use of speech is to transfer our mental discourse into verbal, or the train of our thoughts into a train of words, and that for two commodities; whereof one is the registering of the consequences of our thoughts, which being apt to slip out of our memory and put us to a new labour, may again be recalled by such words as they were marked by. So that the first use of names is to serve for marks or notes of remembrance. Another is when many use the same words to signify, by their connexion and order one to another, what they conceive or think of each matter; and also what they desire, fear, or have any other passion for. And for this use they are called signs. Special uses of speech are these: first, to register what by cogitation we find to be the cause of anything, present or past; and what we find things present or past may produce, or effect; which, in sum, is acquiring of arts. Secondly, to show to others that knowledge which we have attained; which is to counsel and teach one another. Thirdly, to make known to others our wills and purposes that we may have the mutual help of one another. Fourthly, to please and delight ourselves, and others, by playing with our words, for pleasure or ornament, innocently.

To these uses, there are also four correspondent abuses. First, when men register their thoughts wrong by the inconstancy of the signification of their words; by which they register for their conceptions that which they never conceived, and so deceive themselves. Secondly, when they use words metaphorically; that is, in other sense than that they are ordained for, and thereby deceive others. Thirdly, when by words they declare that to be their will which is not. Fourthly, when they use them to grieve one another: for seeing nature hath armed living creatures, some with teeth, some with horns, and some with hands, to grieve an enemy, it is but an abuse of speech to grieve him with the tongue, unless it be one whom we are obliged to govern; and then it is not to grieve, but to correct and amend. . . .

Chapter 5
Of Reason and Science

WHEN man reasoneth, he does nothing else but conceive a sum total, from addition of parcels; or conceive a remainder, from subtraction of one sum from another: which, if it be done by words, is conceiving of the consequence of the names of all the parts, to the name of the whole; or from the names of the whole and one part, to the name of the other part. And though in some things, as in numbers, besides adding and subtracting, men name other operations, as multiplying and dividing; yet they are the same: for multiplication is but adding together of things equal; and division, but subtracting of one thing, as often as we can.

These operations are not incident to numbers only, but to all manner of things that can be added together, and taken one out of another. For as arithmeticians teach to add and subtract in numbers, so the geometricians teach the same in lines, figures (solid and superficial), angles, proportions, times, degrees of swiftness, force, power, and the like; the logicians teach the same in consequences of words, adding together two names to make an affirmation, and two affirmations to make a syllogism, and many syllogisms to make a demonstration; and from the sum, or conclusion of a syllogism, they subtract one proposition to find the other. Writers of politics add together pactions to find men's duties; and lawyers, laws and facts to find what is right and wrong in the actions of private men. In sum, in what matter soever there is place for addition and subtraction, there also is place for reason; and where these have no place, there reason has nothing at all to do.

Out of all which we may define (that is to say determine) what that is which is meant by this word reason when we reckon it amongst the faculties of the mind. For reason, in this sense, is nothing but reckoning (that is, adding and subtracting) of the consequences of general names agreed upon for the marking and signifying of our thoughts; I say marking them, when we reckon by ourselves; and signifying, when we demonstrate or approve our reckonings to other men.

And as in arithmetic unpractised men must, and professors themselves may often, err, and cast up false; so also in any other subject of reasoning, the ablest, most attentive, and most practised men may deceive themselves, and infer false conclusions; not but that reason itself is always right reason, as well as arithmetic is a certain and infallible art: but no one man's reason, nor the reason of any one number of men, makes the certainty; no more than an account is therefore well cast up because a great many men have unanimously approved it. And therefore, as when there is a controversy in an account, the parties must by their own accord set up for right reason the reason of some arbitrator, or judge, to whose sentence they will both stand, or their controversy must either come to blows, or be undecided, for want of a right reason constituted by Nature; so is it also in all debates of what kind soever: and when men that think themselves wiser than all others clamour and demand right reason for judge, yet seek no more but that things should be determined by no other men's reason but their own, it is as intolerable in the society of men, as it is in play after trump is turned to use for trump on every occasion that suit whereof they have most in their hand. For they do nothing else, that will have every of their passions, as it comes to bear sway in them, to be taken for right reason, and that in their own controversies: betraying their want of right reason by the claim they lay to it.

The use and end of reason is not the finding of the sum and truth of one, or a few consequences, remote from the first definitions and settled significations of names; but to begin at these, and proceed from one consequence to another. For there can be no certainty of the last conclusion without a certainty of all those affirmations and negations on which it was grounded and inferred. As when a master of a family, in taking an account, casteth up the sums of all the bills of expense into one sum; and not regarding how each bill is summed up, by those that give them in account, nor what it is he pays for, he advantages himself no more than if he allowed the account in gross, trusting to every of the accountant's skill and honesty: so also in reasoning of all other things, he that takes up conclusions on the trust of authors, and doth not fetch them from the first items in every reckoning (which are the significations of names settled by definitions), loses his labour, and does not know anything, but only believeth.

When a man reckons without the use of words, which may be done in particular things, as when upon the sight of any one thing, we conjecture what was likely to have preceded, or is likely to follow upon it; if that which he thought likely to follow follows not, or that which he thought likely to have preceded it hath not preceded it, this is called error; to which even the most prudent men are subject. But when we reason in words of general signification, and fall upon a general inference which is false; though it be commonly called error, it is indeed an absurdity, or senseless speech. For error is but a deception, in presuming that somewhat is past, or to come; of which, though it were not past, or not to come, yet there was no impossibility discoverable. But when we make a general assertion, unless it be a true one, the possibility of it is inconceivable. And words whereby we conceive nothing but the sound are those we call absurd, insignificant, and nonsense. And therefore if a man should talk to me of a round quadrangle; or accidents of bread in cheese; or immaterial substances; or of a free subject; a free will; or any free but free from being hindered by opposition; I should not say he were in an error, but that his words were without meaning; that is to say, absurd.

I have said before, in the second chapter, that a man did excel all other animals in this faculty, that when he conceived anything whatsoever, he was apt to enquire the consequences of it, and what effects he could do with it. And now I add this other degree of the same excellence, that he can by words reduce the consequences he finds to general rules, called theorems, or aphorisms; that is, he can reason, or reckon, not only in number, but in all other things whereof one may be added unto or subtracted from another.

But this privilege is allayed by another; and that is by the privilege of absurdity, to which no living creature is subject, but men only. And of men, those are of all most subject to it that profess philosophy. For it is most true that Cicero saith of them somewhere; that there can be nothing so absurd but may be found in the books of philosophers. And the reason is manifest. For there is not one of them that begins his ratiocination from the definitions or explications of the names they are to use; which is a method that hath been used only in geometry, whose conclusions have thereby been made indisputable. . . .

Chapter 6
Of the Interior Beginnings of Voluntary Motions, Commonly Called the Passions

THERE be in animals two sorts of motions peculiar to them: One called vital, begun in generation, and continued without interruption through their whole life; such as are the course of the blood, the pulse, the breathing, the concoction, nutrition, excretion, etc.; to which motions there needs no help of imagination: the other is animal motion, otherwise called voluntary motion; as to go, to speak, to move any of our limbs, in such manner as is first fancied in our minds. That sense is motion in the organs and interior parts of man's body, caused by the action of the things we see, hear, etc., and that fancy is but the relics of the same motion, remaining after sense, has been already said in the first and second chapters. And because going, speaking, and the like voluntary motions depend always upon a precedent thought of whither, which way, and what, it is evident that the imagination is the first internal beginning of all voluntary motion. And although unstudied men do not conceive any motion at all to be there, where the thing moved is invisible, or the space it is moved in is, for the shortness of it, insensible; yet that doth not hinder but that such motions are. For let a space be never so little, that which is moved over a greater space, whereof that little one is part, must first be moved over that. These small beginnings of motion within the body of man, before they appear in walking, speaking, striking, and other visible actions, are commonly called endeavour.

This endeavour, when it is toward something which causes it, is called appetite, or desire, the latter being the general name, and the other oftentimes restrained to signify the desire of food, namely hunger and thirst. And when the endeavour is from ward something, it is generally called aversion. These words appetite and aversion we have from the Latins; and they both of them signify the motions, one of approaching, the other of retiring. So also do the Greek words for the same, which are *orme* and *aphorme*. For Nature itself does often press upon men those truths which afterwards, when they look for somewhat beyond Nature, they stumble at. For the Schools find in mere appetite to go, or move, no actual motion at all; but because some motion they must acknowledge, they call it metaphorical motion, which is but an absurd speech; for though words may be called metaphorical, bodies and motions cannot.

That which men desire they are said to love, and to hate those things for which they have aversion. So that desire and love are the same thing; save that by desire, we signify the absence of the object; by love, most commonly the presence of the same. So also by aversion, we signify the absence; and by hate, the presence of the object.

Of appetites and aversions, some are born with men; as appetite of food, appetite of excretion, and exoneration (which may also and more properly be called aversions, from somewhat they feel in their bodies), and some other appetites, not many. The rest, which are appetites of particular things, proceed from experience and trial of their effects upon themselves or other men. For of things we know not at all, or believe not to be, we can have no further desire than to taste and try. But aversion we have for things, not only which we know have hurt us, but also that we do not know whether they will hurt us, or not.

Those things which we neither desire nor hate, we are said to contemn: contempt being nothing else but an immobility or contumacy of the heart in resisting the action of certain things; and proceeding from that the heart is already moved otherwise, by other more potent objects, or from want of experience of them.

And because the constitution of a man's body is in continual mutation, it is impossible that all the same things should always cause in him the same appetites and aversions: much less can all men consent in the desire of almost any one and the same object.

But whatsoever is the object of any man's appetite or desire, that is it which he for his part calleth good; and the object of his hate and aversion, evil; and of his contempt, vile and inconsiderable. For these words of good, evil, and contemptible are ever used with relation to the person that useth them: there being nothing simply and absolutely so; nor any common rule of good and evil to be taken from the nature of the objects themselves; but from the person of the man, where there is no Commonwealth; or, in a Commonwealth, from the person that representeth it; or from an arbitrator or judge, whom men disagreeing shall by consent set up and make his sentence the rule thereof.

The Latin tongue has two words whose significations approach to those of good and evil, but are not precisely the same; and those are *pulchrum* and *turpe*. Whereof the former signifies that which by some apparent signs promiseth good; and the latter, that which promiseth evil. But in our tongue we have not so general names to express them by. But for *pulchrum* we say in some things, fair; in others, beautiful, or handsome, or gallant, or honourable, or comely, or amiable: and for *turpe*; foul, deformed, ugly, base, nauseous, and the like, as the subject shall require; all which words, in their proper places, signify nothing else but the mien, or countenance, that promiseth good and evil. So that of good there be three kinds: good in the promise, that is *pulchrum*; good in effect, as the end desired, which is called *jucundum*, delightful; and good as the means, which is called utile, profitable; and as many of evil: for evil in promise is that they call *turpe*; evil in effect and end is *molestum*, unpleasant, troublesome; and evil in the means, inutile, unprofitable, hurtful.

As in sense that which is really within us is, as I have said before, only motion, caused by the action of external objects but in appearance; to the sight, light and colour; to the ear, sound; to the nostril, odour, etc.: so, when the action of the same object is continued from the eyes, ears, and other organs to the heart, the real effect there is nothing but motion, or endeavour; which consisteth in appetite or aversion to or from the object moving. But the appearance or sense of that motion is that we either call delight or trouble of mind.

This motion, which is called appetite, and for the appearance of it delight and pleasure, seemeth to be a corroboration of vital motion, and a help thereunto; and therefore such things as caused delight were not improperly called *jucunda*, from helping or fortifying; and the contrary, *molesta*, offensive, from hindering and troubling the motion vital.

Pleasure therefore, or delight, is the appearance or sense of good; and molestation or displeasure, the appearance or sense of evil. And consequently all appetite, desire, and love is accompanied with some delight more or less; and all hatred and aversion with more or less displeasure and offence. . . .

In deliberation, the last appetite, or aversion, immediately adhering to the action, or to the omission thereof, is that we call the will; the act, not the faculty, of willing. And beasts that have deliberation must necessarily also have will. The definition of the will, given commonly by the Schools, that it is a rational appetite, is not good. For if it were, then could there be no voluntary act against reason. For a voluntary act is that which proceedeth from the will, and no other. But if instead of a rational appetite, we shall say an appetite resulting from a precedent deliberation, then the definition is the same that I have given here. Will, therefore, is the last appetite in deliberating. And though we say in common discourse, a man had a will once to do a thing, that nevertheless he forbore to do; yet that is properly but an inclination, which makes no action voluntary; because the action depends not of it, but of the last inclination, or appetite. For if the intervenient appetites make any action voluntary, then by the same reason all intervenient aversions should make the same action involuntary; and so one and the same action should be both voluntary and involuntary.

By this it is manifest that, not only actions that have their beginning from covetousness, ambition, lust, or other appetites to the thing propounded, but also those that have their beginning from aversion, or fear of those consequences that follow the omission, are voluntary actions.

The forms of speech by which the passions are expressed are partly the same and partly different from those by which we express our thoughts. And first generally all passions may be expressed indicatively; as, I love, I fear, I joy, I deliberate, I will, I command: but some of them have particular expressions by themselves, which nevertheless are not affirmations, unless it be when they serve to make other inferences besides that of the passion they proceed from. Deliberation is expressed subjunctively; which is a speech proper to signify suppositions, with their consequences; as, If this be done, then this will follow; and differs not from the language of reasoning, save that reasoning is in general words, but deliberation for the most part is of particulars. The language of desire, and aversion, is imperative; as, Do this, forbear that; which when the party is obliged to do, or forbear, is command; otherwise prayer; or else counsel. The language of vainglory, of indignation, pity and revengefulness, optative: but of the desire to know, there is a peculiar expression called interrogative; as, What is it, when shall it, how is it done, and why so? Other language of the passions I find none: for cursing, swearing, reviling, and the like do not signify as speech, but as the actions of a tongue accustomed.

These forms of speech, I say, are expressions or voluntary significations of our passions: but certain signs they be not; because they may be used arbitrarily, whether they that use them have such passions or not. The best signs of passions present are either in the countenance, motions of the body, actions, and ends, or aims, which we otherwise know the man to have.

And because in deliberation the appetites and aversions are raised by foresight of the good and evil consequences, and sequels of the action whereof we deliberate, the good or evil effect thereof dependeth on the foresight of a long chain of consequences, of which very seldom any man is able to see to the end. But for so far as a man seeth, if the good in those consequences be greater than the evil, the whole chain is that which writers call apparent or seeming good. And contrarily, when the evil exceedeth the good, the whole is apparent or seeming evil: so that he who hath by experience, or reason, the greatest and surest prospect of consequences, deliberates best himself; and is able, when he will, to give the best counsel unto others.

Continual success in obtaining those things which a man from time to time desireth, that is to say, continual prospering, is that men call felicity; I mean the felicity of this life. For there is no such thing as perpetual tranquillity of mind, while we live here; because life itself is but motion, and can never be without desire, nor without fear, no more than without sense. What kind of felicity God hath ordained to them that devoutly honour him, a man shall no sooner know than enjoy; being joys that now are as incomprehensible as the word of Schoolmen, beatifical vision, is unintelligible.

The form of speech whereby men signify their opinion of the goodness of anything is praise. That whereby they signify the power and greatness of anything is magnifying. And that whereby they signify the opinion they have of a man's felicity is by the Greeks called makarismos, for which we have no name in our tongue. And thus much is sufficient for the present purpose to have been said of the passions.

BENEDICT SPINOZA

Ethics Demonstrated in Geometrical Order

Translated by Jonathan Bennett

Part 1
God

Definitions

D1: In calling something 'cause of itself' I mean that its essence involves existence, i.e. that its nature can't be conceived except as existing.

D2: A thing is said to be 'finite in its own kind' if it can be limited by something else of the same nature. For example, every body counts as 'finite in its own kind' because we can always conceive another body that is even bigger. And a thought can be limited by—i.e. can count as finite because of—another thought that somehow exceeds it. But a body can't be limited by a thought or a thought by a body.

D3: By 'substance' I understand: what is in itself and is conceived through itself, i.e. that whose concept doesn't have to be formed out of the concept of something else.

D4: By 'attribute' I understand: what the intellect perceives of a substance as constituting its essence.

D5: By 'mode' I understand: a state of a substance, i.e. something that exists in and is conceived through something else.

D6: By 'God' I understand: a thing that is absolutely infinite, i.e. a substance consisting of an infinity of attributes, each of which expresses an eternal and infinite essence. I say 'absolutely infinite' in contrast to 'infinite in its own kind'. If something is infinite only in its own kind, there can be attributes that it doesn't have; but if something is absolutely infinite its essence ·or nature· contains every positive way in which a thing can exist—·which means that it has all possible attributes·.

D7: A thing is called 'free' if its own nature—with no input from anything else—•makes it necessary for it to exist and causes it to act as it does. We say that a thing is 'compelled' if something other than itself makes it exist and causes it to act in this or that specific way.

D8: By 'eternity' I understand: existence itself when conceived to follow necessarily from the definition of the eternal thing. A thing is eternal only if it is absolutely (logically) necessary that the thing exists; for something to be eternal it isn't merely a matter of its existing at all times—it must necessarily exist.

Axioms

A1: Whatever exists is either in itself or in something else. As we have already seen, a substance is in itself, a mode is in something else.

A2: What can't be conceived through something else must be conceived through itself.

A3: From a given determinate cause the effect follows necessarily; and, conversely, if there is no determinate cause no effect can follow.

A4: Knowledge of an effect depends on, and involves, knowledge of its cause.

A5: If two things have nothing in common, they can't be understood through one another—that is, the concept of one doesn't involve the concept of the other.

A6: A true idea must agree with its object.

A7: If a thing can be conceived as not existing then its essence doesn't involve existence.

Propositions

1: A substance is prior in nature to its states. This is evident from D3 and D5.

2: Two substances having different attributes have nothing in common with one another. This also evident from D3. For each substance must be in itself and be conceived through itself, which is to say that the concept of the one doesn't involve the concept of the other.

3: If things have nothing in common with one another, one of them can't be the cause of the other. If they have nothing in common with one another, then (by A5) they can't be understood through one another, and so (by A4) one can't be the cause of the other.

4: Two or more things are made distinct from one another either by a difference in their attributes or by a difference in their states.

Whatever exists is either in itself or in something else (by A1), which is to say (by D3 and D5) that outside the intellect there is nothing except substances and their states. So there is nothing outside the intellect through which things can be distinguished from one another except substances (which is to say (by D4) their attributes) and their states.

5: In Nature there cannot be two or more substances having the same nature or attribute. If there were two or more distinct substances, they would have to be distinguished from one another by a difference either in their attributes or in their states (by 4). If they are distinguished only by a difference in their attributes, then any given attribute can be possessed by only one of them. Suppose, then, that they are distinguished by a difference in their states.

But a substance is prior in nature to its states (by 1), so we can set the states aside and consider the substance in itself; and then there is nothing left through which one substance can be conceived as distinguished from another, which by 4 amounts to saying that we don't have two or more substances with a single attribute, but only one.

6: One substance can't be produced by another substance. In Nature there can't be two substances that share an attribute (by 5), that is (by 2), there can't be two substances that have something in common with each other. Therefore (by 3) one substance can't be the cause of another, or be caused by it.

Corollary: A substance can't be produced by anything else. In Nature there are only substances and their states (as is evident from A1, D3, and D5). But a substance can't be produced by another substance (by 6). Therefore, a substance can't be produced by anything else at all.

This corollary is demonstrated even more easily from the absurdity of its contradictory. If a substance could be produced by something else, the knowledge of it would have to depend on the knowledge of its cause (by 4). And so (by D3) it wouldn't be a substance.

7: It pertains to the nature of a substance to exist. A substance can't be produced by anything else (by the corollary to 6), so it must be its own cause; and that, by D1, is to say that its essence necessarily involves existence, i.e. it pertains to its nature to exist.

8: Every substance is necessarily infinite. [The difficult demonstration of 8 has this at its core: if x is finite then it is limited by something of the same kind as itself, i.e. something that shares an attribute with it; but no substance shares an attribute with any other substance, so no substance can be limited in this way, so every substance is infinite.]

First note on 7 and 8: Since finiteness is partly negative, while being infinite is an unqualifiedly positive affirmation of the existence of some nature, it follows from 7 alone that every substance must be infinite; for in calling a substance 'finite' we partly, because of the negative element in finiteness, deny existence to its nature, and according to 7 that is absurd.

Second note on 7 and 8: I'm sure that the proof of 7 will be found difficult to grasp by people who judge things confusedly and haven't been accustomed to understanding things through their first causes. Such people don't distinguish the qualities of substances from the substances themselves, and they don't know how things are produced. This brings it about that they fictitiously ascribe to substances the sort of beginning that they see natural things to have; for those who don't know the true causes of things confuse everything, and have no difficulty supposing that both trees and men speak, that men are formed both from stones and from seed, and that anything can be changed into anything else! So, also, those who confuse the divine nature with human nature easily ascribe human character-traits to God, particularly when they are also ignorant of how those traits are produced in the human mind.

But if men would attend to the nature of substance, they would have no doubt of the truth of 7. Indeed, this proposition would be an axiom for everyone. For by 'substance' they would understand what is in itself and is conceived through itself, i.e. that the knowledge of which doesn't require the knowledge of anything else; and by 'quality' they would understand what is in something else, something the concept of which is formed from the concept of the thing in which it is.

Hence, if someone said that he had a clear and distinct (i.e. true) idea of a substance, and nevertheless wondered whether such a substance existed, that would amount to saying that he had a true idea and wondered whether it was false. (You'll see that this is right if you think about it.) Or if someone says that a substance has been created, he is saying that a false idea has become true! Of course nothing more absurd can be conceived. So it must be admitted that the existence of a substance is an eternal truth, just as its essence is.

This lets us infer in another way that a single nature can be possessed by only one substance —I think the inference is worth presenting in the remainder of this Note. Four needed preliminaries to the argument:

1. The true definition of each thing neither involves nor expresses anything except the nature of the thing defined. From which it follows that:

2. No definition involves or expresses any certain number of individuals, since a definition expresses only the nature of the thing defined. For example, the definition of triangle expresses only the simple nature of the triangle, not any particular number of triangles. It should also be noted that

3. There must be, for each existing thing, a certain cause for its existing.

Finally, 4. The cause on account of which a thing exists must either be contained in the very nature and definition of the existing thing (which means that it pertains to the nature of the thing to exist) or be outside it. From these propositions it follows that if in Nature a certain number of individuals exists, there must be a cause why just those individuals exist and not more or fewer.

For example, if twenty men exist in Nature—and for clarity's sake let's assume that they are the first men to exist and that they all exist at the same time—how are we to explain this? To show why there are exactly twenty men, no more and no fewer, it doesn't suffice to show the cause of human nature in general. For (by 3) there must be a cause why each particular man exists. But this cause (by 2 and 3) can't be contained in human nature itself, since the true definition of man doesn't involve the number twenty. So (by 4) the cause why these twenty men exist—and thus why each of them exists— must lie outside each of them.

From that it follows that if something has a nature such that there can be many individuals of that nature, there must be an external cause of its existing. Now since it pertains to the nature of a substance to exist (already shown in this note), its definition must involve necessary existence, and so its existence must be inferred from its definition alone. But, as we have shown in 2 and 3, the existence of a number of substances can't follow from a definition. So it follows that there can exist only one substance having a given nature.

9: The more reality or being each thing has, the more attributes belong to it. This is evident from D4.

10: Each attribute of a substance must be conceived through itself.

An attribute is what the intellect perceives concerning a substance, as constituting its essence (by D4); so (by D3) it must be conceived through itself. . . .

Note on 10: From these propositions it is evident that although two attributes can be conceived to be really distinct (each conceived without the aid of the other), we still can't infer from that that they constitute two different substances. . . . It is far from absurd to ascribe many attributes to one substance. Indeed, nothing in Nature is clearer than that each thing must be conceived under some attribute, and the more reality a thing has the more attributes it has—attributes that express necessity, or eternity and infinity. So it is utterly clear that an absolutely infinite thing must be defined (as in D6) as a thing that consists of infinite attributes, each of which expresses a certain eternal and infinite essence. If you want to know how we can tell when there are many substances, read on: in the following propositions I shall show that in Nature there exists only one substance, which is absolutely infinite. So there is nothing to 'tell'.

11: God, or a substance consisting of infinite attributes each of which expresses eternal and infinite essence, necessarily exists.

If God didn't exist, then (by A7) God's essence would not involve existence; and (by 7) that is absurd. Therefore God necessarily exists.

A second proof: For each thing there must be assigned a cause or reason for its existence (if it exists) and for its nonexistence (if it doesn't). This reason or cause must be either contained in, or lie outside of, the nature of the thing. For example, the very nature of a square circle indicates the reason why it doesn't exist, namely because it involves a contradiction; and the very nature of a substance explains why it does exist, because that nature involves existence (see 7). But the reason why [changing the example] a coin exists, or why it doesn't exist, does not follow from its nature but from the order of the whole of the physical world. For from this ·order· it must follow either that the coin necessarily exists now or that it is impossible for it to exist now. These things are self-evident. From them it follows that a thing necessarily exists if there is no reason or cause that prevents it from existing. So if there is no reason or cause that prevents God from existing or takes God's existence away, it certainly follows that God necessarily exists.

But if there were such a reason or cause, it would have to be either in God's very nature or outside it and in another substance of a different nature. It couldn't be in a substance of the same nature as God's, for the supposition that there is such a substance is, itself, the supposition that God exists. So it would have to be a substance of a nature different from God's; but such a substance would have nothing in common with God (by 2) and so could neither give existence to God nor take it away. So a reason or cause that takes away God's existence couldn't lie outside the divine nature.

It would, then, have to be in God's nature itself. That would mean that God's nature involved a contradiction, like the square circle. But it is absurd to affirm this of a thing that is absolutely infinite and supremely perfect. (That is because a contradiction must involve something of the form 'P and not-P—a 'square circle' would be something that was 'square and not square' because 'not square is contained in the meaning of 'circle'—and a thing that is infinite and perfect is one whose nature involves nothing negative, so nothing of the contradictory form.) So there is no cause or reason—either in God or outside God—that takes God's existence away. Therefore God necessarily exists.

A third proof: To be unable to exist is to lack power, and conversely to be able to exist is to have power (this is self-evident). Now, suppose that God doesn't exist but some finite things do exist necessarily. In that case, these finite things are more powerful than an absolutely infinite thing (because they can exist and the absolutely infinite thing can't). But this is self-evidently absurd. So either nothing exists or an absolutely infinite thing also exists. But we exist, either in ourselves as substances that necessarily exist or as qualities of something else that necessarily exists (see A1 and 7). Therefore an absolutely infinite thing—that is (by D6) God—necessarily exists. . . .

So there is nothing of whose existence we can be more certain than we are of the existence of an absolutely infinite thing, i.e. a perfect thing, i.e. God. For since God's essence excludes all imperfection and involves absolute perfection, by that very fact it removes every cause of doubting God's existence and gives the greatest certainty concerning it. I think this will be clear to you even if you are only moderately attentive! . . .

14: God is the only substance that can exist or be conceived.

Since God is an absolutely infinite thing, of whom no attribute expressing an essence of substance can be denied (by 6), and God necessarily exists (by 11), if there were a substance other than God it would have to be explained through some attribute of God; but explanations can flow only within attributes, not from one attribute to another; and so two substances with an attribute in common would exist, which (by 5) is absurd. So no substance other than God can exist; and none such can be conceived either, for if it could be conceived it would have to be conceived as existing, and the first part of this demonstration shows that to be absurd. Therefore, God is the only substance that can exist or be conceived.

First corollary: God is unique, i.e. (by 6) in Nature there is only one substance, and it is absolutely infinite. . . .

15: Whatever exists is in God, and nothing can exist or be conceived without God.

Proposition 14 secures that apart from God there cannot exist (or be conceived) any substance, i.e. (by D3) any thing that is in itself and is conceived through itself. But (by D5) modes can't exist or be conceived without a substance that they are modes of. So modes can exist only in the divine nature, and can be conceived only through that nature. But (by A1) substances and modes are all there is. Therefore, everything is in God and nothing can be or be conceived without God.

Note on 15:

(1) Some people imagine a God who is like a man, consisting of a body and a mind, and subject to passions. But how far they wander from the true knowledge of God is shown well enough by what I have already demonstrated, and I shan't talk about them any more. Everyone who has to any extent contemplated the divine nature denies that God is corporeal. This is best proved from the fact that by 'a body' we understand a quantity that has length, breadth, and depth, by some specific shape. Nothing could be more absurd than to say this about God, i.e. about a thing that is infinite [i.e., unlimited.]

In trying to demonstrate this same conclusion by different arguments from mine, some people clearly show that as well as denying that God is or has a body they conclude that the divine nature doesn't in any way involve corporeal or extended substance. They maintain that the corporeal world, rather than being part of God's nature, has been created by God. But by what divine power could it be created? They have no answer to that, which shows clearly that they don't understand what they are saying.

At any rate, I have demonstrated clearly enough—in my judgment, at least—that no substance can be produced or created by any other (see the corollary to 6 and the second note on 8). Next, I have shown (14) that God is the only substance that can exist or be conceived, and from this I have inferred in the second corollary to 14 that extended substance is one of God's infinite attributes. To explain all this more fully, I shall refute my opponents' arguments, which all come down to these two.

(2) First, they think that corporeal substance, insofar as it is substance, consists of parts. From this they infer that it cannot be infinite, and thus cannot pertain to God. They explain this through many examples, of which I shall mention three.

If corporeal substance is infinite, they say, let us conceive it to be divided into two parts. If each part is finite, then an infinite is composed of two finite parts, which is absurd. If each part is infinite, then there is one infinite twice as large as another, which is also absurd.

Again, if an infinite quantity is measured by parts each equal to a foot, it will consist of infinitely many of them, as it will also if it is measured by parts each equal to an inch. So one infinite number will be twelve times as great as another, which is no less absurd.

Finally, suppose that from one point in something of infinite extent two lines are extended to infinity. Although near the beginning they are a certain determinate distance apart, the distance between them is continuously increased as they lengthen, until finally it stops being determinate and becomes indeterminable; which is also absurd. Since these absurdities follow—so they think—from the supposition of an infinite quantity, they infer that corporeal substance must be finite and consequently cannot pertain to God's essence.

(3) Their second argument is also drawn from God's supreme perfection. For, they say, God as a supremely perfect thing cannot be acted on. But corporeal substance, since it is divisible, can be acted on; ·anything that is divisible can be pulled apart by outside forces·. So it follows that corporeal substance does not pertain to God's essence.

(4) These are the arguments that I find being used by authors who want to show that corporeal substance is unworthy of the divine nature, and cannot have anything to do with it. But anyone who is properly attentive will find that I have already replied to them, since these arguments are based wholly on the supposition that corporeal substance is composed of parts, which I have already (12 and corollary to 13) shown to be absurd. Anyone who wants to consider the matter rightly will see that all those absurdities (if indeed that's what they are) from which they infer that extended substance is finite don't at all follow from the supposition of an infinite quantity, but from supposing that an infinite quantity might be measurable and composed of finite parts. All they are entitled to infer from the absurdities they have uncovered is that infinite quantity is not measurable and is not composed of finite parts. This is just what I have already demonstrated above (12, etc.). So the weapon they aim at me turns against themselves.

Others, imagining that a line is composed of points, know how to invent many arguments showing that a line can't be divided to infinity. And indeed it is just as absurd to say that corporeal substance is composed of bodies, or parts, as it is to say that a body is composed of surfaces, the surfaces of lines, and the lines of points.

This must be admitted by all those who know that clear reason is infallible, and especially those who deny that there is a vacuum. For if corporeal substance could be divided into parts that were really distinct, why couldn't one part be annihilated while the rest remained interrelated as before (thus creating a vacuum)? Why must they all be so fitted together that there is no vacuum? If two things are really distinct from one another rather than being different modes or aspects of a single substance, one of them can stay where it is whatever the other does. But there isn't any vacuum in Nature (a subject I discuss elsewhere); all the parts of Nature do have to hang together so that there is no vacuum; so it follows that those parts are not really distinct from one another, ·i.e. that they are not distinct things·, which is to say that corporeal substance, insofar as it is a substance, cannot be divided.

(5) Why are we by nature so inclined to divide quantity? The answer involves the fact that we have two ways of thinking about quantity: we can think of it abstractly or superficially, which is how we depict it to ourselves in our imagination; and we can also think of it as substance, which is done by the intellect alone without help from the imagination. If we attend to quantity as it is in the imagination—which we often do, finding it easy—it will be found to be finite, divisible, and composed of parts; but if we attend to it as it is in the intellect, and conceive it insofar as it is a substance—which we don't do often, finding it hard—then (as I have already sufficiently demonstrated) it will be found to be infinite, unique, and indivisible.

This will be clear enough to anyone who knows how to distinguish the intellect from the imagination—particularly if he bears in mind that matter is everywhere the same, and that parts are distinguished in it only through our conceiving it to have different qualities, so that its parts are distinguished only modally but not really. [That is, the parts are not genuinely and deeply distinct things.]

For example, we conceive that water is divided and its parts separated from one another—considered as water, but not considered as corporeal substance, for considered as substance it is neither separated nor divided. Again, water considered as water can come into existence and go out of existence, but considered as substance it can do neither. When water considered as water goes out of existence, what happens at the level of substance is, roughly speaking, that an area in the one extended substance changes from being wet to being dry.

(6) I think this also answers the second argument—the one in III above—because that is based on the supposition that matter, insofar as it is substance, is divisible and made up of parts. Even if this reply were not sufficient, ·the argument would not succeed, because· there is no reason why divisibility should be unworthy of the divine nature. For (by 14) apart from God there can be no substance by which the divine nature would be acted on, and so God's being made up of parts would not bring with it a vulnerability to a dismantling attack from the outside, so to speak. All things, I repeat, are in God, and whatever happens does so through the laws of God's infinite nature and follows (as I'll show) from the necessity of God's essence. So it can't be said in any way that God is acted on by something else, or that extension is unworthy of the divine nature—even if it is supposed to be divisible—provided that God is granted to be eternal and infinite.

16: From the necessity of the divine nature there must follow infinitely many things in infinitely many ways, i.e., everything that can fall under an unlimited intellect.

This proposition must be plain to anyone who attends to the fact that the intellect infers from a thing's definition a number of properties that really do follow necessarily from it (i.e., from the very essence of the thing); and that the more reality the definition of the thing expresses, i.e., the more reality the essence of the defined thing involves, the more properties the intellect infers. But the divine nature has absolutely infinite attributes (by D6), each of which also expresses an essence that is infinite in its own kind, and so from its necessity there must follow infinitely many things in infinite ways (i.e. everything that can fall under an unlimited intellect).

First corollary to 16: God is the efficient cause of all things that can fall under an unlimited intellect.

Second corollary to 16: God is a cause through himself/itself and not an accidental cause.

Third corollary to 16: God is the absolutely first cause.

17: God acts from the laws of the divine nature alone, and is not compelled by anything.

I have just shown (16) that from the necessity of the divine nature alone, or (what is the same thing) from the laws of God's nature alone, absolutely infinite things follow; and in 15 I have demonstrated that nothing can be or be conceived without God—that all things are in God. So there can't be anything outside God by which God could be caused or compelled to act. Therefore, God acts from the laws of the divine nature alone, and is not compelled by anything.

First corollary to 17: There is no cause, either extrinsically or intrinsically, which prompts God to action, except the perfection of the divine nature.

Second corollary to 17: God alone is a free cause. God alone exists only from the necessity of the divine nature (by 11 and first corollary to 14), and acts from the necessity of the divine nature (by 17). Therefore (by D7) God alone is a free cause.

Note on 17:

(1) Some people think, regarding the things that I have said follow from God's nature (i.e. are in God's power), that God could bring it about that they don't happen, are not produced by God; from which they infer that God is a free cause. But this is tantamount to saying that God can bring it about that the nature of a triangle doesn't require that its three angles are equal to two right angles, or that from a given cause the effect would not follow—which is absurd.

Further, I shall show later, without help from 17, that God's nature doesn't involve either intellect or will. I know of course that many think they can demonstrate that a supreme intellect and a free will pertain to God's nature; for, they say, they know nothing they can ascribe to God more perfect than what is the highest perfection in us.

Moreover, while thinking of God as actually understanding things in the highest degree, they don't believe that God can bring it about that all those understood things exist. For they think that would destroy God's power. If God had created all the things in the divine intellect (they say), then God couldn't have created anything more, which they believe to be incompatible with God's omnipotence. So these thinkers prefer to maintain that God has no leanings in any direction, not creating anything except what God has decreed to create by some fundamental free choice.

But I think I have shown clearly enough (see 16) that from God's supreme power or infinite nature infinitely many things in infinitely many ways—that is, all possible things—have necessarily flowed or do always follow, with the same necessity and in the same way as from the nature of a triangle it follows from eternity that its three angles equal two right angles. So God's omnipotence has been actual from eternity and will remain actual to eternity. I think that this maintains God's omnipotence better than does the view that there are things God could do but chooses not to.

Indeed—to be frank about it—my opponents seem to deny God's omnipotence. For they have to admit that God understands infinitely many creatable things which nevertheless God will never be able to create. For creating everything that God understands to be creatable would (according to them) exhaust God's omnipotence and render God imperfect. To maintain that God is perfect, therefore, they are driven to maintaining that God cannot bring about everything that lies within the scope of the divine power. I don't see how anything more absurd than this, or more contrary to God's omnipotence, could be dreamed up!

(2) I shall add a point about the intellect and will that are commonly attributed to God. If 'will' and 'intellect' do pertain to the eternal essence of God, we must understand by each of these something different from what men commonly understand by them. For the 'intellect' and 'will' that would constitute God's essence would have to differ entirely from our intellect and will, not agreeing with them in anything but the name. They wouldn't match one another any more than Sirius the 'dog-star' matches the dog that is a barking animal. I shall demonstrate this.

We have intellect, and what we understand through it is either earlier than the act of understanding (as most people think) or simultaneous with it; but if the divine nature includes intellect, it can't be like ours in this respect, because God is prior in causality to all things (by the first corollary to 16). So far from its being the case that God's intellect represents something because the thing exists, the fundamental nature of things is what it is because God's intellect represents it in that way. So God's intellect, conceived as constituting the divine essence, is really the cause of the essence and of the existence of things. Some writers seem to have realized this—the ones who have said that God's intellect, will and power are one and the same.

Therefore, since God's intellect is the only cause of things—of their essence as well as of their existence—God must differ from other things both in essence and in existence. I shall explain this. Something that is caused differs from its cause precisely in what it gets from the cause. For example, a man may be the cause of the existence of another man, but not of his essence—that is, not of the human nature that he has, not of the-possibility-of-being-human—for the latter is an eternal truth. So they can agree entirely in their essence, having the very same human nature. But they must differ in their existences: if one of the men goes out of existence, that need not destroy the other's existence. But if the essence of one could be destroyed and become false—that is, if it could become the case that there was no such thing as human nature, no possibility-of-being-human—then the essence of the other would also be destroyed.

So if something causes both the essence and the existence of some effect, it must differ in essence and existence from the effect. But God's intellect is the cause both of the essence and of the existence of our intellect. Therefore God's intellect, conceived as constituting the divine essence, differs from our intellect both in essence and in existence and can't agree with it in anything but in name—which is what I said. It is easy to see that there is a similar proof regarding God's will and our will.

18: God is the in-dwelling and not the going-across cause of all things.

In-dwelling because: everything that exists is in God and must be conceived through God (by 15), and so (by the first corollary to 16) God is the cause of all things that are in God. Not going-across because: by 14 there can't be anything outside God for God to act on. So God is the in-dwelling and not the going-across cause of all things. [The expressions 'in-dwelling- and 'going-across' render technical terms of Spinoza's that are usually translated by 'immanent' and 'transeunt' respectively. The distinction itself is plain: I am the in-dwelling cause of my hand's moving when I move it, and the going-across cause of the fall of the tumbler that I knock off the table.] . . .

[So:]

(1) God is absolutely the proximate cause of the things produced immediately by God, and not a proximate cause in God's own kind, as they say. For God's effects can neither be nor be conceived without their cause (by 15 and 24C).

(2) God cannot properly be called the 'remote' cause of singular things (except perhaps to distinguish them from things that God has produced immediately, i.e. that follow from God's absolute nature). A 'remote' cause is one that isn't conjoined in any way with its effect; but every existing thing is in God, and depends on God in such a way that it can't exist or be conceived without God.

29: In Nature there is nothing contingent; all things have been caused by the necessity of the divine nature to exist and produce an effect in a certain way.

Whatever exists is in God (by 15); and (by 11) God exists necessarily, not contingently. Next, the modes of the divine nature—the ways in which God exists—have also followed from that nature necessarily (by 16)—either following from the divine nature just in itself (by 21) or following from it considered as caused to act in a certain way (by 28). Further, God is the cause not only of the existence of these modes (by corollary to 24) but also of their having such-and-such causal powers. For if they hadn't been caused by God, then (by 26) they could not possibly have caused themselves. And conversely (by 27) if they have been caused by God, it is impossible that they should render themselves uncaused. So all things have been caused from the necessity of the divine nature not only to exist but to exist in a certain way, and to produce effects in a certain way; and all of this is necessary, not contingent. There is nothing contingent.

32: The will cannot be called a free cause, but only a necessary one.

The will, like the intellect, is only a certain mode ·or way· of thinking. And so (by 28) each volition—each act of the will—can exist and be fit to produce an effect only if it is caused by another cause, and this cause again by another, and so on, to infinity. So the will requires a cause by which it is caused to exist and produce an effect; and so (by D7) it cannot be called a 'free' cause but only a necessary or compelled one. That was based on the will's being a finite entity to which 28 applies. Suppose it is infinite, making 28 irrelevant to it. Then it falls under 23, which means that it has to be caused to exist and produce an effect by God—this time by God-as-having-the-infinite-and-eternal-essence-of-thought rather than God-as-having-this-or-that-temporary-and-local-quality. So on this supposition also the will is not a free cause but a compelled one.

Corollary to 32: God doesn't produce any effect through freedom of the will.

Second corollary to 32: Will and intellect are related to God's nature as motion and rest are, and as are absolutely all natural things, which (by 29) must be caused by God to exist and produce an effect in a certain way.

The will, like everything else, requires a cause by which it is caused to exist and produce an effect in a certain way. And although from a given will or intellect infinitely many things may follow, God still can't be said on that account to act from freedom of the will, any more than God can be said to act from 'freedom of motion and rest' on account of the things that follow from motion and rest! So will doesn't pertain to God's nature any more than do other natural things; it is related to God in the same way as motion and rest. In short: acts of the will, such as human choices and decisions, are natural events with natural causes, just as are (for example) collisions of billiard balls. And to attribute will to God, saying that because the cause of each volition is God (= Nature) therefore God has choices and makes decisions, is as absurd as to suppose that God is rattling around on the billiard table.

33: Things could not have been produced by God in any way or in any order other than that in which they have been produced.

All things have necessarily followed from God's given nature (by 16), and have been caused from the necessity of God's nature to exist and produce an effect in a certain way (by 29). To think of them as possibly being different in some way is, therefore, to think of God as possibly being different; that is to think that there is some other nature that God could have—some other divine nature—and if such a nature is possible then it is actually instantiated, which means that there are two Gods. But it is absurd to suppose that there could have been two Gods. So things could not have been produced in any other way or in any other order than they have been produced.

Note on 33:

(1) Since by these propositions I have made it as clear as day that there is absolutely nothing in things on the basis of which they can be called contingent, I wish now to explain briefly what we should understand by 'contingent'— but first, what we should understand by 'necessary' and 'impossible'. A thing is called 'necessary' either by reason of its essence or by reason of its cause. For a thing's existence follows necessarily either from its essence and definition or from a given efficient cause. And a thing is also called 'impossible' for these same reasons—namely, either because its essence or definition involves a contradiction, or because no external cause has been caused to produce such a thing in which case the external causes that do exist will have been enough to prevent the thing from existing.

A thing is called 'contingent' only because of a lack of our knowledge. If we don't know that the thing's essence involves a contradiction, or if we know quite well that its essence doesn't involve a contradiction, but we can't say anything for sure about its existence because the order of causes is hidden from us, it can't seem to us either necessary or impossible. So we call it 'contingent' or 'merely possible'.

(2) From this it clearly follows that things have been produced by God with the highest perfection, since they have followed necessarily from a most perfect nature. God's producing everything there is doesn't mean that God is in any way imperfect. The suggestion that God could have acted differently is, as I have shown, absurd.

I'm sure that many people will reject my view as absurd, without even being willing to examine it. Of course they will! because they have been accustomed to credit God with having an absolute will—that is, with just non-causally deciding what to do—which attributes to God a 'freedom' quite different from what I have taught (D7). But I am also sure that if they would consent to reflect on the matter, and pay proper attention to my chain of our demonstrations, they would end up utterly rejecting the 'freedom' they now attribute to God, not only as futile but as a great obstacle to science. I needn't repeat here what I said in the note on 17.

Still, to please them or at least meet them half-way, I shall argue on the basis that God's essence does involve will, and shall still prove that it follows from God's perfection that things could not have been created by God in any other way or any other order. It will be easy to show this if we consider two things. First, as my opponents concede, it depends on God's decree and will alone that each thing is what it is; for otherwise God wouldn't be the cause of all things. Secondly, all God's decrees have been established by God from eternity; for otherwise God would be convicted of imperfection and inconstancy. But since in eternity there is neither when, nor before, nor after, it follows purely from God's perfection that God could never have decreed anything different. It is a mistake to think of God as having existed for a while without making any decrees and then making some.

The opponents will say that in supposing God to have made another nature of things, or supposing that from eternity God had decreed something else concerning Nature and its order, one is not implicitly supposing any imperfection in God.

Still, if they say this, they will have to concede also that God's decrees can be changed by their maker. Their supposition that God could have decreed Nature and its order to be different from how they actually are involves supposing that God could have had a different intellect and will from those that God actually has; and they—the opponents—hold that this could have been the case without any change of God's essence or of God's perfection. But if that is right, why can't God now change

God's decrees concerning created things while remaining just as perfect? It is absurd to suppose that God can do this—e.g., that from now on the laws of physics will be slightly different every second Tuesday—but my opponents have left themselves with no basis for ruling this out as the absurdity that it really is.

Therefore, since things could not have been produced by God in any other way or any other order, and since the truth of this follows from God's supreme perfection, we have to accept that God willed to create all the things that are in God's intellect, with the same perfection with which God understands them.

The opponents will say that there is no perfection or imperfection in things: what is to count in things as making them perfect or imperfect, and thus called 'good' or 'bad', depends only on God's will. So God could have brought it about, simply by willing it, that what is now perfection would have been the greatest imperfection, and conversely that what is now an imperfection in things would have been the most perfect. Thus the opponents. But God necessarily understands what God wills; so what the opponents say here is tantamount to saying outright that God could bring it about through an act of will that God understands things in a different way from how God does understand them. And this, as I have just shown, is a great absurdity.

I confess that this opinion that subjects all things to a certain unguided will of God and makes everything depend on God's whim is nearer the truth than the view of those who maintain that God does all things for the sake of the good. For the latter seem to suppose something outside God, something not depending on God, to which God in acting attends as a model and at which God aims as at a goal. This is simply to subject God to fate. Nothing more absurd can be maintained about God —shown by me to be the first and only free cause of the essence of all things and of their existence. I shan't waste any more time refuting this absurdity. . . .

Appendix to Part One

With these demonstrations I have explained God's nature and properties: God exists necessarily; God is unique; God exists and acts solely from the necessity of the divine nature; God is the free cause of all things (and I have shown how); all things are in God and depend on God in such a way that without God they can't exist or be conceived; all things have been precaused by God, not from freedom of the will or absolute ·whim or· good pleasure, but from God's absolute nature or infinite power.

Further, I have taken care, whenever the occasion arose, to remove prejudices that could prevent my demonstrations from being grasped. But because many prejudices remain that could—that can—be a great obstacle to men's understanding my way of explaining how things hang together, I have thought it worthwhile to consider those prejudices here, subjecting them to the scrutiny of reason. All the prejudices I here undertake to expose depend on the common supposition that all natural things act, as men do, on account of an end. Indeed, people maintain as a certainty that God directs all things to some definite end, this being implicit in their view that God has made all things for man and has made man to worship God.

So I shall begin by considering this one prejudice, asking first why most people are satisfied that it is true and so inclined by nature to embrace it. Then I shall show its falsity, and finally show how from this prejudices have arisen concerning good and evil, merit and wrong-doing, praise and blame, order and confusion, beauty and ugliness, and other things of this kind.

(1) Of course this is not the place to derive my explanations from the nature of the human mind. It will suffice here to build on two things that everyone must admit to be true: that all men are born ignorant of the causes of things, and that all men want to seek their own advantage and are conscious of wanting this.

From these premises it follows that men think themselves free, because they are conscious of their choices and their desires, are ignorant of the causes that incline them to want and to choose, and thus never give the faintest thought—even in their dreams!—to those causes. It follows also that men act always on account of a goal, specifically on account of their advantage, which they seek. Putting these two together, men are in a frame of mind from which efficient causes—that is, real causes—are almost totally absent, and which is saturated by thought about final causes, goals or ends or purposes. So the only explanations they look for are ones in terms of final causes—in asking 'Why did that happen?' they are asking 'For what purpose did that happen?'—and when they have heard that they are satisfied, having nothing more to ask. But if they can't get such explanations from others they have to turn to themselves, and to reflect on the ends by which they are usually led to do such things; so they necessarily judge the temperament of other men from their own temperament.

Furthermore, they find—both in themselves and outside themselves—many means that are very helpful in seeking their own advantage: eyes for seeing, teeth for chewing, plants and animals for food, the sun for light, the sea for supporting fish, and similarly with almost everything else whose natural causes—that is, whose efficient causes— they are not curious about. This leads them to consider all natural things as means to their own advantage. And knowing that they had found these means, not provided them for themselves, they had reason to think there was someone else who had prepared these means for human use. So they inferred that one or more rulers of Nature, endowed with human freedom, had taken care of all things for them, and made all things for their (human) use.

And since they had never heard anything about the character of these rulers, they had to judge it from their own characters; so they maintained that the Gods direct everything for the use of men in order to bind men to them and be held by men in the highest honour! So it has come about that each man has thought up—on the basis of his own character—his own way of worshipping God, so that God might love him above all the rest, and direct the whole of Nature according to the needs of his blind desire and insatiable greed. Thus this prejudice changed into superstition, and struck deep roots in men's minds. This is why everyone tried so hard to understand and explain the final causes—the purposes—of all things.

But while trying to show that Nature does nothing in vain (meaning: nothing that isn't useful to men), they seem to have shown only that Nature and the Gods are as mad as men are! Look at how they ended up! Along with many conveniences in Nature they couldn't avoid finding many inconveniences—storms, earthquakes, diseases, etc. They hold that these happen because the Gods—whom they judge on the basis of themselves—are angry with men for wronging them or making mistakes in their worship. And though their daily experience contradicted this, and though countless examples showed that conveniences and inconveniences happen indiscriminately to the pious and the impious alike, that didn't lead them to give up their longstanding prejudice. It was easier for them to put the Gods' reasons for· this among the other unknown things whose uses they were ignorant of, thus remaining in the state of ignorance in which they had been born, than to destroy that whole construction and think up a new one.

So they maintained it as certain that the Gods' judgments far surpass man's grasp. This alone would have caused the truth to be hidden from the human race for ever, if mathematics hadn't shown them another standard of truth. It could do this because it isn't involved in the final-causes muddle, because· it is concerned not with ends but only with the essential properties of figures. In addition to mathematics there have also been a few other things (I needn't list them here) which have enabled a few men to notice these common prejudices and be led to the true knowledge of things.

(2) That is enough on what I promised in the first place, namely, to explain why men are so inclined to believe that all things act for an end. I don't need many words to show that Nature has no end set before it, and that all final causes are nothing but human fictions. I think I have already sufficiently established it, both by my explanation of the origins of this prejudice and also by 16, the corollaries to 32, and all the propositions by which I have shown that everything happens by a certain eternal necessity of Nature and with the greatest perfection.

Still, I shall add this: this doctrine about ends turns Nature completely upside down. For what is really a cause it considers as an effect, and conversely what is an effect it considers as a cause. What by Nature comes first it makes follow. And finally, what is supreme and most perfect it makes imperfect.

The first two points are self-evident. Again, this doctrine takes away God's perfection. For if God acts for the sake of an end, it must be that God wants something and therefore lacks something.

And though the theologians and metaphysicians distinguish different kinds of ends, that doesn't help them with the present difficulty. They say that God did everything for God's own sake and not for the sake of the things God was going to create. For before the creation that they believe in they can't find anything for the sake of which God could act—except God! And so they have to admit that God willed to make things happen as means to things that God wanted and lacked. This is self-evident.

I should also mention that the followers of this doctrine about ends, wanting to show off their cleverness in saying what things are for, have called to their aid a new form of argument: instead of reducing things to the impossible, they reduce them to ignorance! Their resorting to this shows that no other way of defending their doctrine was open to them.

For example, if a slate falls from a roof onto someone's head and kills him, they will argue that the slate fell in order to kill the man. Here is how their argument goes: If it didn't fall for that purpose because God wanted the man to be killed, how could so many circumstances have come together by chance? You may answer that it happened because the wind was blowing hard and the man was walking that way. But why was the wind blowing hard just then? Why was the man walking by just then? If you answer that the wind arose then because on the preceding day, while the weather was still calm, the sea began to toss, and that the man had been invited somewhere by a friend, then we will ask: Why was the sea tossing? Why was the man invited at just that time?

And on it goes! They won't stop asking for the causes of causes until you take refuge in the will of God, which is the haven of unacknowledged ignorance.

Similarly, when they see the structure of the human body, these people are struck by a foolish wonder; and because they don't know the causes of this elaborate structure they conclude that it is constructed not by mechanical processes but by divine or supernatural skill, and constituted as it is so that the parts won't injure another.

So it comes about that someone who seeks the true causes of 'miracles' and is eager (like an educated man) to understand natural things, not (like a fool) to wonder at them, is denounced as an impious heretic by those whom the people honour as interpreters of Nature and of the Gods. For the denouncers know that if ignorance is taken away and replaced by real knowledge of mechanical processes, then foolish wonder is also taken away, depriving them of their only means for arguing and defending their authority. Enough of this; I now pass on to what I decided to treat here in the third place.

(3) After men convinced themselves that whatever happens does so on their account, they had to judge as most important in each thing whatever is most useful to them, and to rate as most excellent all the things by which they were most pleased. So they had to develop the notions: good, bad, order, confusion, warm, cold, beauty, ugliness, in terms of which they 'explained' natural things. I shall briefly discuss these here.

Whatever contributes to health and to the worship of God they have called 'good', and what is contrary to these they call 'bad'. Those who don't understand the real nature of things, and have only a pictorial grasp of them, mistake their own imaginings for intellectual thought; they really have nothing to say about things, but in their ignorance of things and of their own natures they firmly believe that there is an order in things. When a number of items are set out in such a way that when they're presented to us through the senses we can easily imagine them—can easily depict them to ourselves—and so can easily remember them, we say that they are 'orderly'; but if the opposite is true we say that they are 'disorderly' or 'confused'.

And since the things we can easily imagine are especially pleasing to us, men prefer 'order' to 'confusion', as if order were something in Nature more than a relation to our imagination! They also say that God has created all things to be orderly (thus unknowingly attributing imagination to God, unless they mean that God has disposed things so that men can easily imagine them). Perhaps they won't be deterred—though they should be—by the fact that we find infinitely many things that far surpass our imagination, and many that confuse it on account of its weakness. But enough of this.

The other notions are also nothing but various states of the imagination; yet ignorant people consider them to be chief attributes of things. This is because, as I have already said, they believe that all things were made for their sake, and call the nature of a thing 'good' or 'bad', 'sound' or 'rotten' and 'corrupt', according to how it affects them. For example, if the motion the nerves receive from objects presented through the eyes is conducive to health, the objects that cause it are called 'beautiful'; those that cause a contrary motion are called 'ugly'. Those that move the sensory apparatus through the nose they call 'pleasant-smelling' or 'stinking'; through the tongue, 'sweet' or 'bitter', 'tasty' or 'tasteless'; through touch, 'hard' or 'soft', 'rough' or 'smooth', etc.; and finally those that affect us through the ears are said to produce 'noise', 'sound' or 'harmony'. Some men have been mad enough to believe that God is pleased by harmony!

All these things show well enough that each person has judged things according to the disposition of his own brain; or rather, has accepted states of the imagination as things. So it is no wonder (I note in passing) that we find so many controversies to have arisen among men, and that they have finally given rise to scepticism. For although human bodies are alike in many ways, they still differ in very many. And for that reason what seems good to one seems bad to another; what seems ordered to one seems confused to another; what seems pleasing to one seems displeasing to another, and so on.

I pass over the other notions here, both because this is not the place to treat them at length and because everyone has experienced this variability sufficiently for himself. That is why we have such sayings as 'So many heads, so many attitudes', 'Everyone is well pleased with his own opinion', and 'Brains differ as much as palates do'. These proverbs show well enough that men judge things according to the disposition of their brain, and imagine things rather than understanding them. For if men had understood natural things they would at least have been convinced ·of the truth about them·, even if they weren't all attracted by it. The example of mathematics shows this. So we see that all the notions by which ordinary people are accustomed to explain Nature are only states of the imagination, and don't indicate the nature of anything except the imagination.

Many people are accustomed to arguing in this way: If all things have followed from the necessity of God's most perfect nature, why are there so many imperfections in Nature? why are things so rotten that they stink? so ugly that they make us sick? why is there confusion, evil, and wrongdoing? I repeat that those who argue like this are easily answered. For the perfection of things is to be judged solely from their nature and power; things are not more or less perfect because they please or offend men's senses, or because they are useful or harmful to human nature.

But to those who ask 'Why didn't God create all men so that they would be governed by the command of reason?' I answer only: 'Because God had the material to create all things, from the highest degree of perfection to the lowest'; or, to put it more accurately, 'Because the laws of God's nature have been so ample that they sufficed for producing all things that can be conceived by an unlimited intellect' (as I demonstrated in 16)—that is, producing everything that is conceivable or possible.

Part 2
The Nature and Origin of the Mind

I now move on to explain things that must necessarily follow from the essence of God, i.e. the essence of the infinite and eternal thing—not, indeed, all of them (for I have demonstrated (by I.16) that infinitely many things must follow from it in infinitely many ways), but only those that can lead us by the hand, as it were, to the knowledge of the human mind and its highest happiness.

Definitions

D1: By 'body' I understand a mode that in a certain and determinate way expresses God's essence with God is considered as an extended thing (see corollary to I.25).

D2: I say that to the 'essence' of a thing x belongs anything without which x can neither exist nor be conceived, and which can neither exist nor be conceived without x.

D3: By 'idea' I understand a concept that a mind forms because it is a thinking thing.

Explanation: I say 'concept' rather than 'perception' because the word 'perception' seems to indicate that the mind is acted on by the object, whereas 'concept' seems to express not the mind's being acted on but its acting.

D4: By 'adequate idea' I understand an idea which, considered in itself and without relation to an object, has all the properties or intrinsic marks of a true idea.

I say 'intrinsic' to exclude the idea's agreement with its object, which is extrinsic.

D5: Duration is an indefinite continuation of existing.

Explanation: I say 'indefinite' because you can't work out how long a thing will last from its own nature, or from its efficient cause, because the cause implies the existence of the thing and not its non-existence.

D6: By 'reality' and 'perfection' I understand the same thing.

D7: By 'particular things' I understand things that are finite and have a determinate [i.e., 'limited'] existence. If a number of individuals work together in one process so that together they are all the cause of one effect, I consider them all as being to that extent one particular thing.

Axioms

A1: The essence of man does not involve necessary existence; whether this or that man exists or doesn't exist depends on the order of Nature and not on the man's essence.

A2: Men think.

A3: Whenever there is a mental state such as love, desire, or anything else that can be called an 'affect' of the mind, the individual who has it must also have an idea of the thing that is loved, desired, etc. But the idea can occur without any other mental state, and thus without any corresponding affect.

A4: Each of us feels that a certain body is affected in many ways.

A5: We neither feel nor perceive any particular things except bodies and modes of thinking. See the postulates after 13.

Propositions

1: Thought is an attribute of God; that is, God is a thinking thing.

Particular thoughts are modes that express God's nature in a certain and determinate way (by corollary to I.25). Therefore (by I.D5) God has an attribute the concept of which is involved in all particular thoughts, and through which they are conceived. So thought is one of God's infinite attributes.

2: Extension is an attribute of God; that is, God is an extended thing. The demonstration of this proceeds in the same way as that of 1.

3: In God there is necessarily an idea of God's essence and of everything that necessarily follows from God's essence.

God can think infinitely many things in infinitely many ways (by 1); that is God can form the idea of God's essence and of everything that necessarily follows from it (I.16 implies that these are the same thing). But whatever is in God's power necessarily exists (by I.35); therefore, such an idea must exist, and (by I.15) it must be God that has it.

Note on 3: By 'God's power' ordinary people understand God's free will and God's power of decision over everything that exists, things which on that account are commonly thought to be contingent. For people say that God has the power of destroying all things and reducing them to nothing; and they often compare God's power with the power of kings. But I have refuted this in the corollaries to I.32.5, and have shown in I.16 that God acts with the same necessity by which God understands

God; that is, just as it follows from the necessity of the divine nature (everyone agrees about this) that God understands God, with the same necessity it also follows that God does infinitely many things in infinitely many ways. And then I have shown in I.34 that God's power is nothing but God's active essence.

So we can no more conceive of God as not acting than we can conceive of God as not existing. If it were all right to pursue these matters further, I could also show here that the power that ordinary people fictitiously ascribe to God is not only human (which shows that ordinary people conceive God as a man, or as like a man), but also involves lack of power. But I don't want to speak so often about the same topic. I do ask you to reflect repeatedly on what I have said about this in Part I, from I.16 to the end; for you won't be able to command a clear view of what I am saying unless you are careful not to confuse God's power with the human power of kings.

4: God's idea, from which infinitely many things follow in infinitely many ways, must be unique. God is unique (by the first corollary to I.14. Therefore God's idea, from which infinitely many things follow in infinitely many modes, must be unique.

5: The intrinsic being of ideas can be caused by God only considered as a thinking thing, and not considered under any other attribute. That is to say, the efficient cause of an idea cannot be the non-mental thing it is *of*, and can only be something belonging to the realm of thought, i.e., God considered as a thinking thing. This is evident from 3.

Another way of demonstrating 5 is the following. The intrinsic being of an idea is (self-evidently) a mode or manner of thinking, that is (by the corollary to I.25), a mode that expresses in a certain way God's nature as a thinking thing. And so (by I.10) it doesn't involve the concept of any other attribute of God, and consequently (by I.A4) isn't an effect of any other attribute. So the intrinsic being of ideas admits God as its cause insofar as God is considered only as a thinking thing, etc.

6: The modes or special cases or instances of each attribute have God for their cause only considered under the attribute of which they are modes, and not considered under any other attribute.

Each attribute is conceived through itself, having no conceptual overlap with any other attribute (by I.10). So the modes of each attribute involve the concept of their own attribute but not of any other; and so (by I.A4) they have God for their cause only considered under the attribute of which they are modes, and not considered under any other attribute.

Corollary: The intrinsic being of things that are not modes of thinking does not follow from the divine nature because God has first known the things, because that would mean that a mentalistic cause had a non-mentalistic effect; rather, they follow from their own attributes in the same way, and by the same necessity, as I have shown that ideas follow from the attribute of thought. For example: Why are there any plants? Don't say 'Because God wanted, willed, or planned that there be plants', for that explains something material in terms of something mental. The existence of plants has to come from facts about the material realm—God considered as extended. This still involves causation by God, but not the mental causation of a personal God, as most people think.

7: The order and connection of ideas is the same as the order and connection of things.

This is clear from I.A4. For the idea of each thing that is caused depends on the knowledge of the cause of which it is the effect.

Corollary: God's power of thinking is equal to God's power of acting. That is, whatever follows intrinsically from God's infinite nature follows representatively in God from God's idea in the same order and with the same connection.

Note on 7: Before we go on, I should recall here what I showed in Part I, namely that any attribute—that is, whatever an unlimited intellect can perceive as constituting an essence of a substance—belongs to one substance only, and consequently that the thinking substance and the extended substance are one and the same substance, which is comprehended now under this attribute, now under that. So also a mode of extension and the idea of that mode are one and the same thing, but expressed in two ways. For example, a coin existing in Nature and the idea of that coin (which is also in God, that is, which is also a part of Nature) are one and the same thing, which is thought or explained through different attributes. So whether we conceive Nature under the attribute of extension or under thought or under any other attribute, we shall find one and the same order, or one and the same connection of causes; that is, we shall find the same or parallel or analogous causal chains under all the attributes.

When I said that only as a thinking thing is God the cause of the idea of a coin (for example), and that only as an extended thing is God the cause of the coin, my point was that the intrinsic being of the idea of the coin can be perceived only through another mode of thinking as its proximate cause, and that mode again through another, and so on to infinity. So long as things are considered as modes of thinking, we must explain the order of the whole of Nature—the entire connection of causes—through the attribute of thought alone. And insofar as they are considered as modes of extension, the order of the whole of Nature must be explained through the attribute of extension alone. I maintain the same thing concerning other attributes.

8: The ideas of particular things (or modes or ways of being) that don't exist must be comprehended in God's infinite idea in the same way that the essences of the particular things (or modes or ways of being) are contained in God's attributes.

This proposition is evident from 7, but is understood more clearly from the note on 7.

Corollary: So long as particular things exist only by being comprehended in God's attributes, the ideas of them exist only because God's infinite idea exists. And when a particular thing is said to exist for a certain period of time, the idea of it also exists for that period of time.

Note on 8: If you want me to explain this further by an example, I can't of course give one that adequately explains the point I am making, since it is unique.

9: The idea of an actually existing particular thing has God for a cause. But not God considered as an infinite thing. Rather, God considered as having another idea of a particular thing which actually exists; And the cause of this second idea is also God considered as having a third idea, and so on to infinity.

The idea of a particular thing that actually exists is a particular mode of thinking, and distinct from the others (by the corollary and note on 8), and so (by 6) has God for a cause only insofar as God is a thinking thing. But (by I.28) it doesn't have God for a cause just because God is a thinking thing but because God has another determinate mode of thinking. And God is also the cause of this mode because God has a third mode of thinking, and so on backwards to infinity. But the order and connection of ideas (by 7) is the same as the order and connection of causes. So the cause of one particular idea is another idea, or God-as-having-another-idea; and of this also God is the cause because God is has a third, and so on backwards to infinity.

Corollary: Whatever happens in the particular object of any idea, there is knowledge of it in God only insofar as God has the idea of the same object.

10: The being of substance does not pertain to the essence of man; that is, substance does not constitute the form of man.

The being of substance involves necessary existence (by I.7). So if the being of substance pertained to the essence of man, then. . . man would exist necessarily, which (by A1) is absurd.

Note on 10: This proposition also follows from I.5, which says that there are not two substances of the same nature. Since a number of men can exist, what constitutes the form of man is not the being of substance. This proposition is also obvious from the other properties of substance, namely that a substance is by its nature infinite, immutable, indivisible, and so on.

Corollary: The essence of man is constituted by certain states of God's attributes—or, more precisely, certain states of God that fall under, or are special cases of, God's attributes. The being of substance doesn't pertain to the essence of man (by 10). So (by I.15) it is something that is in God and can neither exist nor be conceived without God, or (by the corollary to I.25) it is a quality or mode that expresses God's nature in a certain and determinate way.

Note on 10 and its corollary: Of course everyone must concede that nothing can either exist or be conceived without God. For everyone agrees that God is the only cause of all things, both of their essence and of their existence. That is, God is the cause not only of things' coming into existence but also of their being ·what they are·. But many people say that if x can't exist or be conceived without y, then y pertains to the nature of x. If they follow through on this consistently (which they usually don't), they will be led to believe either that the nature of God pertains to the essence of created things, or that created things can be or be conceived without God.

I think they were led into this by neglecting the ·proper· order of philosophizing. They believed that the divine nature—which they should have contemplated before anything else, because it comes first both in knowledge and in nature—is last in the order of knowledge, and that the so-called 'objects of the senses' come first. That is why when they thought about natural things they paid no attention at all to the divine nature; and when later they turned their minds to the divine nature, they entirely ignored the first fictions on which they had based their knowledge of natural things, because these could not assist knowledge of the divine nature. So it is no wonder that they have generally contradicted themselves. No more of that.

All I wanted here was to give a reason why I didn't say that anything without which a thing can neither exist nor be conceived pertains to its nature—namely, for the reason that particular things can neither exist nor be conceived without God, yet God doesn't pertain to their essence. Here is what I have said does constitute the essence of a thing: it is that which is given if the thing is given, and is taken away if the thing is taken away. In other words: x is the essence of y if x can neither exist nor be conceived without y, and vice versa.

11: The first thing that constitutes the actual being of a human mind is nothing but the idea of a particular thing that actually exists.

Corollary: Any human mind is a part of the infinite intellect of God. Therefore, when we say that a human mind perceives this or that, we are merely saying that God has this or that idea; not God-as-infinite, but God-as-explained-through-the-nature-of-that-human- mind, or God-as-providing-the-essence-of-that-human-mind. And when we say that this or that idea is had by God-as-providing-the-nature-of-a-mind-together-with-x (where x is something other than that mind), then we are saying that that human mind perceives x only partially or inadequately.

Note on 11 and corollary: Here, no doubt, you will come to a halt and think of many things that will give you pause. I ask you to continue with me slowly, step by step, and to make no judgment on these matters until you have read through them all.

12: Whatever happens in the object of the idea constituting a human mind must be perceived by that human mind (which is to say that there must be an idea of that thing in the mind in question). So if the object of the idea constituting a human mind is a body, everything that happens in that body must be perceived by that mind.

Whatever happens in the object of any idea, the knowledge of it must (by the corollary to 9) be in God-as-having-the-idea-of-that-object, i.e., (by 11) it must be in God-as-constituting-the mind-of-some-thing.

Note on 12: This proposition is also evident, and more clearly understood, from the note on 7, which you should consult.

13: The object of the idea constituting a human mind is the corresponding body, or a certain mode of extension that actually exists, and nothing else.

If the object of your mind were not your body, the ideas of the states of your body would (by the corollary to 9) not be in God-as-constituting-your-mind, but in God-as-constituting-the mind-of-something-else; that is (by the corollary to 11), the ideas of the states of your body would not be in your mind; but (by A4) you do have ideas of the states of your body. Therefore, the object of the idea that constitutes your human mind is your body, and (by 11) it actually exists.

Corollary: A man consists of a mind and a body, and the human body exists as we are aware of it.

Note on 13: From these propositions we understand not only that the human mind is united to the body, but also what that union of mind and body consists in. But no one will be able to understand this adequately or clearly unless he first knows enough about the nature of our body. For the things I have shown up to here have been completely general and apply not only to man but to other individuals (though all individuals are to some degree alive). Of each thing there must be an idea in God, of which God is the cause in the same way as God causes the idea of the human body; so everything I have said so far about the idea of the human body also holds for the idea of any thing.

Still, we can't deny that ideas differ among themselves, just as the objects of ideas do, and that one idea is more excellent and contains more reality than another idea, just as the object of the former is more excellent and contains more reality than the object of the latter. And so (I repeat) to determine how the human mind differs from the others, and how it excels them, we must know the nature of its object, that is, of the human body. I can't explain this here, nor do I need to for the things I want to demonstrate.

But I shall make this general remark: To the extent that a body is more capable than others of doing many things at once, or of being acted on in many ways at once, to that extent its mind is more capable than others of perceiving many things at once. And to the extent that the actions of a body depend more on itself alone, and less on input from other bodies, to that extent its mind is more capable of understanding clearly.

From this we can know the excellence of one mind over the others, and also see why we have only a completely confused knowledge of our body, and many other things that I shall deduce in the following propositions. For this reason I have thought it worthwhile to explain and demonstrate these things more accurately. To do this I need first to premise a few things about the nature of bodies. . . .

[Interlude on Body]

LEMMA 4: When a body or individual loses some of its parts which are replaced by others of the same nature, the body or individual will retain its nature as before, with no change in its form.

Bodies are not distinguished by difference of substance; what constitutes the form of the individual consists in the union of the bodies that are its parts (by The Definition); and this union is retained even if a continual change of constituent bodies occurs. So the individual will retain its nature, as before, through such a change.

L5: If the parts composing an individual become larger or smaller, but in such a proportion that they all keep the same ratio of motion and rest to each other as before, then the individual will retain its nature, as before, without any change of form. The demonstration of this is the same as that of L4.

L6: If certain bodies composing an individual are compelled to alter the direction of their motion, but in such a way that they continue their motions and communicate them to each other in the same ratio as before, the individual will retain its nature, without any change of form.

L7: Such an individual retains its nature so long as each part retains its motion and communicates it to the other parts as before, whether it as a whole moves or is at rest, and in whatever direction it moves.

Note on L4–7: Now we can see how a composite individual can be altered in many ways while still preserving its nature. So far we have been thinking of an individual that is composed only of the simplest bodies, namely ones differing from one another only by motion and rest, speed and slowness. If we now turn to an individual composed of a number of individuals with different natures, we shall find that this ·too· can be altered in a great many other ways while still preserving its nature. For since each part of it is composed of a number of simpler bodies, each part (by L7) can without any change of its nature move at varying speeds and consequently communicate its motion at varying speeds to the others.

If we now turn to a third kind of individual, composed of many individuals of the second kind, we shall find that it also can be altered in many other ways while still retaining its form. And if we carry this line of thought on to infinity, we shall easily grasp that the whole of Nature is one individual whose parts—that is, all bodies—vary in infinite ways without any change of the whole individual. . . .

Postulates

P1. A human body is composed of a great many individuals of different natures, each of which is highly composite.

P2. Some of the individuals of which a human body is composed are fluid, some soft, some hard.

P3. The individuals composing a human body are affected by external bodies in very many ways, and so, therefore, is the body as a whole.

P4. For a human body to be preserved, it needs a great many other bodies by which it is continually regenerated, so to speak.

P5. When a fluid part of a human body is acted on by an external body so that it frequently pushes against a soft part ·of the body·, it changes its surface and impresses ·on the soft part· certain traces of the external body.

P6. A human body can move and arrange external bodies in a great many ways.

⌈Back to the Mind⌉

14: A human mind can perceive many things, and the more ways its body can be arranged the greater is its ability to perceive things.

A human body (by P3 and P6) is affected in a great many ways by external bodies, and is disposed to affect external bodies in a great many ways. But the human mind must perceive everything that happens in the human body (by 12). So 14 follows.

15: The idea that constitutes the intrinsic being of a human mind is not simple, but is composed of a great many ideas.

The idea that constitutes the intrinsic being of a human mind is the idea of a body (by 13), which (by P1) is composed of a great many highly composite individuals. But (by the corollary to 8) there must be an idea in God of each individual composing the body. Therefore (by 7) the idea of a human body is composed of these many ideas of the parts composing the body.

16: The idea of any effect that external bodies have on a human body must involve the natures both of that human body and of the external bodies.

The ways in which a body is affected follow from the natures of both the affected body and the affecting body (by A1" in the Physical Interlude). So the ideas of those effects will (by I.A4) necessarily involve the nature of each body. And so 16 follows.

Corollary 1: A human mind perceives the nature of many bodies together with the nature of its own body.

Corollary 2: The ideas that we have of external bodies are more informative about the condition of our own body than about the nature of the external bodies. I have explained this by many examples in the Appendix of Part I.

17: If a human body is in a state that involves the nature of an external body, the corresponding human mind will regard that external body as actually existing, or as present to it, until the body is put into a state that excludes the existence or presence of that body.

This is obvious. For as long as the human body is in that state, the ·corresponding· human mind (by 12) will perceive that state of the body, that is (by 16), it will have an idea that involves the nature of the external body, an idea that doesn't exclude but affirms the existence or presence of the external body. And so (by the first corollary to 16) the mind will regard the external body as actually existing, or as present, until it is put into a state etc.

Corollary: Even if the external bodies by which a human body was once affected neither exist nor are present, the corresponding mind will still be able to regard them as if they were present.

Note on 17: So we see how it can happen (as it often does) that we regard as present things that don't exist. This can happen from other causes also, but I am content here to have shown one cause through which I can explain the phenomenon as if I had shown it through its true cause. I don't in fact think I have wandered far from the true cause, because my 'postulates' contain hardly anything that isn't established by experience that we can't doubt once we have shown that the human body exists as we are aware of it (see corollary to 13).

Furthermore from the corollary to 17 and the second corollary to 16 we clearly understand how the idea of Peter that constitutes the essence of Peter's mind differs from the idea of Peter that Paul has. The former directly expresses the essence of Peter's body, and it involves existence only so long as Peter exists; but the latter indicates the condition of Paul's body more than it does Peter's nature, so while Paul's body remains in that condition his mind will still regard Peter as present to itself even if Peter doesn't exist.

The states of the human body whose ideas present external bodies as present to us I shall—so as to stay with ordinary usage—call 'images' of the bodies, even if they don't reproduce the shapes of the bodies themselves. And when the mind regards bodies in this way I shall say that it 'imagines', and the states it is in when it imagines I shall call 'imaginings'.

As a start on understanding what error is, I ask you to note that the imaginings of the mind, considered in themselves, contain no error; what puts the mind into error is never just its imagining things that don't exist, but rather its lacking an idea that excludes the existence of the things that it imagines to be present to it. For if the mind imagines nonexistent things as present to it while at the same time knowing that those things don't exist, it would regard this power of imagining not as a vice but as a virtue of its nature—especially if this faculty of imagining depends only on its own nature, i.e., if the mind's faculty of imagining is free.

18: If a human body has once been affected by two or more bodies at the same time, then when the corresponding mind subsequently imagines one of them it will immediately recollect the others also.

Note on 18: From this we clearly understand what memory is. For it is nothing but a certain connection of ideas involving the nature of things outside the human body—a connection that is in the mind according to the order and connection of the states of the corresponding human body. I say, first, that this connection is only of ideas that involve the nature of things outside the human body, not of the ideas that explain the nature of those things. For they are really (by 16) ideas of states of the human body which involve both its nature and that of external bodies. I say, second, that this connection happens according to the order and connection of the states of the human body in order to distinguish it from the connection of ideas that happens according to the order of the intellect, by which the mind perceives things through their first causes, and which is the same in all men.

From this we clearly understand why the mind immediately passes from the thought of one thing to the thought of another that is quite unlike the first: for example, from the thought of the word *pomum* a Roman will immediately pass to the thought of an apple, which has no similarity to that articulate sound; the two have nothing in common except that the body of the Roman has often been affected by these two at the same time, hearing the word *pomum* while he saw the fruit. In this way each of us will pass from one thought to another, according to how the images have come to be associated in the body. For example, a soldier who sees hoof-prints in the sand will immediately think of a horse, then a horseman, then a war, and so on; while a farmer will think of a horse, then a plough, then a field, and so on.

19: The only way in which a human mind knows the ·corresponding· human body—and the only way it knows that the body exists—is through ideas of the states of that body.

20: There is also in God an idea of the human mind—i.e. knowledge of the human mind—which follows in God in the same way and is related to God in the same way as the idea (i.e., knowledge) of the human body.

Thought is an attribute of God (by 1), and so (by 3) there must be in God an idea both of thought in general and of every specific state of affairs that involves thought, and consequently (by 11) of each human mind also. Now, this idea (i.e., knowledge) of the mind is caused not by God's nature as an unlimited thinking thing, but rather by God considered as having some other idea of a particular thing (by 9). But the order and connection of ideas is the same as the order and connection of causes (by 7). Therefore, this idea (i.e., knowledge) of the mind follows in God and is related to God in the same way as the idea (i.e., knowledge) of the body.

21: This idea of the mind is united to the mind in the same way as the mind is united to the body. I have shown that what unites a mind to its body is the fact that the body is the object of the mind (see 12 and 13); and so by the same reasoning the idea of the mind must be united with its own object, i.e., with the mind itself, just as the mind is united with the body.

Note on 21: This proposition is understood far more clearly from what I said in the note on 7; for there I showed that a body and the idea of it (which by 13 is the corresponding mind) are one and the same individual, which can be conceived as a mind under the attribute of thought or as a body under the attribute of extension. So the mind and the idea of it are one and the same thing, which is conceived under one and the same attribute, namely thought. The mind and the idea of it follow in God from the same power of thinking and by the same necessity. For the idea of the mind (i.e., the idea of an idea) is nothing but the form of the idea considered as a mode of thinking without relation to an object. For as soon as someone knows something, he thereby knows that he knows it, and at the same time knows that he knows that he knows, and so on, to infinity. But more on these matters later.

22: A human mind perceives not only the states of the corresponding body but also the ideas of these states.

The ideas of the ideas of the states follow in God in the same way and are related to God in the same way as the ideas of the states (this is demonstrated in the same way as 20). But the ideas of the states of a body are in the corresponding human mind (by 12), that is, they are (by the corollary to 11) in God-as-constituting-the-essence-of-that-human-mind. So the ideas of these ideas will be in God insofar as God has the knowledge (i.e., the idea) of the human mind in question, which is to say (by 21) that they will be in that human mind itself, which for that reason perceives not only the states of the body but also the ideas of the states.

23: A mind knows itself only through perceiving the ideas of the states of the corresponding body.

24: A human mind does not involve adequate knowledge of the parts composing the corresponding human body.

The parts composing a human body contribute to the essence of that body itself only insofar as they communicate their motions to one another in a certain fixed manner (see The Definition on page 30); they can be considered as individuals, without relation to the human body, but that aspect of them is irrelevant to the human body's being the body that it is. For (by P1) the parts of a human body are themselves highly composite individuals, whose parts (by L4) can be separated from the human body and go their own way, communicating their motions (see A1" after L3) to other bodies in some other way, while the human body in question completely preserves its own nature and form.

So the idea (that is, the knowledge) of each part will be in God (by 3) insofar as God is considered to have another idea of a particular thing (by 9), a particular thing which is prior in the order of nature to the part itself (by 7). This holds for each part of the individual which is a human body. And so, the knowledge of each part composing a human body is in God insofar as God has a great many ideas of things, and not insofar as God has only the idea of the human body, i.e., (by 13), the idea that constitutes the nature of the human mind. And so, by (the corollary to 11) the human mind does not involve adequate knowledge of the parts composing the human body.

25: The idea of any state of a human body does not involve adequate knowledge of an external body.

I have shown (16) that the idea of a state of a human body involves the nature of an external body to the extent that the external body causes that human body to be in that state. But the adequate idea (or knowledge) of the external body.

26: The only way a human mind perceives any external body as actually existing is through the ideas of the states of its own body.

Insofar as a human body is affected by an external body in some way, to that extent the mind in question (by 16 and its first corollary) perceives the external body. But if a human body is not affected by an external body in any way, then (by 7) the idea of that human body—that is (by 13), the corresponding human mind—is also not affected in any way by the idea of that body; which is to say that it does not perceive the existence of that external body in any way.

Corollary: Insofar as a human mind imagines an external body, it does not have adequate knowledge of it.

27: The idea of any state of a human body does not involve adequate knowledge of the human body itself.

Any idea of any state of a human body involves the nature of that body insofar as it is considered to be in a certain definite qualitative state (see 16). But insofar as the human body is an individual which can be—and indeed is—in many other states, the idea of this one state must omit the others, and thus cannot be adequate. See the demonstration of 25.

28: The ideas of the states of a human body, insofar as they are related only to the corresponding human mind, are not clear and distinct, but confused.

The ideas of the states of a human body involve the nature of external bodies as much as that of the human body (by 16), and must involve the nature not only of that human body as a whole but also of its parts; for the states are (by P3) ways in which the parts of the human body and consequently the whole of it are affected. But (by 24 and 25) adequate knowledge of external bodies and of the parts composing a human body is in God—not God as having the idea that constitutes the human mind, but God as having other ideas.

Or, in different words: adequate ideas of the external bodies and of the parts of the human body occur in the mental realm only as corresponding to those bodies and body-parts; so they don't occur in the mind corresponding to that human body. Therefore any ideas of a human body's states that occur in the corresponding mind are not adequate because they don't include ideas of all the causes of the states in question; and so they are like conclusions without premises, which as anyone can see is equivalent to saying that they are confused ideas.

Note on 28: In the same way we can demonstrate that the idea that constitutes the nature of a human mind is not, considered in itself alone, clear and distinct.

29: The idea of the idea of any state of a human body doesn't involve adequate knowledge of the human mind.

The idea of a state of a human body (by 27) doesn't involve adequate knowledge of that body itself (meaning that it doesn't express the body's nature adequately), that is (by 13),it doesn't agree adequately with the nature of the mind; and so (by I.6) the idea of this idea doesn't express the nature of the human mind adequately, or doesn't involve adequate knowledge of it.

Corollary: So long as a human mind perceives things from the common order of nature, it does not have an adequate but only a confused and mutilated knowledge of itself, of its own body, and of external bodies.

A mind knows itself only by perceiving ideas of the states of the corresponding body (by 23). But (by 19) it perceives its own body only through ideas of that body's states and that is also how it perceives external bodies (by 26). So its having these ideas doesn't give it adequate knowledge either of itself (by 29) or of its own body (by 27) or of external bodies (by 25); such knowledge as it has of these is (by 28 and the note on it) mutilated and confused.

Note on 29: To spell this out a little: A mind has not an adequate but only a confused and mutilated knowledge of itself, of its own body, and of external bodies, so long as it perceives things from the common order of Nature, i.e. so long as what happens in it is caused from the outside through chance encounters with things; but not when, regarding a number of things at once, it is caused internally to understand their agreements, differences, and oppositions. For when its set of mind is caused from within, it is regarding things clearly and distinctly, as I shall show below.

30: We can have only an entirely inadequate knowledge of the duration of our body.

Our body's duration depends neither on its essence (by A1), nor even on God's absolute nature (by I.21). But (by I.28) it is caused to exist and produce an effect by other causes that are also caused by others, and so on to infinity. So the duration of our body depends on the common order of Nature and the constitution of things. But adequate knowledge of how things are constituted is in God considered as having the ideas of everything, and not in God considered only as having the idea of a human body (by the corollary to 9). So the knowledge of the duration of our body is quite inadequate in God considered as constituting only the nature of the human mind, which is to say (by the corollary to 11) that this knowledge is quite inadequate in our mind.

31: We can have only an entirely inadequate knowledge of the duration of particular things outside us.

Each particular thing, like the human body, must be caused by another particular thing to exist and produce effects in some definite way, and this again by another, and so to infinity (by I.28). But in 30 I demonstrated from this common property of particular things that we have only a very inadequate knowledge of the duration of our body; so we have to draw the same conclusion concerning the duration of particular things outside us, namely that we can have only a very inadequate knowledge of their duration.

Corollary: All particular things are contingent and destructible. We can have no adequate knowledge of their duration (by 31), and that is what we must understand by things' being 'contingent' and by their being 'destructible' (see the first note on I.33). For (by I.29) there is no contingency other than that.

32: All ideas, insofar as they are related to God, are true.

All ideas that are in God agree entirely with their objects (by the corollary to 7), and so (by I.A6) they are all true.

33: There is nothing positive in ideas on account of which they are called false.

If you deny this, try to conceive a positive way of thinking that embodies the form of error, or falsity. This way of thinking cannot be in God (by 32). But it can't either be or be conceived outside God either (by I.15). So there can be nothing positive in ideas on account of which they are called false.

34: Every idea that in us is absolute (or adequate and perfect) is true.

When we say that there is in us an adequate and perfect idea, we are saying only that (by the corollary to 11) there is an adequate and perfect idea in God insofar as God constitutes the essence of our mind; so (by 32) we are saying only that such an idea is true.

35: Falsity consists in the lack of knowledge that inadequate (or mutilated and confused) ideas involve.

There is nothing positive in ideas that embodies the form of falsity (by 33). Then what can falsity (or error) consist in? It can't consist merely in lacking something; for minds are said to err or to be deceived while bodies are not, yet anything relevant that minds lack is also lacked by bodies. Minds are said to be 'ignorant', while bodies are not; but falsity or error can't consist in merely being ignorant either; for ignorance and error are different. So it consists in the lack of knowledge that is involved in inadequate and confused ideas.

Note on 35: In the note on 17 I explained how error consists in the lack of knowledge. But to explain the matter more fully I shall give one or two examples: men are deceived in thinking themselves free—that is, they think that of their own free will they can either do a thing or refrain from doing it—an opinion that consists only in this, that they are conscious of their actions and ignorant of the causes that make them act as they do. So this—their not knowing any cause of their actions—is their idea of freedom! Of course they say that human actions 'depend on the will', but these are only words for which they have no idea and thus have no meaning. For nobody knows what 'the will' is, or how it moves the body.

Similarly, when we look at the sun, we imagine it as about 200 feet away from us, an error that doesn't consist simply in this imagining, but in our imagining it in this way while being ignorant of its true distance and of the cause of our imagining it as we do. Don't think that the cause of our imagining is the fact that we don't know any better, i.e. don't know how far away the sun really is. For even if we later come to know that it is more than 600 diameters of the earth away from us, we nevertheless imagine it—we picture it—as near. For we imagine the sun as so near not because we don't know its true distance but because the sun causes our body to be in a certain state.

36: Inadequate and confused ideas follow with the same necessity as adequate (or clear and distinct) ideas.

All ideas are in God (by I.15); and so far as their relation to God goes they are true (by 32) and adequate (by the corollary to 7). So the only way ideas can be inadequate or confused is in relation to some particular person's mind (see 24 and 28). So all ideas—both the adequate and the inadequate—follow with the same necessity (by the corollary to 6).

37: What is common to all things (see Lemma 2), and is equally in the part and in the whole, does not constitute the essence of any particular thing.

Try to conceive something (call it A) that is common to all things and is equally in the part and in the whole, and that does constitute the essence of some particular thing, call it B. Then (by D2) A can neither be nor be conceived without B. But this is contrary to the hypothesis that A is common to all etc. and that B is merely one particular thing. So A does not pertain to the essence of B and does not constitute the essence of any other particular thing either.

38: Things that are common to all, and are equally in the part and in the whole, can only be conceived adequately.

Corollary: Certain ideas or notions are common to all men. For (by Lemma 2) all bodies agree in certain things, which (by 38) must be perceived adequately (that is, clearly and distinctly) by everyone.

39: If something is common to a human body and certain external bodies by which that human body is usually affected, and is equally in the part and in the whole of each of them, its idea will also be adequate in the ·corresponding· mind.

Corollary: A mind is the more capable of perceiving many things adequately as its body has many things in common with other bodies.

40: Whatever ideas follow in the mind from ideas that are adequate in the mind are also adequate.

This is obvious. For when we say that an idea in a human mind follows from ideas that are adequate in it, we are saying only (by the corollary to 11) that the cause of this idea is not God-considered-as-infinite or God-considered-as-involving-many-particular-things but just God-considered-as-including-the-essence-of-that-human-mind; so it must be adequate.

Notes on 37–40:

(1) With this I have explained the cause of so-called 'common notions', which are the foundations of our reasoning. But some axioms or notions result from other causes which it would be helpful to explain by my method. For my explanations would enable us to establish which notions are more useful than the others, and which are nearly useless; and then to show which are 'common', which are clear and distinct only to those who have no prejudices, and finally which have no good basis. Moreover, we could establish what is the origin of the so-called 'second notions' and thus of the axioms

based on them, and other things I have thought about from time to time concerning these matters. But since I have set these aside for another treatise, and don't want to annoy you with too long a discussion, I have decided to pass over them here.

But I don't want to omit anything that you need to know, so I shall briefly add something about the source of the so-called 'transcendental' terms—I mean ones like 'being, 'thing' and 'something'. These terms arise from the fact that a human body, being limited, can form distinctly only a certain number of images at the same time (I have explained what an image is—especially that it is a bodily state—in the note on 17). If that number is exceeded, the images will begin to be confused, and when the excess becomes big enough the images will all be completely confused with one another.

Since this is so, it is evident from the corollary to 17 and from 18 that a human mind will be able to imagine distinctly, at the same time, as many bodies as there can be ·distinct· images formed at the same time in its body. But when the images in the body are completely confused, the mind will imagine all the bodies confusedly, running them all together, and treat them as though they all fall under one attribute, namely the 'attribute' of being, thing, etc. This also follows from the fact that images are not always equally vigorous, and from other such facts; but I needn't go into these here. For my purposes the one I have chosen is enough, for all the reasons come down to this: these 'transcendental' terms signify ideas that are highly confused.

The notions they call 'universal', like man, horse, dog etc., have arisen from similar causes. To take one example: So many images of men are formed at one time in a human body that they surpass the power of imagining, to the extent that the ·corresponding· mind can't imagine slight differences amongst the particular men (such as the colour and size of each one) or their determinate number, and imagines distinctly only what is common to them all in their effects on the body in question. For the body has been affected most forcefully by what is common to all the men, since each particular man has affected it by this property. And the mind expresses this what-is-common by the word 'man', and predicates it of countless particulars.

These 'universal' notions are not formed by all people in the same way, but vary from one person to another, depending on what the body of each person has more often been affected by, and on what the mind of each imagines or recollects more easily. For example, those who have mostly been impressed by men's stature will understand by the word 'man' an animal that stands upright. But those who have generally focused on something else will form another common image of men—e.g. that man is an animal capable of laughter, or a featherless biped, or a rational animal. And similarly with the others—each will form universal images of things according to the disposition of his body. Hence it is not surprising that so many controversies have arisen among the philosophers, who have wished to explain natural things by mere images of things.

(2) From what I have said above, it is clear that we perceive many things and form universal notions:

1. from particular things which have been represented to us through the senses in a way that is mutilated, confused, and without order for the intellect (see corollary to 29); for that reason I have been accustomed to call such perceptions knowledge from random experience;

2. from signs, e.g. from the fact that, having heard or read certain words, we recollect things and form certain ideas of them that resemble them, through which we imagine the things (note on 18). These two ways of regarding things I shall from now on call 'knowledge of the first kind', 'opinion' or 'imagination';

3. from the fact that we have common notions and adequate ideas of the properties of things (see the corollary to 38, and 39 and its corollary, and 40). This I shall call 'reason' and 'the second kind of knowledge'.

4. In addition to these two kinds of knowledge, there is (as I shall show in what follows) a third kind, which I shall call 'intuitive knowledge'. This kind of knowing goes from an adequate idea of the formal essence of certain attributes of God to adequate knowledge of the intrinsic essences of things. I shall explain all these with one example.

Suppose there are three numbers, and the problem is to find a fourth which is to the third as the second is to the first. Merchants don't hesitate to multiply the second by the third, and divide the product by the first, because [2] they haven't yet forgotten what their teacher told them (without proving it), or because [1] they have often found that this works with the simplest numbers, or [3] from the force of Euclid's demonstration of proposition 7 in Book 7—that is, from the common property of proportionals. But with the simplest numbers none of this is necessary.

Given the numbers 1, 2, and 3, no one fails [4] to see that the fourth proportional number is, and we see this much more clearly because we infer the fourth number from the ratio which we see at a glance the first number to have to the second.

41: Knowledge of the first kind is the only cause of falsity, whereas knowledge of the second and third kinds is necessarily true.

I said in the preceding note that all the ideas that are inadequate and confused pertain to knowledge of the first kind, and so (by 35) this kind of knowledge is the only cause of falsity. Next, I have said that adequate ideas pertain to knowledge of the second and third kinds, and so (by 34) this knowledge is necessarily true.

42: Knowledge of the second and third kinds, and not of the first kind, teaches us to distinguish the true from the false.

This proposition is self-evident, For someone who knows how to distinguish between the true and the false must have an adequate idea of the true and of the false, that is (second note on 37–40), he must know the true and the false by the second or third kind of knowledge.

43: He who has a true idea at the same time knows that he has a true idea, and cannot doubt the truth of the thing.

Note on 43: In the note on 21 I have explained what an idea of an idea is, ·which may help you with the foregoing demonstration·. But it should be noted that ·the demonstration wasn't really needed, because· the truth of 43 is pretty obvious. No one who has a true idea is unaware that a true idea involves the highest certainty; for to have a true idea means knowing a thing perfectly or in the best way. No one can doubt this unless he thinks that an idea is something mute, like a picture on a tablet, and not a mode of thinking—namely, the very act of understanding. That is, for a mind to 'have an idea in it' is not for it to contain some kind of mental lump, but rather for it to do something of a certain sort. And I ask, who can know that he understands something unless he first understands it? That is, who can know that he is certain about something unless he is first certain about it? What can there be which is clearer and more certain than a true idea, to serve as a standard of truth? As the light makes both itself and the darkness plain, so truth is the standard both of itself and of falsehood.

Here are three questions that are sometimes asked:

(1) If a true idea is distinguished from a false one not intrinsically but only because it agrees with its object, so that a true idea has no more reality or perfection than a false one because 'true' marks it off not intrinsically but only through its relation to something else, does the man who has true ideas have any more reality or perfection than the one who has only false ideas?

(2) Why do men have false ideas?

(3) How can someone know for sure that he has ideas that agree with their objects?

To these questions I think I have already replied.

(1) As regards the difference between a true and a false idea, it is established from 35 that the true is related to the false as existence is to nonexistence.

(2) And in the passage from 19 through the note on 35 I have shown most clearly the causes of falsity. From this it is also clear how a man who has true ideas differs from one who has only false ideas.

(3) As for 'How can someone know for sure that he has ideas that agree with their objects?', I have just shown more than adequately that this arises solely from his having an idea that does agree with its object—or that truth is its own standard. Furthermore, insofar as our mind perceives things truly it is part of the infinite intellect of God (by the corollary to 11), so it is necessary that the mind's clear and distinct are true as that God's are.

44: It is of the nature of reason to regard things as necessary, not as contingent.

It is of the nature of reason to perceive things truly (by 41), that is (by I.A6), as they are in themselves, that is (by I.29), not as contingent but as necessary.

First corollary: It depends only on the imagination that we regard things as contingent, both in respect to the past and in respect to the future.

Note on 44: I shall explain briefly how this happens. I have shown above (by 17 and its corollary) that even if a thing doesn't exist the mind still imagines it as present to itself unless causes occur that exclude its present existence. Next, I have shown (18) that if a human body has once been affected by two external bodies at the same time, then afterwards when the corresponding mind imagines one of them it will immediately recollect the other also—that is, will regard both as present to itself unless causes occur that exclude their present existence. Moreover, no one doubts that our sense of time comes from the imagination, specifically from the fact that we imagine ·or experience· bodies as moving at various speeds.

Let us suppose, then, a child who saw Peter for the first time yesterday in the morning, saw Paul at noon, and saw Simon in the evening, and today again saw Peter in the morning. It is clear from 18 that as soon as he sees the morning light, he will immediately imagine the sun taking the same course through the sky as he saw the day yesterday; that is, he will imagine the whole day, and Peter together with the morning, Paul with noon, and Simon with the evening. That is, he will imagine the existence of Paul and of Simon with a relation to future time. On the other hand, if he sees Simon in the evening, he will relate Paul and Peter to the time past by imagining them together with past time. And the more often he has seen them in this same order the more uniformly he will do this. But if it should happen that on some other evening he sees James instead of Simon, then on the following morning he will imagine the coming evening time accompanied now by Simon, now by James, but not by both at once. (I am stipulating that he has seen them on different evenings, never both together.) So his imagination will vacillate and he will imagine now this one, now that one, with the future evening time. That is, he will regard neither of them as certainly future but both of them as contingently future.

And the imagination will vacillate in this way whenever it imagines things that we regard as related to past time or to present time in this manner. So we shall imagine things as contingent in relation to present time as well as to past and future time.

Second corollary: It is of the nature of reason to perceive things as in a certain way eternal.

It is of the nature of reason to regard things as necessary and not as contingent (by 44). And it perceives this necessity of things truly (by 41), that is (by I.A6), as it is in itself. But (by I.16) this necessity of things is the very necessity of God's eternal nature. Therefore, it is of the nature of reason to regard things as in this way eternal. Add to this that the foundations of reason are notions (by 38) of the qualities that are common to all, and (by 37) not of the essence of any particular thing. So they must be conceived without any relation to time but as in a certain way eternal.

eternal

45: Each idea of each body, or of each particular thing that actually exists, necessarily involves an eternal and infinite essence of God.

The idea of a particular thing x that actually exists necessarily involves both the essence of x and its existence (by corollary to 8). But particular things (by I.15) can't be conceived without God; indeed, (by 6) the idea of x has for a cause God-considered-as-A where A is the attribute under which x is a mode; so the idea of x must involve the concept of A (by I.A4), that is (by I.D6), must involve an eternal and infinite essence of God. E.g., your mind involves thought and your body involves extension; each of those is an attribute, and thus an eternal and infinite essence of God.

Note on 45: By 'existence' here I don't mean duration, that is, existence conceived abstractly as a certain sort of quantity ('How long will it exist?'). Rather, I am speaking of the very nature of existence, which is attributed to particular things because infinitely many things follow from the eternal necessity of God's nature in infinitely many ways (see I.16)—the very existence of particular things insofar as they are in God. For even if each one is caused by another particular thing to exist in a certain way, still the force by which each one stays in existence follows from the eternal necessity of God's nature. Concerning this, see the corollary to I.24.

46: The knowledge of God's eternal and infinite essence which each idea involves is adequate and perfect.

The demonstration of 45 is universal: the idea of anything, whether thought of as a part or as a whole, involves God's eternal and infinite essence. So a source of knowledge of an eternal and infinite essence of God is common to all, and is equally in the part and in the whole. And so (by 38) this knowledge will be adequate.

47: Any human mind has an adequate knowledge of God's eternal and infinite essence.

A human mind has ideas (by 22) from which it perceives as actually existing (by 23) itself, (by 19) its own body, and (by the first corollary to 16 and by 17) external bodies. So (by 45 and 46) it has an adequate knowledge of God's eternal and infinite essence.

Note on 47: From this we see that God's infinite essence and God's eternity are known to everyone. And since all things are in God and are conceived through God, it follows that we can deduce from this knowledge a great many things that we know adequately, and so can form that third kind of knowledge of which I spoke in the second note on 37-40.

Why do men have a less clear knowledge of God than of the common notions? It is because they cannot imagine God, as they can bodies, and they have joined the name 'God' to images of things that they are used to seeing. Men can hardly avoid this because they are continually affected by bodies. Indeed, most errors consist only in our not rightly applying names to things. For when someone says 'The lines drawn from the centre of a circle to its circumference are unequal', he must (at least at that moment) be meaning by 'circle' something different from what mathematicians understand by it. Similarly, when men err in calculating they have certain numbers in their mind and different ones on the paper: attending only to what they have in mind, they don't really err, but they seem to do so because we think they have in their mind the numbers that are on the paper.

If we didn't think this, we wouldn't believe that they were erring, because we distinguish mere verbal mishaps from downright error. Recently I heard someone exclaim 'My courtyard has just flown into my neighbour's hen!'; and although this was absurd I didn't think he was in error, because I had no doubt that what he meant was that his hen had flown into his neighbour's courtyard. Most controversies have arisen from men's failure to explain their own mind, or to interpret the mind of someone else. For really, when they contradict one another most energetically they either have the same thoughts or they are thinking of different things, so that what each thinks are errors and absurdities in the other are not.

48: In the mind there is no absolute (that is, free) will; rather, the mind is caused to will this or that by a cause which is also caused by another, and this again by another, and so to infinity.

A mind is a certain and determinate mode of thinking (by 11), and so (by the second corollary to I.17) it can't be a free cause of its own actions, that is, it can't have an absolute [= unconditioned] ability to will or not will. Rather, when it wills it must be caused to do so (by I.28) by a cause which is also caused by another, and this cause again by another, etc.

Note on 48: It can be shown in the same way that there is in the mind no absolute ability to understand, desire, love, etc. From this it follows that the ·so-called· 'faculties' of intellect, will, etc. are either complete fictions or merely metaphysical beings—that is, universals that we customarily form from particulars. So the relation between these: intellect—a particular idea, will—a particular act of volition Is the same as that between 'stone-ness'—a particular pebble, humanity—a particular man. The crucial point is that intellect, will, etc. are not agents or causes or anything like that; so crediting a man with having intellect is saying that he thinks or has ideas, and is not saying more than that. Analogously, to credit the thing in my hand with having stone-ness is to say that it is a stone, and not say anything more.

I have explained in the Appendix of Part I the cause of men's thinking themselves free. But before I go on I should point out here that by 'will' I understand a capacity for affirming and denying, and not a capacity for desiring. I take 'will' to be the faculty by which the mind affirms or denies something true or something false, and not the desire by which the mind wants a thing or avoids it.

Having demonstrated that these so-called 'faculties' are universal notions that aren't anything over and above the particulars from which we form the notions, we must now investigate whether the volitions themselves are anything over and above the mere ideas of things. Does a mind engage in any affirmation or negation other than what is involved in the idea itself just because it is an idea? (On this see 49 and also D3.) If it does, then our thoughts—our ideas—are just pictures. Perhaps ideas would be just pictures if they were the bodily images that I introduced in the note on 17. But it certainly isn't right to claim a pictorial status for them on that basis. For by 'ideas' I understand not the images that are formed at the back of the eye (and, if you like, in the middle of the brain), but concepts of thought.

49: In a mind no volition—that is, no affirmation or negation—occurs except that which the idea involves just because it is an idea.

In a mind (by 48) there is no absolute faculty of willing and not willing, but only particular volitions—this and that affirmation, this and that negation. Let us take the example of some particular volition, say a mode of thinking by which a mind affirms that the three angles of a triangle are equal to two right angles. This affirmation involves the concept—the idea—of the triangle; so the volition can't be conceived without the idea of the triangle. (For to say that A must involve the concept of B is the same as to say that A can't be conceived without B.) Further, this affirmation (by A3) can't exist without the idea of the triangle. Therefore, this affirmation can neither be nor be conceived without the idea of the triangle.

Furthermore, this idea of the triangle must involve this same affirmation, namely that its three angles equal two right angles. So conversely, this idea of the triangle also can neither be nor be conceived without this affirmation.

So (by D2) this affirmation belongs to the essence of the idea of the triangle, and is nothing over and above that essence. And this demonstration didn't bring in any special features of the example, so what it shows concerning this volition (or affirmation) applies to every volition, namely that it is nothing over and above the idea.

Corollary: The will and the intellect are one and the same. Will and intellect are nothing apart from particular volitions and ideas (by 48 and its note). But these are one and the same (by 49). Therefore the will and the intellect are one and the same.

Concluding Note to Part Two

By this I have cleared away what is commonly maintained to be the cause of error. Moreover, I have shown [in 35 and its note] that falsity consists only in the lack ·of knowledge· that mutilated and confused ideas involve. So a false idea, just because it is false, does not involve certainty. When we say that a man stands by some false ideas and doesn't doubt them, we aren't saying that he is certain, but only that he doesn't doubt, or that his false ideas stay with him because nothing causes him to doubt them.

Therefore, however stubbornly a man may cling to something false, I shall still never say that he is certain of it. For by 'certainty' I understand something positive (see 43 and its note), not the mere absence of doubt. But by 'lack of certainty' I do understand falsity.

However, to explain the preceding proposition more fully, I should give you some warnings. Then I must reply to the objections that can be made against this doctrine of mine; and finally, to remove every uneasiness, I thought it worthwhile to indicate some of the doctrine's advantages.

I begin, therefore, by warning you to distinguish accurately between an idea or concept of the mind and the images of things that we imagine, and between ideas and the words by which we signify things. Many people either completely confuse these three—ideas, images, and words—or don't distinguish them accurately enough or carefully enough; and that has left them completely ignorant of this doctrine concerning the will. But one needs to know it, both for the sake of philosophical theory and in order to arrange one's life wisely.

Indeed, those who think that ideas consist in images that are formed in us through encounters with external bodies are convinced that the ideas of things of which we can't form a similar image are not ideas but only fictions that we make up through a free choice of the will. They look on ideas, that is, as dumb pictures on a panel; and being in the grip of this prejudice they don't see that an idea, just because it is an idea, involves an affirmation or negation.

And then those who confuse words with ideas, or with the affirmations that ideas involve, think that they can will something contrary to what they are aware of, when really they only affirm or deny with words something contrary to what they are aware of. But you can easily put these prejudices aside if you will attend to the nature of thought, which doesn't in any way involve the concept of extension. You will then understand clearly that an idea (since it is a way of thinking) is not to be identified with either an image or a series of words; for the essence of words and of images is constituted purely by bodily events, which don't at all involve the concept of thought.

⌜Four objections⌝

(1) The first objection comes from people who think it clear that the will extends more widely than the intellect, and so is different from the intellect. Why do they think the will extends more widely than the intellect? They say that it is because they know by experience that their actual faculty of assenting (that is, affirming and denying) is sufficient to enable them to assent to countless thoughts which they don't yet have, but that to have some of those thoughts they do require a greater faculty of understanding than they actually possess. Some enlargements of our stock of propositional thoughts will require a greater understanding than we have; but when such enlargement has occurred, we will be able to say yes or no without needing any enlargement of our abilities of that sort. In short: the will is distinguished from the intellect because the intellect is limited and the will is not.

(2) It can be objected against me that experience seems to teach us most clearly that we can suspend our judgment so as not to affirm or deny thoughts that we have in our minds. This also seems to be confirmed from the fact that no one is said to be deceived just because of some thought that he has, but only if he assents or dissents. Someone who feigns a winged horse—that is, merely entertains the thought of a winged horse—does not thereby affirm that there is a winged horse, and isn't deceived in entertaining that thought. Thus, experience makes it utterly clear that the will, or faculty of assenting, is free and is different from the faculty of understanding.

(3) It can be objected that one affirmation (it seems) doesn't contain more reality than another: we don't (it seems) require a greater power to affirm of something true that it is true than to affirm of something false that it is true. But with ideas it is different, for we perceive that one idea has more reality—that is, more perfection—than another. As some objects are more excellent than others, so also some ideas of objects are more perfect than others. This also seems to establish a difference between the will and the intellect.

(4) It can be objected that if man doesn't act from freedom of the will, what will happen if he is in a state of equilibrium, like Buridan's ass? ⌜The ass was equidistant between food and drink, and equally in need of each, so that it couldn't choose between them.⌝ Will he die of hunger and of thirst? If I concede that he will, I would seem to be thinking of an ass or a statue of a man, not a real man. But if I deny that he will die of hunger and thirst, then I am admitting that he will determine himself, and thus that he has the capacity for going where he wants and doing what he wants.

Perhaps other objections can also be made. But I don't have to burden you with everything that anyone may dream up; so I shall confine myself to these four, replying to them as briefly as I can.

⌜Four replies⌝

(1) I grant that the will extends more widely than the intellect, if by 'intellect' the objector refers only to clear and distinct ideas. But I deny that the will extends more widely than 'intellect' in the sense of our capacity for having thoughts. And indeed, I don't see why our capacity for willing should be called unlimited when our capacity for sensing is not. For just as the former will enable us to

affirm endlessly many things (one after another, for we can't affirm so many things all at once), so also the latter enables us to sense (that is, to perceive) endlessly many bodies one after another.

If the objectors say that there are infinitely many things that we can't perceive, I reply that since we can't reach those things by any thought we can't reach them by our faculty of willing either. 'But if God wanted to bring it about that we did have those thoughts,' they say, 'he would have to increase our faculty of perceiving, but not our faculty of willing.' This line of thought is based on the old mistake of thinking of a 'faculty' as some kind of agent or cause or mechanism. I have shown that 'the will' is not a concrete thing of any kind but a universal being or idea, something that gathers together all the particular volitions by expressing what is common to them all. Understood properly, then, the will is in a trivial way infinite: it is a universal that applies to any and all of the infinitely many actual and possible particular acts of volition!

But that is not the kind of infinity the objectors had in mind, as can be seen from looking at the other half of their objection—the one about 'intellect'. They say that for us to understand things that we now don't understand our intellect would have to be enlarged; whereas actually what would be needed is for us to have ideas that we don't now have. In employing that enlarged stock of ideas, we would still be thinking; that is, our activity with them would fall under the universal idea of intellect just as our present thinking activities do; so it would be the same intellect as we now have. In short, in the only sense in which the will 'is infinite', the intellect 'is infinite' too.

(2) I reply to the second objection by denying that we have a free power of suspending judgment. For when we say that someone 'suspends judgment', all we are saying is that he sees that he doesn't perceive the thing adequately. So suspension of judgment is really a perception, not an act of free will.

To understand this clearly, let us conceive a child imagining a winged horse while not perceiving anything else. Since this imagining involves the existence of the horse (by the corollary to 17), and the child doesn't perceive anything else that excludes the existence of the horse, he will necessarily think the horse is there in front of him. And he won't be able to doubt its existence, though he won't be certain of it.

We find this daily in our dreams, and I don't think anyone believes that while he is dreaming he has a free power of suspending judgment about the things he dreams, and of bringing it about that he doesn't dream the things he dreams he sees. Yet it does sometimes happen that even in dreams we 'suspend judgment'—namely, when we dream that we are dreaming.

Next, I agree that no one is deceived just because of what he perceives; that is, I agree that the imaginings of the mind in themselves involve no error. But I deny that a man affirms nothing in perceiving. For what is perceiving a winged horse other than affirming wings of the horse? If a mind perceived a winged horse and nothing else, it would regard the horse as present to it, and would have no cause for doubting its existence, and no ability to dissent from the proposition that there is a winged horse on the scene. The mind can't dissent from that proposition unless either its imagining of the winged horse is joined to an idea that excludes the existence of that horse or the mind perceives that its idea of a winged horse is inadequate. And then it will be compelled to deny the horse's existence (in the former case) or to doubt it (in the latter).

(3) I think that the third objection is answered by something I have already said, namely that 'the will' is something universal—merely a way of referring to something that is common to all ideas, namely affirmation—so that its complete essence must be in each idea, and in this way must be the same in all. But that holds only when 'the will' is thus conceived abstractly, so that saying 'The will is the same in every idea' is just saying that 'Every idea involves an affirmation'. The will's being the same in every idea, understood in this way, doesn't imply that there are no differences between the affirmations involved in different ideas; for in fact particular affirmations differ from one another as much as the ideas themselves do.

For example, the affirmation involved in the idea of a circle differs from the affirmation involved in the idea of a triangle as much as the idea of the circle differs from the idea of the triangle. Next, I flatly deny that affirming of what is true that it is true requires as much power of thinking as does affirming of what is false that it is true. Looked at just in terms of the mind, these two activities are related to one another as existence is to non-existence. For there is nothing positive in ideas that constitutes the form of falsity (see 35 and its note, and the note on 47). So the thing to note here, above all, is how easily we are deceived when we confuse universals with particulars, and beings of reason and abstractions with real things.

(4) As far as the fourth objection is concerned, I say that I agree entirely that a man placed in such an equilibrium—experiencing nothing but thirst and hunger, with food and drink equally distant from him—will die of hunger and thirst. If the objectors ask me whether such a man shouldn't be thought an ass rather than a man, I say that I don't know—just as I don't know how greatly we should admire someone who hangs himself, or children, fools, and madmen, etc.

[Four advantages of the doctrine]

It remains now to indicate how greatly the knowledge of this doctrine is to our advantage in life. We shall see this easily from the following four considerations. The doctrine is good for us because:

(1) It teaches that we act only from God's command, that we share in the divine nature, and that the more perfect our actions are and the more thoroughly we understand God the more thoroughly we share in the divine nature. This doctrine, then, as well as giving us complete peace of mind, also teaches us what our greatest happiness consists in—namely, in the knowledge of God alone, which leads us to do only the things that love and morality advise. This shows clearly how far people stray from the true valuation of virtue when they expect to be honoured by God with the greatest rewards for their virtue and best actions, this attitude being the greatest bondage—as if virtue itself and the service of God were not happiness itself, and the greatest freedom!

(2) It teaches us how we must conduct ourselves concerning matters of luck, or things that are not in our power—that is, things that don't follow solely from our nature, and thus depend at least in part on events external to us. What it teaches is that we must expect and bear calmly both good luck and bad. For everything that happens follows from God's eternal decree with the same necessity as it follows from the essence of a triangle that its three angles are equal to two right angles.

(3) This doctrine contributes to communal life by teaching us not to hate, to disesteem, to mock, to be angry at, or to envy anyone, and also by teaching that each of us should be content with what he has, and should be helpful to his neighbour, not from soft-hearted compassion or favouritism or superstition, but from the guidance of reason, as the time and occasion demand.

(4) Finally, this doctrine also contributes greatly to the common society by teaching how citizens are to be governed and led, not so that they may be slaves, but so that they may freely do what is best.

That completes what I had decided to treat in this note, and brings Part II to an end. In it I think I have explained the nature and properties of the human mind in enough detail, and as clearly as the difficulty of the subject allows, and that I have set out doctrines from which we can infer many excellent things that are highly useful and necessary to know. . . .

DAVID HUME

An Enquiry Concerning Human Understanding

Section 1
Of the Different Species of Philosophy

Moral philosophy, or the science of human nature, may be treated after two different manners; each of which has its peculiar merit, and may contribute to the entertainment, instruction, and reformation of mankind. The one considers man chiefly as born for action; and as influenced in his measures by taste and sentiment; pursuing one object, and avoiding another, according to the value which these objects seem to possess, and according to the light in which they present themselves. As virtue, of all objects, is allowed to be the most valuable, this species of philosophers paint her in the most amiable colours; borrowing all helps from poetry and eloquence, and treating their subject in an easy and obvious manner, and such as is best fitted to please the imagination, and engage the affections. They select the most striking observations and instances from common life; place opposite characters in a proper contrast; and alluring us into the paths of virtue by the views of glory and happiness, direct our steps in these paths by the soundest precepts and most illustrious examples. They make us *feel* the difference between vice and virtue; they excite and regulate our sentiments; and so they can but bend our hearts to the love of probity and true honour, they think, that they have fully attained the end of all their labours.

2. The other species of philosophers consider man in the light of a reasonable rather than an active being, and endeavour to form his understanding more than cultivate his manners. They regard human nature as a subject of speculation; and with a narrow scrutiny examine it, in order to find those principles, which regulate our understanding, excite our sentiments, and make us approve or blame any particular object, action, or behaviour. They think it a reproach to all literature, that philosophy should not yet have fixed, beyond controversy, the foundation of morals, reasoning, and criticism; and should for ever talk of truth and falsehood, vice and virtue, beauty and deformity, without being able to determine the source of these distinctions. While they attempt this arduous task, they are deterred by no difficulties; but proceeding from particular instances to general principles, they still push on their enquiries to principles more general, and rest not satisfied till they arrive at those original principles, by which, in every science, all human curiosity must be bounded. Though their speculations seem abstract, and even unintelligible to common readers, they aim at the approbation of the learned and the wise; and think themselves sufficiently compensated for the labour of their whole lives, if they can discover some hidden truths, which may contribute to the instruction of posterity.

3. It is certain that the easy and obvious philosophy will always, with the generality of mankind, have the preference above the accurate and abstruse; and by many will be recommended, not only as more agreeable, but more useful than the other. It enters more into common life; moulds the heart and affections; and, by touching those principles which actuate men, reforms their conduct, and brings them nearer to that model of perfection which it describes. On the contrary, the abstruse philosophy, being founded on a turn of mind, which cannot enter into business and action, vanishes when the philosopher leaves the shade, and comes into open day; nor can its principles easily retain any influence over our conduct and behaviour. The feelings of our heart, the agitation of our passions, the vehemence of our affections, dissipate all its conclusions, and reduce the profound philosopher to a mere plebeian.

4. This also must be confessed, that the most durable, as well as justest fame, has been acquired by the easy philosophy, and that abstract reasoners seem hitherto to have enjoyed only a momentary reputation, from the caprice or ignorance of their own age, but have not been able to support their renown with more equitable posterity. It is easy for a profound philosopher to commit a mistake in his subtile reasonings; and one mistake is the necessary parent of another, while he pushes on his consequences, and is not deterred from embracing any conclusion, by its unusual appearance, or its contradiction to popular opinion. But a philosopher, who purposes only to represent the common sense of mankind in more beautiful and more engaging colours, if by accident he falls into error, goes no farther; but renewing his appeal to common sense, and the natural sentiments of the mind, returns into the right path, and secures himself from any dangerous illusions. The fame of Cicero flourishes at

present; but that of Aristotle is utterly decayed. La Bruyere passes the seas, and still maintains his reputation: But the glory of Malebranche is confined to his own nation, and to his own age. And Addison, perhaps, will be read with pleasure, when Locke shall be entirely forgotten.

The mere philosopher is a character, which is commonly but little acceptable in the world, as being supposed to contribute nothing either to the advantage or pleasure of society; while he lives remote from communication with mankind, and is wrapped up in principles and notions equally remote from their comprehension. On the other hand, the mere ignorant is still more despised; nor is any thing deemed a surer sign of an illiberal genius in an age and nation where the sciences flourish, than to be entirely destitute of all relish for those noble entertainments. The most perfect character is supposed to lie between those extremes; retaining an equal ability and taste for books, company, and business; preserving in conversation that discernment and delicacy which arise from polite letters; and in business, that probity and accuracy which are the natural result of a just philosophy. In order to diffuse and cultivate so accomplished a character, nothing can be more useful than compositions of the easy style and manner, which draw not too much from life, require no deep application or retreat to be comprehended, and send back the student among mankind full of noble sentiments and wise precepts, applicable to every exigence of human life. By means of such compositions, virtue becomes amiable, science agreeable, company instructive, and retirement entertaining.

Man is a reasonable being; and as such, receives from science his proper food and nourishment: But so narrow are the bounds of human understanding, that little satisfaction can be hoped for in this particular, either from the extent of security or his acquisitions. Man is a sociable, no less than a reasonable being: But neither can he always enjoy company agreeable and amusing, or preserve the proper relish for them. Man is also an active being; and from that disposition, as well as from the various necessities of human life, must submit to business and occupation: But the mind requires some relaxation, and cannot always support its bent to care and industry. It seems, then, that nature has pointed out a mixed kind of life as most suitable to the human race, and secretly admonished them to allow none of these biases to *draw* too much, so as to incapacitate them for other occupations and entertainments. Indulge your passion for science, says she, but let your science be human, and such as may have a direct reference to action and society. Abstruse thought and profound researches I prohibit, and will severely punish, by the pensive melancholy which they introduce, by the endless uncertainty in which they involve you, and by the cold reception which your pretended discoveries shall meet with, when communicated. Be a philosopher; but, amidst all your philosophy, be still a man.

5. Were the generality of mankind contented to prefer the easy philosophy to the abstract and profound, without throwing any blame or contempt on the latter, it might not be improper, perhaps, to comply with this general opinion, and allow every man to enjoy, without opposition, his own taste and sentiment. But as the matter is often carried farther, even to the absolute rejecting of all profound reasonings, or what is commonly called *metaphysics*, we shall now proceed to consider what can reasonably be pleaded in their behalf.

We may begin with observing, that one considerable advantage, which results from the accurate and abstract philosophy, is, its subserviency to the easy and humane; which, without the former, can never attain a sufficient degree of exactness in its sentiments, precepts, or reasonings. All polite letters are nothing but pictures of human life in various attitudes and situations; and inspire us with different sentiments, of praise or blame, admiration or ridicule, according to the qualities of the object, which they set before us. An artist must be better qualified to succeed in this undertaking, who, besides a delicate taste and a quick apprehension, possesses an accurate knowledge of the internal fabric, the operations of the understanding, the workings of the passions, and the various species of sentiment which discriminate vice and virtue.

How painful soever this inward search or enquiry may appear, it becomes, in some measure, requisite to those, who would describe with success the obvious and outward appearances of life and manners. The anatomist presents to the eye the most hideous and disagreeable objects; but his science is useful to the painter in delineating even a Venus or an Helen. While the latter employs all the richest colours of his art, and gives his figures the most graceful and engaging airs; he must still carry his attention to the inward structure of the human body, the position of the muscles, the fabric of the bones, and the use and figure of every part or organ. Accuracy is, in every case, advantageous to beauty, and just reasoning to delicate sentiment. In vain would we exalt the one by depreciating the other.

Besides, we may observe, in every art or profession, even those which most concern life or action, that a spirit of accuracy, however acquired, carries all of them nearer their perfection, and renders them more subservient to the interests of society. And though a philosopher may live remote from business, the genius of philosophy, if carefully cultivated by several, must gradually diffuse itself throughout the whole society, and bestow a similar correctness on every art and calling. The politician will acquire greater foresight and subtility, in the subdividing and balancing of power; the lawyer more method and finer principles in his reasonings; and the general more regularity in his discipline, and more caution in his plans and operations. The stability of modern governments above the ancient, and the accuracy of modern philosophy, have improved, and probably will still improve, by similar gradations.

6. Were there no advantage to be reaped from these studies, beyond the gratification of an innocent curiosity, yet ought not even this to be despised; as being one accession to those few safe and harmless pleasures, which are bestowed on human race. The sweetest and most inoffensive path of life leads through the avenues of science and learning; and whoever can either remove any obstructions in this way, or open up any new prospect, ought so far to be esteemed a benefactor to mankind. And though these researches may appear painful and fatiguing, it is with some minds as with some bodies, which being endowed with vigorous and florid health, require severe exercise, and reap a pleasure from what, to the generality of mankind, may seem burdensome and laborious. Obscurity, indeed, is painful to the mind as well as to the eye; but to bring light from obscurity, by whatever labour, must needs be delightful and rejoicing.

But this obscurity in the profound and abstract philosophy, is objected to, not only as painful and fatiguing, but as the inevitable source of uncertainty and error. Here indeed lies the justest and most plausible objection against a considerable part of metaphysics, that they are not properly a science; but arise either from the fruitless efforts of human vanity, which would penetrate into subjects utterly inaccessible to the understanding, or from the craft of popular superstitions, which, being unable to defend themselves on fair ground, raise these intangling brambles to cover and protect their weakness. Chaced from the open country, these robbers fly into the forest, and lie in wait to break in upon every unguarded avenue of the mind, and overwhelm it with religious fears and prejudices. The stoutest antagonist, if he remit his watch a moment, is oppressed. And many, through cowardice and folly, open the gates to the enemies, and willingly receive them with reverence and submission, as their legal sovereigns.

7. But is this a sufficient reason, why philosophers should desist from such researches, and leave superstition still in possession of her retreat? Is it not proper to draw an opposite conclusion, and perceive the necessity of carrying the war into the most secret recesses of the enemy? In vain do we hope, that men, from frequent disappointment, will at last abandon such airy sciences, and discover the proper province of human reason. For, besides, that many persons find too sensible an interest in perpetually recalling such topics; besides this, I say, the motive of blind despair can never reasonably have place in the sciences; since, however unsuccessful former attempts may have proved, there is still room to hope, that the industry, good fortune, or improved sagacity of succeeding generations may reach discoveries unknown to former ages. Each adventurous genius will still leap at the arduous prize, and find himself stimulated, rather that discouraged, by the failures of his predecessors; while he hopes that the glory of achieving so hard an adventure is reserved for him alone.

The only method of freeing learning, at once, from these abstruse questions, is to enquire seriously into the nature of human understanding, and show, from an exact analysis of its powers and capacity, that it is by no means fitted for such remote and abstruse subjects. We must submit to this fatigue, in order to live at ease ever after: And must cultivate true metaphysics with some care, in order to destroy the false and adulterate. Indolence, which, to some persons, affords a safeguard against this deceitful philosophy, is, with others, overbalanced by curiosity; and despair, which, at some moments, prevails, may give place afterwards to sanguine hopes and expectations. Accurate and just reasoning is the only catholic remedy, fitted for all persons and all dispositions; and is alone able to subvert that abstruse philosophy and metaphysical jargon, which, being mixed up with popular superstition, renders it in a manner impenetrable to careless reasoners, and gives it the air of science and wisdom.

8. Besides this advantage of rejecting, after deliberate enquiry, the most uncertain and disagreeable part of learning, there are many positive advantages, which result from an accurate scrutiny into the powers and faculties of human nature. It is remarkable concerning the operations of the mind, that, though most intimately present to us, yet, whenever they become the object of reflexion, they seem involved in obscurity; nor can the eye readily find those lines and boundaries, which discriminate and distinguish them. The objects are too fine to remain long in the same aspect or situation; and must be apprehended in an instant, by a superior penetration, derived from nature, and improved by habit and reflexion. It becomes, therefore, no inconsiderable part of science barely to know the different operations of the mind, to separate them from each other, to class them under their proper heads, and to correct all that seeming disorder, in which they lie involved, when made the object of reflexion and enquiry. This talk of ordering and distinguishing, which has no merit, when performed with regard to external bodies, the objects of our senses, rises in its value, when directed towards the operations of the mind, in proportion to the difficulty and labour, which we meet with in performing it. And if we can go no farther than this mental geography, or delineation of the distinct parts and powers of the mind, it is at least a satisfaction to go so far; and the more obvious this science may appear (and it is by no means obvious) the more contemptible still must the ignorance of it be esteemed, in all pretenders to learning and philosophy.

Nor can there remain any suspicion, that this science is uncertain and chimerical; unless we should entertain such a scepticism as is entirely subversive of all speculation, and even action. It cannot be doubted, that the mind is endowed with several powers and faculties, that these powers are distinct from each other, that what is really distinct to the immediate perception may be distinguished by reflexion; and consequently, that there is a truth and falsehood in all propositions on this subject, and a truth and falsehood, which lie not beyond the compass of human understanding. There are many obvious distinctions of this kind, such as those between the will and understanding, the imagination and passions, which fall within the comprehension of every human creature; and the finer and more philosophical distinctions are no less real and certain, though more difficult to be comprehended. Some instances, especially late ones, of success in these enquiries, may give us a juster notion of the certainty and solidity of this branch of learning. And shall we esteem it worthy the labour of a philosopher to give us a true system of the planets, and adjust the position and order of those remote bodies; while we affect to overlook those, who, with so much success, delineate the parts of the mind, in which we are so intimately concerned?

9. But may we not hope, that philosophy, if cultivated with care, and encouraged by the attention of the public, may carry its researches still farther, and discover, at least in some degree, the secret springs and principles, by which the human mind is actuated in its operations? Astronomers had long contented themselves with proving, from the phaenomena, the true motions, order, and magnitude of the heavenly bodies: Till a philosopher, at last, arose, who seems, from the happiest reasoning, to have also determined the laws and forces, by which the revolutions of the planets are governed and directed. The like has been performed with regard to other parts of nature. And there is no reason to despair of equal success in our enquiries concerning the mental powers and economy, if prosecuted with equal capacity and caution. It is probable, that one operation and principle of the mind depends on another; which, again, may be resolved into one more general and universal: And how far these researches may possibly be carried, it will be difficult for us, before, or even after, a careful trial, exactly to determine. This is certain, that attempts of this kind are every day made even by those who philosophize the most negligently: And nothing can be more requisite than to enter upon the enterprize with thorough care and attention; that, if it lie within the compass of human understanding, it may at last be happily achieved; if not, it may, however, be rejected with some confidence and security.

This last conclusion, surely, is not desirable; nor ought it to be embraced too rashly. For how much must we diminish from the beauty and value of this species of philosophy, upon such a supposition? Moralists have hitherto been accustomed, when they considered the vast multitude and diversity of those actions that excite our approbation or dislike, to search for some common principle, on which this variety of sentiments might depend. And though they have sometimes carried the matter too far, by their passion for some one general principle; it must, however, be confessed, that they are excusable in expecting to find some general principles, into which all the vices and virtues were justly to be resolved. The like has been the endeavour of critics, logicians, and even politicians: Nor have their attempts been wholly unsuccessful; though perhaps longer time, greater accuracy, and more ardent application may bring these sciences still nearer their perfection. To throw up at once all pretensions of this kind may justly be deemed more rash, precipitate, and dogmatical, than even the boldest and most affirmative philosophy, that has ever attempted to impose its crude dictates and principles on mankind.

10. What though these reasonings concerning human nature seem abstract, and of difficult comprehension? This affords no presumption of their falsehood. On the contrary, it seems impossible, that what has hitherto escaped so many wise and profound philosophers can be very obvious and easy. And whatever pains these researches may cost us, we may think ourselves sufficiently rewarded, not only in point of profit but of pleasure, if, by that means, we can make any addition to our stock of knowledge, in subjects of such unspeakable importance.

But as, after all, the abstractedness of these speculations is no recommendation, but rather a disadvantage to them, and as this difficulty may perhaps be surmounted by care and art, and the avoiding of all unnecessary detail, we have, in the following enquiry, attempted to throw some light upon subjects, from which uncertainty has hitherto deterred the wise, and obscurity the ignorant. Happy, if we can unite the boundaries of the different species of philosophy, by reconciling profound enquiry with clearness, and truth with novelty! And still more happy, if, reasoning in this easy manner, we can undermine the foundations of an abstruse philosophy, which seems to have hitherto served only as a shelter to superstition, and a cover to absurdity and error!

Section 2
Of the Origin of Ideas

11. Every one will readily allow, that there is a considerable difference between the perceptions of the mind, when a man feels the pain of excessive heat, or the pleasure of moderate warmth, and when he afterwards recalls to his memory this sensation, or anticipates it by his imagination. These faculties may mimic or copy the perceptions of the senses; but they never can entirely reach the force and vivacity of the original sentiment. The utmost we say of them, even when they operate with greatest vigour, is, that they represent their object in so lively a manner, that we could *almost* say we feel or see it: But, except the mind be disordered by disease or madness, they never can arrive at such a pitch of vivacity, as to render these perceptions altogether undistinguishable. All the colours of poetry, however splendid, can never paint natural objects in such a manner as to make the description be taken for a real landskip. The most lively thought is still inferior to the dullest sensation.

We may observe a like distinction to run through all the other perceptions of the mind. A man in a fit of anger, is actuated in a very different manner from one who only thinks of that emotion. If you tell me, that any person is in love, I easily understand your meaning, and form a just conception of his situation; but never can mistake that conception for the real disorders and agitations of the passion. When we reflect on our past sentiments and affections, our thought is a faithful mirror, and copies its objects truly; but the colours which it employs are faint and dull, in comparison of those in which our original perceptions were clothed. It requires no nice discernment or metaphysical head to mark the distinction between them.

12. Here therefore we may divide all the perceptions of the mind into two classes or species, which are distinguished by their different degrees of force and vivacity. The less forcible and lively are commonly denominated *Thoughts* or *Ideas*. The other species want a name in our language, and in most others; I suppose, because it was not requisite for any, but philosophical purposes, to rank them under a general term or appellation. Let us, therefore, use a little freedom, and call them *Impressions*; employing that word in a sense somewhat different from the usual. By the term *impression*, then, I mean all our more lively perceptions, when we hear, or see, or feel, or love, or hate, or desire, or will. And impressions are distinguished from ideas, which are the less lively perceptions, of which we are conscious, when we reflect on any of those sensations or movements above mentioned.

13. Nothing, at first view, may seem more unbounded than the thought of man, which not only escapes all human power and authority, but is not even restrained within the limits of nature and reality. To form monsters, and join incongruous shapes and appearances, costs the imagination no more trouble than to conceive the most natural and familiar objects. And while the body is confined to one planet, along which it creeps with pain and difficulty; the thought can in an instant transport us into the most distant regions of the universe; or even beyond the universe, into the unbounded chaos, where nature is supposed to lie in total confusion. What never was seen, or heard of, may yet be conceived; nor is any thing beyond the power of thought, except what implies an absolute contradiction.

But though our thought seems to possess this unbounded liberty, we shall find, upon a nearer examination, that it is really confined within very narrow limits, and that all this creative power of the mind amounts to no more than the faculty of compounding, transposing, augmenting, or diminishing the materials afforded us by the senses and experience. When we think of a golden mountain, we only join two consistent ideas, *gold*, and *mountain*, with which we were formerly acquainted. A virtuous horse we can conceive; because, from our own feeling, we can conceive virtue; and this we may unite to the figure and shape of a horse, which is an animal familiar to us. In short, all the materials of thinking are derived either from our outward or inward sentiment: the mixture and composition of these belongs alone to the mind and will. Or, to express myself in philosophical language, all our ideas or more feeble perceptions are copies of our impressions or more lively ones.

14. To prove this, the two following arguments will, I hope, be sufficient. First, when we analyze our thoughts or ideas, however compounded or sublime, we always find that they resolve themselves into such simple ideas as were copied from a precedent feeling or sentiment. Even those ideas, which, at first view, seem the most wide of this origin, are found, upon a nearer scrutiny, to be derived from it. The idea of God, as meaning an infinitely intelligent, wise, and good Being, arises from reflecting on the operations of our own mind, and augmenting, without limit, those qualities of goodness and wisdom. We may prosecute this enquiry to what length we please; where we shall always find, that every idea which we examine is copied from a similar impression. Those who would assert that this position is not universally true nor without exception, have only one, and that an easy method of refuting it; by producing that idea, which, in their opinion, is not derived from this source. It will then be incumbent on us, if we would maintain our doctrine, to produce the impression, or lively perception, which corresponds to it.

15. Secondly. If it happen, from a defect of the organ, that a man is not susceptible of any species of sensation, we always find that he is as little susceptible of the correspondent ideas. A blind man can form no notion of colours; a deaf man of sounds. Restore either of them that sense in which he is deficient; by opening this new inlet for his sensations, you also open an inlet for the ideas; and he finds no difficulty in conceiving these objects. The case is the same, if the object, proper for exciting any sensation, has never been applied to the organ. A Laplander or Negro has no notion of the relish of wine. And though there are few or no instances of a like deficiency in the mind, where a person has never felt or is wholly incapable of a sentiment or passion that belongs to his species; yet we find the same observation to take place in a less degree. A man of mild manners can form no idea of inveterate revenge or cruelty; nor can a selfish heart easily conceive the heights of friendship and generosity. It is readily allowed, that other beings may possess many senses of which we can have no conception; because the ideas of them have never been introduced to us in the only manner by which an idea can have access to the mind, to wit, by the actual feeling and sensation.

16. There is, however, one contradictory phenomenon, which may prove that it is not absolutely impossible for ideas to arise, independent of their correspondent impressions. I believe it will readily be allowed, that the several distinct ideas of colour, which enter by the eye, or those of sound, which are conveyed by the ear, are really different from each other; though, at the same time, resembling. Now if this be true of different colours, it must be no less so of the different shades of the same colour; and each shade produces a distinct idea, independent of the rest. For if this should be denied, it is possible, by the continual gradation of shades, to run a colour insensibly into what is most remote from it; and if you will not allow any of the means to be different, you cannot, without absurdity, deny the extremes to be the same. Suppose, therefore, a person to have enjoyed his sight for thirty years, and to have become perfectly acquainted with colours of all kinds except one particular shade of

blue, for instance, which it never has been his fortune to meet with. Let all the different shades of that colour, except that single one, be placed before him, descending gradually from the deepest to the lightest; it is plain that he will perceive a blank, where that shade is wanting, and will be sensible that there is a greater distance in that place between the contiguous colours than in any other. Now I ask, whether it be possible for him, from his own imagination, to supply this deficiency, and raise up to himself the idea of that particular shade, though it had never been conveyed to him by his senses? I believe there are few but will be of opinion that he can: and this may serve as a proof that the simple ideas are not always, in every instance, derived from the correspondent impressions; though this instance is so singular, that it is scarcely worth our observing, and does not merit that for it alone we should alter our general maxim.

17. Here, therefore, is a proposition, which not only seems, in itself, simple and intelligible; but, if a proper use were made of it, might render every dispute equally intelligible, and banish all that jargon, which has so long taken possession of metaphysical reasonings, and drawn disgrace upon them. All ideas, especially abstract ones, are naturally faint and obscure: the mind has but a slender hold of them: they are apt to be confounded with other resembling ideas; and when we have often employed any term, though without a distinct meaning, we are apt to imagine it has a determinate idea annexed to it. On the contrary, all impressions, that is, all sensations, either outward or inward, are strong and vivid: the limits between them are more exactly determined: nor is it easy to fall into any error or mistake with regard to them. When we entertain, therefore, any suspicion that a philosophical term is employed without any meaning or idea (as is but too frequent), we need but enquire, *from what impression is that supposed idea derived?* And if it be impossible to assign any, this will serve to confirm our suspicion. By bringing ideas into so clear a light we may reasonably hope to remove all dispute, which may arise, concerning their nature and reality.

Section 3
Of the Association of Ideas

18. It is evident that there is a principle of connexion between the different thoughts or ideas of the mind, and that, in their appearance to the memory or imagination, they introduce each other with a certain degree of method and regularity. In our more serious thinking or discourse this is so observable that any particular thought, which breaks in upon the regular tract or chain of ideas, is immediately remarked and rejected. And even in our wildest and most wandering reveries, nay in our very dreams, we shall find, if we reflect, that the imagination ran not altogether at adventures, but that there was still a connexion upheld among the different ideas, which succeeded each other. Were the loosest and freest conversation to be transcribed, there would immediately be observed something which connected it in all its transitions. Or where this is wanting, the person who broke the thread of discourse might still inform you, that there had secretly revolved in his mind a succession of thought, which had gradually led him from the subject of conversation. Among different languages, even where we cannot suspect the least connexion or communication, it is found, that the words, expressive of ideas, the most compounded, do yet nearly correspond to each other: a certain proof that the simple ideas, comprehended in the compound ones, were bound together by some universal principle, which had an equal influence on all mankind.

19. Though it be too obvious to escape observation, that different ideas are connected together; I do not find that any philosopher has attempted to enumerate or class all the principles of association; a subject, however, that seems worthy of curiosity. To me, there appear to be only three principles of connexion among ideas, namely, *Resemblance*, *Contiguity* in time or place, and *Cause or Effect*.

That these principles serve to connect ideas will not, I believe, be much doubted. A picture naturally leads our thoughts to the original [*resemblance*]: the mention of one apartment in a building naturally introduces an enquiry or discourse concerning the others [*contiguity*]: and if we think of a wound, we can scarcely forbear reflecting on the pain which follows it [*cause and effect*]. But that this enumeration is complete, and that there are no other principles of association except these, may be difficult to prove to the satisfaction of the reader, or even to a man's own satisfaction. All we can do, in such cases, is to run over several instances, and examine carefully the principle which binds the different thoughts to each other, never stopping till we render the principle as general as possible. The more instances we examine, and the more care we employ, the more assurance shall we acquire, that the enumeration, which we form from the whole, is complete and entire.

Section 4
Sceptical Doubts Concerning the Operations of the Understanding

Part 1

20. All the objects of human reason or enquiry may naturally be divided into two kinds, to wit, *Relations of Ideas*, and *Matters of Fact*. Of the first kind are the sciences of Geometry, Algebra, and Arithmetic; and in short, every affirmation which is either intuitively or demonstratively certain. *That the square of the hypothenuse is equal to the square of the two sides*, is a proposition which expresses a relation between these figures. *That three times five is equal to the half of thirty*, expresses a relation between these numbers. Propositions of this kind are discoverable by the mere operation of thought, without dependence on what is anywhere existent in the universe. Though there never were a circle or triangle in nature, the truths demonstrated by Euclid would for ever retain their certainty and evidence.

21. Matters of fact, which are the second objects of human reason, are not ascertained in the same manner; nor is our evidence of their truth, however great, of a like nature with the foregoing. The contrary of every matter of fact is still possible; because it can never imply a contradiction, and is conceived by the mind with the same facility and distinctness, as if ever so conformable to reality. *That the sun will not rise to-morrow* is no less intelligible a proposition, and implies no more contradiction than the affirmation, *that it will rise*. We should in vain, therefore, attempt to demonstrate its falsehood. Were it demonstratively false, it would imply a contradiction, and could never be distinctly conceived by the mind.

It may, therefore, be a subject worthy of curiosity, to enquire what is the nature of that evidence which assures us of any real existence and matter of fact, beyond the present testimony of our senses, or the records of our memory. This part of philosophy, it is observable, has been little cultivated, either by the ancients or moderns; and therefore our doubts and errors, in the prosecution of so important an enquiry, may be the more excusable; while we march through such difficult paths without any guide or direction. They may even prove useful, by exciting curiosity, and destroying that implicit faith and security, which is the bane of all reasoning and free enquiry. The discovery of defects in the common philosophy, if any such there be, will not, I presume, be a discouragement, but rather an incitement, as is usual, to attempt something more full and satisfactory than has yet been proposed to the public.

22. All reasonings concerning matter of fact seem to be founded on the relation of *Cause and Effect*. By means of that relation alone we can go beyond the evidence of our memory and senses. If you were to ask a man, why he believes any matter of fact, which is absent; for instance, that his friend is in the country, or in France; he would give you a reason; and this reason would be some other fact; as a letter received from him, or the knowledge of his former resolutions and promises. A man finding a watch or any other machine in a desert island, would conclude that there had once been men in that island. All our reasonings concerning fact are of the same nature. And here it is constantly supposed that there is a connexion between the present fact and that which is inferred from it. Were there nothing to bind them together, the inference would be entirely precarious. The hearing of an articulate voice and rational discourse in the dark assures us of the presence of some person: Why? because these are the effects of the human make and fabric, and closely connected with it. If we anatomize all the other reasonings of this nature, we shall find that they are founded on the relation of cause and effect, and that this relation is either near or remote, direct or collateral. Heat and light are collateral effects of fire, and the one effect may justly be inferred from the other.

23. If we would satisfy ourselves, therefore, concerning the nature of that evidence, which assures us of matters of fact, we must enquire how we arrive at the knowledge of cause and effect.

I shall venture to affirm, as a general proposition, which admits of no exception, that the knowledge of this relation is not, in any instance, attained by reasonings a priori; but arises entirely from experience, when we find that any particular objects are constantly conjoined with each other. Let an object be presented to a man of ever so strong natural reason and abilities; if that object be entirely new to him, he will not be able, by the most accurate examination of its sensible qualities, to discover any of its causes or effects. Adam, though his rational faculties be supposed, at the very first, entirely perfect, could not have inferred from the fluidity and transparency of water that it would suffocate him, or from the light and warmth of fire that it would consume him. No object ever discovers, by the qualities which appear to the senses, either the causes which produced it, or the effects which will arise from it; nor can our reason, unassisted by experience, ever draw any inference concerning real existence and matter of fact.

24. This proposition, *that causes and effects are discoverable, not by reason but by experience*, will readily be admitted with regard to such objects, as we remember to have once been altogether unknown to us; since we must be conscious of the utter inability, which we then lay under, of foretelling what would arise from them. Present two smooth pieces of marble to a man who has no tincture of natural philosophy; he will never discover that they will adhere together in such a manner as to require great force to separate them in a direct line, while they make so small a resistance to a lateral pressure. Such events, as bear little analogy to the common course of nature, are also readily confessed to be known only by experience; nor does any man imagine that the explosion of gunpowder, or the attraction of a loadstone, could ever be discovered by arguments a priori. In like manner, when an effect is supposed to depend upon an intricate machinery or secret structure of parts, we make no difficulty in attributing all our knowledge of it to experience. Who will assert that he can give the ultimate reason, why milk or bread is proper nourishment for a man, not for a lion or a tiger?

But the same truth may not appear, at first sight, to have the same evidence with regard to events, which have become familiar to us from our first appearance in the world, which bear a close analogy to the whole course of nature, and which are supposed to depend on the simple qualities of objects, without any secret structure of parts. We are apt to imagine that we could discover these effects by the mere operation of our reason, without experience. We fancy, that were we brought on a sudden into this world, we could at first have inferred that one Billiard-ball would communicate motion to another upon impulse; and that we needed not to have waited for the event, in order to pronounce with certainty concerning it. Such is the influence of custom, that, where it is strongest, it not only covers our natural ignorance, but even conceals itself, and seems not to take place, merely because it is found in the highest degree.

25. But to convince us that all the laws of nature, and all the operations of bodies without exception, are known only by experience, the following reflections may, perhaps, suffice. Were any object presented to us, and were we required to pronounce concerning the effect, which will result from it, without consulting past observation; after what manner, I beseech you, must the mind proceed in this operation? It must invent or imagine some event, which it ascribes to the object as its effect; and it is plain that this invention must be entirely arbitrary. The mind can never possibly find the effect in the supposed cause, by the most accurate scrutiny and examination. For the effect is totally different from the cause, and consequently can never be discovered in it. Motion in the second Billiard-ball is a quite distinct event from motion in the first; nor is there anything in the one to suggest the smallest hint of the other. A stone or piece of metal raised into the air, and left without any support, immediately falls: but to consider the matter a priori, is there anything we discover in this situation which can beget the idea of a downward, rather than an upward, or any other motion, in the stone or metal?

As the first imagination or invention of a particular effect, in all natural operations, is arbitrary, where we consult not experience; so must we also esteem the supposed tie or connexion between the cause and effect, which binds them together, and renders it impossible that any other effect could result from the operation of that cause. When I see, for instance, a Billiard-ball moving in a straight line towards another; even suppose motion in the second ball should by accident be suggested to me, as the result of their contact or impulse; may I not conceive, that a hundred different events might as well follow from that cause? May not both these balls remain at absolute rest? May not the first ball return in a straight line, or leap off from the second in any line or direction? All these suppositions are consistent and conceivable. Why then should we give the preference to one, which is no more consistent or conceivable than the rest? All our reasonings a priori will never be able to show us any foundation for this preference.

In a word, then, every effect is a distinct event from its cause. It could not, therefore, be discovered in the cause, and the first invention or conception of it, a priori, must be entirely arbitrary. And even after it is suggested, the conjunction of it with the cause must appear equally arbitrary; since there are always many other effects, which, to reason, must seem fully as consistent and natural. In vain, therefore, should we pretend to determine any single event, or infer any cause or effect, without the assistance of observation and experience.

26. Hence we may discover the reason why no philosopher, who is rational and modest, has ever pretended to assign the ultimate cause of any natural operation, or to show distinctly the action of that power, which produces any single effect in the universe. It is confessed, that the utmost effort of human reason is to reduce the principles, productive of natural phenomena, to a greater simplicity, and to resolve the many particular effects into a few general causes, by means of reasonings from analogy, experience, and observation. But as to the causes of these general causes, we should in vain attempt their discovery; nor shall we ever be able to satisfy ourselves, by any particular explication of them. These ultimate springs and principles are totally shut up from human curiosity and enquiry. Elasticity, gravity, cohesion of parts, communication of motion by impulse; these are probably the ultimate causes and principles which we shall ever discover in nature; and we may esteem ourselves sufficiently happy, if, by accurate enquiry and reasoning, we can trace up the particular phenomena to, or near to, these general principles. The most perfect philosophy of the natural kind only staves off our ignorance a little longer: as perhaps the most perfect philosophy of the moral or metaphysical kind serves only to discover larger portions of it. Thus the observation of human blindness and weakness is the result of all philosophy, and meets us at every turn, in spite of our endeavours to elude or avoid it.

27. Nor is geometry, when taken into the assistance of natural philosophy, ever able to remedy this defect, or lead us into the knowledge of ultimate causes, by all that accuracy of reasoning for which it is so justly celebrated. Every part of mixed mathematics proceeds upon the supposition that certain laws are established by nature in her operations; and abstract reasonings are employed, either to assist experience in the discovery of these laws, or to determine their influence in particular instances, where it depends upon any precise degree of distance and quantity. Thus, it is a law of motion, discovered by experience, that the moment or force of any body in motion is in the compound ratio or proportion of its solid contents and its velocity; and consequently, that a small force may remove the greatest obstacle or raise the greatest weight, if, by any contrivance or machinery, we can increase the velocity of that force, so as to make it an overmatch for its antagonist. Geometry assists us in the application of this law, by giving us the just dimensions of all the parts and figures which can enter into any species of machine; but still the discovery of the law itself is owing merely to experience, and all the abstract reasonings in the world could never lead us one step towards the knowledge of it. When we reason a priori, and consider merely any object or cause, as it appears to the mind, independent of all observation, it never could suggest to us the notion of any distinct object, such as its effect; much less, show us the inseparable and inviolable connexion between them. A man must be very sagacious who could discover by reasoning that crystal is the effect of heat, and ice of cold, without being previously acquainted with the operation of these qualities.

Part 2

28. But we have not yet attained any tolerable satisfaction with regard to the question first proposed. Each solution still gives rise to a new question as difficult as the foregoing, and leads us on to farther enquiries. When it is asked, *What is the nature of all our reasonings concerning matter of fact?* the proper answer seems to be, that they are founded on the relation of cause and effect. When again it is asked, *What is the foundation of all our reasonings and conclusions concerning that relation?* it may be replied in one word, Experience. But if we still carry on our sifting humour, and ask, *What is the foundation of all conclusions from experience?* this implies a new question, which may be of more difficult solution and explication. Philosophers, that give themselves airs of superior wisdom and sufficiency, have a hard task when they encounter persons of inquisitive dispositions, who push them from every corner to which they retreat, and who are sure at last to bring them to some dangerous dilemma. The best ex-

pedient to prevent this confusion, is to be modest in our pretensions; and even to discover the difficulty ourselves before it is objected to us. By this means, we may make a kind of merit of our very ignorance.

I shall content myself, in this section, with an easy task, and shall pretend only to give a negative answer to the question here proposed. I say then, that, even after we have experience of the operations of cause and effect, our conclusions from that experience are *not* founded on reasoning, or any process of the understanding. This answer we must endeavour both to explain and to defend.

29. It must certainly be allowed, that nature has kept us at a great distance from all her secrets, and has afforded us only the knowledge of a few superficial qualities of objects; while she conceals from us those powers and principles on which the influence of those objects entirely depends. Our senses inform us of the colour, weight, and consistence of bread; but neither sense nor reason can ever inform us of those qualities which fit it for the nourishment and support of a human body. Sight or feeling conveys an idea of the actual motion of bodies; but as to that wonderful force or power, which would carry on a moving body for ever in a continued change of place, and which bodies never lose but by communicating it to others; of this we cannot form the most distant conception. But notwithstanding this ignorance of natural powers and principles, we always presume, when we see like sensible qualities, that they have like secret powers, and expect that effects, similar to those which we have experienced, will follow from them. If a body of like colour and consistence with that bread, which we have formerly eat, be presented to us, we make no scruple of repeating the experiment, and foresee, with certainty, like nourishment and support.

Now this is a process of the mind or thought, of which I would willingly know the foundation. It is allowed on all hands that there is no known connexion between the sensible qualities and the secret powers; and consequently, that the mind is not led to form such a conclusion concerning their constant and regular conjunction, by anything which it knows of their nature. As to past *Experience*, it can be allowed to give *direct* and *certain* information of those precise objects only, and that precise period of time, which fell under its cognizance: but why this experience should be extended to future times, and to other objects, which for aught we know, may be only in appearance similar; this is the main question on which I would insist. The bread, which I formerly eat, nourished me; that is, a body of such sensible qualities was, at that time, endued with such secret powers: but does it follow, that other bread must also nourish me at another time, and that like sensible qualities must always be attended with like secret powers?

The consequence seems nowise necessary. At least, it must be acknowledged that there is here a consequence drawn by the mind; that there is a certain step taken; a process of thought, and an inference, which wants to be explained. These two propositions are far from being the same, *I have found that such an object has always been attended with such an effect*, and *I foresee, that other objects, which are, in appearance, similar, will be attended with similar effects.* I shall allow, if you please, that the one proposition may justly be inferred from the other: I know, in fact, that it always is inferred. But if you insist that the inference is made by a chain of reasoning, I desire you to produce that reasoning. The connexion between these propositions is not intuitive. There is required a medium, which may enable the mind to draw such an inference, if indeed it be drawn by reasoning and argument. What that medium is, I must confess, passes my comprehension; and it is incumbent on those to produce it, who assert that it really exists, and is the origin of all our conclusions concerning matter of fact.

30. This negative argument must certainly, in process of time, become altogether convincing, if many penetrating and able philosophers shall turn their enquiries this way and no one be ever able to discover any connecting proposition or intermediate step, which supports the understanding in this conclusion. But as the question is yet new, every reader may not trust so far to his own penetration, as to conclude, because an argument escapes his enquiry, that therefore it does not really exist. For this reason it may be requisite to venture upon a more difficult task; and enumerating all the branches of human knowledge, endeavour to show that none of them can afford such an argument.

All reasonings may be divided into two kinds, namely, demonstrative reasoning, or that concerning relations of ideas, and moral reasoning, or that concerning matter of fact and existence. That there are no demonstrative arguments in the case seems evident; since it implies no contradiction that the course of nature may change, and that an object, seemingly like those which we have experienced, may be attended with different or contrary effects. May I not clearly and distinctly conceive that a body, falling from the clouds, and which, in all other respects, resembles snow, has yet the taste of salt or feeling of fire? Is there any more intelligible proposition than to affirm, that all the trees will flourish in December and January, and decay in May and June? Now whatever is intelligible, and can be distinctly conceived, implies no contradiction, and can never be proved false by any demonstrative argument or abstract reasoning a priori.

If we be, therefore, engaged by arguments to put trust in past experience, and make it the standard of our future judgement, these arguments must be probable only, or such as regard matter of fact and real existence, according to the division above mentioned. But that there is no argument of this kind, must appear, if our explication of that species of reasoning be admitted as solid and satisfactory. We have said that all arguments concerning existence are founded on the relation of cause and effect; that our knowledge of that relation is derived entirely from experience; and that all our experimental conclusions proceed upon the supposition that the future will be conformable to the past. To endeavour, therefore, the proof of this last supposition by probable arguments, or arguments regarding existence, must be evidently going in a circle, and taking that for granted, which is the very point in question.

31. In reality, all arguments from experience are founded on the similarity which we discover among natural objects, and by which we are induced to expect effects similar to those which we have found to follow from such objects. And though none but a fool or madman will ever pretend to dispute the authority of experience, or to reject that great guide of human life, it may surely be allowed a philosopher to have so much curiosity at least as to examine the principle of human nature, which gives this mighty authority to experience, and makes us draw advantage from that similarity which nature has placed among different objects. From causes which appear *similar* we expect similar effects. This is the sum of all our experimental conclusions.

Now it seems evident that, if this conclusion were formed by reason, it would be as perfect at first, and upon one instance, as after ever so long a course of experience. But the case is far otherwise. Nothing so like as eggs; yet no one, on account of this appearing similarity, expects the same taste and relish in all of them. It is only after a long course of uniform experiments in any kind, that we attain a firm reliance and security with regard to a particular event. Now where is that process of reasoning which, from one instance, draws a conclusion, so different from that which it infers from a hundred instances that are nowise different from that single one? This question I propose as much for the sake of information, as with an intention of raising difficulties. I cannot find, I cannot imagine any such reasoning. But I keep my mind still open to instruction, if any one will vouchsafe to bestow it on me.

32. Should it be said that, from a number of uniform experiments, we *infer* a connexion between the sensible qualities and the secret powers; this, I must confess, seems the same difficulty, couched in different terms. The question still recurs, on what process of argument this *inference* is founded? Where is the medium, the interposing ideas, which join propositions so very wide of each other? It is confessed that the colour, consistence, and other sensible qualities of bread appear not, of themselves, to have any connexion with the secret powers of nourishment and support. For otherwise we could infer these secret powers from the first appearance of these sensible qualities, without the aid of experience; contrary to the sentiment of all philosophers, and contrary to plain matter of fact. Here, then, is our natural state of ignorance with regard to the powers and influence of all objects. How is this remedied by experience? It only shows us a number of uniform effects, resulting from certain objects, and teaches us that those particular objects, at that particular time, were endowed with such powers and forces. When a new object, endowed with similar sensible qualities, is produced, we expect similar powers and forces, and look for a like effect. From a body of like colour and consistence with bread we expect like nourishment and support.

But this surely is a step or progress of the mind, which wants to be explained. When a man says, *I have found, in all past instances, such sensible qualities conjoined with such secret powers*: And when he says, *Similar sensible qualities will always be conjoined with similar secret powers*, he is not guilty of a tautology, nor are these propositions in any respect the same. You say that the one proposition is an inference from the other. But you must confess that the inference is not intuitive; neither is it demonstrative: Of what nature is it, then? To say it is experimental, is begging the question. For all inferences from experience suppose, as their foundation, that the future will resemble the past, and that similar powers will be conjoined with similar sensible qualities. If there be any suspicion that the course of nature may change, and that the past may be no rule for the future, all experience becomes useless, and can give rise to no inference or conclusion. It is impossible, therefore, that any arguments from experience can prove this resemblance of the past to the future; since all these arguments are founded on the supposition of that resemblance. Let the course of things be allowed hitherto ever so regular; that alone, without some new argument or inference, proves not that, for the future, it will continue so.

In vain do you pretend to have learned the nature of bodies from your past experience. Their secret nature, and consequently all their effects and influence, may change, without any change in their sensible qualities. This happens sometimes, and with regard to some objects: Why may it not happen always, and with regard to all objects? What logic, what process of argument secures you against this supposition? My practice, you say, refutes my doubts. But you mistake the purport of my question. As an agent, I am quite satisfied in the point; but as a philosopher, who has some share of curiosity, I will not say scepticism, I want to learn the foundation of this inference. No reading, no enquiry has yet been able to remove my difficulty, or give me satisfaction in a matter of such importance. Can I do better than propose the difficulty to the public, even though, perhaps, I have small hopes of obtaining a solution? We shall at least, by this means, be sensible of our ignorance, if we do not augment our knowledge.

33. I must confess that a man is guilty of unpardonable arrogance who concludes, because an argument has escaped his own investigation, that therefore it does not really exist. I must also confess that, though all the learned, for several ages, should have employed themselves in fruitless search upon any subject, it may still, perhaps, be rash to conclude positively that the subject must, therefore, pass all human comprehension. Even though we examine all the sources of our knowledge, and conclude them unfit for such a subject, there may still remain a suspicion, that the enumeration is not complete, or the examination not accurate. But with regard to the present subject, there are some considerations which seem to remove all this accusation of arrogance or suspicion of mistake.

It is certain that the most ignorant and stupid peasants—nay infants, nay even brute beasts—improve by experience, and learn the qualities of natural objects, by observing the effects which result from them. When a child has felt the sensation of pain from touching the flame of a candle, he will be careful not to put his hand near any candle; but will expect a similar effect from a cause which is similar in its sensible qualities and appearance. If you assert, therefore, that the understanding of the child is led into this conclusion by any process of argument or ratiocination, I may justly require you to produce that argument; nor have you any pretence to refuse so equitable a demand. You cannot say that the argument is abstruse, and may possibly escape your enquiry; since you confess that it is obvious to the capacity of a mere infant. If you hesitate, therefore, a moment, or if, after reflection, you produce any intricate or profound argument, you, in a manner, give up the question, and confess that it is not reasoning which engages us to suppose the past resembling the future, and to expect similar effects from causes which are, to appearance, similar.

This is the proposition which I intended to enforce in the present section. If I be right, I pretend not to have made any mighty discovery. And if I be wrong, I must acknowledge myself to be indeed a very backward scholar; since I cannot now discover an argument which, it seems, was perfectly familiar to me long before I was out of my cradle.

Section 5
Sceptical Solution of these Doubts

Part 1

34. The passion for philosophy, like that for religion, seems liable to this inconvenience, that, though it aims at the correction of our manners, and extirpation of our vices, it may only serve, by imprudent management, to foster a predominant inclination, and push the mind, with more determined resolution, towards that side which already *draws* too much, by the bias and propensity of the natural temper. It is certain that, while we aspire to the magnanimous firmness of the philosophic sage, and endeavour to confine our pleasures altogether within our own minds, we may, at last, render our philosophy like that of Epictetus, and other Stoics, only a more refined system of selfishness, and reason

ourselves out of all virtue as well as social enjoyment. While we study with attention the vanity of human life, and turn all our thoughts towards the empty and transitory nature of riches and honours, we are, perhaps, all the while flattering our natural indolence, which, hating the bustle of the world, and drudgery of business, seeks a pretence of reason to give itself a full and uncontrolled indulgence.

There is, however, one species of philosophy which seems little liable to this inconvenience, and that because it strikes in with no disorderly passion of the human mind, nor can mingle itself with any natural affection or propensity; and that is the Academic or Sceptical philosophy. The academics always talk of doubt and suspense of judgement, of danger in hasty determinations, of confining to very narrow bounds the enquiries of the understanding, and of renouncing all speculations which lie not within the limits of common life and practice. Nothing, therefore, can be more contrary than such a philosophy to the supine indolence of the mind, its rash arrogance, its lofty pretensions, and its superstitious credulity. Every passion is mortified by it, except the love of truth; and that passion never is, nor can be, carried to too high a degree. It is surprising, therefore, that this philosophy, which, in almost every instance, must be harmless and innocent, should be the subject of so much groundless reproach and obloquy. But, perhaps, the very circumstance which renders it so innocent is what chiefly exposes it to the public hatred and resentment. By flattering no irregular passion, it gains few partizans: By opposing so many vices and follies, it raises to itself abundance of enemies, who stigmatize it as libertine profane, and irreligious.

Nor need we fear that this philosophy, while it endeavours to limit our enquiries to common life, should ever undermine the reasonings of common life, and carry its doubts so far as to destroy all action, as well as speculation. Nature will always maintain her rights, and prevail in the end over any abstract reasoning whatsoever. Though we should conclude, for instance, as in the foregoing section, that, in all reasonings from experience, there is a step taken by the mind which is not supported by any argument or process of the understanding; there is no danger that these reasonings, on which almost all knowledge depends, will ever be affected by such a discovery. If the mind be not engaged by argument to make this step, it must be induced by some other principle of equal weight and authority; and that principle will preserve its influence as long as human nature remains the same. What that principle is may well be worth the pains of enquiry.

35. Suppose a person, though endowed with the strongest faculties of reason and reflection, to be brought on a sudden into this world; he would, indeed, immediately observe a continual succession of objects, and one event following another; but he would not be able to discover anything farther. He would not, at first, by any reasoning, be able to reach the idea of cause and effect; since the particular powers, by which all natural operations are performed, never appear to the senses; nor is it reasonable to conclude, merely because one event, in one instance, precedes another, that therefore the one is the cause, the other the effect. Their conjunction may be arbitrary and casual. There may be no reason to infer the existence of one from the appearance of the other. And in a word, such a person, without more experience, could never employ his conjecture or reasoning concerning any matter of fact, or be assured of anything beyond what was immediately present to his memory and senses.

Suppose, again, that he has acquired more experience, and has lived so long in the world as to have observed familiar objects or events to be constantly conjoined together; what is the consequence of this experience? He immediately infers the existence of one object from the appearance of the other. Yet he has not, by all his experience, acquired any idea or knowledge of the secret power by which the one object produces the other; nor is it, by any process of reasoning, he is engaged to draw this inference. But still he finds himself determined to draw it: And though he should be convinced that his understanding has no part in the operation, he would nevertheless continue in the same course of thinking. There is some other principle which determines him to form such a conclusion.

36. This principle is Custom or Habit. For wherever the repetition of any particular act or operation produces a propensity to renew the same act or operation, without being impelled by any reasoning or process of the understanding, we always say, that this propensity is the effect of *Custom*. By employing that word, we pretend not to have given the ultimate reason of such a propensity. We only point out a principle of human nature, which is universally acknowledged, and which is well known by its effects. Perhaps we can push our enquiries no farther, or pretend to give the cause of this cause; but must rest contented with it as the ultimate principle, which we can assign, of all our conclu-

sions from experience. It is sufficient satisfaction, that we can go so far, without repining at the narrowness of our faculties because they will carry us no farther.

And it is certain we here advance a very intelligible proposition at least, if not a true one, when we assert that, after the constant conjunction of two objects—heat and flame, for instance, weight and solidity—we are determined by custom alone to expect the one from the appearance of the other. This hypothesis seems even the only one which explains the difficulty, why we draw, from a thousand instances, an inference which we are not able to draw from one instance, that is, in no respect, different from them. Reason is incapable of any such variation. The conclusions which it draws from considering one circle are the same which it would form upon surveying all the circles in the universe. But no man, having seen only one body move after being impelled by another, could infer that every other body will move after a like impulse. All inferences from experience, therefore, are effects of custom, not of reasoning.

The same distinction between reason and experience is maintained in all our deliberations concerning the conduct of life; while the experienced statesman, general, physician, or merchant is trusted and followed; and the unpractised novice, with whatever natural talents endowed, neglected and despised. Though it be allowed, that reason may form very plausible conjectures with regard to the consequences of such a particular conduct in such particular circumstances; it is still supposed imperfect, without the assistance of experience, which is alone able to give stability and certainty to the maxims, derived from study and reflection.

But notwithstanding that this distinction be thus universally received, both in the active speculative scenes of life, I shall not scruple to pronounce, that it is, at bottom, erroneous, at least, superficial.

If we examine those arguments, which, in any of the sciences above mentioned, are supposed to be the mere effects of reasoning and reflection, they will be found to terminate, at last, in some general principle or conclusion, for which we can assign no reason but observation and experience. The only difference between them and those maxims, which are vulgarly esteemed the result of pure experience, is, that the former cannot be established without some process of thought, and some reflection on what we have observed, in order to distinguish its circumstances, and trace its consequences: Whereas in the latter, the experienced event is exactly and fully familiar to that which we infer as the result of any particular situation. The history of a TIBERIUS or a NERO makes us dread a like tyranny, were our monarchs freed from the restraints of laws and senates: But the observation of any fraud or cruelty in private life is sufficient, with the aid of a little thought, to give us the same apprehension; while it serves as an instance of the general corruption of human nature, and shows us the danger which we must incur by reposing an entire confidence in mankind. In both cases, it is experience which is ultimately the foundation of our inference and conclusion.

There is no man so young and unexperienced, as not to have formed, from observation, many general and just maxims concerning human affairs and the conduct of life; but it must be confessed, that, when a man comes to put these in practice, he will be extremely liable to error, till time and farther experience both enlarge these maxims, and teach him their proper use and application. In every situation or incident, there are many particular and seemingly minute circumstances, which the man of greatest talent is, at first, apt to overlook, though on them the justness of his conclusions, and consequently the prudence of his conduct, entirely depend. Not to mention, that, to a young beginner, the general observations and maxims occur not always on the proper occasions, nor can be immediately applied with due calmness and distinction. The truth is, an unexperienced reasoner could be no reasoner at all, were he absolutely unexperienced; and when we assign that character to any one, we mean it only in a comparative sense, and suppose him possessed of experience, in a smaller and more imperfect degree.

Custom, then, is the great guide of human life. It is that principle alone which renders our experience useful to us, and makes us expect, for the future, a similar train of events with those which have appeared in the past.

Without the influence of custom, we should be entirely ignorant of every matter of fact beyond what is immediately present to the memory and senses. We should never know how to adjust means to ends, or to employ our natural powers in the production of any effect. There would be an end at once of all action, as well as of the chief part of speculation.

37. But here it may be proper to remark, that though our conclusions from experience carry us beyond our memory and senses, and assure us of matters of fact which happened in the most distant places and most remote ages, yet some fact must always be present to the senses or memory, from which we may first proceed in drawing these conclusions. A man, who should find in a desert country the remains of pompous buildings, would conclude that the country had, in ancient times, been cultivated by civilized inhabitants; but did nothing of this nature occur to him, he could never form such an inference. We learn the events of former ages from history; but then we must peruse the volumes in which this instruction is contained, and thence carry up our inferences from one testimony to another, till we arrive at the eyewitnesses and spectators of these distant events.

In a word, if we proceed not upon some fact, present to the memory or senses, our reasonings would be merely hypothetical; and however the particular links might be connected with each other, the whole chain of inferences would have nothing to support it, nor could we ever, by its means, arrive at the knowledge of any real existence. If I ask why you believe any particular matter of fact, which you relate, you must tell me some reason; and this reason will be some other fact, connected with it. But as you cannot proceed after this manner, *in infinitum*, you must at last terminate in some fact, which is present to your memory or senses; or must allow that your belief is entirely without foundation.

38. What, then, is the conclusion of the whole matter? A simple one; though, it must be confessed, pretty remote from the common theories of philosophy. All belief of matter of fact or real existence is derived merely from some object, present to the memory or senses, and a customary conjunction between that and some other object. Or in other words; having found, in many instances, that any two kinds of objects—flame and heat, snow and cold—have always been conjoined together; if flame or snow be presented anew to the senses, the mind is carried by custom to expect heat or cold, and to *believe* that such a quality does exist, and will discover itself upon a nearer approach. This belief is the necessary result of placing the mind in such circumstances. It is an operation of the soul, when we are so situated, as unavoidable as to feel the passion of love, when we receive benefits; or hatred, when we meet with injuries. All these operations are a species of natural instincts, which no reasoning or process of the thought and understanding is able either to produce or to prevent.

At this point, it would be very allowable for us to stop our philosophical researches. In most questions we can never make a single step farther; and in all questions we must terminate here at last, after our most restless and curious enquiries. But still our curiosity will be pardonable, perhaps commendable, if it carry us on to still farther researches, and make us examine more accurately the nature of this *belief*, and of the *customary conjunction*, whence it is derived. By this means we may meet with some explications and analogies that will give satisfaction; at least to such as love the abstract sciences, and can be entertained with speculations, which, however accurate, may still retain a degree of doubt and uncertainty. As to readers of a different taste; the remaining part of this section is not calculated for them, and the following enquiries may well be understood, though it be neglected.

Part 2

39. Nothing is more free than the imagination of man; and though it cannot exceed that original stock of ideas furnished by the internal and external senses, it has unlimited power of mixing, compounding, separating, and dividing these ideas, in all the varieties of fiction and vision. It can feign a train of events, with all the appearance of reality, ascribe to them a particular time and place, conceive them as existent, and paint them out to itself with every circumstance, that belongs to any historical fact, which it believes with the greatest certainty. Wherein, therefore, consists the difference between such a fiction and belief? It lies not merely in any peculiar idea, which is annexed to such a conception as commands our assent, and which is wanting to every known fiction. For as the mind has authority over all its ideas, it could voluntarily annex this particular idea to any fiction, and consequently be able to believe whatever it pleases; contrary to what we find by daily experience. We can, in our conception, join the head of a man to the body of a horse; but it is not in our power to believe that such an animal has ever really existed.

It follows, therefore, that the difference between *fiction* and *belief* lies in some sentiment or feeling, which is annexed to the latter, not to the former, and which depends not on the will, nor can be commanded at pleasure. It must be excited by nature, like all other sentiments; and must arise from the particular situation, in which the mind is placed at any particular juncture. Whenever any object is presented to the memory or senses, it immediately, by the force of custom, carries the imagination to conceive that object, which is usually conjoined to it; and this conception is attended with a feeling or sentiment, different from the loose reveries of the fancy. In this consists the whole nature of belief. For as there is no matter of fact which we believe so firmly that we cannot conceive the contrary, there would be no difference between the conception assented to and that which is rejected, were it not for some sentiment which distinguishes the one from the other. If I see a billiard-ball moving towards another, on a smooth table, I can easily conceive it to stop upon contact. This conception implies no contradiction; but still it feels very differently from that conception by which I represent to myself the impulse and the communication of motion from one ball to another.

40. Were we to attempt a *definition* of this sentiment, we should, perhaps, find it a very difficult, if not an impossible task; in the same manner as if we should endeavour to define the feeling of cold or passion of anger, to a creature who never had any experience of these sentiments. Belief is the true and proper name of this feeling; and no one is ever at a loss to know the meaning of that term; because every man is every moment conscious of the sentiment represented by it. It may not, however, be improper to attempt a *description* of this sentiment; in hopes we may, by that means, arrive at some analogies, which may afford a more perfect explication of it. I say, then, that belief is nothing but a more vivid, lively, forcible, firm, steady conception of an object, than what the imagination alone is ever able to attain. This variety of terms, which may seem so unphilosophical, is intended only to express that act of the mind, which renders realities, or what is taken for such, more present to us than fictions, causes them to weigh more in the thought, and gives them a superior influence on the passions and imagination. Provided we agree about the thing, it is needless to dispute about the terms.

The imagination has the command over all its ideas, and can join and mix and vary them, in all the ways possible. It may conceive fictitious objects with all the circumstances of place and time. It may set them, in a manner, before our eyes, in their true colours, just as they might have existed. But as it is impossible that this faculty of imagination can ever, of itself, reach belief, it is evident that belief consists not in the peculiar nature or order of ideas, but in the *manner* of their conception, and in their *feeling* to the mind. I confess, that it is impossible perfectly to explain this feeling or manner of conception. We may make use of words which express something near it. But its true and proper name, as we observed before, is *belief*; which is a term that every one sufficiently understands in common life.

And in philosophy, we can go no farther than assert, that *belief* is something felt by the mind, which distinguishes the ideas of the judgement from the fictions of the imagination. It gives them more weight and influence; makes them appear of greater importance; enforces them in the mind; and renders them the governing principle of our actions. I hear at present, for instance, a person's voice, with whom I am acquainted; and the sound comes as from the next room. This impression of my senses immediately conveys my thought to the person, together with all the surrounding objects. I paint them out to myself as existing at present, with the same qualities and relations, of which I formerly knew them possessed. These ideas take faster hold of my mind than ideas of an enchanted castle. They are very different to the feeling, and have a much greater influence of every kind, either to give pleasure or pain, joy or sorrow.

Let us, then, take in the whole compass of this doctrine, and allow, that the sentiment of belief is nothing but a conception more intense and steady than what attends the mere fictions of the imagination, and that this *manner* of conception arises from a customary conjunction of the object with something present to the memory or senses: I believe that it will not be difficult, upon these suppositions, to find other operations of the mind analogous to it, and to trace up these phenomena to principles still more general.

41. We have already observed that nature has established connexions among particular ideas, and that no sooner one idea occurs to our thoughts than it introduces its correlative, and carries our attention towards it, by a gentle and insensible movement. These principles of connexion or association we have reduced to three, namely, *Resemblance*, *Contiguity* and *Causation*; which are the only bonds

that unite our thoughts together, and beget that regular train of reflection or discourse, which, in a greater or less degree, takes place among all mankind. Now here arises a question, on which the solution of the present difficulty will depend. Does it happen, in all these relations, that, when one of the objects is presented to the senses or memory, the mind is not only carried to the conception of the correlative, but reaches a steadier and stronger conception of it than what otherwise it would have been able to attain? This seems to be the case with that belief which arises from the relation of cause and effect. And if the case be the same with the other relations or principles of associations, this may be established as a general law, which takes place in all the operations of the mind.

We may, therefore, observe, as the first experiment to our present purpose, that, upon the appearance of the picture of an absent friend, our idea of him is evidently enlivened by the *resemblance*, and that every passion, which that idea occasions, whether of joy or sorrow, acquires new force and vigour. In producing this effect, there concur both a relation and a present impression. Where the picture bears him no resemblance, at least was not intended for him, it never so much as conveys our thought to him: And where it is absent, as well as the person, though the mind may pass from the thought of the one to that of the other, it feels its idea to be rather weakened than enlivened by that transition. We take a pleasure in viewing the picture of a friend, when it is set before us; but when it is removed, rather choose to consider him directly than by reflection in an image, which is equally distant and obscure. . . .

42. We may add force to these experiments by others of a different kind, in considering the effects of *contiguity* as well as of *resemblance*. It is certain that distance diminishes the force of every idea, and that, upon our approach to any object; though it does not discover itself to our senses; it operates upon the mind with an influence, which imitates an immediate impression. The thinking on any object readily transports the mind to what is contiguous; but it is only the actual presence of an object, that transports it with a superior vivacity. When I am a few miles from home, whatever relates to it touches me more nearly than when I am two hundred leagues distant; though even at that distance the reflecting on any thing in the neighbourhood of my friends or family naturally produces an idea of them. But as in this latter case, both the objects of the mind are ideas; notwithstanding there is an easy transition between them; that transition alone is not able to give a superior vivacity to any of the ideas, for want of some immediate impression.

43. No one can doubt but causation has the same influence as the other two relations of resemblance and contiguity. Superstitious people are fond of the reliques of saints and holy men, for the same reason, that they seek after types or images, in order to enliven their devotion, and give them a more intimate and strong conception of those exemplary lives, which they desire to imitate. Now it is evident, that one of the best reliques, which a devotee could procure, would be the handywork of a saint; and if his cloaths and furniture are ever to be considered in this light, it is because they were once at his disposal, and were moved and affected by him; in which respect they are to be considered as imperfect effects, and as connected with him by a shorter chain of consequences than any of those, by which we learn the reality of his existence.

Suppose, that the son of a friend, who had been long dead or absent, were presented to us; it is evident, that this object would instantly revive its correlative idea, and recal to our thoughts all past intimacies and familiarities, in more lively colours than they would otherwise have appeared to us. This is another phaenomenon, which seems to prove the principle above mentioned.

44. We may observe, that, in these phaenomena, the belief of the correlative object is always presupposed; without which the relation could have no effect. The influence of the picture supposes, that we *believe* our friend to have once existed. Contiguity to home can never excite our ideas of home, unless we *believe* that it really exists. Now I assert, that this belief, where it reaches beyond the memory or senses, is of a similar nature, and arises from similar causes, with the transition of thought and vivacity of conception here explained. When I throw a piece of dry wood into a fire, my mind is immediately carried to conceive, that it augments, not extinguishes the flame.

This transition of thought from the cause to the effect proceeds not from reason. It derives its origin altogether from custom and experience. And as it first begins from an object, present to the senses, it renders the idea or conception of flame more strong and lively than any loose, floating reverie of the imagination. That idea arises immediately. The thought moves instantly towards it, and conveys to it all that force of conception, which is derived from the impression present to the senses. When a sword is levelled at my breast, does not the idea of wound and pain strike me more strongly, than when a glass of wine is presented to me, even though by accident this idea should occur after the appearance of the latter object?

But what is there in this whole matter to cause such a strong conception, except only a present object and a customary transition to the idea of another object, which we have been accustomed to conjoin with the former? This is the whole operation of the mind, in all our conclusions concerning matter of fact and existence; and it is a satisfaction to find some analogies, by which it may be explained. The transition from a present object does in all cases give strength and solidity to the related idea.

Here, then, is a kind of pre-established harmony between the course of nature and the succession of our ideas; and though the powers and forces, by which the former is governed, be wholly unknown to us; yet our thoughts and conceptions have still, we find, gone on in the same train with the other works of nature. Custom is that principle, by which this correspondence has been effected; so necessary to the subsistence of our species, and the regulation of our conduct, in every circumstance and occurrence of human life. Had not the presence of an object, instantly excited the idea of those objects, commonly conjoined with it, all our knowledge must have been limited to the narrow sphere of our memory and senses; and we should never have been able to adjust means to ends, or employ our natural powers, either to the producing of good, or avoiding of evil. Those, who delight in the discovery and contemplation of *final causes*, have here ample subject to employ their wonder and admiration.

45. I shall add, for a further confirmation of the foregoing theory, that, as this operation of the mind, by which we infer like effects from like causes, and *vice versa*, is so essential to the subsistence of all human creatures, it is not probable, that it could be trusted to the fallacious deductions of our reason, which is slow in its operations; appears not, in any degree, during the first years of infancy; and at best is, in every age and period of human life, extremely liable to error and mistake. It is more conformable to the ordinary wisdom of nature to secure so necessary an act of the mind, by some instinct or mechanical tendency, which may be infallible in its operations, may discover itself at the first appearance of life and thought, and may be independent of all the laboured deductions of the understanding. As nature has taught us the use of our limbs, without giving us the knowledge of the muscles and nerves, by which they are actuated; so has she implanted in us an instinct, which carries forward the thought in a correspondent course to that which she has established among external objects; though we are ignorant of those powers and forces, on which this regular course and succession of objects totally depends. . . .

Section 8
Of Liberty and Necessity

Part 1

62. It might reasonably be expected in questions which have been canvassed and disputed with great eagerness, since the first origin of science and philosophy, that the meaning of all the terms, at least, should have been agreed upon among the disputants; and our enquiries, in the course of two thousand years, been able to pass from words to the true and real subject of the controversy. For how easy may it seem to give exact definitions of the terms employed in reasoning, and make these definitions, not the mere sound of words, the object of future scrutiny and examination?

But if we consider the matter more narrowly, we shall be apt to draw a quite opposite conclusion. From this circumstance alone, that a controversy has been long kept on foot, and remains still undecided, we may presume that there is some ambiguity in the expression, and that the disputants affix different ideas to the terms employed in the controversy. For as the faculties of the mind are supposed to be naturally alike in every individual; otherwise nothing could be more fruitless than to reason or dispute together; it were impossible, if men affix the same ideas to their terms, that they could so long form different opinions of the same subject; especially when they communicate their views, and each party turn themselves on all sides, in search of arguments which may give them the victory over their antagonists.

It is true, if men attempt the discussion of questions which lie entirely beyond the reach of human capacity, such as those concerning the origin of worlds, or the economy of the intellectual system or region of spirits, they may long beat the air in their fruitless contests, and never arrive at any determinate conclusion. But if the question regard any subject of common life and experience, nothing, one would think, could preserve the dispute so long undecided but some ambiguous expressions, which keep the antagonists still at a distance, and hinder them from grappling with each other.

63. This has been the case in the long disputed question concerning liberty and necessity; and to so remarkable a degree that, if I be not much mistaken, we shall find, that all mankind, both learned and ignorant, have always been of the same opinion with regard to this subject, and that a few intelligible definitions would immediately have put an end to the whole controversy. I own that this dispute has been so much canvassed on all hands, and has led philosophers into such a labyrinth of obscure sophistry, that it is no wonder, if a sensible reader indulge his ease so far as to turn a deaf ear to the proposal of such a question, from which he can expect neither instruction or entertainment. But the state of the argument here proposed may, perhaps, serve to renew his attention; as it has more novelty, promises at least some decision of the controversy, and will not much disturb his ease by any intricate or obscure reasoning.

I hope, therefore, to make it appear that all men have ever agreed in the doctrine both of necessity and of liberty, according to any reasonable sense, which can be put on these terms; and that the whole controversy has hitherto turned merely upon words. We shall begin with examining the doctrine of necessity.

64. It is universally allowed that matter, in all its operations, is actuated by a necessary force, and that every natural effect is so precisely determined by the energy of its cause that no other effect, in such particular circumstances, could possibly have resulted from it. The degree and direction of every motion is, by the laws of nature, prescribed with such exactness that a living creature may as soon arise from the shock of two bodies as motion in any other degree or direction than what is actually produced by it. Would we, therefore, form a just and precise idea of *necessity*, we must consider whence that idea arises when we apply it to the operation of bodies.

It seems evident that, if all the scenes of nature were continually shifted in such a manner that no two events bore any resemblance to each other, but every object was entirely new, without any similitude to whatever had been seen before, we should never, in that case, have attained the least idea of necessity, or of a connexion among these objects. We might say, upon such a supposition, that one object or event has followed another; not that one was produced by the other. The relation of cause and effect must be utterly unknown to mankind. Inference and reasoning concerning the operations of nature would, from that moment, be at an end; and the memory and senses remain the only canals, by which the knowledge of any real existence could possibly have access to the mind.

Our idea, therefore, of necessity and causation arises entirely from the uniformity observable in the operations of nature, where similar objects are constantly conjoined together, and the mind is determined by custom to infer the one from the appearance of the other. These two circumstances form the whole of that necessity, which we ascribe to matter. Beyond the constant *conjunction* of similar objects, and the consequent *inference* from one to the other, we have no notion of any necessity or connexion.

If it appear, therefore, that all mankind have ever allowed, without any doubt or hesitation, that these two circumstances take place in the voluntary actions of men, and in the operations of mind; it must follow, that all mankind have ever agreed in the doctrine of necessity, and that they have hitherto disputed, merely for not understanding each other.

65. As to the first circumstance, the constant and regular conjunction of similar events, we may possibly satisfy ourselves by the following considerations. It is universally acknowledged that there is a great uniformity among the actions of men, in all nations and ages, and that human nature remains still the same, in its principles and operations. The same motives always produce the same actions. The same events follow from the same causes. Ambition, avarice, self-love, vanity, friendship, generosity, public spirit: these passions, mixed in various degrees, and distributed through society, have been, from the beginning of the world, and still are, the source of all the actions and enterprises, which have ever been observed among mankind. Would you know the sentiments, inclinations, and

course of life of the Greeks and Romans? Study well the temper and actions of the French and English: You cannot be much mistaken in transferring to the former *most* of the observations which you have made with regard to the latter.

Mankind are so much the same, in all times and places, that history informs us of nothing new or strange in this particular. Its chief use is only to discover the constant and universal principles of human nature, by showing men in all varieties of circumstances and situations, and furnishing us with materials from which we may form our observations and become acquainted with the regular springs of human action and behaviour. These records of wars, intrigues, factions, and revolutions, are so many collections of experiments, by which the politician or moral philosopher fixes the principles of his science, in the same manner as the physician or natural philosopher becomes acquainted with the nature of plants, minerals, and other external objects, by the experiments which he forms concerning them. Nor are the earth, water, and other elements, examined by Aristotle, and Hippocrates, more like to those which at present lie under our observation than the men described by Polybius and Tacitus are to those who now govern the world.

Should a traveller, returning from a far country, bring us an account of men, wholly different from any with whom we were ever acquainted; men, who were entirely divested of avarice, ambition, or revenge; who knew no pleasure but friendship, generosity, and public spirit; we should immediately, from these circumstances, detect the falsehood, and prove him a liar, with the same certainty as if he had stuffed his narration with stories of centaurs and dragons, miracles and prodigies. And if we would explode any forgery in history, we cannot make use of a more convincing argument, than to prove, that the actions ascribed to any person are directly contrary to the course of nature, and that no human motives, in such circumstances, could ever induce him to such a conduct. The veracity of Quintus Curtius is as much to be suspected, when he describes the supernatural courage of Alexander, by which he was hurried on singly to attack multitudes, as when he describes his supernatural force and activity, by which he was able to resist them. So readily and universally do we acknowledge a uniformity in human motives and actions as well as in the operations of body.

Hence likewise the benefit of that experience, acquired by long life and a variety of business and company, in order to instruct us in the principles of human nature, and regulate our future conduct, as well as speculation. By means of this guide, we mount up to the knowledge of men's inclinations and motives, from their actions, expressions, and even gestures; and again descend to the interpretation of their actions from our knowledge of their motives and inclinations. The general observations treasured up by a course of experience, give us the clue of human nature, and teach us to unravel all its intricacies. Pretexts and appearances no longer deceive us. Public declarations pass for the specious colouring of a cause. And though virtue and honour be allowed their proper weight and authority, that perfect disinterestedness, so often pretended to, is never expected in multitudes and parties; seldom in their leaders; and scarcely even in individuals of any rank or station.

But were there no uniformity in human actions, and were every experiment which we could form of this kind irregular and anomalous, it were impossible to collect any general observations concerning mankind; and no experience, however accurately digested by reflection, would ever serve to any purpose. Why is the aged husbandman more skilful in his calling than the young beginner but because there is a certain uniformity in the operation of the sun, rain, and earth towards the production of vegetables; and experience teaches the old practitioner the rules by which this operation is governed and directed.

66. We must not, however, expect that this uniformity of human actions should be carried to such a length as that all men, in the same circumstances, will always act precisely in the same manner, without making any allowance for the diversity of characters, prejudices, and opinions. Such a uniformity in every particular, is found in no part of nature. On the contrary, from observing the variety of conduct in different men, we are enabled to form a greater variety of maxims, which still suppose a degree of uniformity and regularity.

Are the manners of men different in different ages and countries? We learn thence the great force of custom and education, which mould the human mind from its infancy and form it into a fixed and established character. Is the behaviour and conduct of the one sex very unlike that of the other? Is it thence we become acquainted with the different characters which nature has impressed upon the sexes, and which she preserves with constancy and regularity? Are the actions of the same person much diversified in the different periods of his life, from infancy to old age? This affords room for many general observations concerning the gradual change of our sentiments and inclinations, and the different maxims which prevail in the different ages of human creatures. Even the characters, which are peculiar to each individual, have a uniformity in their influence; otherwise our acquaintance with the persons and our observation of their conduct could never teach us their dispositions, or serve to direct our behaviour with regard to them.

67. I grant it possible to find some actions, which seem to have no regular connexion with any known motives, and are exceptions to all the measures of conduct which have ever been established for the government of men. But if we would willingly know what judgement should be formed of such irregular and extraordinary actions, we may consider the sentiments commonly entertained with regard to those irregular events which appear in the course of nature, and the operations of external objects. All causes are not conjoined to their usual effects with like uniformity. An artificer, who handles only dead matter, may be disappointed of his aim, as well as the politician, who directs the conduct of sensible and intelligent agents.

The vulgar, who take things according to their first appearance, attribute the uncertainty of events to such an uncertainty in the causes as makes the latter often fail of their usual influence; though they meet with no impediment in their operation. But philosophers, observing that, almost in every part of nature, there is contained a vast variety of springs and principles, which are hid, by reason of their minuteness or remoteness, find, that it is at least possible the contrariety of events may not proceed from any contingency in the cause, but from the secret operation of contrary causes. This possibility is converted into certainty by farther observation, when they remark that, upon an exact scrutiny, a contrariety of effects always betrays a contrariety of causes, and proceeds from their mutual opposition. A peasant can give no better reason for the stopping of any clock or watch than to say that it does not commonly go right: But an artist easily perceives that the same force in the spring or pendulum has always the same influence on the wheels; but fails of its usual effect, perhaps by reason of a grain of dust, which puts a stop to the whole movement. From the observation of several parallel instances, philosophers form a maxim that the connexion between all causes and effects is equally necessary, and that its seeming uncertainty in some instances proceeds from the secret opposition of contrary causes.

Thus, for instance, in the human body, when the usual symptoms of health or sickness disappoint our expectation; when medicines operate not with their wonted powers; when irregular events follow from any particular cause; the philosopher and physician are not surprised at the matter, nor are ever tempted to deny, in general, the necessity and uniformity of those principles by which the animal economy is conducted. They know that a human body is a mighty complicated machine: That many secret powers lurk in it, which are altogether beyond our comprehension: That to us it must often appear very uncertain in its operations: And that therefore the irregular events, which outwardly discover themselves, can be no proof that the laws of nature are not observed with the greatest regularity in its internal operations and government.

68. The philosopher, if he be consistent, must apply the same reasoning to the actions and volitions of intelligent agents. The most irregular and unexpected resolutions of men may frequently be accounted for by those who know every particular circumstance of their character and situation. A person of an obliging disposition gives a peevish answer: But he has the toothache, or has not dined. A stupid fellow discovers an uncommon alacrity in his carriage: But he has met with a sudden piece of good fortune. Or even when an action, as sometimes happens, cannot be particularly accounted for, either by the person himself or by others; we know, in general, that the characters of men are, to a certain degree, inconstant and irregular. This is, in a manner, the constant character of human nature; though it be applicable, in a more particular manner, to some persons who have no fixed rule for their conduct, but proceed in a continued course of caprice and inconstancy. The internal principles and motives may operate in a uniform manner, notwithstanding these seeming irregularities; in the same manner as the winds, rain, clouds, and other variations of the weather are supposed to be governed by steady principles; though not easily discoverable by human sagacity and enquiry.

69. Thus it appears, not only that the conjunction between motives and voluntary actions is as regular and uniform as that between the cause and effect in any part of nature; but also that this regular conjunction has been universally acknowledged among mankind, and has never been the subject of dispute, either in philosophy or common life. Now, as it is from past experience that we draw all inferences concerning the future, and as we conclude that objects will always be conjoined together which we find to have always been conjoined; it may seem superfluous to prove that this experienced uniformity in human actions is a source whence we draw *inferences* concerning them. But in order to throw the argument into a greater variety of lights we shall also insist, though briefly, on this latter topic.

The mutual dependence of men is so great in all societies that scarce any human action is entirely complete in itself, or is performed without some reference to the actions of others, which are requisite to make it answer fully the intention of the agent. The poorest artificer, who labours alone, expects at least the protection of the magistrate, to ensure him the enjoyment of the fruits of his labour. He also expects that, when he carries his goods to market, and offers them at a reasonable price, he shall find purchasers, and shall be able, by the money he acquires, to engage others to supply him with those commodities which are requisite for his subsistence. In proportion as men extend their dealings, and render their intercourse with others more complicated, they always comprehend, in their schemes of life, a greater variety of voluntary actions, which they expect, from the proper motives, to co-operate with their own.

In all these conclusions they take their measures from past experience, in the same manner as in their reasonings concerning external objects; and firmly believe that men, as well as all the elements, are to continue, in their operations, the same that they have ever found them. A manufacturer reckons upon the labour of his servants for the execution of any work as much as upon the tools which he employs, and would be equally surprised were his expectations disappointed. In short, this experimental inference and reasoning concerning the actions of others enters so much into human life that no man, while awake, is ever a moment without employing it. Have we not reason, therefore, to affirm that all mankind have always agreed in the doctrine of necessity according to the foregoing definition and explication of it?

70. Nor have philosophers ever entertained a different opinion from the people in this particular. For, not to mention that almost every action of their life supposes that opinion, there are even few of the speculative parts of learning to which it is not essential. What would become of *history*, had we not a dependence on the veracity of the historian according to the experience which we have had of mankind? How could *politics* be a science, if laws and forms of goverment had not a uniform influence upon society? Where would be the foundation of *morals*, if particular characters had no certain or determinate power to produce particular sentiments, and if these sentiments had no constant operation on actions? And with what pretence could we employ our *criticism* upon any poet or polite author, if we could not pronounce the conduct and sentiments of his actors either natural or unnatural to such characters, and in such circumstances? It seems almost impossible, therefore, to engage either in science or action of any kind without acknowledging the doctrine of necessity, and this *inference* from motive to voluntary actions, from characters to conduct.

And indeed, when we consider how aptly *natural* and *moral* evidence link together, and form only one chain of argument, we shall make no scruple to allow that they are of the same nature, and derived from the same principles. A prisoner who has neither money nor interest, discovers the impossibility of his escape, as well when he considers the obstinacy of the gaoler, as the walls and bars with which he is surrounded; and, in all attempts for his freedom, chooses rather to work upon the stone and iron of the one, than upon the inflexible nature of the other. The same prisoner, when conducted to the scaffold, foresees his death as certainly from the constancy and fidelity of his guards, as from the operation of the axe or wheel. His mind runs along a certain train of ideas: The refusal of the soldiers to consent to his escape; the action of the executioner; the separation of the head and body; bleeding, convulsive motions, and death.

Here is a connected chain of natural causes and voluntary actions; but the mind feels no difference between them in passing from one link to another: Nor is less certain of the future event than if it were connected with the objects present to the memory or senses, by a train of causes, cemented together by what we are pleased to call a *physical* necessity. The same experienced union has the same effect on the mind, whether the united objects be motives, volition, and actions; or figure and motion. We may change the name of things; but their nature and their operation on the understanding never change.

Were a man, whom I know to be honest and opulent, and with whom I live in intimate friendship, to come into my house, where I am surrounded with my servants, I rest assured that he is not to stab me before he leaves it in order to rob me of my silver standish; and I no more suspect this event than the falling of the house itself, which is new, and solidly built and founded.—*But he may have been seized with a sudden and unknown frenzy.*— So may a sudden earthquake arise, and shake and tumble my house about my ears. I shall therefore change the suppositions. I shall say that I know with certainty that he is not to put his hand into the fire and hold it there till it be consumed: And this event, I think I can foretell with the same assurance, as that, if he throw himself out at the window, and meet with no obstruction, he will not remain a moment suspended in the air. No suspicion of an unknown frenzy can give the least possibility to the former event, which is so contrary to all the known principles of human nature. A man who at noon leaves his purse full of gold on the pavement at Charing-Cross, may as well expect that it will fly away like a feather, as that he will find it untouched an hour after. Above one half of human reasonings contain inferences of a similar nature, attended with more or less degrees of certainty proportioned to our experience of the usual conduct of mankind in such particular situations.

71. I have frequently considered, what could possibly be the reason why all mankind, though they have ever, without hesitation, acknowledged the doctrine of necessity in their whole practice and reasoning, have yet discovered such a reluctance to acknowledge it in words, and have rather shown a propensity, in all ages, to profess the contrary opinion. The matter, I think, may be accounted for after the following manner. If we examine the operations of body, and the production of effects from their causes, we shall find that all our faculties can never carry us farther in our knowledge of this relation than barely to observe that particular objects are *constantly conjoined* together, and that the mind is carried, by a *customary transition*, from the appearance of one to the belief of the other. But though this conclusion concerning human ignorance be the result of the strictest scrutiny of this subject, men still entertain a strong propensity to believe that they penetrate farther into the powers of nature, and perceive something like a necessary connexion between the cause and the effect.

When again they turn their reflections towards the operations of their own minds, and *feel* no such connexion of the motive and the action; they are thence apt to suppose, that there is a difference between the effects which result from material force, and those which arise from thought and intelligence. But being once convinced that we know nothing farther of causation of any kind than merely the *constant conjunction* of objects, and the consequent *inference* of the mind from one to another, and finding that these two circumstances are universally allowed to have place in voluntary actions; we may be more easily led to own the same necessity common to all causes.

And though this reasoning may contradict the systems of many philosophers, in ascribing necessity to the determinations of the will, we shall find, upon reflection, that they dissent from it in words only, not in their real sentiment. Necessity, according to the sense in which it is here taken, has never yet been rejected, nor can ever, I think, be rejected by any philosopher. It may only, perhaps, be pretended that the mind can perceive, in the operations of matter, some farther connexion between the cause and effect; and connexion that has not place in voluntary actions of intelligent beings. Now whether it be so or not, can only appear upon examination; and it is incumbent on these philosophers to make good their assertion, by defining or describing that necessity, and pointing it out to us in the operations of material causes.

72. It would seem, indeed, that men begin at the wrong end of this question concerning liberty and necessity, when they enter upon it by examining the faculties of the soul, the influence of the understanding, and the operations of the will. Let them first discuss a more simple question, namely, the operations of body and of brute unintelligent matter; and try whether they can there form any idea of causation and necessity, except that of a constant conjunction of objects, and subsequent inference of the mind from one to another. If these circumstances form, in reality, the whole of that necessity, which we conceive in matter, and if these circumstances be also universally acknowledged to take place

in the operations of the mind, the dispute is at an end; at least, must be owned to be thenceforth merely verbal.

But as long as we will rashly suppose, that we have some farther idea of necessity and causation in the operations of external objects; at the same time, that we can find nothing farther in the voluntary actions of the mind; there is no possibility of bringing the question to any determinate issue, while we proceed upon so erroneous a supposition. The only method of undeceiving us is to mount up higher; to examine the narrow extent of science when applied to material causes; and to convince ourselves that all we know of them is the constant conjunction and inference above mentioned. We may, perhaps, find that it is with difficulty we are induced to fix such narrow limits to human understanding: But we can afterwards find no difficulty when we come to apply this doctrine to the actions of the will. For as it is evident that these have a regular conjunction with motives and circumstances and characters, and as we always draw inferences from one to the other, we must be obliged to acknowledge in words that necessity, which we have already avowed, in every deliberation of our lives, and in every step of our conduct and behaviour.

73. But to proceed in this reconciling project with regard to the question of liberty and necessity; the most contentious question of metaphysics, the most contentious science; it will not require many words to prove, that all mankind have ever agreed in the doctrine of liberty as well as in that of necessity, and that the whole dispute, in this respect also, has been hitherto merely verbal. For what is meant by liberty, when applied to voluntary actions? We cannot surely mean that actions have so little connexion with motives, inclinations, and circumstances, that one does not follow with a certain degree of uniformity from the other, and that one affords no inference by which we can conclude the existence of the other. For these are plain and acknowledged matters of fact. By liberty, then, we can only mean *a power of acting or not acting, according to the determinations of the will*; that is, if we choose to remain at rest, we may; if we choose to move, we also may. Now this hypothetical liberty is universally allowed to belong to every one who is not a prisoner and in chains. Here, then, is no subject of dispute.

74. Whatever definition we may give of liberty, we should be careful to observe two requisite circumstances; *first*, that it be consistent with plain matter of fact; *secondly*, that it be consistent with itself. If we observe these circumstances, and render our definition intelligible, I am persuaded that all mankind will be found of one opinion with regard to it.

It is universally allowed that nothing exists without a cause of its existence, and that chance, when strictly examined, is a mere negative word, and means not any real power which has anywhere a being in nature. But it is pretended that some causes are necessary, some not necessary. Here then is the advantage of definitions. Let any one *define* a cause, without comprehending, as a part of the definition, a *necessary connexion* with its effect; and let him show distinctly the origin of the idea, expressed by the definition; and I shall readily give up the whole controversy. But if the foregoing explication of the matter be received, this must be absolutely impracticable. Had not objects a regular conjunction with each other, we should never have entertained any notion of cause and effect; and this regular conjunction produces that inference of the understanding, which is the only connexion, that we can have any comprehension of. Whoever attempts a definition of cause, exclusive of these circumstances, will be obliged either to employ unintelligible terms or such as are synonymous to the term which he endeavours to define. And if the definition above mentioned be admitted; liberty, when opposed to necessity, not to constraint, is the same thing with chance; which is universally allowed to have no existence.

Part 2

75. There is no method of reasoning more common, and yet none more blameable, than, in philosophical disputes, to endeavour the refutation of any hypothesis, by a pretence of its dangerous consequences to religion and morality. When any opinion leads to absurdities, it is certainly false; but it is not certain that an opinion is false, because it is of dangerous consequence. Such topics, therefore, ought entirely to be forborne; as serving nothing to the discovery of truth, but only to make the person of an antagonist odious. This I observe in general, without pretending to draw any advantage from it. I frankly submit to an examination of this kind, and shall venture to affirm that the doctrines, both of necessity and of liberty, as above explained, are not only consistent with morality, but are absolutely essential to its support.

Necessity may be defined two ways, conformably to the two definitions of *cause*, of which it makes an essential part. It consists either in the constant conjunction of like objects, or in the inference of the understanding from one object to another. Now necessity, in both these senses, (which, indeed, are at bottom the same) has universally, though tacitly, in the schools, in the pulpit, and in common life, been allowed to belong to the will of man; and no one has ever pretended to deny that we can draw inferences concerning human actions, and that those inferences are founded on the experienced union of like actions, with like motives, inclinations, and circumstances.

The only particular in which any one can differ, is, that either, perhaps, he will refuse to give the name of necessity to this property of human actions: But as long as the meaning is understood, I hope the word can do no harm: Or that he will maintain it possible to discover something farther in the operations of matter. But this, it must be acknowledged, can be of no consequence to morality or religion, whatever it may be to natural philosophy or metaphysics. We may here be mistaken in asserting that there is no idea of any other necessity or connexion in the actions of body: But surely we ascribe nothing to the actions of the mind, but what everyone does, and must readily allow of. We change no circumstance in the received orthodox system with regard to the will, but only in that with regard to material objects and causes. Nothing, therefore, can be more innocent, at least, than this doctrine.

76. All laws being founded on rewards and punishments, it is supposed as a fundamental principle, that these motives have a regular and uniform influence on the mind, and both produce the good and prevent the evil actions. We may give to this influence what name we please; but, as it is usually conjoined with the action, it must be esteemed a *cause*, and be looked upon as an instance of that necessity, which we would here establish.

The only proper object of hatred or vengeance is a person or creature, endowed with thought and consciousness; and when any criminal or injurious actions excite that passion, it is only by their relation to the person, or connexion with him. Actions are, by their very nature, temporary and perishing; and where they proceed not from some *cause* in the character and disposition of the person who performed them, they can neither redound to his honour, if good; nor infamy, if evil. The actions themselves may be blameable; they may be contrary to all the rules of morality and religion: But the person is not answerable for them; and as they proceeded from nothing in him that is durable and constant, and leave nothing of that nature behind them, it is impossible he can, upon their account, become the object of punishment or vengeance. According to the principle, therefore, which denies necessity, and consequently causes, a man is as pure and untainted, after having committed the most horrid crime, as at the first moment of his birth, nor is his character anywise concerned in his actions, since they are not derived from it, and the wickedness of the one can never be used as a proof of the depravity of the other.

Men are not blamed for such actions as they perform ignorantly and casually, whatever may be the consequences. Why? but because the principles of these actions are only momentary, and terminate in them alone. Men are less blamed for such actions as they perform hastily and unpremeditately than for such as proceed from deliberation. For what reason? but because a hasty temper, though a constant cause or principle in the mind, operates only by intervals, and infects not the whole character. Again, repentance wipes off every crime, if attended with a reformation of life and manners. How is this to be accounted for? but by asserting that actions render a person criminal merely as they are proofs of criminal principles in the mind; and when, by an alteration of these principles, they cease to be just proofs, they likewise cease to be criminal. But, except upon the doctrine of necessity, they never were just proofs, and consequently never were criminal.

77. It will be equally easy to prove, and from the same arguments, that *liberty*, according to that definition above mentioned, in which all men agree, is also essential to morality, and that no human actions, where it is wanting, are susceptible of any moral qualities, or can be the objects either of approbation or dislike. For as actions are objects of our moral sentiment, so far only as they are indications of the internal character, passions, and affections; it is impossible that they can give rise either to praise or blame, where they proceed not from these principles, but are derived altogether from external violence.

78. I pretend not to have obviated or removed all objections to this theory, with regard to necessity and liberty. I can foresee other objections, derived from topics which have not here been treated of. It may be said, for instance, that, if voluntary actions be subjected to the same laws of necessity with the operations of matter, there is a continued chain of necessary causes, pre-ordained and pre-determined, reaching from the original cause of all to every single volition of every human creature. No contingency anywhere in the universe; no indifference; no liberty. While we act, we are, at the same time, acted upon. The ultimate Author of all our volitions is the Creator of the world, who first bestowed motion on this immense machine, and placed all beings in that particular position, whence every subsequent event, by an inevitable necessity, must result.

Human actions, therefore, either can have no moral turpitude at all, as proceeding from so good a cause; or if they have any turpitude, they must involve our Creator in the same guilt, while he is acknowledged to be their ultimate cause and author. For as a man, who fired a mine, is answerable for all the consequences whether the train he employed be long or short; so wherever a continued chain of necessary causes is fixed, that Being, either finite or infinite, who produces the first, is likewise the author of all the rest, and must both bear the blame and acquire the praise which belong to them. Our clear and unalterable ideas of morality establish this rule, upon unquestionable reasons, when we examine the consequences of any human action; and these reasons must still have greater force when applied to the volitions and intentions of a Being infinitely wise and powerful. Ignorance or impotence may be pleaded for so limited a creature as man; but those imperfections have no place in our Creator. He foresaw, he ordained, he intended all those actions of men, which we so rashly pronounce criminal. And we must therefore conclude, either that they are not criminal, or that the Deity, not man, is accountable for them. But as either of these positions is absurd and impious, it follows, that the doctrine from which they are deduced cannot possibly be true, as being liable to all the same objections. An absurd consequence, if necessary, proves the original doctrine to be absurd; in the same manner as criminal actions render criminal the original cause, if the connexion between them be necessary and evitable.

This objection consists of two parts, which we shall examine separately; *First*, that, if human actions can be traced up, by a necessary chain, to the Deity, they can never be criminal; on account of the infinite perfection of that Being from whom they are derived, and who can intend nothing but what is altogether good and laudable. Or, *Secondly*, if they be criminal, we must retract the attribute of perfection, which we ascribe to the Deity, and must acknowledge him to be the ultimate author of guilt and moral turpitude in all his creatures.

79. The answer to the first objection seems obvious and convincing. There are many philosophers who, after an exact scrutiny of all the phenomena of nature, conclude, that the WHOLE, considered as one system, is, in every period of its existence, ordered with perfect benevolence; and that the utmost possible happiness will, in the end, result to all created beings, without any mixture of positive or absolute ill or misery. Every physical ill, say they, makes an essential part of this benevolent system, and could not possibly be removed, even by the Deity himself, considered as a wise agent, without giving entrance to greater ill, or excluding greater good, which will result from it. From this theory, some philosophers, and the ancient Stoics among the rest, derived a topic of consolation under all afflictions, while they taught their pupils that those ills under which they laboured were, in reality, goods to the universe; and that to an enlarged view, which could comprehend the whole system of nature, every event became an object of joy and exultation.

But though this topic be specious and sublime, it was soon found in practice weak and ineffectual. You would surely more irritate than appease a man lying under the racking pains of the gout by preaching up to him the rectitude of those general laws, which produced the malignant humours in his body, and led them through the proper canals, to the sinews and nerves, where they now excite such acute torments. These enlarged views may, for a moment, please the imagination of a speculative man, who is placed in ease and security; but neither can they dwell with constancy on his mind, even though undisturbed by the emotions of pain or passion; much less can they maintain their ground when attacked by such powerful antagonists. The affections take a narrower and more natural survey of their object; and by an economy, more suitable to the infirmity of human minds, regard alone the beings around us, and are actuated by such events as appear good or ill to the private system.

80. The case is the same with *moral* as with *physical* ill. It cannot reasonably be supposed, that those remote considerations, which are found of so little efficacy with regard to one, will have a more powerful influence with regard to the other. The mind of man is so formed by nature that, upon the appearance of certain characters, dispositions, and actions, it immediately feels the sentiment of approbation or blame; nor are there any emotions more essential to its frame and constitution. The characters which engage our approbation are chiefly such as contribute to the peace and security of human society; as the characters which excite blame are chiefly such as tend to public detriment and disturbance: Whence it may reasonably be presumed, that the moral sentiments arise, either mediately or immediately, from a reflection of these opposite interests.

What though of philosophical meditations [that purport to] establish a different opinion or conjecture; that everything is right with regard to the WHOLE, and that the qualities, which disturb society, are, in the main, as beneficial, and are as suitable to the primary intention of nature as those which more directly promote its happiness and welfare? Are such remote and uncertain speculations able to counterbalance the sentiments which arise from the natural and immediate view of the objects? A man who is robbed of a considerable sum; does he find his vexation for the loss anywise diminished by these sublime reflections? Why then should his moral resentment against the crime be supposed incompatible with them? Or why should not the acknowledgment of a real distinction between vice and virtue be reconcileable to all speculative systems of philosophy, as well as that of a real distinction between personal beauty and deformity? Both these distinctions are founded in the natural sentiments of the human mind: And these sentiments are not to be controuled or altered by any philosophical theory or speculation whatsoever.

81. The *second* objection admits not of so easy and satisfactory an answer; nor is it possible to explain distinctly, how the Deity can be the mediate cause of all the actions of men, without being the author of sin and moral turpitude. These are mysteries, which mere natural and unassisted reason is very unfit to handle; and whatever system she embraces, she must find herself involved in inextricable difficulties, and even contradictions, at every step which she takes with regard to such subjects. To reconcile the indifference and contingency of human actions with prescience; or to defend absolute decrees, and yet free the Deity from being the author of sin, has been found hitherto to exceed all the power of philosophy. Happy, if she be thence sensible of her temerity, when she pries into these sublime mysteries; and leaving a scene so full of obscurities and perplexities, return, with suitable modesty, to her true and proper province, the examination of common life; where she will find difficulties enough to employ her enquiries, without launching into so boundless an ocean of doubt, uncertainty, and contradiction! . . .

Section 10
Of Miracles

Part 1

86. There is, in Dr. Tillotson's writings, an argument against the *real presence*, which is as concise, and elegant, and strong as any argument can possibly be supposed against a doctrine, so little worthy of a serious refutation. It is acknowledged on all hands, says that learned prelate, that the authority, either of the scripture or of tradition, is founded merely in the testimony of the apostles, who were eye-witnesses to those miracles of our Saviour, by which he proved his divine mission. Our evidence, then, for the truth of the Christian religion is less than the evidence for the truth of our senses; because, even in the first authors of our religion, it was no greater; and it is evident it must diminish in passing from them to their disciples; nor can any one rest such confidence in their testimony, as in the immediate object of his senses.

But a weaker evidence can never destroy a stronger; and therefore, were the doctrine of the real presence ever so clearly revealed in scripture, it were directly contrary to the rules of just reasoning to give our assent to it. It contradicts sense, though both the scripture and tradition, on which it is supposed to be built, carry not such evidence with them as sense; when they are considered merely as external evidences, and are not brought home to every one's breast, by the immediate operation of the Holy Spirit.

Nothing is so convenient as a decisive argument of this kind, which must at least *silence* the most arrogant bigotry and superstition, and free us from their impertinent solicitations. I flatter myself, that I have discovered an argument of a like nature, which, if just, will, with the wise and learned, be an everlasting check to all kinds of superstitious delusion, and consequently, will be useful as long as the world endures. For so long, I presume, will the accounts of miracles and prodigies be found in all history, sacred and profane.

87. Though experience be our only guide in reasoning concerning matters of fact; it must be acknowledged, that this guide is not altogether infallible, but in some cases is apt to lead us into errors. One, who in our climate, should expect better weather in any week of June than in one of December, would reason justly, and conformably to experience; but it is certain, that he may happen, in the event, to find himself mistaken. However, we may observe, that, in such a case, he would have no cause to complain of experience; because it commonly informs us beforehand of the uncertainty, by that contrariety of events, which we may learn from a diligent observation. All effects follow not with like certainty from their supposed causes. Some events are found, in all countries and all ages, to have been constantly conjoined together: Others are found to have been more variable, and sometimes to disappoint our expectations; so that, in our reasonings concerning matter of fact, there are all imaginable degrees of assurance, from the highest certainty to the lowest species of moral evidence.

A wise man, therefore, proportions his belief to the evidence. In such conclusions as are founded on an infallible experience, he expects the event with the last degree of assurance, and regards his past experience as a full *proof* of the future existence of that event. In other cases, he proceeds with more caution: He weighs the opposite experiments: He considers which side is supported by the greater number of experiments: to that side he inclines, with doubt and hesitation; and when at last he fixes his judgement, the evidence exceeds not what we properly call *probability*. All probability, then, supposes an opposition of experiments and observations, where the one side is found to overbalance the other, and to produce a degree of evidence, proportioned to the superiority. A hundred instances or experiments on one side, and fifty on another, afford a doubtful expectation of any event; though a hundred uniform experiments, with only one that is contradictory, reasonably beget a pretty strong degree of assurance. In all cases, we must balance the opposite experiments, where they are opposite, and deduct the smaller number from the greater, in order to know the exact force of the superior evidence.

88. To apply these principles to a particular instance; we may observe, that there is no species of reasoning more common, more useful, and even necessary to human life, than that which is derived from the testimony of men, and the reports of eye-witnesses and spectators. This species of reasoning, perhaps, one may deny to be founded on the relation of cause and effect. I shall not dispute about a word. It will be sufficient to observe that our assurance in any argument of this kind is derived from no other principle than our observation of the veracity of human testimony, and of the usual conformity of facts to the reports of witnesses. It being a general maxim, that no objects have any discoverable connexion together, and that all the inferences, which we can draw from one to another, are founded merely on our experience of their constant and regular conjunction; it is evident, that we ought not to make an exception to this maxim in favour of human testimony, whose connexion with any event seems, in itself, as little necessary as any other. Were not the memory tenacious to a certain degree, had not men commonly an inclination to truth and a principle of probity; were they not sensible to shame, when detected in a falsehood: Were not these, I say, discovered by experience to be qualities, inherent in human nature, we should never repose the least confidence in human testimony. A man delirious, or noted for falsehood and villany, has no manner of authority with us.

And as the evidence, derived from witnesses and human testimony, is founded on past experience, so it varies with the experience, and is regarded either as a *proof* or a *probability*, according as the conjunction between any particular kind of report and any kind of object has been found to be constant or variable. There are a number of circumstances to be taken into consideration in all judgements of this kind; and the ultimate standard, by which we determine all disputes, that may arise concerning them, is always derived from experience and observation. Where this experience is not entirely uniform on any side, it is attended with an unavoidable contrariety in our judgements, and with the same opposition and mutual destruction of argument as in every other kind of evidence. We frequently hesitate concerning the reports of others. We balance the opposite circumstances, which cause any doubt or uncertainty; and when we discover a superiority on any side, we incline to it; but still with a diminution of assurance, in proportion to the force of its antagonist.

89. This contrariety of evidence, in the present case, may be derived from several different causes; from the opposition of contrary testimony; from the character or number of the witnesses; from the manner of their delivering their testimony; or from the union of all these circumstances. We entertain a suspicion concerning any matter of fact, when the witnesses contradict each other; when they are but few, or of a doubtful character; when they have an interest in what they affirm; when they deliver their testimony with hesitation, or on the contrary, with too violent asseverations. There are many other particulars of the same kind, which may diminish or destroy the force of any argument, derived from human testimony.

Suppose, for instance, that the fact, which the testimony endeavours to establish, partakes of the extraordinary and the marvellous; in that case, the evidence, resulting from the testimony, admits of a diminution, greater or less, in proportion as the fact is more or less unusual. The reason why we place any credit in witnesses and historians, is not derived from any *connexion*, which we perceive a priori, between testimony and reality, but because we are accustomed to find a conformity between them. But when the fact attested is such a one as has seldom fallen under our observation, here is a contest of two opposite experiences; of which the one destroys the other, as far as its force goes, and the superior can only operate on the mind by the force, which remains. The very same principle of experience, which gives us a certain degree of assurance in the testimony of witnesses, gives us also, in this case, another degree of assurance against the fact, which they endeavour to establish; from which contradition there necessarily arises a counterpoize, and mutual destruction of belief and authority.

I should not believe such a story were it told me by Cato, was a proverbial saying in Rome, even during the lifetime of that philosophical patriot. The incredibility of a fact, it was allowed, might invalidate so great an authority. The Indian prince, who refused to believe the first relations concerning the effects of frost, reasoned justly; and it naturally required very strong testimony to engage his assent to facts, that arose from a state of nature, with which he was unacquainted, and which bore so little analogy to those events, of which he had had constant and uniform experience. Though they were not contrary to his experience, they were not conformable to it.

90. But in order to encrease the probability against the testimony of witnesses, let us suppose, that the fact, which they affirm, instead of being only marvellous, is really miraculous; and suppose also, that the testimony considered apart and in itself, amounts to an entire proof; in that case, there is proof against proof, of which the strongest must prevail, but still with a diminution of its force, in proportion to that of its antagonist.

A miracle is a violation of the laws of nature; and as a firm and unalterable experience has established these laws, the proof against a miracle, from the very nature of the fact, is as entire as any argument from experience can possibly be imagined. Why is it more than probable, that all men must die; that lead cannot, of itself, remain suspended in the air; that fire consumes wood, and is extinguished by water; unless it be, that these events are found agreeable to the laws of nature, and there is required a violation of these laws, or in other words, a miracle to prevent them? Nothing is esteemed a miracle, if it ever happen in the common course of nature. It is no miracle that a man, seemingly in good health, should die on a sudden: because such a kind of death, though more unusual than any other, has yet been frequently observed to happen. But it is a miracle, that a dead man should come to life; because that has never been observed in any age or country. There must, therefore, be a uniform experience against every miraculous event, otherwise the event would not merit that appellation. And as a uniform experience amounts to a proof, there is here a direct and full *proof*, from the nature of the fact, against the existence of any miracle; nor can such a proof be destroyed, or the miracle rendered credible, but by an opposite proof, which is superior.

91. The plain consequence is (and it is a general maxim worthy of our attention), 'That no testimony is sufficient to establish a miracle, unless the testimony be of such a kind, that its falsehood would be more miraculous, than the fact, which it endeavours to establish; and even in that case there is a mutual destruction of arguments, and the superior only gives us an assurance suitable to that degree of force, which remains, after deducting the inferior.' When anyone tells me, that he saw a dead man restored to life, I immediately consider with myself, whether it be more probable, that this person

should either deceive or be deceived, or that the fact, which he relates, should really have happened. I weigh the one miracle against the other; and according to the superiority, which I discover, I pronounce my decision, and always reject the greater miracle. If the falsehood of his testimony would be more miraculous, than the event which he relates; then, and not till then, can he pretend to command my belief or opinion.

Part 2

92. In the foregoing reasoning we have supposed, that the testimony, upon which a miracle is founded, may possibly amount to an entire proof, and that the falsehood of that testimony would be a real prodigy: But it is easy to shew, that we have been a great deal too liberal in our concession, and that there never was a miraculous event established on so full an evidence.

For *first*, there is not to be found, in all history, any miracle attested by a sufficient number of men, of such unquestioned good-sense, education, and learning, as to secure us against all delusion in themselves; of such undoubted integrity, as to place them beyond all suspicion of any design to deceive others; of such credit and reputation in the eyes of mankind, as to have a great deal to lose in case of their being detected in any falsehood; and at the same time, attesting facts performed in such a public manner and in so celebrated a part of the world, as to render the detection unavoidable: All which circumstances are requisite to give us a full assurance in the testimony of men.

93. *Secondly*. We may observe in human nature a principle which, if strictly examined, will be found to diminish extremely the assurance, which we might, from human testimony, have, in any kind of prodigy. The maxim, by which we commonly conduct ourselves in our reasonings, is, that the objects, of which we have no experience, resembles those, of which we have; that what we have found to be most usual is always most probable; and that where there is an opposition of arguments, we ought to give the preference to such as are founded on the greatest number of past observations.

But though, in proceeding by this rule, we readily reject any fact which is unusual and incredible in an ordinary degree; yet in advancing farther, the mind observes not always the same rule; but when anything is affirmed utterly absurd and miraculous, it rather the more readily admits of such a fact, upon account of that very circumstance, which ought to destroy all its authority. The passion of *surprise* and *wonder*, arising from miracles, being an agreeable emotion, gives a sensible tendency towards the belief of those events, from which it is derived. And this goes so far, that even those who cannot enjoy this pleasure immediately, nor can believe those miraculous events, of which they are informed, yet love to partake of the satisfaction at second-hand or by rebound, and place a pride and delight in exciting the admiration of others.

With what greediness are the miraculous accounts of travellers received, their descriptions of sea and land monsters, their relations of wonderful adventures, strange men, and uncouth manners? But if the spirit of religion join itself to the love of wonder, there is an end of common sense; and human testimony, in these circumstances, loses all pretensions to authority. A religionist may be an enthusiast, and imagine he sees what has no reality: he may know his narrative to be false, and yet persevere in it, with the best intentions in the world, for the sake of promoting so holy a cause: or even where this delusion has not place, vanity, excited by so strong a temptation, operates on him more powerfully than on the rest of mankind in any other circumstances; and self-interest with equal force. His auditors may not have, and commonly have not, sufficient judgement to canvass his evidence: what judgement they have, they renounce by principle, in these sublime and mysterious subjects: or if they were ever so willing to employ it, passion and a heated imagination disturb the regularity of its operations. Their credulity increases his impudence: and his impudence overpowers their credulity.

Eloquence, when at its highest pitch, leaves little room for reason or reflection; but addressing itself entirely to the fancy or the affections, captivates the willing hearers, and subdues their understanding. Happily, this pitch it seldom attains. But what a Tully or a Demosthenes could scarcely effect over a Roman or Athenian audience, every *Capuchin*, every itinerant or stationary teacher can perform over the generality of mankind, and in a higher degree, by touching such gross and vulgar passions.

The many instances of forged miracles, and prophecies, and supernatural events, which, in all ages, have either been detected by contrary evidence, or which detect themselves by their absurdity, prove sufficiently the strong propensity of mankind to the extraordinary and the marvellous, and ought reasonably to beget a suspicion against all relations of this kind. This is our natural way of thinking, even with regard to the most common and most credible events. For instance: There is no kind of report which rises so easily, and spreads so quickly, especially in country places and provincial towns, as those concerning marriages; insomuch that two young persons of equal condition never see each other twice, but the whole neighbourhood immediately join them together. The pleasure of telling a piece of news so interesting, of propagating it, and of being the first reporters of it, spreads the intelligence. And this is so well known, that no man of sense gives attention to these reports, till he find them confirmed by some greater evidence. Do not the same passions, and others still stronger, incline the generality of mankind to believe and report, with the greatest vehemence and assurance, all religious miracles?

94. *Thirdly.* It forms a strong presumption against all supernatural and miraculous relations, that they are observed chiefly to abound among ignorant and barbarous nations; or if a civilized people has ever given admission to any of them, that people will be found to have received them from ignorant and barbarous ancestors, who transmitted them with that inviolable sanction and authority, which always attend received opinions. When we peruse the first histories of all nations, we are apt to imagine ourselves transported into some new world; where the whole frame of nature is disjointed, and every element performs its operations in a different manner, from what it does at present. Battles, revolutions, pestilence, famine and death, are never the effect of those natural causes, which we experience. Prodigies, omens, oracles, judgements, quite obscure the few natural events, that are intermingled with them. But as the former grow thinner every page, in proportion as we advance nearer the enlightened ages, we soon learn, that there is nothing mysterious or supernatural in the case, but that all proceeds from the usual propensity of mankind towards the marvellous, and that, though this inclination may at intervals receive a check from sense and learning, it can never be thoroughly extirpated from human nature.

It is strange, a judicious reader is apt to say, upon the perusal of these wonderful historians, *that such prodigious events never happen in our days.* But it is nothing strange, I hope, that men should lie in all ages. You must surely have seen instances enough of that frailty. You have yourself heard many such marvellous relations started, which, being treated with scorn by all the wise and judicious, have at last been abandoned even by the vulgar. Be assured, that those renowned lies, which have spread and flourished to such a monstrous height, arose from like beginnings; but being sown in a more proper soil, shot up at last into prodigies almost equal to those which they relate.

It was a wise policy in that false prophet, Alexander, who though now forgotten, was once so famous, to lay the first scene of his impostures in Paphlagonia, where, as Lucian tells us, the people were extremely ignorant and stupid, and ready to swallow even the grossest delusion. People at a distance, who are weak enough to think the matter at all worth enquiry, have no opportunity of receiving better information. The stories come magnified to them by a hundred circumstances. Fools are industrious in propagating the imposture; while the wise and learned are contented, in general, to deride its absurdity, without informing themselves of the particular facts, by which it may be distinctly refuted. And thus the impostor above mentioned was enabled to proceed, from his ignorant Paphlagonians, to the enlisting of votaries, even among the Grecian philosophers, and men of the most eminent rank and distinction in Rome: nay, could engage the attention of that sage emperor Marcus Aurelius; so far as to make him trust the success of a military expedition to his delusive prophecies.

The advantages are so great, of starting an imposture among an ignorant people, that, even though the delusion should be too gross to impose on the generality of them (*which, though seldom, is sometimes the case*) it has a much better chance for succeeding in remote countries, than if the first scene had been laid in a city renowned for arts and knowledge. The most ignorant and barbarous of these barbarians carry the report abroad. None of their countrymen have a large correspondence, or sufficient credit and authority to contradict and beat down the delusion. Men's inclination to the marvellous has full opportunity to display itself. And thus a story, which is universally exploded in the place where it was first started, shall pass for certain at a thousand miles distance. But had Alexander fixed his residence at Athens, the philosophers of that renowned mart of learning had immediately spread, throughout the whole Roman empire, their sense of the matter; which, being supported by so great authority, and displayed by all the force of reason and eloquence, had entirely opened the eyes of mankind. It is true; Lucian, passing by chance through Paphlagonia, had an opportunity of performing this good office. But, though much to be wished, it does not always happen, that every Alexander meets with a Lucian, ready to expose and detect his impostures.

95. I may add as a *fourth* reason, which diminishes the authority of prodigies, that there is no testimony for any, even those which have not been expressly detected, that is not opposed by an infinite number of witnesses; so that not only the miracle destroys the credit of testimony, but the testimony destroys itself. To make this the better understood, let us consider, that, in matters of religion, whatever is different is contrary; and that it is impossible the religions of ancient Rome, of Turkey, of Siam, and of China should, all of them, be established on any solid foundation. Every miracle, therefore, pretended to have been wrought in any of these religions (and all of them abound in miracles), as its direct scope is to establish the particular system to which it is attributed; so has it the same force, though more indirectly, to overthrow every other system. In destroying a rival system, it likewise destroys the credit of those miracles, on which that system was established; so that all the prodigies of different religions are to be regarded as contrary facts, and the evidences of these prodigies, whether weak or strong, as opposite to each other.

According to this method of reasoning, when we believe any miracle of Mahomet or his successors, we have for our warrant the testimony of a few barbarous Arabians: And on the other hand, we are to regard the authority of Titus Livius, Plutarch, Tacitus, and, in short, of all the authors and witnesses, Grecian, Chinese, and Roman Catholic, who have related any miracle in their particular religion; I say, we are to regard their testimony in the same light as if they had mentioned that Mahometan miracle, and had in express terms contradicted it, with the same certainty as they have for the miracle they relate. This argument may appear over subtile and refined; but is not in reality different from the reasoning of a judge, who supposes, that the credit of two witnesses, maintaining a crime against any one, is destroyed by the testimony of two others, who affirm him to have been two hundred leagues distant, at the same instant when the crime is said to have been committed.

96. One of the best attested miracles in all profane history, is that which Tacitus reports of Vespasian, who cured a blind man in Alexandria, by means of his spittle, and a lame man by the mere touch of his foot; in obedience to a vision of the god Serapis, who had enjoined them to have recourse to the Emperor, for these miraculous cures. The story may be seen in that fine historian; where every circumstance seems to add weight to the testimony, and might be displayed at large with all the force of argument and eloquence, if any one were now concerned to enforce the evidence of that exploded and idolatrous superstition. The gravity, solidity, age, and probity of so great an emperor, who, through the whole course of his life, conversed in a familiar manner with his friends and courtiers, and never affected those extraordinary airs of divinity assumed by Alexander and Demetrius. The historian, a contemporary writer, noted for candour and veracity, and withal, the greatest and most penetrating genius, perhaps, of all antiquity; and so free from any tendency to credulity, that he even lies under the contrary imputation, of atheism and profaneness: The persons, from whose authority he related the miracle, of established character for judgement and veracity, as we may well presume; eye-witnesses of the fact, and confirming their testimony, after the Flavian family was despoiled of the empire, and could no longer give any reward, as the price of a lie. To which if we add the public nature of the facts, as related, it will appear, that no evidence can well be supposed stronger for so gross and so palpable a falsehood.

97. Is the consequence just, because some human testimony has the utmost force and authority in some cases, when it relates the battle of Philippi or Pharsalia for instance; that therefore all kinds of testimony must, in all cases, have equal force and authority? Suppose that the Caesarean and Pompeian factions had, each of them, claimed the victory in these battles, and that the historians of each party had uniformly ascribed the advantage to their own side; how could mankind, at this distance, have been able to determine between them? The contrariety is equally strong between the miracles related by Herodotus or Plutarch, and those delivered by Mariana, Bede, or any monkish historian.

The wise lend a very academic faith to every report which favours the passion of the reporter; whether it magnifies his country, his family, or himself, or in any other way strikes in with his natural inclinations and propensities. But what greater temptation than to appear a missionary, a prophet, an ambassador from heaven? Who would not encounter many dangers and difficulties, in order to attain so sublime a character? Or if, by the help of vanity and a heated imagination, a man has first made a convert of himself, and entered seriously into the delusion; who ever scruples to make use of pious frauds, in support of so holy and meritorious a cause?

The smallest spark may here kindle into the greatest flame; because the materials are always prepared for it. The *avidum genus auricularum*, the gazing populace, receive greedily, without examination, whatever sooths superstition, and promotes wonder. How many stories of this nature have, in all ages, been detected and exploded in their infancy? How many more have been celebrated for a time, and have afterwards sunk into neglect and oblivion? Where such reports, therefore, fly about, the solution of the phenomenon is obvious; and we judge in conformity to regular experience and observation, when we account for it by the known and natural principles of credulity and delusion. And shall we, rather than have a recourse to so natural a solution, allow of a miraculous violation of the most established laws of nature?

I need not mention the difficulty of detecting a falsehood in any private or even public history, at the place, where it is said to happen; much more when the scene is removed to ever so small a distance. Even a court of judicature, with all the authority, accuracy, and judgement, which they can employ, find themselves often at a loss to distinguish between truth and falsehood in the most recent actions. But the matter never comes to any issue, if trusted to the common method of altercations and debate and flying rumours; especially when men's passions have taken part on either side.

In the infancy of new religions, the wise and learned commonly esteem the matter too inconsiderable to deserve their attention or regard. And when afterwards they would willingly detect the cheat, in order to undeceive the deluded multitude, the season is now past, and the records and witnesses, which might clear up the matter, have perished beyond recovery.

No means of detection remain, but those which must be drawn from the very testimony itself of the reporters: and these, though always sufficient with the judicious and knowing, are commonly too fine to fall under the comprehension of the vulgar.

98. Upon the whole, then, it appears, that no testimony for any kind of miracle has ever amounted to a probability, much less to a proof; and that, even supposing it amounted to a proof, it would be opposed by another proof; derived from the very nature of the fact, which it would endeavour to establish. It is experience only, which gives authority to human testimony; and it is the same experience, which assures us of the laws of nature. When, therefore, these two kinds of experience are contrary, we have nothing to do but substract the one from the other, and embrace an opinion, either on one side or the other, with that assurance which arises from the remainder. But according to the principle here explained, this substraction, with regard to all popular religions, amounts to an entire annihilation; and therefore we may establish it as a maxim, that no human testimony can have such force as to prove a miracle, and make it a just foundation for any such system of religion.

99. I beg the limitations here made may be remarked, when I say, that a miracle can never be proved, so as to be the foundation of a system of religion. For I own, that otherwise, there may possibly be miracles, or violations of the usual course of nature, of such a kind as to admit of proof from human testimony; though, perhaps, it will be impossible to find any such in all the records of history. Thus, suppose, all authors, in all languages, agree, that, from the first of January 1600, there was a total darkness over the whole earth for eight days: suppose that the tradition of this extraordinary event is still strong and lively among the people: that all travellers, who return from foreign countries, bring us accounts of the same tradition, without the least variation or contradiction: it is evident, that our present philosophers, instead of doubting the fact, ought to receive it as certain, and ought to search for the causes whence it might be derived. The decay, corruption, and dissolution of nature, is an event rendered probable by so many analogies, that any phenomenon, which seems to have a tendency towards that catastrophe, comes within the reach of human testimony, if that testimony be very extensive and uniform.

But suppose, that all the historians who treat of England, should agree, that, on the first of January 1600, Queen Elizabeth died; that both before and after her death she was seen by her physicians and the whole court, as is usual with persons of her rank; that her successor was acknowledged and proclaimed by the parliament; and that, after being interred a month, she again appeared, resumed the throne, and governed England for three years: I must confess that I should be surprised at the concurrence of so many odd circumstances, but should not have the least inclination to believe so miraculous an event. I should not doubt of her pretended death, and of those other public circumstances that followed it: I should only assert it to have been pretended, and that it neither was, nor possibly could be real. You would in vain object to me the difficulty, and almost impossibility of deceiving the world in an affair of such consequence; the wisdom and solid judgement of that renowned queen; with the little or no advantage which she could reap from so poor an artifice: All this might astonish me; but I would still reply, that the knavery and folly of men are such common phenomena, that I should rather believe the most extraordinary events to arise from their concurrence, than admit of so signal a violation of the laws of nature.

But should this miracle be ascribed to any new system of religion; men, in all ages, have been so much imposed on by ridiculous stories of that kind, that this very circumstance would be a full proof of a cheat, and sufficient, with all men of sense, not only to make them reject the fact, but even reject it without farther examination. Though the Being to whom the miracle is ascribed, be, in this case, Almighty, it does not, upon that account, become a whit more probable; since it is impossible for us to know the attributes or actions of such a Being, otherwise than from the experience which we have of his productions, in the usual course of nature. This still reduces us to past observation, and obliges us to compare the instances of the violation of truth in the testimony of men, with those of the violation of the laws of nature by miracles, in order to judge which of them is most likely and probable. As the violations of truth are more common in the testimony concerning religious miracles, than in that concerning any other matter of fact; this must diminish very much the authority of the former testimony, and make us form a general resolution, never to lend any attention to it, with whatever specious pretence it may be covered.

Lord Bacon seems to have embraced the same principles of reasoning. 'We ought,' says he, 'to make a collection or particular history of all monsters and prodigious births or productions, and in a word of every thing new, rare, and extraordinary in nature. But this must be done with the most severe scrutiny, lest we depart from truth. Above all, every relation must be considered as suspicious, which depends in any degree upon religion, as the prodigies of Livy: And no less so, every thing that is to be found in the writers of natural magic or alchimy, or such authors, who seem, all of them, to have an unconquerable appetite for falsehood and fable.'

100. I am the better pleased with the method of reasoning here delivered, as I think it may serve to confound those dangerous friends or disguised enemies to the Christian Religion, who have undertaken to defend it by the principles of human reason. Our most holy religion is founded on *Faith*, not on reason; and it is a sure method of exposing it to put it to such a trial as it is, by no means, fitted to endure. To make this more evident, let us examine those miracles, related in scripture; and not to lose ourselves in too wide a field, let us confine ourselves to such as we find in the *Pentateuch*, which we shall examine, according to the principles of these pretended Christians, not as the word or testimony of God himself, but as the production of a mere human writer and historian.

Here then we are first to consider a book, presented to us by a barbarous and ignorant people, written in an age when they were still more barbarous, and in all probability long after the facts which it relates, corroborated by no concurring testimony, and resembling those fabulous accounts, which every nation gives of its origin. Upon reading this book, we find it full of prodigies and miracles. It gives an account of a state of the world and of human nature entirely different from the present: Of our fall from that state: Of the age of man, extended to near a thousand years: Of the destruction of the world by a deluge: Of the arbitrary choice of one people, as the favourites of heaven; and that people the countrymen of the author: Of their deliverance from bondage by prodigies the most astonishing imaginable: I desire any one to lay his hand upon his heart, and after a serious consideration declare, whether he thinks that the falsehood of such a book, supported by such a testimony, would be more extraordinary and miraculous than all the miracles it relates; which is, however, necessary to make it be received, according to the measures of probability above established.

101. What we have said of miracles may be applied, without any variation, to prophecies; and indeed, all prophecies are real miracles, and as such only, can be admitted as proofs of any revelation. If it did not exceed the capacity of human nature to foretell future events, it would be absurd to employ any prophecy as an argument for a divine mission or authority from heaven. So that, upon the whole,

we may conclude, that the Christian Religion not only was at first attended with miracles, but even at this day cannot be believed by any reasonable person without one. Mere reason is insufficient to convince us of its veracity: And whoever is moved by *Faith* to assent to it, is conscious of a continued miracle in his own person, which subverts all the principles of his understanding, and gives him a determination to believe what is most contrary to custom and experience.

Section 11
Of a Particular Providence and of a Future State

102. I was lately engaged in conversation with a friend who loves sceptical paradoxes; where, though he advanced many principles, of which I can by no means approve, yet as they seem to be curious, and to bear some relation to the chain of reasoning carried on throughout this enquiry, I shall here copy them from my memory as accurately as I can, in order to submit them to the judgement of the reader.

Our conversation began with my admiring the singular good fortune of philosophy, which, as it requires entire liberty above all other privileges, and chiefly flourishes from the free opposition of sentiments and argumentation, received its first birth in an age and country of freedom and toleration, and was never cramped, even in its most extravagant principles, by any creeds, concessions, or penal statutes. For, except the banishment of Protagoras, and the death of Socrates, which last event proceeded partly from other motives, there are scarcely any instances to be met with, in ancient history, of this bigotted jealousy, with which the present age is so much infested. Epicurus lived at Athens to an advanced age, in peace and tranquillity: Epicureans were even admitted to receive the sacerdotal character, and to officiate at the altar, in the most sacred rites of the established religion: And the public encouragement of pensions and salaries was afforded equally, by the wisest of all the Roman emperors, to the professors of every sect of philosophy. How requisite such kind of treatment was to philosophy, in her early youth, will easily be conceived, if we reflect, that, even at present, when she may be supposed more hardy and robust, she bears with much difficulty the inclemency of the seasons, and those harsh winds of calumny and persecution, which blow upon her.

You admire, says my friend, as the singular good fortune of philosophy, what seems to result from the natural course of things, and to be unavoidable in every age and nation. This pertinacious bigotry, of which you complain, as so fatal to philosophy, is really her offspring, who, after allying with superstition, separates himself entirely from the interest of his parent, and becomes her most inveterate enemy and persecutor. Speculative dogmas of religion, the present occasions of such furious dispute, could not possibly be conceived or admitted in the early ages of the world; when mankind, being wholly illiterate, formed an idea of religion more suitable to their weak apprehension, and composed their sacred tenets of such tales chiefly as were the objects of traditional belief, more than of argument or disputation. After the first alarm, therefore, was over, which arose from the new paradoxes and principles of the philosophers; these teachers seem ever after, during the ages of antiquity, to have lived in great harmony with the established superstition, and to have made a fair partition of mankind between them; the former claiming all the learned and wise, the latter possessing all the vulgar and illiterate.

103. It seems then, say I, that you leave politics entirely out of the question, and never suppose, that a wise magistrate can justly be jealous of certain tenets of philosophy, such as those of Epicurus, which, denying a divine existence, and consequently a providence and a future state, seem to loosen, in a great measure, the ties of morality, and may be supposed, for that reason, pernicious to the peace of civil society.

I know, replied he, that in fact these persecutions never, in any age, proceeded from calm reason, or from experience of the pernicious consequences of philosophy; but arose entirely from passion and prejudice. But what if I should advance farther, and assert, that if Epicurus had been accused before the people, by any of the *sycophants* or informers of those days, he could easily have defended his cause, and proved his principles of philosophy to be as salutary as those of his adversaries, who endeavoured, with such zeal, to expose him to the public hatred and jealousy?

I wish, said I, you would try your eloquence upon so extraordinary a topic, and make a speech for Epicurus, which might satisfy, not the mob of Athens, if you will allow that ancient and polite city to have contained any mob, but the more philosophical part of his audience, such as might be supposed capable of comprehending his arguments.

The matter would not be difficult, upon such conditions, replied he: And if you please, I shall suppose myself Epicurus for a moment, and make you stand for the Athenian people, and shall deliver you such an harangue as will fill all the urn with white beans, and leave not a black one to gratify the malice of my adversaries.

Very well: Pray proceed upon these suppositions.

104. I come hither, O ye Athenians, to justify in your assembly what I maintained in my school, and I find myself impeached by furious antagonists, instead of reasoning with calm and dispassionate enquirers. Your deliberations, which of right should be directed to questions of public good, and the interest of the commonwealth, are diverted to the disquisitions of speculative philosophy; and these magnificent, but perhaps fruitless enquiries, take place of your more familiar but more useful occupations. But so far as in me lies, I will prevent this abuse. We shall not here dispute concerning the origin and government of worlds. We shall only enquire how far such questions concern the public interest. And if I can persuade you, that they are entirely indifferent to the peace of society and security of government, I hope that you will presently send us back to our schools, there to examine, at leisure, the question the most sublime, but at the same time, the most speculative of all philosophy.

The religious philosophers, not satisfied with the tradition of your forefathers, and doctrine of your priests (in which I willingly acquiesce), indulge a rash curiosity, in trying how far they can establish religion upon the principles of reason; and they thereby excite, instead of satisfying, the doubts, which naturally arise from a diligent and scrutinous enquiry. They paint, in the most magnificent colours, the order, beauty, and wise arrangement of the universe; and then ask, if such a glorious display of intelligence could proceed from the fortuitous concourse of atoms, or if chance could produce what the greatest genius can never sufficiently admire. I shall not examine the justness of this argument. I shall allow it to be as solid as my antagonists and accusers can desire. It is sufficient, if I can prove, from this very reasoning, that the question is entirely speculative, and that, when, in my philosophical disquisitions, I deny a providence and a future state, I undermine not the foundations of society, but advance principles, which they themselves, upon their own topics, if they argue consistently, must allow to be solid and satisfactory.

105. You then, who are my accusers, have acknowledged, that the chief or sole argument for a divine existence (which I never questioned) is derived from the order of nature; where there appear such marks of intelligence and design, that you think it extravagant to assign for its cause, either chance, or the blind and unguided force of matter. You allow, that this is an argument drawn from effects to causes. From the order of the work, you infer, that there must have been project and forethought in the workman. If you cannot make out this point, you allow, that your conclusion fails; and you pretend not to establish the conclusion in a greater latitude than the phenomena of nature will justify. These are your concessions. I desire you to mark the consequences.

When we infer any particular cause from an effect, we must proportion the one to the other, and can never be allowed to ascribe to the cause any qualities, but what are exactly sufficient to produce the effect. A body of ten ounces raised in any scale may serve as a proof, that the counterbalancing weight exceeds ten ounces; but can never afford a reason that it exceeds a hundred. If the cause, assigned for any effect, be not sufficient to produce it, we must either reject that cause, or add to it such qualities as will give it a just proportion to the effect. But if we ascribe to it farther qualities, or affirm it capable of producing other effects, we can only indulge the licence of conjecture, and arbitrarily suppose the existence of qualities and energies, without reason or authority.

The same rule holds, whether the cause assigned be brute unconscious matter, or a rational intelligent being. If the cause be known only by the effect, we never ought to ascribe to it any qualities, beyond what are precisely requisite to produce the effect: Nor can we, by any rules of just reasoning, return back from the cause, and infer other effects from it, beyond those by which alone it is known to us. No one, merely from the sight of one of Zeuxis's pictures, could know, that he was also a statuary or architect, and was an artist no less skilful in stone and marble than in colours. The talents and taste, displayed in the particular work before us; these we may safely conclude the workman to be possessed of. The cause must be proportioned to the effect; and if we exactly and precisely proportion it, we shall never find in it any qualities, that point farther, or afford an inference concerning any other design or performance. Such qualities must be somewhat beyond what is merely requisite for producing the effect, which we examine.

106. Allowing, therefore, the gods to be the authors of the existence or order of the universe; it follows, that they possess that precise degree of power, intelligence, and benevolence, which appears in their workmanship; but nothing farther can ever be proved, except we call in the assistance of exaggeration and flattery to supply the defects of argument and reasoning. So far as the traces of any attributes, at present, appear, so far may we conclude these attributes to exist. The supposition of farther attributes is mere hypothesis; much more the supposition, that, in distant regions of space or periods of time, there has been, or will be, a more magnificent display of these attributes, and a scheme of administration more suitable to such imaginary virtues. We can never be allowed to mount up from the universe, the effect, to Jupiter, the cause; and then descend downwards, to infer any new effect from that cause; as if the present effects alone were not entirely worthy of the glorious attributes, which we ascribe to that deity. The knowledge of the cause being derived solely from the effect, they must be exactly adjusted to each other; and the one can never refer to anything farther, or be the foundation of any new inference and conclusion.

You find certain phenomena in nature. You seek a cause or author. You imagine that you have found him. You afterwards become so enamoured of this offspring of your brain, that you imagine it impossible, but he must produce something greater and more perfect than the present scene of things, which is so full of ill and disorder. You forget, that this superlative intelligence and benevolence are entirely imaginary, or, at least, without any foundation in reason; and that you have no ground to ascribe to him any qualities, but what you see he has actually exerted and displayed in his productions. Let your gods, therefore, O philosophers, be suited to the present appearances of nature: and presume not to alter these appearances by arbitrary suppositions, in order to suit them to the attributes, which you so fondly ascribe to your deities.

107. When priests and poets, supported by your authority, O Athenians, talk of a golden or silver age, which preceded the present state of vice and misery, I hear them with attention and with reverence. But when philosophers, who pretend to neglect authority, and to cultivate reason, hold the same discourse, I pay them not, I own, the same obsequious submission and pious deference. I ask; who carried them into the celestial regions, who admitted them into the councils of the gods, who opened to them the book of fate, that they thus rashly affirm, that their deities have executed, or will execute, any purpose beyond what has actually appeared? If they tell me, that they have mounted on the steps or by the gradual ascent of reason, and by drawing inferences from effects to causes, I still insist, that they have aided the ascent of reason by the wings of imagination; otherwise they could not thus change their manner of inference, and argue from causes to effects; presuming, that a more perfect production than the present world would be more suitable to such perfect beings as the gods, and forgetting that they have no reason to ascribe to these celestial beings any perfection or any attribute, but what can be found in the present world.

Hence all the fruitless industry to account for the ill appearances of nature, and save the honour of the gods; while we must acknowledge the reality of that evil and disorder, with which the world so much abounds. The obstinate and intractable qualities of matter, we are told, or the observance of general laws, or some such reason, is the sole cause, which controlled the power and benevolence of Jupiter, and obliged him to create mankind and every sensible creature so imperfect and so unhappy. These attributes then, are, it seems, beforehand, taken for granted, in their greatest latitude. And upon that supposition, I own that such conjectures may, perhaps, be admitted as plausible solutions of the ill phenomena. But still I ask; Why take these attributes for granted, or why ascribe to the cause any qualities but what actually appear in the effect? Why torture your brain to justify the course of nature upon suppositions, which, for aught you know, may be entirely imaginary, and of which there are to be found no traces in the course of nature?

The religious hypothesis, therefore, must be considered only as a particular method of accounting for the visible phenomena of the universe: but no just reasoner will ever presume to infer from it any single fact, and alter or add to the phenomena, in any single particular. If you think, that the appearances of things prove such causes, it is allowable for you to draw an inference concerning the existence of these causes. In such complicated and sublime subjects, every one should be indulged in the liberty of conjecture and argument. But here you ought to rest. If you come backward, and arguing from your inferred causes, conclude, that any other fact has existed, or will exist, in the course of nature, which may serve as a fuller display of particular attributes; I must admonish you, that you have departed from the method of reasoning, attached to the present subject, and have certainly added something to the attributes of the cause, beyond what appears in the effect; otherwise you could never, with tolerable sense or propriety, add anything to the effect, in order to render it more worthy of the cause.

108. Where, then, is the odiousness of that doctrine, which I teach in my school, or rather, which I examine in my gardens? Or what do you find in this whole question, wherein the security of good morals, or the peace and order of society, is in the least concerned?

I deny a providence, you say, and supreme governor of the world, who guides the course of events, and punishes the vicious with infamy and disappointment, and rewards the virtuous with honour and success, in all their undertakings. But surely, I deny not the course itself of events, which lies open to every one's inquiry and examination. I acknowledge, that, in the present order of things, virtue is attended with more peace of mind than vice, and meets with a more favourable reception from the world. I am sensible, that, according to the past experience of mankind, friendship is the chief joy of human life, and moderation the only source of tranquillity and happiness. I never balance between the virtuous and the vicious course of life; but am sensible, that, to a well-disposed mind, every advantage is on the side of the former. And what can you say more, allowing all your suppositions and reasonings?

You tell me, indeed, that this disposition of things proceeds from intelligence and design. But whatever it proceeds from, the disposition itself, on which depends our happiness or misery, and consequently our conduct and deportment in life is still the same. It is still open for me, as well as you, to regulate my behaviour, by my experience of past events. And if you affirm, that, while a divine providence is allowed, and a supreme distributive justice in the universe, I ought to expect some more particular reward of the good, and punishment of the bad, beyond the ordinary course of events; I here find the same fallacy, which I have before endeavoured to detect. You persist in imagining, that, if we grant that divine existence, for which you so earnestly contend, you may safely infer consequences from it, and add something to the experienced order of nature, by arguing from the attributes which you ascribe to your gods. You seem not to remember, that all your reasonings on this subject can only be drawn from effects to causes; and that every argument, deducted from causes to effects, must of necessity be a gross sophism; since it is impossible for you to know anything of the cause, but what you have antecedently, not inferred, but discovered to the full, in the effect.

109. But what must a philosopher think of those vain reasoners, who, instead of regarding the present scene of things as the sole object of their contemplation, so far reverse the whole course of nature, as to render this life merely a passage to something farther; a porch, which leads to a greater, and vastly different building; a prologue, which serves only to introduce the piece, and give it more grace and propriety? Whence, do you think, can such philosophers derive their idea of the gods? From their own conceit and imagination surely. For if they derived it from the present phenomena, it would never point to anything farther, but must be exactly adjusted to them. That the divinity may *possibly* be endowed with attributes, which we have never seen exerted; may be governed by principles of action, which we cannot discover to be satisfied: all this will freely be allowed. But still this is mere *possibility* and hypothesis. We never can have reason to *infer* any attributes, or any principles of action in him, but so far as we know them to have been exerted and satisfied.

Are there any marks of a distributive justice in the world? If you answer in the affirmative, I conclude, that, since justice here exerts itself, it is satisfied. If you reply in the negative, I conclude, that you have then no reason to ascribe justice, in our sense of it, to the gods. If you hold a medium between affirmation and negation, by saying, that the justice of the gods, at present, exerts itself in part, but not in its full extent; I answer, that you have no reason to give it any particular extent, but only so far as you see it, *at present*, exert itself.

110. Thus I bring the dispute, O Athenians, to a short issue with my antagonists. The course of nature lies open to my contemplation as well as to theirs. The experienced train of events is the great standard, by which we all regulate our conduct. Nothing else can be appealed to in the field, or in the senate. Nothing else ought ever to be heard of in the school, or in the closet. In vain would our limited understanding break through those boundaries, which are too narrow for our fond imagination. While we argue from the course of nature, and infer a particular intelligent cause, which first bestowed, and still preserves order in the universe, we embrace a principle, which is both uncertain and useless. It is uncertain; because the subject lies entirely beyond the reach of human experience. It is useless; because our knowledge of this cause being derived entirely from the course of nature, we can never, according to the rules of just reasoning, return back from the cause with any new inference, or making additions to the common and experienced course of nature, establish any new principles of conduct and behaviour.

111. I observe (said I, finding he had finished his harangue) that you neglect not the artifice of the demagogues of old; and as you were pleased to make me stand for the people, you insinuate yourself into my favour by embracing those principles, to which, you know, I have always expressed a particular attachment. But allowing you to make experience (as indeed I think you ought) the only standard of our judgement concerning this, and all other questions of fact; I doubt not but, from the very same experience, to which you appeal, it may be possible to refute this reasoning, which you have put into the mouth of Epicurus. If you saw, for instance, a half-finished building, surrounded with heaps of brick and stone and mortar, and all the instruments of masonry; could you not *infer* from the effect, that it was a work of design and contrivance?

And could you not return again, from this inferred cause, to infer new additions to the effect, and conclude, that the building would soon be finished, and receive all the further improvements, which art could bestow upon it? If you saw upon the sea-shore the print of one human foot, you would conclude, that a man had passed that way, and that he had also left the traces of the other foot, though effaced by the rolling of the sands or inundation of the waters. Why then do you refuse to admit the same method of reasoning with regard to the order of nature? Consider the world and the present life only as an imperfect building, from which you can infer a superior intelligence; and arguing from that superior intelligence, which can leave nothing imperfect; why may you not infer a more finished scheme or plan, which will receive its completion in some distant point of space or time? Are not these methods of reasoning exactly similar? And under what pretence can you embrace the one, while you reject the other?

112. The infinite difference of the subjects, replied he, is a sufficient foundation for this difference in my conclusions. In works of art and contrivance, it is allowable to advance from the effect to the cause, and returning back from the cause, to form new inferences concerning the effect, and examine the alterations, which it has probably undergone, or may still undergo. But what is the foundation of this method of reasoning? Plainly this; that man is a being, whom we know by experience, whose motives and designs we are acquainted with, and whose projects and inclinations have a certain connexion and coherence, according to the laws which nature has established for the government of such a creature. When, therefore, we find, that any work has proceeded from the skill and industry of man; as we are otherwise acquainted with the nature of the animal, we can draw a hundred inferences concerning what may be expected from him; and these inferences will all be founded in experience and observation.

But did we know man only from the single work or production which we examine, it were impossible for us to argue in this manner; because our knowledge of all the qualities, which we ascribe to him, being in that case derived from the production, it is impossible they could point to anything farther, or be the foundation of any new inference. The print of a foot in the sand can only prove, when considered alone, that there was some figure adapted to it, by which it was produced: but the print of a human foot proves likewise, from our other experience, that there was probably another foot, which also left its impression, though effaced by time or other accidents. Here we mount from the effect to the cause; and descending again from the cause, infer alterations in the effect; but this is not a continuation of the same simple chain of reasoning. We comprehend in this case a hundred other experiences and observations, concerning the *usual* figure and members of that species of animal, without which this method of argument must be considered as fallacious and sophistical.

113. The case is not the same with our reasonings from the works of nature. The Deity is known to us only by his productions, and is a single being in the universe, not comprehended under any species or genus, from whose experienced attributes or qualities, we can, by analogy, infer any attribute or quality in him. As the universe shews wisdom and goodness, we infer wisdom and goodness. As it shews a particular degree of these perfections, we infer a particular degree of them, precisely adapted to the effect which we examine. But farther attributes or farther degrees of the same attributes, we can never be authorised to infer or suppose, by any rules of just reasoning. Now, without some such licence of supposition, it is impossible for us to argue from the cause, or infer any alteration in the effect, beyond what has immediately fallen under our observation. Greater good produced by this Being must still prove a greater degree of goodness: a more impartial distribution of rewards and punishments must proceed from a greater regard to justice and equity. Every supposed addition to the works of nature makes an addition to the attributes of the Author of nature; and consequently, being entirely unsupported by any reason or argument, can never be admitted but as mere conjecture and hypothesis.

The great source of our mistake in this subject, and of the unbounded licence of conjecture, which we indulge, is, that we tacitly consider ourselves, as in the place of the Supreme Being, and conclude, that he will, on every occasion, observe the same conduct, which we ourselves, in his situation, would have embraced as reasonable and eligible. But, besides that the ordinary course of nature may convince us, that almost everything is regulated by principles and maxims very different from ours; besides this, I say, it must evidently appear contrary to all rules of analogy to reason, from the intentions and projects of men, to those of a Being so different, and so much superior. In human nature, there is a certain experienced coherence of designs and inclinations; so that when, from any fact, we have discovered one intention of any man, it may often be reasonable, from experience, to infer another, and draw a long chain of conclusions concerning his past or future conduct.

But this method of reasoning can never have place with regard to a Being, so remote and incomprehensible, who bears much less analogy to any other being in the universe than the sun to a waxen taper, and who discovers himself only by some faint traces or outlines, beyond which we have no authority to ascribe to him any attribute or perfection. What we imagine to be a superior perfection, may really be a defect. Or were it ever so much a perfection, the ascribing of it to the Supreme Being, where it appears not to have been really exerted, to the full, in his works, savours more of flattery and panegyric, than of just reasoning and sound philosophy.

All the philosophy, therefore, in the world, and all the religion, which is nothing but a species of philosophy, will never be able to carry us beyond the usual course of experience, or give us measures of conduct and behaviour different from those which are furnished by reflections on common life. No new fact can ever be inferred from the religious hypothesis; no event foreseen or foretold; no reward or punishment expected or dreaded, beyond what is already known by practice and observation. So that my apology for Epicurus will still appear solid and satisfactory; nor have the political interests of society any connexion with the philosophical disputes concerning metaphysics and religion.

114. There is still one circumstance, replied I, which you seem to have overlooked. Though I should allow your premises, I must deny your conclusion. You conclude, that religious doctrines and reasonings *can* have no influence on life, because they *ought* to have no influence; never considering, that men reason not in the same manner you do, but draw many consequences from the belief of a divine Existence, and suppose that the Deity will inflict punishments on vice, and bestow rewards on virtue, beyond what appear in the ordinary course of nature. Whether this reasoning of theirs be just or not, is no matter. Its influence on their life and conduct must still be the same. And, those, who attempt to disabuse them of such prejudices, may, for aught I know, be good reasoners, but I cannot allow them to be good citizens and politicians; since they free men from one restraint upon their passions, and make the infringement of the laws of society, in one respect, more easy and secure.

After all, I may, perhaps, agree to your general conclusion in favour of liberty, though upon different premises from those, on which you endeavour to found it. I think, that the state ought to tolerate every principle of philosophy; nor is there an instance, that any government has suffered in its political interests by such indulgence. There is no enthusiasm among philosophers; their doctrines are not very alluring to the people; and no restraint can be put upon their reasonings, but what must be of dangerous consequence to the sciences, and even to the state, by paving the way for persecution and oppression in points, where the generality of mankind are more deeply interested and concerned.

115. But there occurs to me (continued I) with regard to your main topic, a difficulty, which I shall just propose to you without insisting on it; lest it lead into reasonings of too nice and delicate a nature. In a word, I much doubt whether it be possible for a cause to be known only by its effect (as you have all along supposed) or to be of so singular and particular a nature as to have no parallel and no similarity with any other cause or object, that has ever fallen under our observation. It is only when two *species* of objects are found to be constantly conjoined, that we can infer the one from the other; and were an effect presented, which was entirely singular, and could not be comprehended under any known *species*, I do not see, that we could form any conjecture or inference at all concerning its cause.

If experience and observation and analogy be, indeed, the only guides which we can reasonably follow in inferences of this nature; both the effect and cause must bear a similarity and resemblance to other effects and causes, which we know, and which we have found, in many instances, to be conjoined with each other. I leave it to your own reflection to pursue the consequences of this principle. I shall just observe, that, as the antagonists of Epicurus always suppose the universe, an effect quite singular and unparalleled, to be the proof of a Deity, a cause no less singular and unparalleled; your reasonings, upon that supposition, seem, at least, to merit our attention. There is, I own, some difficulty, how we can ever return from the cause to the effect, and, reasoning from our ideas of the former, infer any alteration on the latter, or any addition to it.

Section 12
Of the Academical or Sceptical Philosophy

Part 1

116. There is not a greater number of philosophical reasonings, displayed upon any subject, than those, which prove the existence of a Deity, and refute the fallacies of Atheists; and yet the most religious philosophers still dispute whether any man can be so blinded as to be a speculative atheist. How shall we reconcile these contradictions? The knights-errant, who wandered about to clear the world of dragons and giants, never entertained the least doubt with regard to the existence of these monsters.

The Sceptic is another enemy of religion, who naturally provokes the indignation of all divines and graver philosophers; though it is certain, that no man ever met with any such absurd creature, or conversed with a man, who had no opinion or principle concerning any subject, either of action or speculation. This begets a very natural question; What is meant by a sceptic? And how far it is possible to push these philosophical principles of doubt and uncertainty?

There is a species of scepticism, *antecedent* to all study and philosophy, which is much inculcated by Des Cartes and others, as a sovereign preservative against error and precipitate judgement. It recommends an universal doubt, not only of all our former opinions and principles, but also of our very faculties; of whose veracity, say they, we must assure ourselves, by a chain of reasoning, deduced from some original principle, which cannot possibly be fallacious or deceitful. But neither is there any such original principle, which has a prerogative above others, that are self-evident and convincing: or if there were, could we advance a step beyond it, but by the use of those very faculties, of which we are supposed to be already diffident. The Cartesian doubt, therefore, were it ever possible to be attained by any human creature (as it plainly is not) would be entirely incurable; and no reasoning could ever bring us to a state of assurance and conviction upon any subject.

It must, however, be confessed, that this species of scepticism, when more moderate, may be understood in a very reasonable sense, and is a necessary preparative to the study of philosophy, by preserving a proper impartiality in our judgements, and weaning our mind from all those prejudices, which we may have imbibed from education or rash opinion. To begin with clear and self-evident principles, to advance by timorous and sure steps, to review frequently our conclusions, and examine accurately all their consequences; though by these means we shall make both a slow and a short progress in our systems; are the only methods, by which we can ever hope to reach truth, and attain a proper stability and certainty in our determinations.

117. There is another species of scepticism, *consequent* to science and enquiry, when men are supposed to have discovered, either the absolute fallaciousness of their mental faculties, or their unfitness to reach any fixed determination in all those curious subjects of speculation, about which they are commonly employed. Even our very senses are brought into dispute, by a certain species of philosophers; and the maxims of common life are subjected to the same doubt as the most profound principles or conclusions of metaphysics and theology. As these paradoxical tenets (if they may be called tenets) are to be met with in some philosophers, and the refutation of them in several, they naturally excite our curiosity, and make us enquire into the arguments, on which they may be founded.

I need not insist upon the more trite topics, employed by the sceptics in all ages, against the evidence of *sense*; such as those which are derived from the imperfection and fallaciousness of our organs, on numberless occasions; the crooked appearance of an oar in water; the various aspects of objects, according to their different distances; the double images which arise from the pressing one eye; with many other appearances of a like nature. These sceptical topics, indeed, are only sufficient to prove, that the senses alone are not implicitly to be depended on; but that we must correct their evidence by reason, and by considerations, derived from the nature of the medium, the distance of the object, and the disposition of the organ, in order to render them, within their sphere, the proper *criteria* of truth and falsehood. There are other more profound arguments against the senses, which admit not of so easy a solution.

118. It seems evident, that men are carried, by a natural instinct or prepossession, to repose faith in their senses; and that, without any reasoning, or even almost before the use of reason, we always suppose an external universe, which depends not on our perception, but would exist, though we and every sensible creature were absent or annihilated. Even the animal creation are governed by a like opinion, and preserve this belief of external objects, in all their thoughts, designs, and actions.

It seems also evident, that, when men follow this blind and powerful instinct of nature, they always suppose the very images, presented by the senses, to be the external objects, and never entertain any suspicion, that the one are nothing but representations of the other. This very table, which we see white, and which we feel hard, is believed to exist, independent of our perception, and to be something external to our mind, which perceives it. Our presence bestows not being on it: our absence does not annihilate it. It preserves its existence uniform and entire, independent of the situation of intelligent beings, who perceive or contemplate it.

But this universal and primary opinion of all men is soon destroyed by the slightest philosophy, which teaches us, that nothing can ever be present to the mind but an image or perception, and that the senses are only the inlets, through which these images are conveyed, without being able to produce any immediate intercourse between the mind and the object. The table, which we see, seems to diminish, as we remove farther from it: but the real table, which exists independent of us, suffers no alteration: it was, therefore, nothing but its image, which was present to the mind. These are the obvious dictates of reason; and no man, who reflects, ever doubted, that the existences, which we consider, when we say, *this house* and *that tree*, are nothing but perceptions in the mind, and fleeting copies or representations of other existences, which remain uniform and independent.

119. So far, then, are we necessitated by reasoning to contradict or depart from the primary instincts of nature, and to embrace a new system with regard to the evidence of our senses. But here philosophy finds herself extremely embarrassed, when she would justify this new system, and obviate the cavils and objections of the sceptics. She can no longer plead the infallible and irresistible instinct of nature: for that led us to a quite different system, which is acknowledged fallible and even erroneous. And to justify this pretended philosophical system, by a chain of clear and convincing argument, or even any appearance of argument, exceeds the power of all human capacity.

By what argument can it be proved, that the perceptions of the mind must be caused by external objects, entirely different from them, though resembling them (if that be possible) and could not arise either from the energy of the mind itself, or from the suggestion of some invisible and unknown spirit, or from some other cause still more unknown to us? It is acknowledged, that, in fact, many of these perceptions arise not from anything external, as in dreams, madness, and other diseases. And nothing can be more inexplicable than the manner, in which body should so operate upon mind as ever to convey an image of itself to a substance, supposed of so different, and even contrary a nature.

It is a question of fact, whether the perceptions of the senses be produced by external objects, resembling them: how shall this question be determined? By experience surely; as all other questions of a like nature. But here experience is, and must be entirely silent. The mind has never anything present to it but the perceptions, and cannot possibly reach any experience of their connexion with objects. The supposition of such a connexion is, therefore, without any foundation in reasoning.

120. To have recourse to the veracity of the supreme Being, in order to prove the veracity of our senses, is surely making a very unexpected circuit. If his veracity were at all concerned in this matter, our senses would be entirely infallible; because it is not possible that he can ever deceive. Not to mention, that, if the external world be once called in question, we shall be at a loss to find arguments, by which we may prove the existence of that Being or any of his attributes.

121. This is a topic, therefore, in which the profounder and more philosophical sceptics will always triumph, when they endeavour to introduce an universal doubt into all subjects of human knowledge and enquiry. Do you follow the instincts and propensities of nature, may they say, in assenting to the veracity of sense? But these lead you to believe that the very perception or sensible image is the external object. Do you disclaim this principle, in order to embrace a more rational opinion, that the perceptions are only representations of something external? You here depart from your natural propensities and more obvious sentiments; and yet are not able to satisfy your reason, which can never find any convincing argument from experience to prove, that the perceptions are connected with any external objects.

122. There is another sceptical topic of a like nature, derived from the most profound philosophy; which might merit our attention, were it requisite to dive so deep, in order to discover arguments and reasonings, which can so little serve to any serious purpose. It is universally allowed by modern enquirers, that all the sensible qualities of objects, such as hard, soft, hot, cold, white, black, &c. are merely secondary, and exist not in the objects themselves, but are perceptions of the mind, without any external archetype or model, which they represent. If this be allowed, with regard to secondary qualities, it must also follow, with regard to the supposed primary qualities of extension and solidity; nor can the latter be any more entitled to that denomination than the former.

The idea of extension is entirely acquired from the senses of sight and feeling; and if all the qualities, perceived by the senses, be in the mind, not in the object, the same conclusion must reach the idea of extension, which is wholly dependent on the sensible ideas or the ideas of secondary qualities. Nothing can save us from this conclusion, but the asserting, that the ideas of those primary qualities are attained by *Abstraction*, an opinion, which, if we examine it accurately, we shall find to be unintelligible, and even absurd. An extension, that is neither tangible nor visible, cannot possibly be conceived: and a tangible or visible extension, which is neither hard nor soft, black nor white, is equally beyond the reach of human conception. Let any man try to conceive a triangle in general, which is neither *Isosceles* nor *Scalenum*, nor has any particular length or proportion of sides; and he will soon perceive the absurdity of all the scholastic notions with regard to abstraction and general ideas.

123. Thus the first philosophical objection to the evidence of sense or to the opinion of external existence consists in this, that such an opinion, if rested on natural instinct, is contrary to reason, and if referred to reason, is contrary to natural instinct, and at the same time carries no rational evidence with it, to convince an impartial enquirer. The second objection goes farther, and represents this opinion as contrary to reason: at least, if it be a principle of reason, that all sensible qualities are in the mind, not in the object. Bereave matter of all its intelligible qualities, both primary and secondary, you in a manner annihilate it, and leave only a certain unknown, inexplicable *something*, as the cause of our perceptions; a notion so imperfect, that no sceptic will think it worth while to contend against it. . . .

Part 3

129. There is, indeed, a more *mitigated* scepticism or *academical* philosophy, which may be both durable and useful, and which may, in part, be the result of this Pyrrhonism, or *excessive* scepticism, when its undistinguished doubts are, in some measure, corrected by common sense and reflection. The greater part of mankind are naturally apt to be affirmative and dogmatical in their opinions; and while they see objects only on one side, and have no idea of any counterpoising argument, they throw themselves precipitately into the principles, to which they are inclined; nor have they any indulgence for those who entertain opposite sentiments. To hesitate or balance perplexes their understanding, checks their passion, and suspends their action. They are, therefore, impatient till they escape from a state, which to them is so uneasy: and they think, that they could never remove themselves far enough from it, by the violence of their affirmations and obstinacy of their belief.

But could such dogmatical reasoners become sensible of the strange infirmities of human understanding, even in its most perfect state, and when most accurate and cautious in its determinations; such a reflection would naturally inspire them with more modesty and reserve, and diminish their fond opinion of themselves, and their prejudice against antagonists. The illiterate may reflect on the disposition of the learned, who, amidst all the advantages of study and reflection, are commonly still diffident in their determinations: and if any of the learned be inclined, from their natural temper, to haughtiness and obstinacy, a small tincture of Pyrrhonism might abate their pride, by showing them, that the few advantages, which they may have attained over their fellows, are but inconsiderable, if compared with the universal perplexity and confusion, which is inherent in human nature. In general, there is a degree of doubt, and caution, and modesty, which, in all kinds of scrutiny and decision, ought for ever to accompany a just reasoner.

130. Another species of *mitigated* scepticism which may be of advantage to mankind, and which may be the natural result of the Pyrrhonian doubts and scruples, is the limitation of our enquiries to such subjects as are best adapted to the narrow capacity of human understanding. The *imagination* of man is naturally sublime, delighted with whatever is remote and extraordinary, and running, without control, into the most distant parts of space and time in order to avoid the objects, which custom has rendered too familiar to it. A correct *Judgement* observes a contrary method, and avoiding all distant and high enquiries, confines itself to common life, and to such subjects as fall under daily practice and experience; leaving the more sublime topics to the embellishment of poets and orators, or to the arts of priests and politicians.

To bring us to so salutary a determination, nothing can be more serviceable, than to be once thoroughly convinced of the force of the Pyrrhonian doubt, and of the impossibility, that anything, but the strong power of natural instinct, could free us from it. Those who have a propensity to philosophy, will still continue their researches; because they reflect, that, besides the immediate pleasure, attending such an occupation, philosophical decisions are nothing but the reflections of common life, methodized and corrected. But they will never be tempted to go beyond common life, so long as they consider the imperfection of those faculties which they employ, their narrow reach, and their inaccurate operations. While we cannot give a satisfactory reason, why we believe, after a thousand experiments, that a stone will fall, or fire burn; can we ever satisfy ourselves concerning any determination, which we may form, with regard to the origin of worlds, and the situation of nature, from, and to eternity?

This narrow limitation, indeed, of our enquiries, is, in every respect, so reasonable, that it suffices to make the slightest examination into the natural powers of the human mind and to compare them with their objects, in order to recommend it to us. We shall then find what are the proper subjects of science and enquiry.

131. It seems to me, that the only objects of the abstract science or of demonstration are quantity and number, and that all attempts to extend this more perfect species of knowledge beyond these bounds are mere sophistry and illusion. As the component parts of quantity and number are entirely similar, their relations become intricate and involved; and nothing can be more curious, as well as useful, than to trace, by a variety of mediums, their equality or inequality, through their different appearances. But as all other ideas are clearly distinct and different from each other, we can never advance farther, by our utmost scrutiny, than to observe this diversity, and, by an obvious reflection, pronounce one thing not to be another.

Or if there be any difficulty in these decisions, it proceeds entirely from the undeterminate meaning of words, which is corrected by juster definitions. That *the square of the hypothenuse is equal to the squares of the other two sides*, cannot be known, let the terms be ever so exactly defined, without a train of reasoning and enquiry. But to convince us of this proposition, *that where there is no property, there can be no injustice*, it is only necessary to define the terms, and explain injustice to be a violation of property. This proposition is, indeed, nothing but a more imperfect definition. It is the same case with all those pretended syllogistical reasonings, which may be found in every other branch of learning, except the sciences of quantity and number; and these may safely, I think, be pronounced the only proper objects of knowledge and demonstration.

132. All other enquiries of men regard only matter of fact and existence; and these are evidently incapable of demonstration. Whatever *is* may *not be*. No negation of a fact can involve a contradiction. The non-existence of any being, without exception, is as clear and distinct an idea as its existence. The proposition, which affirms it not to be, however false, is no less conceivable and intelligible, than that which affirms it to be. The case is different with the sciences, properly so called. Every proposition, which is not true, is there confused and unintelligible. That the cube root of 64 is equal to the half of 10, is a false proposition, and can never be distinctly conceived. But that Caesar, or the angel Gabriel, or any being never existed, may be a false proposition, but still is perfectly conceivable, and implies no contradiction.

The existence, therefore, of any being can only be proved by arguments from its cause or its effect; and these arguments are founded entirely on experience. If we reason a priori, anything may appear able to produce anything. The falling of a pebble may, for aught we know, extinguish the sun; or the wish of a man control the planets in their orbits. It is only experience, which teaches us the nature and bounds of cause and effect, and enables us to infer the existence of one object from that of another. Such is the foundation of moral reasoning, which forms the greater part of human knowledge, and is the source of all human action and behaviour.

Moral reasonings are either concerning particular or general facts. All deliberations in life regard the former; as also all disquisitions in history, chronology, geography, and astronomy.

The sciences, which treat of general facts, are politics, natural philosophy, physic, chemistry, &c. where the qualities, causes and effects of a whole species of objects are enquired into.

Divinity or Theology, as it proves the existence of a Deity, and the immortality of souls, is composed partly of reasonings concerning particular, partly concerning general facts. It has a foundation in *reason*, so far as it is supported by experience. But its best and most solid foundation is *faith* and divine revelation.

Morals and criticism are not so properly objects of the understanding as of taste and sentiment. Beauty, whether moral or natural, is felt, more properly than perceived. Or if we reason concerning it, and endeavour to fix its standard, we regard a new fact, to wit, the general tastes of mankind, or some such fact, which may be the object of reasoning and enquiry.

When we run over libraries, persuaded of these principles, what havoc must we make? If we take in our hand any volume; of divinity or school metaphysics, for instance; let us ask, *Does it contain any abstract reasoning concerning quantity or number?* No. *Does it contain any experimental reasoning concerning matter of fact and existence?* No. Commit it then to the flames: for it can contain nothing but sophistry and illusion.

FRIEDRICH NIETZSCHE
Twilight of the Idols

Translated by Jack Miller

The Problem of Socrates

§1

Concerning life, the wisest men of all ages have judged alike: it is no good. Always and everywhere one has heard the same sound from their mouths—a sound full of doubt, full of melancholy, full of weariness of life, full of resistance to life. Even Socrates said, as he died: "To live—that means to be sick a long time: I owe Asclepius the Savior a rooster." Even Socrates was tired of it. What does that evidence? What does it evince? Formerly one would have said (—oh, it has been said, and loud enough, and especially by our pessimists): "At least something of all this must be true! The consensus of the sages evidences the truth." Shall we still talk like that today? May we? "At least something must be sick here," we retort. These wisest men of all ages—they should first be scrutinized closely. Were they all perhaps shaky on their legs? late? tottery? decadents? Could it be that wisdom appears on earth as a raven, inspired by a little whiff of carrion?

§2

This irreverent thought that the great sages are types of decline first occurred to me precisely in a case where it is most strongly opposed by both scholarly and unscholarly prejudice: I recognized Socrates and Plato to be symptoms of degeneration, tools of the Greek dissolution, pseudo-Greek, anti-Greek. The consensus of the sages—I comprehended this ever more clearly—proves least of all that they were right in what they agreed on: it shows rather that they themselves, these wisest men, agreed in some physiological respect, and hence adopted the same negative attitude to life—had to adopt it. Judgments, judgments of value, concerning life, for it or against it, can, in the end, never be true: they have value only as symptoms, they are worthy of consideration only as symptoms; in themselves such judgments are stupidities. One must by all means stretch out one's fingers and make the attempt to grasp this amazing finesse, that the value of life cannot be estimated. Not by the living, for they are an interested party, even a bone of contention, and not judges; not by the dead, for a different reason. For a philosopher to see a problem in the value of life is thus an objection to him, a question mark concerning his wisdom, an un-wisdom. Indeed? All these great wise men—they were not only decadents but not wise at all? But I return to the problem of Socrates.

§3

In origin, Socrates belonged to the lowest class: Socrates was plebs. We know, we can still see for ourselves, how ugly he was. But ugliness, in itself an objection, is among the Greeks almost a refutation. Was Socrates a Greek at all? Ugliness is often enough the expression of a development that has been crossed, thwarted by crossing. Or it appears as declining development. The anthropologists among the criminologists tell us that the typical criminal is ugly. But the criminal is a decadent. Was Socrates a typical criminal? At least that would not be contradicted by the famous judgment of the physiognomist which sounded so offensive to the friends of Socrates. A foreigner who knew about faces once passed through Athens and told Socrates to his face that he was a monstrum—that he harbored in himself all the bad vices and appetites. And Socrates merely answered: "You know me, sir!"

§4

Socrates' decadence is suggested not only by the admitted wantonness and anarchy of his instincts, but also by the hypertrophy of the logical faculty and that sarcasm of the rachitic which distinguishes him. Nor should we forget those auditory hallucinations which, as "the daimon of Socrates," have been interpreted religiously. Everything in him is exaggerated, buffo, a caricature; everything is at the same time concealed, ulterior, subterranean. I seek to comprehend what idiosyncrasy begot that Socratic equation of reason, virtue, and happiness: that most bizarre of all equations which, moreover, is opposed to all the instincts of the earlier Greeks.

§5

With Socrates, Greek taste changes in favor of dialectics. What really happened there? Above all, a noble taste is thus vanquished; with dialectics the plebs come to the top. Before Socrates, dialectic manners were repudiated in good society: they were considered bad manners, they were compromising. The young were warned against them. Furthermore, all such presentations of one's reasons were distrusted. Honest things, like honest men, do not carry their reasons in their hands like that. It is indecent to show all five fingers. What must first be proved is worth little. Wherever authority still forms part of good bearing, where one does not give reasons but commands, the dialectician is a kind of buffoon: one laughs at him, one does not take him seriously. Socrates was the buffoon who got himself taken seriously: what really happened there?

§6

One chooses dialectic only when one has no other means. One knows that one arouses mistrust with it, that it is not very persuasive. Nothing is easier to erase than a dialectical effect: the experience of every meeting at which there are speeches proves this. It can only be self-defense for those who no longer have other weapons. One must have to enforce one's right: until one reaches that point, one makes no use of it. The Jews were dialecticians for that reason; Reynard the Fox was one—and Socrates too?

§7

Is the irony of Socrates an expression of revolt? Of plebeian *ressentiment*? Does he, as one oppressed, enjoy his own ferocity in the knife-thrusts of his syllogisms? Does he avenge himself on the noble people whom he fascinates? As a dialectician, one holds a merciless tool in one's hand; one can become a tyrant by means of it; one compromises those one conquers. The dialectician leaves it to his opponent to prove that he is no idiot: he makes one furious and helpless at the same time. The dialectician renders the intellect of his opponent powerless. Indeed? Is dialectic only a form of revenge in Socrates?

§8

I have given to understand how it was that Socrates could repel: it is therefore all the more necessary to explain his fascination. That he discovered a new kind of agon, that he became its first fencing master for the noble circles of Athens, is one point. He fascinated by appealing to the agonistic impulse of the Greeks—he introduced a variation into the wrestling match between young men and youths. Socrates was also a great erotic.

§9

But Socrates guessed even more. He saw through his noble Athenians; he comprehended that his own case, his idiosyncrasy, was no longer exceptional. The same kind of degeneration was quietly developing everywhere: old Athens was coming to an end. And Socrates understood that all the world needed him—his means, his cure, his personal artifice of self-preservation. Everywhere the instincts were in anarchy everywhere one was within five paces of excess: monstrum in animo was the general danger. "The impulses want to play the tyrant; one must invent a counter-tyrant who is stronger. When the physiognomist had revealed to Socrates who he was—a cave of bad appetites—the great master of irony let slip another word which is the key to his character. "This is true," he said, "but I mastered them all." How did Socrates become master over himself? His case was, at bottom, merely the extreme case, only the most striking instance of what was then beginning to be a universal distress: no one was any longer master over himself, the instincts turned against each other. He fascinated, being this extreme case; his awe-inspiring ugliness proclaimed him as such to all who could see: he fascinated, of course, even more as an answer, a solution, an apparent cure of this case.

§10

When one finds it necessary to turn reason into a tyrant, as Socrates did, the danger cannot be slight that something else will play the tyrant. Rationality was then hit upon as the savior; neither Socrates nor his "patients" had any choice about being rational: it was de rigeur, it was their last resort.

The fanaticism with which all Greek reflection throws itself upon rationality betrays a desperate situation; there was danger, there was but one choice: either to perish or—to be absurdly rational. The moralism of the Greek philosophers from Plato on is pathologically conditioned; so is their esteem of dialectics. Reason = virtue = happiness, that means merely that one must imitate Socrates and counter the dark appetites with a permanent daylight—the daylight of reason. One must be clever, clear, bright at any price: any concession to the instincts, to the unconscious, leads downward.

§11

I have given to understand how it was that Socrates fascinated: he seemed to be a physician, a savior. Is it necessary to go on to demonstrate the error in his faith in "rationality at any price"? It is a self-deception on the part of philosophers and moralists if they believe that they are extricating themselves from decadence when they merely wage war against it. Extrication lies beyond their strength: what they choose as a means, as salvation, is itself but another expression of decadence; they change its expression, but they do not get rid of decadence itself. Socrates was a misunderstanding; the whole improvement-morality, including the Christian, was a misunderstanding. The most blinding daylight; rationality at any price; life, bright, cold, cautious, conscious, without instinct, in opposition to the instincts—all this too was a mere disease, another disease, and by no means a return to "virtue," to "health," to happiness. To have to fight the instincts—that is the formula of decadence: as long as life is ascending, happiness equals instinct.

§12

Did he himself still comprehend this, this most brilliant of all self-outwitters? Was this what he said to himself in the end, in the wisdom of his courage to die? Socrates wanted to die: not Athens, but he himself chose the hemlock; he forced Athens to sentence him. "Socrates is no physician," he said softly to himself, "here death alone is the physician. Socrates himself has merely been sick a long time."

"Reason" in Philosophy

§1

You ask me which of the philosophers' traits are really idiosyncrasies? For example, their lack of historical sense, their hatred of the very idea of becoming, their Egypticism. They think that they show their respect for a subject when they de-historicize it, *sub specie aeternitas*—when they turn it into a mummy. All that philosophers have handled for thousands of years have-been concept-mummies; nothing real escaped their grasp alive. When these honorable idolators of concepts worship something, they kill it and stuff it; they threaten the life of everything they worship. Death, change, old age, as well as procreation and growth, are to their minds objections—even refutations. Whatever has being does not become; whatever becomes does not have being. Now they all believe, desperately even, in what has being. But since they never grasp it, they seek for reasons why it is kept from them. "There must be mere appearance, there must be some deception which prevents us from perceiving that which has being: where is the deceiver?"

"We have found him," they cry ecstatically; "it is the senses! These senses, which are so immoral in other ways too, deceive us concerning the true world. Moral: let us free ourselves from the deception of the senses, from becoming, from history, from lies; history is nothing but faith in the senses, faith in lies. Moral: let us say No to all who have faith in the senses, to all the rest of mankind; they are all 'mob.' Let us be philosophers! Let us be mummies!" Let us represent monotono-theism by adopting the expression of a gravedigger! And above all, away with the body, this wretched *idée fixe* of the senses, disfigured by all the fallacies of logic, refuted, even impossible, although it is impudent enough to behave as if it were real!"

§2

With the highest respect, I except the name of Heraclitus. When the rest of the philosophic folk rejected the testimony of the senses because they showed multiplicity and change, he rejected their testimony because they showed things as if they had permanence and unity. Heraclitus too did the senses an injustice. They lie neither in the way the Eleatics believed, nor as he believed—they do not lie at all. What we make of their testimony, that alone introduces lies; for example, the lie of unity, the lie of thinghood, of substance, of permanence. "Reason" is the cause of our falsification of the testimony of the senses. Insofar as the senses show becoming, passing away, and change, they do not lie. But Heraclitus will remain eternally right with his assertion that being is an empty fiction. The "apparent" world is the only one: the "true" world is merely added by a lie.

§3

And what magnificent instruments of observation we possess in our senses! This nose, for example, of which no philosopher has yet spoken with reverence and gratitude, is actually the most delicate instrument so far at our disposal: it is able to detect minimal differences of motion which even a spectroscope cannot detect. Today we possess science precisely to the extent to which we have decided to accept the testimony of the senses--to the extent to which we sharpen them further, arm them, and have learned to think them through. The rest is miscarriage and not-yet-science—in other words, metaphysics, theology, psychology, epistemology—or formal science, a doctrine of signs, such as logic and that applied logic which is called mathematics. In them reality is not encountered at all, not even as a problem—no more than the question of the value of such a sign-convention as logic.

§4

The other idiosyncrasy of the philosophers is no less dangerous; it consists in confusing the last and the first. They place that which comes at the end—unfortunately! for it ought not to come at all!—namely, the "highest concepts," which means the most general, the emptiest concepts, the last smoke of evaporating reality, in the beginning, as the beginning. This again is nothing but their way of showing reverence: the higher may not grow out of the lower, may not have grown at all. Moral: whatever is of the first rank must be *causa sui.* Origin out of something else is considered an objection, a questioning of value. All the highest values are of the first rank; all the highest concepts, that which has being, the unconditional, the good, the true, the perfect—all these cannot have become and must therefore be causes. All these, moreover, cannot be unlike each other or in contradiction to each other. Thus they arrive at their stupendous concept, "God." That which is last, thinnest, and emptiest is put first, as the cause, as *ens realissimum.* Why did mankind have to take seriously the brain afflictions of sick web-spinners? They have paid dearly for it!

§5

At long last, let us contrast the very different manner in which we conceive the problem of error and appearance. (I say "we" for politeness' sake.) Formerly, alteration, change, any becoming at all, were taken as proof of mere appearance, as an indication that there must be something which led us astray. Today, conversely, precisely insofar as the prejudice of reason forces us to posit unity, identity, permanence, substance, cause, thinghood, being, we see ourselves somehow caught in error, compelled into error. So certain are we, on the basis of rigorous examination, that this is where the error lies.

It is no different in this case than with the movement of the sun: there our eye is the constant advocate of error, here it is our language. In its origin language belongs in the age of the most rudimentary form of psychology. We enter a realm of crude fetishism when we summon before consciousness the basic presuppositions of the metaphysics of language, in plain talk, the presuppositions of reason. Everywhere it sees a doer and doing; it believes in will as the cause; it believes in the ego, in the ego as being, in the ego as substance, and it projects this faith in the ego-substance upon all things—only thereby does it first create the concept of "thing." Everywhere "being" is projected by thought, pushed underneath, as the cause; the concept of being follows, and is a derivative of, the concept of ego. In the beginning there is that great calamity of an error that the will is something which is effective, that will is a capacity. Today we know that it is only a word.

Very much later, in a world which was in a thousand ways more enlightened, philosophers, to their great surprise, became aware of the sureness, the subjective certainty, in our handling of the categories of reason: they concluded that these categories could not be derived from anything empirical—for everything empirical plainly contradicted them. Whence, then, were they derived?

And in India, as in Greece, the same mistake was made: "We must once have been at home in a higher world (instead of a very much lower one, which would have been the truth); we must have been divine, for we have reason!" Indeed, nothing has yet possessed a more naive power of persuasion than the error concerning being, as it has been formulated by the Eleatics, for example. After all, every word and every sentence we say speak in its favor. Even the opponents of the Eleatics still succumbed to the seduction of their concept of being: Democritus, among others, when he invented his atom. "Reason" in language—oh, what an old deceptive female she is! I am afraid we are not rid of God because we still have faith in grammar.

§6

It will be appreciated if I condense so essential and so new an insight into four theses. In that way I facilitate comprehension; in that way I provoke contradiction.

First proposition. The reasons for which "this" world has been characterized as "apparent" are the very reasons which indicate its reality; any other kind of reality is absolutely indemonstrable.

Second proposition. The criteria which have been bestowed on the "true being" of things are the criteria of not-being, of naught, the "true world" has been constructed out of contradiction to the actual world: indeed an apparent world, insofar as it is merely a moral-optical illusion.

Third proposition. To invent fables about a world "other" than this one has no meaning at all, unless an instinct of slander, detraction, and suspicion against life has gained the upper hand in us: in that case, we avenge ourselves against life with a phantasmagoria of "another," a "better" life.

Fourth proposition. Any distinction between a "true" and an "apparent" world—whether in the Christian manner or in the manner of Kant (in the end, an underhanded Christian)—is only a suggestion of decadence, a symptom of the decline of life. That the artist esteems appearance higher than reality is no objection to this proposition. For "appearance" in this case means reality once more, only by way of selection, reinforcement, and correction. The tragic artist is no pessimist: he is precisely the one who says Yes to everything questionable, even to the terrible—he is Dionysian.

How the "True World" Finally Became a Fable

The History of an Error

1. The true world--attainable for the sage, the pious, the virtuous man; he lives in it, he is it.

(The oldest form of the idea, relatively sensible, simple, and persuasive. A circumlocution for the sentence, "I, Plato, am the truth.")

2. The true world—unattainable for now, but promised for the sage, the pious, the virtuous man ("for the sinner who repents").

(Progress of the idea: it becomes more subtle, insidious, incomprehensible–it becomes female, it becomes Christian.)

3. The true world—unattainable, indemonstrable, unpromisable; but the very thought of it—a consolation, an obligation, an imperative.

(At bottom, the old sun, but seen through mist and skepticism. The idea has become elusive, pale, Nordic, Königsbergian [Kantian].)

4. The true world—unattainable? At any rate, unattained. And being unattained, also unknown. Consequently, not consoling, redeeming, or obligating: how could something unknown obligate us?

(Gray morning. The first yawn of reason. The cockcrow of positivism.)

5. The "true" world—an idea which is no longer good for anything, not even obligating—an idea which has become useless and superfluous—consequently, a refuted idea: let us abolish it!

(Bright day; breakfast; return of bon sens and cheerfulness; Plato's embarrassed blush; pandemonium of all free spirits.)

6. The true world—we have abolished. What world has remained? The apparent one perhaps? But no! With the true world we have also abolished the apparent one.

(Noon; moment of the briefest shadow; end of the longest error; high point of humanity; INCIPIT ZARATHUSTRA.)

Morality as Anti-Nature

§1

All passions have a phase when they are merely disastrous, when they drag down their victim with the weight of stupidity—and a later, very much later phase when they wed the spirit, when they "spiritualize" themselves. Formerly, in view of the element of stupidity in passion, war was declared on passion itself, its destruction was plotted; all the old moral monsters are agreed on this: *il faut tuer les passions.* The most famous formula for this is to be found in the New Testament, in that Sermon on the Mount, where, incidentally, things are by no means looked at from a height. There it is said, for example, with particular reference to sexuality: "If thy eye offend thee, pluck it out." Fortunately, no Christian acts in accordance with this precept. Destroying the passions and cravings, merely as a preventive measure against their stupidity and the unpleasant consequences of this stupidity—today this itself strikes us as merely another acute form of stupidity. We no longer admire dentists who "pluck out" teeth so that they will not hurt any more.

To be fair, it should be admitted, however, that on the ground out of which Christianity grew, the concept of the "spiritualization of passion" could never have been formed. After all, the first church, as is well known, fought against the "intelligent" in favor of the "poor in spirit." How could one expect from it an intelligent war against passion? The church fights passion with excision in every sense: its practice, its "cure," is castratism. It never asks: "How can one spiritualize, beautify, deify a craving?" It has at all times laid the stress of discipline on extirpation (of sensuality, of pride, of the lust to rule, of avarice, of vengefulness). But an attack on the roots of passion means an attack on the roots of life: the practice of the church is hostile to life.

§2

The same means in the fight against a craving—castration, extirpation—is instinctively chosen by those who are too weak-willed, too degenerate, to be able to impose moderation on themselves; by those who are so constituted that they require La Trappe, to use a figure of speech, or (without any figure of speech) some kind of definitive declaration of hostility, a cleft between themselves and the passion. Radical means are indispensable only for the degenerate; the weakness of the will—or, to speak more definitely, the inability not to respond to a stimulus—is itself merely another form of degeneration. The radical hostility, the deadly hostility against sensuality, is always a symptom to reflect on: it entitles us to suppositions concerning the total state of one who is excessive in this manner.

This hostility, this hatred, by the way, reaches its climax only when such types lack even the firmness for this radical cure, for this renunciation of their "devil." One should survey the whole history of the priests and philosophers, including the artists: the most poisonous things against the senses have been said not by the impotent, nor by ascetics, but by the impossible ascetics, by those who really were in dire need of being ascetics.

§3

The spiritualization of sensuality is called love: it represents a great triumph over Christianity. Another triumph is our spiritualization of hostility. It consists in a profound appreciation of the value of having enemies: in short, it means acting and thinking in the opposite way from that which has been the rule. The church always wanted the destruction of its enemies; we, we immoralists and Antichristians, find our advantage in this, that the church exists. In the political realm too, hostility has now become more spiritual—much more sensible, much more thoughtful, much more considerate. Almost every party understands how it is in the interest of its own self-preservation that the opposition should not lose all strength; the same is true of power politics. A new creation in particular—the new Reich, for example—needs enemies more than friends: in opposition alone does it feel itself necessary, in opposition alone does it become necessary.

Our attitude to the "internal enemy" is no different: here too we have spiritualized hostility; here too we have come to appreciate its value. The price of fruitfulness is to be rich in internal opposition; one remains young only as long as the soul does not stretch itself and desire peace. Nothing has become more alien to us than that desideratum of former times, "peace of soul," the Christian desideratum; there is nothing we envy less than the moralistic cow and the fat happiness of the good conscience. One has renounced the great life when one renounces war.

In many cases, to be sure, "peace of soul" is merely a misunderstanding—something else, which lacks only a more honest name. Without further ado or prejudice, a few examples. "Peace of soul" can be, for one, the gentle radiation of a rich animality into the moral (or religious) sphere. Or the beginning of weariness, the first shadow of evening, of any kind of evening. Or a sign that the air is humid, that south winds are approaching. Or unrecognized gratitude for a good digestion (sometimes called "love of man"). Or the attainment of calm by a convalescent who feels a new relish in all things and waits. Or the state which follows a thorough satisfaction of our dominant passion, the well-being of a rare repletion. Or the senile weakness of our will, our cravings, our vices. Or laziness, persuaded by vanity to give itself moral airs. Or the emergence of certainty, even a dreadful certainty, after long tension and torture by uncertainty. Or the expression of maturity and mastery in the midst of doing, creating, working, and willing—calm breathing, attained "freedom of the will." Twilight of the Idols–who knows? perhaps also only a kind of "peace of soul."

§4

I reduce a principle to a formula. Every naturalism in morality—that is, every healthy morality—is dominated by an instinct of life, some commandment of life is fulfilled by a determinate canon of "shalt" and "shalt not"; some inhibition and hostile element on the path of life is thus removed. Anti-natural morality—that is, almost every morality which has so far been taught, revered, and preached—turns, conversely, against the instincts of life: it is condemnation of these instincts, now secret, now outspoken and impudent. When it says, "God looks at the heart," it says No to both the lowest and the highest desires of life, and posits God as the enemy of life. The saint in whom God delights is the ideal eunuch. Life has come to an end where the "kingdom of God" begins.

§5

Once one has comprehended the outrage of such a revolt against life as has become almost sacrosanct in Christian morality, one has, fortunately, also comprehended something else: the futility, apparentness, absurdity, and mendaciousness of such a revolt. A condemnation of life by the living remains in the end a mere symptom of a certain kind of life: the question whether it is justified or unjustified is not even raised thereby. One would require a position outside of life, and yet have to know it as well as one, as many, as all who have lived it, in order to be permitted even to touch the problem of the value of life: reasons enough to comprehend that this problem is for us an unapproachable problem. When we speak of values, we speak with the inspiration, with the way of looking at things, which is part of life: life itself forces us to posit values; life itself values through us when we posit values. From this it follows that even that anti-natural morality which conceives of God as the counter-concept and condemnation of life is only a value judgment of life—but of what life? of what kind of life? I have already given the answer: of declining, weakened, weary, condemned life. Morality, as it has so far been understood—as it has in the end been formulated once more by Schopenhauer, as "negation of the will to life"—is the very instinct of decadence, which makes an imperative of itself. It says: "Perish!" It is a condemnation pronounced by the condemned.

§6

Let us finally consider how naive it is altogether to say: "Man ought to be such and such!" Reality shows us an enchanting wealth of types, the abundance of a lavish play and change of forms—and some wretched loafer of a moralist comments: "No! Man ought to be different." He even knows what man should be like, this wretched bigot and prig: he paints himself on the wall and comments,

"Ecce homo!" But even when the moralist addresses himself only to the single human being and says to him, "You ought to be such and such!" he does not cease to make himself ridiculous. The single human being is a piece of *fatum* from the front and from the rear, one law more, one necessity more for all that is yet to come and to be. To say to him, "Change yourself!" is to demand that everything be changed, even retroactively. And indeed there have been consistent moralists who wanted man to be different, that is, virtuous—they wanted him remade in their own image, as a prig: to that end, they negated the world! No small madness! No modest kind of immodesty!

Morality, insofar as it condemns for its own sake, and not out of regard for the concerns, considerations, and contrivances of life, is a specific error with which one ought to have no pity—an idiosyncrasy of degenerates which has caused immeasurable harm.

We others, we immoralists, have, conversely, made room in our hearts for every kind of understanding, comprehending, and approving. We do not easily negate; we make it a point of honor to be affirmers. More and more, our eyes have opened to that economy which needs and knows how to utilize everything that the holy witlessness of the priest, the diseased reason in the priest, rejects—that economy in the law of life which finds an advantage even in the disgusting species of the prigs, the priests, the virtuous. What advantage? But we ourselves, we immoralists, are the answer. . . .

What I Owe to the Ancients

§1

In conclusion, a word about that world to which I sought approaches, to which I have perhaps found a new approach—the ancient world. My taste, which may be the opposite of a tolerant taste, is in this case too far from saying Yes indiscriminately: it does not like to say Yes; rather even No; but best of all, nothing. That applies to whole cultures, it applies to books—also to places and landscapes. At bottom it is a very small number of ancient books that counts in my life; the most famous are not among them. My sense of style, for the epigram as a style, was awakened almost instantly when I came into contact with Sallust. I have not forgotten the surprise of my honored teacher, Corssen, when he had to give his worst Latin pupil the best grade: I had finished with one stroke. Compact, severe, with as much substance as possible, a cold sarcasm against "beautiful words" and "beautiful sentiments"—here I found myself. And even in my Zarathustra one will recognize a very serious ambition for a Roman style, for the *aere perennius* [more enduring than bronze] in style.

Nor was my experience any different in my first contact with Horace. To this day, no other poet has given me the same artistic delight that a Horatian ode gave me from the first. In certain languages that which has been achieved here could not even be attempted. This mosaic of words, in which every word—as sound, as place, as concept—pours out its strength right and left and over the whole, this minimum in the extent and number of the signs, and the maximum thereby attained in the energy of the signs—all that is Roman and, if one will believe me, noble par excellence. All the rest of poetry becomes, in contrast, something too popular—a mere garrulity of feelings.

§2

To the Greeks I do not by any means owe similarly strong impressions; and—to come right out with it—they cannot mean as much to us as the Romans. One does not learn from the Greeks—their manner is too foreign, and too fluid, to have an imperative, a "classical" effect. Who could ever have learned to write from a Greek? Who could ever have learned it without the Romans?

For heaven's sake, do not throw Plato at me. I am a complete skeptic about Plato, and I have never been able to join in the admiration for the artist Plato which is customary among scholars. In the end, the subtlest judges of taste among the ancients themselves are here on my side. Plato, it seems to me, throws all stylistic forms together and is thus a first-rate decadent in style: his responsibility is thus comparable to that of the Cynics, who invented the *satura Menippea.* To be attracted by the Platonic dialogue, this horribly self-satisfied and childish kind of dialectic, one must never have read good French writers—Fontenelle, for example. Plato is boring. In the end, my mistrust of Plato goes deep: he represents such an aberration from all the basic instincts of the Hellene, is so moralistic, so pre-existently Christian—he already takes the concept "good" for the highest concept—that for the whole phenomenon of Plato I would sooner use the harsh phrase "higher swindle," or, if it sounds better, "idealism," than any other. We have paid dearly for the fact that this Athenian got his schooling from the Egyptians (or from the Jews in Egypt?). In that great calamity, Christianity, Plato represents that ambiguity and fascination, called an "ideal," which made it possible for the nobler spirits of antiquity to misunderstand themselves and to set foot on the bridge leading to the cross. And how much Plato there still is in the concept "church," in the construction, system, and practice of the church!

My recreation, my preference, my cure from all Platonism has always been Thucydides. Thucydides and, perhaps, Machiavelli's *Principe* are most closely related to myself by the unconditional will not to gull oneself and to see reason in reality—not in "reason," still less in "morality." For the wretched embellishment of the Greeks into an ideal, which the "classically educated" youth carries into life as a prize for his classroom drill, there is no more complete cure than Thucydides. One must follow him line by line and read no less clearly between the lines: there are few thinkers who say so much between the lines. With him the culture of the Sophists, by which I mean the culture of the realists, reaches its perfect expression—this inestimable movement amid the moralistic and idealistic swindle set loose on all sides by the Socratic schools. Greek philosophy: the decadence of the Greek instinct. Thucydides: the great sum, the last revelation of that strong, severe, hard factuality which was instinctive with the older Hellenes. In the end, it is courage in the face of reality that distinguishes a man like Thucydides from Plato: Plato is a coward before reality, consequently he flees into the ideal; Thucydides has control of himself, consequently he also maintains control of things.

§3

To smell out "beautiful souls," "golden means," and other perfections in the Greeks, or to admire their calm in greatness, their ideal cast of mind, their noble simplicity—the psychologist in me protected me against such "noble simplicity," a *niaiserie allemande* [German naievity] anyway. I saw their strongest instinct, the will to power: I saw them tremble before the indomitable force of this drive—I saw how all their institutions grew out of preventive measures taken to protect each other against their inner explosives. This tremendous inward tension then discharged itself in terrible and ruthless hostility to the outside world: the city-states tore each other to pieces so that the citizens of each might find peace from themselves. One needed to be strong: danger was near, it lurked everywhere. The magnificent physical suppleness, the audacious realism and immoralism which distinguished the Hellene constituted a need, not "nature." It only resulted, it was not there from the start. And with festivals and the arts they also aimed at nothing other than to feel on top, to show themselves on top. These are means of glorifying oneself, and in certain cases, of inspiring fear of oneself.

How could one possibly judge the Greeks by their philosophers, as the Germans have done, and use the Philistine moralism of the Socratic schools as a clue to what was basically Hellenic! After all, the philosophers are the decadents of Greek culture, the counter-movement to the ancient, noble taste (to the agonistic instinct, to the polis, to the value of race, to the authority of descent). The Socratic virtues were preached because the Greeks had lost them: excitable, timid, fickle comedians, every one of them, they had a few reasons too many for having morals preached to them. Not that it did any good--but big words and attitudes suit decadents so well.

§4

I was the first to take seriously, for the understanding of the older, the still rich and even overflowing Hellenic instinct, that wonderful phenomenon which bears the name of Dionysus: it is explicable only in terms of an excess of force. Whoever followed the Greeks, like that most profound student of their culture in our time, Jacob Burckhardt in Basel, knew immediately that something had been accomplished thereby; and Burckhardt added a special section on this phenomenon to his *Civilization of the Greeks*. To see the opposite, one should look at the almost amusing poverty of instinct among the German philologists when they approach the Dionysian.

The famous Lobeck, above all, crawled into this world of mysterious states with all the venerable sureness of a worm dried up between books, and persuaded himself that it was scientific of him to be glib and childish to the point of nausea—and with the utmost erudition, Lobeck gave us to understand that all these curiosities really did not amount to anything. In fact, the priests could have told the participants in such orgies some not altogether worthless things; for example, that wine excites lust, that man can under certain circumstances live on fruit, that plants bloom in the spring and wilt in the fall. As regards the astonishing wealth of rites, symbols, and myths of an orgiastic origin, with which the ancient world is literally overrun, this gave Lobeck an opportunity to become still more ingenious.

"The Greeks," he said (*Aglaophamus* I, 672), "when they had nothing else to do, laughed, jumped, and ran around; or, since man sometimes feels that urge too, they sat down, cried, and lamented. Others came later on and sought some reason for this spectacular behavior; and thus there originated, as explanations for these customs, countless traditions concerning feasts and myths. On the other hand, it was believed that this droll ado, which took place on the feast days after all, must also form a necessary part of the festival and therefore it was maintained as an indispensable feature of the religious service." This is contemptible prattle; a Lobeck simply cannot be taken seriously for a moment.

We have quite a different feeling when we examine the concept "Greek" which was developed by Winckelmann and Goethe, and find it incompatible with that element out of which Dionysian art grows—the orgiastic. Indeed I do not doubt that as a matter of principle Goethe excluded a thing of the sort from the possibilities of the Greek soul. Consequently Goethe did not understand the Greeks. For it is only in the Dionysian mysteries, in the psychology of the Dionysian state, that the basic fact of the Hellenic instinct finds expression—its "will to life." What was it that the Hellene guaranteed himself by means of these mysteries? Eternal life, the eternal return of life, the future promised and hallowed in the past; the triumphant Yes to life beyond all death and change; true life as the overall continuation of life through procreation, through the mysteries of sexuality. For the Greeks the sexual symbol was therefore the venerable symbol par excellence, the real profundity in the whole of ancient piety. Every single element in the act of procreation, of pregnancy, and of birth aroused the highest and most solemn feelings. In the doctrine of the mysteries, pain is pronounced holy: the pangs of the woman giving birth hallow all pain; all becoming and growing—all that guarantees a future—involves pain. That there may be the eternal joy of creating, that the will to life may eternally affirm itself, the agony of the woman giving birth must also be there eternally.

All this is meant by the word Dionysus: I know no higher symbolism than this Greek symbolism of the Dionysian festivals. Here the most profound instinct of life, that directed toward the future of life, the eternity of life, is experienced religiously—and the way to life, procreation, as the holy way. It was Christianity, with its ressentiment against life at the bottom of its heart, which first made something unclean of sexuality: it threw filth on the origin, on the presupposition of our life.

§5

The psychology of the orgiastic as an overflowing feeling of life and strength, where even pain still has the effect of a stimulus, gave me the key to the concept of tragic feeling, which had been misunderstood both by Aristotle and, quite especially, by our modern pessimists. Tragedy is so far from proving anything about the pessimism of the Hellenes, in Schopenhauer's sense, that it may, on the contrary, be considered its decisive repudiation and counter-instance. Saying Yes to life even in its strangest and hardest problems, the will to life rejoicing over its own inexhaustibility even in the very sacrifice of its highest types—that is what I called Dionysian, that is what I guessed to be the bridge to the psychology of the tragic poet. Not in order to be liberated from terror and pity, not in order to purge oneself of a dangerous affect by its vehement discharge—Aristotle understood it that way—but in order to be oneself the eternal joy of becoming, beyond all terror and pity—that joy which included even joy in destroying.

And herewith I again touch that point from which I once went forth: The Birth of Tragedy was my first revaluation of all values. Herewith I again stand on the soil out of which my intention, my ability grows—I, the last disciple of the philosopher Dionysus—I, the teacher of the eternal recurrence.

SOURCES

Anaximander, *Fragments*
From John Burnet, *Early Greek Philosophy*, 3rd ed. (London: A & C Black, 1920)
Public Domain

Xenophanes , *Fragments*
From John Burnet, *Early Greek Philosophy*, 3rd ed. (London: A & C Black Ltd., 1920)
Public Domain

Parmenides, *Fragments*
From John Burnet, *Early Greek Philosophy*, 3rd ed. (London: A & C Black, 1920)
Public Domain

Heraclitus, *Fragments*
From John Burnet, *Early Greek Philosophy*, 3rd ed. (London: A & C Black, 1920)
Public Domain

Plato, *Euthphryo*, translated by Benjamin Jowett
eBooks@Adelaide 2007. The University of Adelaide Library, University of Adelaide, South Australia 5005.
This work is licensed under a Creative Commons Licence

Plato, *Apology*, translated by Benjamin Jowett
eBooks@Adelaide 2007. The University of Adelaide Library, University of Adelaide, South Australia 5005.
This work is licensed under a Creative Commons Licence

Plato, *Phaedo*, translated by Benjamin Jowett
eBooks@Adelaide 2007. The University of Adelaide Library, University of Adelaide, South Australia 5005.
This work is licensed under a Creative Commons Licence

Plato, *Symposium*, translated by Benjamin Jowett
eBooks@Adelaide 2007. The University of Adelaide Library, University of Adelaide, South Australia 5005
This work is licensed under a Creative Commons Licence

Plato, *Republic*, translated by Benjamin Jowett
eBooks@Adelaide 2007. The University of Adelaide Library, University of Adelaide, South Australia 5005.
This work is licensed under a Creative Commons Licence

Aristotle, *Metaphysics*, translated by W. D. Ross
eBooks@Adelaide 2007. The University of Adelaide Library, University of Adelaide, South Australia 5005.
This work is licensed under a Creative Commons Licence

Epicurus, *Letter to Menoeceus*
Translated by Erik Anderson
http://www.epicurus.info/etexts/Lives.html#I40

Epicurus, *Principal Doctrines*
Translated by Erik Anderson
http://www.epicurus.info/etexts/PD.html

Epictetus, *Enchiridion*
Translated by Elizabeth Carter
http://classics.mit.edu//Epictetus/epicench.html
The Internet Classics Archive by Daniel C. Stevenson, Web Atomics.. World Wide Web presentation is copyright (C) 1994-2000, Daniel C. Stevenson, Web Atomics. All rights reserved under international and pan-American copyright conventions, including the right of reproduction in whole or in part in any form. Direct permission requests to classics@classics.mit.edu.

Descartes, *Meditations on First Philosophy*
Copyright ©2010–2015 All rights reserved. Jonathan Bennett
www.earlymoderntexts.com

Hobbes, *Leviathan*
eBooks@Adelaide 2007. The University of Adelaide Library, University of Adelaide, South Australia 5005.
This work is licensed under a Creative Commons Licence

Spinoza, *Ethics*
Copyright ©2010–2015 All rights reserved. Jonathan Bennett
www.earlymoderntexts.com

Hume
Extracts from *Enquiry Concerning the Human Understanding*,
Oxford University Press, 1902. May be reprinted only when distributed free of all fees.
Copyright (C) 2001, 2002 by Michael S. Hart.
http://www.gutenberg.org/cache/epub/9662/pg9662.txt

Nietzsche, *Twilight of the Idols*
Translated by Jack Miller
http://nietzsche.holtof.com/Nietzsche_twilight_of_the_idols/the_twilight_of_the_Idols.htm
Public Domain